Real Estate Valuation in Global Markets

Readers of this text may be interested in these related texts published by the Appraisal Institute:

The Appraisal of Real Estate, eleventh edition
Appraising Residential Properties, second edition
The Dictionary of Real Estate Appraisal, third edition
Hotels and Motels
Market Analysis for Valuation Appraisals
The Office Building From Concept to Investment Reality
Shopping Center Appraisal and Analysis

Real Estate

Valuation

in **Global** Markets

Edited by

Howard C. Gelbtuch, MAI

and David Mackmin, FRICS

with Michael R. Milgrim, PhD

**APPRAISAL
INSTITUTE®**

875 North Michigan Avenue
Chicago, IL 60611-1980

For Educational Purposes Only

The material presented in this text has been reviewed by members of the Appraisal Institute, but the opinions and procedures set forth by the authors are not necessarily endorsed as the only methodology consistent with proper appraisal practice. While a great deal of care has been taken to provide accurate and current information, neither the Appraisal Institute nor its editors and staff assume responsibility for the accuracy of the data contained herein. Further, the general principles and conclusions presented in this text are subject to local, state, and federal laws and regulations, court cases, and any revisions of the same. This publication is sold for educational purposes with the understanding that the publisher is not engaged in rendering legal, accounting, or other professional service.

Nondiscrimination Policy

The Appraisal Institute advocates equal opportunity and nondiscrimination in the appraisal profession and conducts its activities in accordance with applicable federal, state, and local laws.

Library of Congress Cataloging-in-Publication Data

Real estate valuation in global markets / edited by Howard C. Gelbtuch and David Mackmin, with
   Michael Milgrim
     p.   cm.
   Includes bibliographical references (p.).
   ISBN 0-922154-42-2
   1. Real property—Valuation. 2. Real estate business.
 I. Gelbtuch, Howard C. II. Mackmin, David. III. Milgrim, Michael. IV. Appraisal Institute (U.S.)

HD1387.R382 1997
333.33`2—dc21
                                      97-34856
                                      CIP

TABLE OF CONTENTS

Foreword

The growth of multinational and international firms, the proliferation of free trade zones, and the development of interactive worldwide financial markets reflect the ever-accelerating globalization of economic activity. This phenomenon continues to impact our lives—as producers and consumers, real estate analysts and consultants, and market participants and investors. More domestic stockholders are finding offshore equities and mutual funds to be attractive investment alternatives, and overseas investment-grade real estate is generating interest among financiers.

Real estate is a fixed asset usually financed by the liquid capital of investment firms, which are oblivious to national boundaries. Whether the real estate asset is located stateside or abroad, investment decisions ultimately depend on current and prospective property valuations. Valuers have been quick to perceive the need for internationally recognized value definitions and practice standards. They must also broaden their understanding of overseas markets and procedures. Obstacles such as a lack of familiarity with foreign languages or the special characteristics of markets abroad must be overcome.

Real Estate Valuation in Global Markets was developed to fill a serious void in the appraisal literature on international practice. The collection looks at valuation practice in 21 different countries around the world, including all major G-7 economies, Russia, and four of the 10 big emerging markets (BEMs). Countries from each of the six inhabited continents are represented. The mix includes developed market economies, former colonial economies entering the ranks of newly industrialized countries (NICs), and economies facing the challenges of transition from state control over the means of production to private enterprise. All of the chapter developers are either valuation experts and nationals of the country they discuss or practitioners with extensive experience in their country of expertise.

Each chapter provides coverage of an individual country's political structure, legally recognized property rights and governmental powers, national currency, units of measure, and outlook for inflation. The state of the local valuation profession is discussed with respect to standards, regulations, and reporting requirements. Lease structure, the bases of valuation, and the approaches to value are described in depth. Each chapter concludes with a list of available data sources and local valuation organizations.

The book is supplemented by three appendices and a glossary, which contain a wealth of information. The appendices include material on international associations of valuers and real estate professionals, international economic pacts, and the International Valuation Standards Committee. The glossary contains more than 450 entries, including English-language variants and foreign language equivalents of essential valuation terms. Extensive cross-referencing enhances the usability of these supplementary sections.

This groundbreaking book will prove to be an indispensable guide for any practitioner interested in taking advantage of emerging valuation opportunities in global markets.

Kenneth L. Nicholson, SRA
1997 President
Appraisal Institute

Introduction

The globalisation of real estate has meant that more real estate valuers and appraisers are working in overseas markets and need to develop an understanding of real estate issues outside their own markets. This book provides an introduction to international valuation practice. Certain limitations must be placed on a book of this nature and all readers are advised to exercise extra caution when reviewing valuation reports prepared by professional valuers practising in other countries. Valuations should not be undertaken in other countries without full knowledge and experience of local markets. Nevertheless, with the growth of international companies and the demand for real estate on a worldwide basis, an appreciation of practice outside one's own national boundaries has become desirable. This book will, we hope, provide some valuable insights.

While each country is unique, one can discern the influence of European colonisation on both land law and valuation practice and the growing influence of North American definitions and standards. Appraisal practice, however, does vary widely.

In some countries, valuers are licensed. They adhere to strict training requirements and belong to self-regulating professional bodies with standards and codes of conduct. In others, appraisers have minimal training and are subject to little or no government control.

In most countries, cost and sales comparison approaches to value are followed and practitioners are aware of the income capitalisation approach and discounted cash flow analysis. But the where, what, when, how, and why of valuation vary around the world. Even in countries that belong to the International Valuation Standards Committee and have adopted the IVSC definition of market value, there are variations in the interpretation of the definition and in the application of methodology.

To comply with the Uniform Standards of Professional Appraisal Practice (USPAP), North American appraisers are required to value real estate based on its highest and best use. Similar requirements exist in countries outside North America, e.g., Japan. Despite the fact that the concept of highest and best use is widely understood, it has not been universally adopted as a basic requirement for market valuations. The concept of highest and best use is interpreted within legal (planning and zoning) and physical (building) constraints as the use which is financially feasible and maximally productive. Elsewhere, definitions of market value encompass bids by purchasers over and above the current "improved" value or existing use value if it can be shown that the market would overbid in view of some latent value or higher and better use, which may not necessarily be the maximally productive use.

This difference is important in countries which practice planning control, but have no specified zoning or density restrictions. In these countries, the highest and best use in terms of planning may only be ascertainable through the submission of planning applications, which is a costly process and not part of the practitioner's valuation brief (guidelines). Market knowledge becomes critical because the valuer must demonstrate that 1) the property (as existing) does not maximise the site potential, 2) further improvement will likely be permitted, and 3) these circumstances are sufficiently obvious in the market for the valuer to be able to justify an opinion of value based on purchase of the property by a developer/entrepreneur with the intent of improving it. In many European countries, central business and residential districts lie within conservation areas. In these areas, limited refurbishment is generally permitted, but interiors as well as exteriors may have to be conserved. While it is possible to find overarching developments that envelope historic frontages (facades), such developments rarely are permitted in historic towns where the historic street scene must be retained.

The adoption in some countries of the current cost accounting concept[1] for corporate annual accounts (corporate annual reports) has given rise to a further point of confusion. Accounting practice in these countries draws a distinction between investment properties and properties requisite to the corporation's operations. Thus, investment properties owned by a corporation are valued at their current open market value. However, an operational property such as a building used in the manufacture of the company's products is, for accounting

---

1. Under this accounting concept, fixed assets are stated at their value to the business in terms of their current, rather than historic, costs.

purposes, valued on the basis of market value under the existing use.[2] Although market value under the existing use may frequently be the same as open market value, this is not always the case.

The accounting basis must show that the asset at its net current replacement cost or deprival value (the loss the business would incur if deprived of the asset) is the value of the asset under the existing use because the asset is requisite to the activities or operations of the company. Under these circumstances, valuers in the United Kingdom are required to provide an alternative use value if a figure substantially different (either higher or lower) than the market value under the existing use could be obtained for the vacant possession sale of the property (a commercial property available for sale with full rights of occupancy). For example, a manufacturer may occupy a property used to bottle soft drinks. However, the property has a very high market value based on development as a shopping centre. The bottling plant is an operational building and, for the purpose of the company's accounts, is valued under the existing use. The valuer, however, will also provide an alternative use value in view of the development potential of the site (its highest and best use) as a shopping centre. If the property becomes surplus to the operational requirements of the company, it would then be valued at open market value, which in this case would be premised on its highest and best use. In many instances, such detailed considerations are beyond the scope of this book, but the reader should be aware that they exist and the unwary should be forewarned.

In some countries, valuation is codified and controlled by statute or government directive. In most, it is prescribed for eminent domain valuations and sometimes for market valuations. In practice, valuation may not mirror price determination. This is particularly true where sales prices are used as a basis for taxation and, as a result, the registered transaction price may differ from the actual exchange price known and agreed to by the vendor (seller) and purchaser. Consequently, data held on sales and lettings (leasings) may be of little use unless one is party to the transaction and has been taken into the confidence of the buyer or seller.

Issues regarding the ownership of title are fundamental. Many countries have some form of freehold (fee simple) title, but there may be variations in the bundle of rights that can be conveyed and, hence, differences in what may be assessed as a transferable right for valuation purposes. The systems of title registration in many countries are poor. In Eastern Europe, significant problems have arisen from

---

2. Valuers in the United Kingdom, countries of the European Community, Australia, and New Zealand follow these practices.

a history of operating a command economy where most land rights were held by the state and disposed of by the state. The attitude toward restitution of ownership in these countries can be a further pitfall for the unwary.

Cultural, social, and behavioural patterns as well as business customs and practices all differ widely so that much of what is assumed or taken for granted by the UK or North American valuer has to be forgotten or relearned to appreciate and understand the position of real estate in another society. Physical factors such as geography, geology, area (size), topography, location, and climate can be measured and expressed in intelligible language. Factors like construction, design, and aesthetics, however, are less easily compared as user requirements vary around the world. A description such as "modern" may call to mind a picture that is far removed from the reality on the ground. Nevertheless, the four forces perceived by many to constitute the bases of real estate appraisal and valuation, i.e., social, economic, political (governmental/legal), and physical (environmental) forces, generally are seen to form the underpinning of the valuation process.

In countries where owner-occupied property far exceeds tenanted property, there is limited rental evidence and limited sale data on investment-grade property. This has promoted the use of the cost approach as the most logical and defensible method. For residential valuations, sales comparison tends to dominate, provided an adequate number of reliable comparables are available. If this is not the case, preference will revert to the cost approach. Only when there is a strong investor market do appraisers place reliance on the income capitalisation approach or DCF analysis.

In preparing this book, we have relied on personal, professional, and academic contacts around the world. Each chapter has a similar structure, but complete conformity was not imposed as we wished to retain some of the local colour added by the chapter authors.

In addition to valuation practice in each country, we have tried to address education, training, and professional standards. Not surprisingly, the variety of presentation is considerable.

While all the continents are represented, there are some obvious omissions in the countries covered. We worked hard to fill these gaps, but eventually had to admit failure. Additional contributions to future editions would be welcomed. In the interim, the overriding message is clear. The broad principles of valuation apply wherever there is a real estate market, but practice can only be understood within the social, political, economic, and legal framework of each individual country.

Howard C. Gelbtuch, MAI, CRE
New York, USA

David Mackmin, B.Sc., M.Sc., FRICS
Sheffield, UK

Editorial Note

In light of the considerable variation in the terminology and notational
systems used around the world, publication of a book on international valuation is an extremely ambitious undertaking. At the outset, the reader should
be aware that the chapters in this collection appear in one of two standard
variants of the English language: North American English or British and Commonwealth English.[1] George Bernard Shaw once quipped that the British and Americans
are two peoples separated by a common language. His observation is equally
relevant to the language of appraisal. A North American first encountering terms
such as *all risks yield, year's purchase, passing rent, council rates, demised
premises, outgoings, rental value,* or *occupational lease* will be puzzled. A Briton,
Australian, or New Zealander will find North American usage similarly discon-
certing.

Further complicating such difficulties are the different categories that North
American and British or Commonwealth valuers use to describe appraisal practice. The North American practitioner speaks of three approaches to value, while
his British or Commonwealth counterpart refers to five methods. To help the
reader, equivalent North American terms are provided in parentheses following
British or Commonwealth expressions that are unlikely to be understood by
North American appraisers. (North American English translations are also pro-

---

1. The editor has relied on *Fowler's Modern English Usage,* 2d. (Oxford: Oxford University Press, 1983) to
   arbitrate matters of British usage and on *The Chicago Manual of Style,* 14th ed. (Chicago: University of
   Chicago Press, 1993) for matters of style.

vided for foreign terms in some of the chapters.) The glossary at the back of the book should assist all readers in identifying equivalent terminology. In addition to North American and British/Commonwealth usage, the glossary contains descriptive entries for basic appraisal terms in several foreign languages, e.g., French, German, Japanese, Russian, and Spanish.

Notation, the use of commas and decimal points in numbers and percentages, represents an additional problem for practitioners involved in international valuation. While the North American, British, and Commonwealth countries follow the same convention, countries on the European continent and in Latin America use an opposite system of notation. For example, a sum in dollars or pounds expressed as $1,499.99 or £1,499.99 would be written in francs or marks as 1.499,99F or 1.499,99DM. Similarly, a percentage expressed as 10.5% in English-speaking countries would become 10,50% on the continent and in Latin America. Since this book is published in English, sums and percentages are expressed in the system of notation common to English-speaking countries.[2]

The reader may find it helpful to read specific groups of chapters together because valuation techniques, legal traditions, and market circumstances are shared by the countries in question, e.g., the Commonwealth countries, Latin American countries, and formerly socialist countries whose economies were centrally planned.

---

2. India has its own system of notation as well as two unique monetary units, the lakh and crore. For more on Indian notational conventions, see Chapter 13.

The United States

Howard C. Gelbtuch, MAI, CRE

Howard C. Gelbtuch is a graduate of New York University with a B.S. degree in finance; he also holds an M.B.A. in real estate from the Bernard M. Baruch College. Mr. Gelbtuch has been a Senior Vice President and head of the Real Estate Evaluation Department at Integrated Resources, Inc.; Director of Research at Morgan Stanley Realty, Inc.; Director in charge of real estate appraisal practice at Coopers & Lybrand; and Senior Director of Jones Lang Wootton USA, where he supervised the firm's valuation activities in North and South America. Currently he is a principal of Greenwich Realty Advisors, Inc., an internationally oriented real estate valuation and counseling firm. In addition to holding the MAI and CRE designations, Mr. Gelbtuch has chaired or served on international committees of the Appraisal Institute, the Counselors of Real Estate, and the National Association of Realtors.® He is a frequent contributor to *The Appraisal Journal* and authored the valuation chapter in *The Office Building: From Concept to Investment Reality.*

The U.S. mainland comprises six geographic regions: the low-lying coastal plain along the Atlantic and Gulf of Mexico, the Appalachian range, the Midwest (the Great Lakes and central plains, drained by the Mississippi and its tributaries), the Rocky Mountains, the intermontane plateau (Great Basin), and the Pacific coastlands (the Cascades, Sierra Nevada, and Central Valley of California). Climate is diverse: the Northeast and Midwest are humid continental; the South is humid subtropical (Florida is tropical); the Southwest is arid steppe or desert; the Northwest is marine; and Southern California is Mediterranean. The eastern and southern coasts are prone to seasonal hurricanes from the Gulf; the Midwest, to tornadoes; and California to earthquakes. Alaska is subarctic or tundra and Hawaii is tropical rain forest. Principal metropolitan centers are New York, Los Angeles, Chicago, Washington-Baltimore, San Francisco-Oakland, Philadelphia, Boston, Detroit, Dallas-Fort Worth, Houston, Miami, Atlanta, Seattle, Cleveland, Minneapolis-St. Paul, San Diego, St. Louis, and Pittsburgh.

Political Structure

The United States has been under democratic rule for more than two centuries and has the oldest federal constitution of any country in the world. The federal government is divided into three branches: the executive branch, which includes the offices of the president and vice president and the various secretaries of the Cabinet; the legislative branch, which encompasses the two houses of Congress; and the judicial branch, which includes the Supreme Court, the highest court in the country.

The president and vice president are elected for four-year terms and are permitted to serve no more than two terms (eight years). The president appoints the 14 Cabinet secretaries, whose responsibilities include foreign affairs (the State Department), the treasury, defense, justice (the Attorney General), the interior, agriculture, commerce, labor, health and human services (social security), housing and urban development, transportation, energy, education, and veterans' affairs.

The U.S. Congress is divided into two houses. The Senate consists of 100 senators, two from each of the 50 states of the United States, each of whom is elected for a six-year term. The House of Representatives has 435 members, each elected for a two-year term. The number of House members representing each state is determined by the state's population, which is counted in a census every 10 years.

The nine justices of the United States Supreme Court are appointed for life terms by the president, subject to approval by the Senate.

In general, governmental authority not specifically delegated to the federal government is reserved for the states. Most regulations governing real estate are formulated at the local level.

Zoning (land use planning) is prevalent throughout the United States, with the notable exception of the city of Houston in the state of Texas. Zoning enables municipalities to regulate the type and density of real estate development.

Property taxes are assessed at the local level. No property taxes are paid to the federal government. For some cities, such as New York, property taxes represent the single largest source of revenue.

Property Rights

Under the fifth amendment to the Constitution, property rights are clearly defined in the United States. The threat of illegal confiscation of property simply does not exist. Ownership of real property is subject to the four powers of government: taxation, eminent domain, police power, and escheat.

- Taxation is the right of government to raise revenue through assessments on goods, products, rights, and interests.

- Eminent domain is the right of the government to take property for public use upon payment of just compensation.

- Police power is the right of government to protect public safety, health, morals, and the general welfare.

- Escheat gives the state ownership of property when its owner dies without a will or ascertainable heirs.

A concept known as *the bundle of rights* is inherent in the ownership of all real estate. The bundle of rights is frequently compared to a bundle of sticks, with each stick representing a right to do something with a property. For example, an owner of property may use it, sell it, lease it, or give it away.

Ownership of all the rights in the bundle is referred to as the *fee simple estate.* This is considered the most complete form of ownership. A fee simple estate implies absolute ownership, unencumbered by any other interest.

A leased fee is an estate in which some rights, such as the rights to use and occupancy, have been transferred to another by means of a lease. Most multi-tenanted buildings are owned in leased fee.

A fairly common form of ownership is a leasehold estate, in which one party leases the land from another party and owns the building (*the improvements*) until the expiration of the lease. The lease, often known as a *ground lease,* typically runs for a long period of time, often 99 years or more.

Language

English is spoken throughout the United States. Although many schoolchildren receive instruction in the use of a second language, usually Spanish or French, citizens of the United States are generally not bilingual.

Currency

The U.S. dollar ($1.00) is the basic monetary unit. All domestic real estate transactions are priced in U.S. dollars.

Units of Measure

The United States uses the English system of measurement.[1] Real estate sizes are quoted in square feet, which may be abbreviated SF, sq. ft., ft.^{2}, or ⊡.

---

1. The pound-foot system is called the *English system* in North America, but the *imperial system* in the United Kingdom and Commonwealth countries.

Both income and expenses are typically quoted in dollars per square foot per year; in the state of California, however, rental amounts are sometimes quoted in dollars per square foot per month.

Inflation

Although annual inflation has varied over the past 20 years, peaking at approximately 13% in the late 1970s and recently averaging 3% to 5%, international real estate practitioners will find that extreme inflation is rare in the United States. Many properties are valued with the discounted cash flow (DCF) technique, in which a presumed rate of inflation is incorporated into the analysis. Inflation is most commonly measured by the change in the Consumer Price Index, or CPI, a measure of the average increase or decrease in the price paid for a fixed market basket of goods and services tracked by the U.S. Bureau of Labor Statistics. Annual and expected rates of inflation are widely reported in the press and are available to all real estate professionals.

In the United States, properties are not valued based on analysis of a "real rate of return." If a forecast of future revenues and expenses is required, a measure of anticipated inflation must be incorporated into the forecast.

Typical Lease Structure

Office

Lease terms for office space can range from three to 20 years or more. Most office leases are written for five- or 10-year terms. Generally, the larger the space, the longer the term of the lease.

Office leases are typically *gross leases,* which means that the tenant is obligated to pay a fixed base rent, expressed in dollars per square foot per year, but paid in monthly installments, plus a proportionate share of the increase in building expenses. The *base year* is typically the year in which the lease begins. Base rent can be fixed for the entire lease term, increase at stipulated intervals, or increase to keep pace with inflation. In weak markets with low demand or an oversupply of space, tenants may be granted *free rent* for a specified period, often six months for a five-year (60-month) lease. This was a typical occurrence in the overbuilt markets of the late 1980s, but has since become less common.

Expense pass-alongs[2] may also be used. For example, if annual building expenses were initially $7.00 per square foot (PSF) and increase by 10% to $7.70 PSF, the tenant is obligated to pay an additional $0.70 PSF in rent the following

---

2. Also called *expense pass-throughs* or *expense recoveries.*

year. Building expenses usually include all costs of operating the property, e.g., cleaning, utilities, maintenance and repairs, property management, and real estate taxes. Typically excluded are capital expenditures such as roof or boiler repairs, tenant improvement costs and leasing commissions, debt service (mortgage) payments, and non-cash expenses such as depreciation.

Certain capital costs are associated with procuring a tenant, namely tenant improvement costs (TIs) and leasing commissions. TIs, usually expressed in dollars PSF, represent the cost of fixing up the space for a new tenant. They can run from only a few dollars for painting and cleaning to $100 or more PSF to attract an upscale tenant in a competitive market. These costs are almost always paid by the landlord, although space may sometimes be rented on an "as is" basis in exchange for a reduced base rent.

Leasing commissions are usually calculated as a percentage of base rent over the lease term and are paid at lease commencement. Typical leasing commissions range from 3% to 5% of the annual rent.

Retail

Lease terms for shopping centers are usually longer than those for office buildings, commonly extending for five, seven, or 10 years or more. The leases signed by anchor or major tenants usually cover a minimum of 20 years, and can sometimes extend for 50 years or more, including options to renew.

In contrast to the gross leases typical of office buildings, leases for retail properties are usually drawn up on a "net" basis, i.e., the tenant agrees to pay a stipulated base rent plus a pro rata share of the shopping center expenses. Building on the expense pass-along example described above, if operating expenses were $7.00 PSF in a given year and $7.70 the following year, the retailer would be obligated to pay the full amount each year (expenses PSF times the tenant's square footage) in addition to the base rent. The same expense categories described for office space also apply to shopping centers, but the operating expenses of retail properties, with the exception of real estate taxes, are referred to as *common area maintenance (CAM)*.

Tenant improvement costs are usually far less for shopping centers than office buildings. In fact, in some retail properties they are solely the obligation of the tenant rather than the landlord. One principal reason retail leases generally run for longer terms than office leases is to give the tenant time to amortize the cost of the tenant improvements over the life of the lease.

A unique feature of most retail leases is the percentage rent clause, which obligates the tenant to pay a portion of annual gross sales above a stipulated level to the landlord. This is known as *percentage rent*. Thus, for a tenant paying $15.00 PSF in base rent with a "natural" breakpoint and percentage rent at 6%, the breakpoint would be estimated at $15.00/0.06, or $250 PSF. This obligates the tenant to pay the landlord percentage rent equal to 6% of sales above $250 PSF. Percentage rent clauses can prove extremely beneficial to the landlord, particularly in an inflationary environment where percentage rent may grow exponentially faster than sales volume. The illustration below shows the amount of annual percentage rent due for a 10,000 SF store based on a 10% annual increase in sales.

Table 1. Calculation of Percentage Rent

Year	Sales PSF	Percentage Rent Payable
1	$227	0
2	250	0
3	275	$15,000*
4	302	31,200
5	332	49,200

*$275 X 10,000 SF = $2,750,000 less $2,500,000 breakpoint = $250,000 X 6% = $15,000 or $1.50 PSF.

Thus, retail tenants usually pay a combination of base rent, CAM charges, real estate taxes, and percentage rent (when applicable).

Industrial

Industrial properties frequently have long-term, flat (level-payment) net leases. Fairly typical would be a 10-year net lease at $3.00 PSF with the tenant paying all the expenses of operating the building with the possible exception of a management fee (usually minor) and capital expenditures.

Valuation Standards

The Appraisal Standards Board (ASB) of The Appraisal Foundation develops, publishes, interprets, and amends the Uniform Standards of Professional Appraisal Practice (USPAP) on behalf of appraisers and users of appraisal services. Since USPAP is used by state and federal regulatory agencies and others, the ASB has adopted an annual publication policy to ensure that all those concerned are informed of interpretations of, and amendments to, USPAP in a regular and timely manner. Each year the ASB publishes a bound edition of the Uniform Standards which includes a history of any changes made the previous year, the full text of USPAP, all Statements on Appraisal Standards, all Advisory Opinions issued for general distribution, and an index. A mid-year supplement is issued and distributed to all purchasers of USPAP.

Licensing/Certification

The Appraisal Institute currently grants the MAI designation to qualified commercial property appraisers and the SRA designation to qualified residential appraisers. Other Appraisal Institute designations include the SRPA, SREA, and RM. Appraisal Institute designations are the most widely recognized professional appraisal designations in the United States. Many lenders require appraisals prepared by MAIs, and many lease documents call for disputes to be resolved with the assistance of an appraiser holding the MAI designation.

Requirements for the MAI designation are summarized below. All candidates must:

- Hold an undergraduate degree from an approved college or university
- Attend the Standards of Professional Practice course
- Attend the Report Writing and Valuation Analysis course
- Pass a comprehensive examination
- Receive a passing grade on a demonstration appraisal report of an income-producing property
- Have 4,500 hours of appraisal experience

Requirements for the SRA designation follow. Each candidate must:

- Hold an undergraduate degree from an approved degree-granting institution of higher education
- Attend the Standards of Professional Practice course
- Receive a passing grade on a demonstration appraisal report of a one- to-four-family residential property
- Have 3,000 hours of residential appraisal experience

In 1989 the U.S. Congress passed the Financial Institutions Reform, Recovery and Enforcement Act, commonly referred to as FIRREA. One purpose of this act was to correct perceived abuses in the appraisal industry by requiring that appraisers be licensed or certified. The responsibility for licensing and certification was delegated to each of the fifty states and the District of Columbia. State licensing and certification of appraisers became mandatory on December 31, 1992, with each state setting its own requirements. Appraisers are now required to be licensed or certified in the state in which the property being appraised is located. This has created problems and a financial burden for many appraisers whose practice spans more than one state.

The Appraisal Institute and each of the states also have continuing education requirements.

Appraisal Reporting Requirements

Users of appraisals, primarily lending institutions and investors, have grown accustomed to receiving thoroughly prepared, well-documented appraisal reports. FlRREA increased the documentation required for most reports. Full narrative appraisal reports are commonly 100 pages or more in length. Set out below is a typical table of contents for a report, as excerpted from the eleventh edition of the Appraisal Institute textbook, *The Appraisal of Real Estate.*

Part One—Introduction

Title page

Letter of transmittal

Table of contents

Certification of value

Summary of important conclusions

Part Two—Premises of the Appraisal

Identification of type of appraisal and report format

Assumptions and limiting conditions

Purpose and use of the appraisal

Definition of value and date of value estimate

Property rights appraised

Scope of the appraisal

Part Three—Presentation of Data

Identification of the property, legal description

Identification of any personal property or other items that are not real property

Area, city, neighborhood, and location data

Site data

Description of improvements

Zoning

Taxes and assessment data

History, including prior sales and current offers or listings

Marketability study, if appropriate

Part Four—Analysis of Data and Conclusions

Highest and best use of the land as though vacant

Highest and best use of the property as improved

Site value

Cost approach

Sales comparison approach

Income capitalization approach

Reconciliation and final value estimate

Estimate of marketing period

Qualifications of the appraiser

Addenda

Detailed legal description, if not included in the presentation of data

Detailed statistical data

Leases or lease summaries

Other appropriate information

Secondary exhibits

Appraisers in the United States are expected to document all the reasoning and analyses in the report and lead the reader to a logical conclusion. This requires a description of the property and its surrounding area, analysis of the market in which it competes, and use of one or more of the three traditional approaches to value. Because of liability concerns as well as reporting requirements, even the shortest reports are five to 10 pages long. All reports must include items such as the assumptions and limiting conditions associated with the value estimate, a certification as to the appraiser's objectivity, and definitions of market value and the property interest appraised.

Definition of Market Value

Although there have been minor variations in the definition of market value over the years, at present the most commonly accepted definition is the one contained in FIRREA. This definition is cited below.

> Market value can be defined as the most probable price which a property should bring in a competitive and open market under all conditions requisite to a fair sale, the buyer and seller each acting prudently and knowledgeably, and assuming the price is not affected by undue stimulus. Implicit in this definition is the consummation of a sale as of a specified date and the passing of title from seller to buyer under conditions whereby:
>
> 1.   Buyer and seller are typically motivated;

2. Both parties are well informed or well advised, and acting in what they consider their best interests;

3. A reasonable time is allowed for exposure in the open market;

4. Payment is made in terms of cash in United States dollars or in terms of financial arrangements comparable thereto; and

5. The price represents the normal consideration for the property sold unaffected by special or creative financing or sales concessions granted by anyone associated with the sale.[3]

Income Approach

Most income-producing properties are bought and sold on the basis of their income-producing potential, which in U.S. appraisal literature is associated with the principle of anticipation, i.e., value is the present worth of future benefits.

A meaningful estimate of cash flow cannot be prepared without a full understanding of the dynamics of the marketplace and the relationship of the subject property to competitive properties in the market. After market investigation, the valuer prepares an estimate of applicable revenue and expense items, either for a single year or for a presumed holding period. The former estimate is used in direct capitalization, while the latter is employed in discounted cash flow (DCF) analysis. The difference between revenues and expenses is called *net operating income (NOI)* or cash flow. Finally, an appropriate capitalization rate or discount rate must be developed for use in the analysis.

Discounted Cash Flow (DCF) Analysis

Income forecasts are commonly based on a presumed 10-year holding period. The subject property is valued with the expectation that the owner will receive 10 years of revenue and then sell the property to a new purchaser. This future sale price is called the *reversion,* and it is calculated by applying a capitalization rate to the estimated *NOI* for the eleventh year. Then these sale proceeds are discounted, along with the 10 years of revenue, to derive an estimate of present value.

---

3. "Appraisal Standards for Federally Related Transactions," *Federal Register,* Vol. 55, No. 165, August 24, 1990, Rules and Regulations, Sections 34, 43.

An accurate forecast of revenues and expenses is key to a proper valuation. In estimating annual revenues and expenses, five steps are generally followed.[4]

1. Base rentals are cataloged. Lease data for existing tenants are entered into a computer on a lease-by-lease basis. A market rent is assigned to vacant space, and a presumed date of lease commencement is entered. Upon lease expiration, a new market base rent is selected from a matrix, expense escalation payments are dropped to zero, and a new base year amount is established in the year of re-leasing.

2. Other sources of revenue such as tenant utility income, escalation payments, and parking revenue are identified.

3. A deduction from income is made to account for collection losses, tenant turnover, and unanticipated vacancies.

4. Reasonable levels of building operating expenses are projected.

5. Capital items such as leasing commissions, the costs of tenant improvements, and a reserve for large, one-time future capital expenses are deducted.

Once the forecast has been prepared and checked for accuracy, the valuer selects an appropriate rate with which to discount the annual cash flows and reversion proceeds to present value. While each property is unique, many published investor surveys are readily available to the appraiser. Surveys published by Peter F. Korpacz & Associates (Frederick, MD), Real Estate Research Corp. (Chicago, IL), and CB Commercial Real Estate Group, Inc. (Los Angeles, CA), among others, provide broad insight into the thinking of market participants. Published rates can be used as a benchmark in selecting a discount rate to apply to the forecast income of the subject property.

Although a discount rate may initially be used to discount future revenues and reversion proceeds to present value, the resultant first year rate of return (expressed as a capitalization rate, as in the example of direct capitalization presented below) is also an important determinant of value, as is the price per square foot of rentable area in the building.

Table 2 illustrates a typical cash flow forecast. Table 3 shows the calculation of property value under a variety of discount and capitalization rates.

---

4. John Robert White, editor-in-chief, *The Office Building From Concept to Investment Reality* (Chicago: Counselors of Real Estate, Appraisal Institute, and Society of Industrial and Office Realtors® Educational Fund, 1993), 557-558.

Table 2. Taton Office Building: Eleven-Year Forecast of Operating Income & Cash Flow

	1997	1998	1999	2000	2001	2002	2003	2004	2005	2006	2007
Income											
Base rent	$2,769,742	$2,902,527	$2,961,726	$3,026,232	$3,127,480	$3,202,927	$3,267,502	$3,292,659	$2,361,683	$2,557,027	$3,982,228
Operating escalation	116,351	210,054	306,701	382,891	445,992	519,463	595,789	653,701	601,821	210,820	63,642
Tenant electric	204,474	216,592	225,256	234,266	243,637	253,382	263,518	268,436	250,529	223,851	298,932
Potential income	$3,090,567	$3,329,173	$3,493,683	$3,643,389	$3,817,109	$3,975,772	$4,126,809	$4,214,796	$3,214,033	$2,991,698	$4,344,802
Credit loss	(92,717)	(99,875)	(104,810)	(109,302)	(114,513)	(119,273)	(123,804)	(126,444)	(96,421)	(89,751)	(130,344)
Total income	$2,997,850	$3,229,298	$3,388,873	$3,534,087	$3,702,596	$3,856,499	$4,003,005	$4,088,352	$3,117,612	$2,901,947	$4,214,458
Expenses											
General operating	$ 436,966	$ 454,445	$ 472,623	$ 491,528	$ 511,189	$ 531,636	$ 552,901	$ 575,017	$ 598,018	$ 621,939	$ 646,816
Real estate taxes	628,680	685,954	745,289	783,224	806,721	838,990	872,549	907,451	943,749	981,499	1,020,759
Utilities	216,780	225,451	234,469	243,848	253,601	263,745	274,295	285,267	296,678	308,545	320,887
Water/sewer	3,867	4,021	4,182	4,350	4,524	4,704	4,893	5,088	5,292	5,504	5,724
Management fees	44,968	48,439	50,833	53,011	55,539	57,847	60,045	61,325	46,764	43,529	63,217
Total expenses	$1,331,261	$1,418,310	$1,507,396	$1,575,961	$1,631,574	$1,696,922	$1,764,683	$1,834,148	$1,890,501	$1,961,016	$2,057,403
Net operating income	$1,666,589	$1,810,988	$1,881,477	$1,958,126	$2,071,022	$2,159,577	$2,238,322	$2,254,204	$1,227,111	$940,931	$2,157,055
Deductions											
Leasing commissions	$ 42,429	$ —	$ —	$ —	$ —	$ —	$ —	$ —	$ 87,512	$ 78,941	$ 65,317
Tenant alterations	75,766	—	—	—	—	—	—	—	66,123	90,507	112,152
Capital reserves	31,366	32,621	33,926	35,283	36,694	38,162	39,688	41,276	42,927	44,644	46,430
Total deductions	$ 149,561	$ 32,621	$ 33,926	$ 35,283	$ 36,694	$ 38,162	$ 39,688	$ 41,276	$ 196,562	$ 214,092	$ 223,899
Net income from operations	$1,517,028	$1,778,367	$1,847,551	$1,922,843	$2,034,328	$2,121,415	$2,198,634	$2,212,928	$1,030,549	$ 726,839	$1,933,156

Table 3. Valuation Analysis

Residual capitalization rate — 10.0%
Net operating income, Period 11 (Year 2007) — $ 2,157,055

Property resale @ 10% cap rate — 21,570,550
Less: 3% commission — 647,116
Net property resale value — $20,923,434

Year	Analysis Period	Annual Cash Flow	PV of Cash Flow @ 11.0% IRR	PV of Cash Flow @ 11.5% IRR	PV of Cash Flow @ 12.0% IRR
Net income from operations					
1997	1	$ 1,517,028	$ 1,366,692	$ 1,360,563	$ 1,354,489
1998	2	1,778,367	1,443,363	1,430,447	1,417,703
1999	3	1,847,551	1,350,913	1,332,821	1,315,050
2000	4	1,922,843	1,266,636	1,244,069	1,222,001
2001	5	2,034,328	1,207,275	1,180,447	1,154,332
2002	6	2,121,415	1,134,195	1,104,019	1,074,775
2003	7	2,198,634	1,058,991	1,026,193	994,550
2004	8	2,212,928	960,248	926,336	893,765
2005	9	1,030,549	402,867	386,897	371,626
2006	10	726,839	255,981	244,731	234,023
Total net income from operations		$17,390,482	$10,447,161	$10,236,522	$10,032,315
Net property resale @ 10% cap rate		20,923,434	7,368,909	7,045,053	6,736,786
Total property present value			$17,816,070	$17,281,575	$16,769,101
Rounded to thousands			$17,816,000	$17,282,000	$16,769,000

Note: **IRR (internal rate of return)** is the annualized yield rate or rate of return on capital that is generated or capable of being generated within an investment or portfolio over a period of ownership.

Direct Capitalization

For properties with long-term, level cash flows and in situations in which investors are reluctant to make assumptions about future, noncontractual increases in revenue, appraisers may want to value property using direct capitalization. This process entails the estimation of a single year's income and expenses—usually the first year of the new purchaser's ownership or the first stabilized year of occupancy—and the application of an overall capitalization, or *cap*, rate (R_O) to *NOI*.

Data on overall capitalization rates, like information on discount rates, are readily available, but again such data must be used with caution. Table 4 illustrates a valuation using direct capitalization.

Table 4. Direct Capitalization			
Potential gross rental income			$2,913,345
Other income			128,520
Parking income			22,440
Total potential gross income			$3,064,305
Vacancy (7% of rental income)			− 203,934
Effective gross income			$2,860,371
Expenses	**Per Sq. Ft.**		
Real estate taxes	$1.49	$408,019	
Insurance	0.12	32,861	
Management fee	0.42	114,415	
Repairs and maintenance	0.30	82,151	
Contract services	0.35	95,843	
Utilities	0.50	136,919	
Salaries	0.79	216,332	
General & administrative	0.55	150,611	
Reserves	0.17	46,552	
Total expenses	$4.69		−$1,283,703
Net operating income	$5.76		$1,576,668
Overall capitalization rate (R_O)			8.5%
Market value ($1,576,668/0.085)			$18,549,035

Sales Comparison Approach

In the sales comparison approach, market value is estimated by comparing the subject property to similar properties that have been sold or are currently being offered for sale. It is based on the principle of substitution, which states that when several, similar properties are available, the one with the lowest price will attract the greatest demand. In the United States, most office, retail, and industrial building sales are quoted on the basis of the price per square foot of rentable area. Hotels are usually compared on a per room or per key basis, while land value may be expressed in terms of price per square foot, per acre, or per square foot of permissible building area.

Although unit comparisons are widely accepted, extreme care should be used because precise building measurements are not prepared by the valuer. Instead, valuers must rely on published directories of significant buildings in major markets, rent rolls, or even figures reported in the press. On rare occasions, exact measurements calculated by an architect are supplied. More commonly, quotations of square footage can vary widely.

For office and retail properties, the appropriate measurement is usually above-grade rentable area; basements are excluded, but first-floor retail areas are counted. One generally accepted custom is to rely on the building's rent roll as an indicator of rentable area. While the rent roll is probably the most accurate and detailed source of information that a valuer can reasonably expect to obtain, even that can change with the signing of a lease that incorporates an area such as a hallway, which was previously common area, into the leased area of a new tenant. Because warehouses and industrial properties are generally constructed much more simply, differences of opinion regarding their size are less common.

For large, investment-grade properties, comparable sales provide a useful check on the results of the income approach. It would be highly unusual for an investor to purchase an income-producing property solely on the basis of its price per square foot.

Cost Approach

The third traditional approach to value, the cost approach, is most applicable to special-purpose buildings, such as schools and churches, and to recently constructed properties that do not suffer from significant amounts of depreciation. Its use as a mainstream appraisal tool has become somewhat controversial. Many users of appraisal reports insist on its inclusion, while an equal number of appraisers call for its demise. Nevertheless, the cost approach is still a recognized valuation technique. An example illustrating the approach is presented in Table 5.

Table 5. Summary of a Cost Approach Appraisal	
Land value	$ 900,000
Replacement cost new	10,500,000
Plus entrepreneurial profit @ 15 % (rounded)	1,700,000
	$13,100,000
Less depreciation	7,700,000
Indicated value	$ 5,400,000

Reconciliation

At the end of the valuation process, the U.S. appraiser takes a step back from his or her analyses and critiques each of the approaches applied before arriving at a final value conclusion. This critique, known in the appraisal report as the *reconciliation*, provides a brief summary of the applicability and reliability of each approach. To arrive at a final estimate of value, the valuer never averages indications derived from different approaches or different comparables. Rather, the valuer gives greater weight to the value or values indicated by the approach most appropriate to the appraisal problem and/or the comparable(s) most similar to the subject.

Availability of Data

Market data are generally easy to obtain in the United States, a fortunate situation given the voluminous requirements that apply to most appraisal reports. In addition, there is a strong sense of camaraderie among appraisers, evidenced by a general willingness to exchange data about comparable sales and rents. Income and expense data about the subject property are almost never disclosed to other appraisers, however, since to do so would violate the appraiser/client relationship. In some instances, appraisers may be asked by their clients to sign confidentiality agreements, restricting access to data even within the appraiser's office to those with a "need to know." The following are some suggested data sources.

Demographic and Economic Data

- Municipal, county, and state offices
- Local chambers of commerce
- Libraries
- Articles in local or business newspapers

Real Estate Market Data (Market Size, Occupancy, Rent Levels)

- Most local offices of real estate brokerage, management, and appraisal firms
- Published reports of larger real estate firms covering major U.S. markets
- Y.T. and Louise Lee Lum Library, Appraisal Institute, Chicago, IL
- International Council of Shopping Centers, New York, NY
- Local real estate boards (Membership may be required.)
- National Association of Realtors® Library, Chicago, IL
- REIS (Real Estate Information Service) Reports, New York, NY
- Urban Land Institute, Washington, DC

Rent and Sale Comparables

- Appraisers (*Directory of Designated Members* available from Appraisal Institute, Chicago, IL.)
- Counselors (Membership directory available from Counselors of Real Estate, Chicago, IL.)
- Locally based real estate brokers and managers

Appraisal Organization

Appraisal Institute
875 North Michigan Avenue
Chicago, IL 60611-1980
Tel. (312) 335-4100
Fax. (312) 335-4400
http://www.realworks.com/ai

Bibliography

The Appraisal Foundation (Appraisal Standards Board). *Uniform Standards of Professional Appraisal Practice.* Washington, DC: The Appraisal Foundation, 1997.

Appraisal Institute. *The Appraisal of Real Estate.* 11th ed. Chicago: Appraisal Institute, 1996.

Appraisal Institute. *Appraising Residential Properties.* 2d ed. Chicago: Appraisal Institute, 1994.

Appraisal Institute. *The Dictionary of Real Estate Appraisal.* 3d ed. Chicago: Appraisal Institute, 1993.

Eaton, J.D. *Real Estate Valuation in Litigation.* 2d ed. Chicago: Appraisal Institute, 1995.

Fanning, Stephen F., Terry V. Grissom, and Thomas D. Pearson. *Market Analysis for Valuation Appraisals.* Chicago: Appraisal Institute, 1992.

White, John Robert. Editor-in-chief. *The Office Building From Concept to Investment Reality.* Chicago: Counselors of Real Estate, Appraisal Institute, and Society of Industrial and Office Realtors® Educational Fund, 1993.

The United Kingdom

David Mackmin, B.Sc., M.Sc., FRICS

David Mackmin, B.Sc.(estate management), M.Sc., and FRICS (Fellow of the Royal Institution of Chartered Surveyors) is a professor of property studies at Sheffield Hallam University. He is the author of *The Valuation and Sale of Residential Property,* published by Routledge (London, 1994) and coauthor with Andrew Baum of *Income Approach to Property Valuation,* also published by Routledge (London, 1989).

The United Kingdom comprises England, Wales, Scotland, and Northern Ireland. England is largely lowland plains with rolling hills (the Cotswolds, Chiltern Hills, and the Downs). In the southeast is the Thames Basin, the location of London. Northern England is dominated by mountains, the Pennines and Cumbrians, site of the Lake District. Wales and Scotland are mainly highland areas, i.e., the Cambrian mountains in Wales and the Grampian mountains with their many lochs in Scotland. Central Scotland is a lowland and the south is an upland. Plains and hills also cover Northern Ireland (Ulster). The moderate maritime climate of the United Kingdom is governed by the Gulf Stream and North Atlantic Drift. Principal cities are London, Manchester, Birmingham, Glasgow, Leeds, Sheffield, Liverpool, Bradford, Edinburgh, Bristol, Belfast, and Cardiff.

Political Structure

The constitution of Great Britain is unwritten and has evolved over the past one thousand years. Key constitutional changes began with the Norman Conquest in 1066. At that time all land in England became vested in the Crown and was held on grant from the Crown in exchange for services.

Today the Crown is still head of state and retains the constitutional power to dissolve Parliament but, in effect, the elected majority party in the House of Commons forms the government for a term of five years. The House of Lords acts as an upper chamber and makes a significant contribution on major legislation, but it has no real power to overrule the work of the House of Commons.

The judiciary is independent of Parliament and acts to protect the rules of natural law and justice. Through precedent, it establishes the legal interpretation of legislation.

As part of the European Community since 1973, the government is bound by the Treaty of Rome, which established the Common Market in 1957-1958.

The law in Scotland is very similar to that of England and Wales, but legislation affecting the United Kingdom may include different provisions for Scotland and Northern Ireland.

Land use control is the responsibility of local governments acting within the framework set down by the central government. The handling of environmental issues increasingly follows European directives. In its strict sense, zoning does not apply in the United Kingdom, but each planning authority is required to formulate broad planning policy. Under planning law in the United Kingdom, there can be no development or material change of use without planning permission being obtained from the local planning authority. Permission for minor changes is generally provided by general development orders. When permission is refused, there is a right of appeal. Appeals are heard by an inspector appointed by the Minister for the Environment.

The concept of highest and best use is familiar to valuers in the United Kingdom. The historic nature of many buildings and areas, however, may preclude further development or redevelopment to the highest and best use. This situation is typical of many parts of Europe. Building regulations approval must also be obtained from the local authority.

Property is subject to various taxes. The transfer of property rights in excess of £60,000 is subject to an ad valorem tax or stamp duty, currently set at 1% of the transfer price. A value-added tax (VAT) is normally payable on rents and service costs. The main property tax on residential property is the council tax. Every house is placed within a *capital value band* and an annual local tax is payable at a rate based on the value band. The council tax is locally determined, but subject to central government *capping.*

On commercial property, the uniform business rate (UBR) is payable. All properties are assessed and a rateable value (RV) is determined. The RV is equivalent to the annual rental value of the property. The level of UBR is centrally determined for England, Scotland, and Wales. Reassessment of RVs occurs every five years.

A capital gains tax is payable on all realised property gains except those from a principal residence. Exemptions exist and roll-over relief will apply in most cases if realised gains are reinvested.

Property Rights

The fee simple absolute, or freehold title, is the principal legal right in real property. Freeholders hold an estate from the Crown in perpetuity and are deemed to own everything beneath and above the surface. In practice, these rights are restricted by law with respect to an individual's right to own and extract certain categories of minerals and by the rights of the air force and civil aviation to use the air space. There are common law rights to provide physical support to adjoining land (i.e., an owner cannot undermine adjoining land) as well as light and air easements and rights of way, where established. Escheat rests with the Crown.

Freeholders have the right to sell the whole or only part of the property to transfer ownership and to create leases and licenses. A lease may be for any number of years up to a maximum of 999 years. A leaseholder's rights are limited by the length of the lease and by the covenants in the lease.

In the nineteenth century, leases were either short (weekly, monthly) leases or long building leases of up to 99 years. Early leases were without rent reviews or break clauses. In our time, most leases have incorporated provisions for rent review. Generally, rent adjustments are upward only. The 1960s saw the establishment of the institutional lease. This market term describes the typical lease granted by property companies and major investors in property. The term of such a lease is 20 or 25 years with rent reviews every three or five years, when rent is adjusted upward to the open market level. The tenant is liable for all repairs, insurances, and other outgoings (expenditures). In the case of multitenanted buildings, each lease is subject to a full service charge. This form of lease may be considered a net lease in investment terms.

The recession has strengthened the bargaining position of tenants. There has been a trend to shorter, 10- to 15-year leases with rent reviews and with the tenant liable for all outgoings (expenses). The next phase may see a shift of liability for structural repairs back to the owner.

The rights of landlords and tenants are sometimes restricted by legislation, particularly in the residential market.[1] In regard to business property in England and Wales, the principal legislation is the Landlord and Tenant Act of 1954, as amended by the Law of Property Act of 1969. These acts give business tenants security of tenure, set out the basis for determining open market rent for new leases, and provide for the payment of compensation if landlords recover possession for their own use and occupation or for redevelopment. This legislation does not apply in Scotland.

Since it is the bundle of legal rights that is valued, it is essential to have a full knowledge of titular rights and obligations and of all legislation that affects the ownership and use of land and buildings. The valuation principles discussed in this chapter must be applied within the specific legal context of the United Kingdom. It is beyond the scope of this text, however, to provide detailed considerations of such issues.

Language

English is the spoken language in most parts of the United Kingdom. Welsh is now spoken by a growing percentage of the population of Wales and is taught in Welsh schools. By law, court and public documents in Wales are now prepared in Welsh and English. Gaelic is still a living language in Scotland, but it is spoken only by a few.

Currency

The pound sterling is the monetary unit. It is divided into 100 pence. All property transactions and valuations are in pounds (£). Scottish banks have the right to print their own notes.

Units of Measure

Metric and imperial measures are used in the United Kingdom. The leading professional bodies have recommended the adoption of metric measures with the imperial equivalents to be provided in brackets. These equivalents are shown in the following table:

---

1. See David Mackmin, *The Valuation and Sale of Residential Property* (London and New York: Routledge, 1994).

Metric	Imperial
1 m	1.0936 yards
0.3048 m	1 foot
0.9144 m	1 yard
1.6093 km	1 mile
1 m^2	10.8 ft^2
0.0920 m^2	1 ft^2
1 hectare (ha)	2.4711 acres

Residential agents (brokers) may be less willing to adopt a metric approach as many properties were designed on an imperial module. Nevertheless, the changeover went into effect in 1996.

Inflation

Inflation is a key factor in the property market. Capital investment which fails to maintain value in real terms is a poor investment. The ability of property to maintain value has been a vital factor in the market since 1940.

Valuation practice in the United Kingdom is largely based on current estimates of rent. However, inflation projections can be built into valuation models if required by the client. Care must be taken in transposing evidence of inflation based on historic movements in the Retail Price Index (RPI), consumer expenditure, or other key indicators because movements in rent are a function of factors in the market for a specific type of property in a specific location. They may not reflect general price movements. Forecasting and economic cycles are now seen as major issues in both property valuation work and in the advice given by agents. In residential and commercial markets, evidence of sale prices has proved that, in the short term, far from maintaining value in real terms, property can lose value in monetary terms. Understanding the underlying social and economic forces in the property market is essential to the education of property valuers and to the fulfillment of the chartered surveyor's analytical and advisory role.

The Valuation Profession

The two principal professional bodies guiding the education and practice of the property valuer are The Royal Institution of Chartered Surveyors and The Incorporated Society of Valuers and Auctioneers, whose members are either associates or fellows and use the designations ARICS/FRICS and ASVA/FSVA.

There are no licence requirements in the United Kingdom so anyone can be called a valuer. In a few cases involving valuations for secured loans and certain asset valuations, the appointed valuer must be a member of the RICS or ISVA. In practice, most valuation work is undertaken by chartered survey-ors or members of the Incorporated Society.

A clear distinction is made in the United Kingdom between the advice rendered by an agent/broker on sale price, which is not regarded as a profes-sional valuation, and the work of a professional valuer.

The minimum education and training period for a chartered surveyor is five years and will normally assume one of the following patterns:

- a three-year, full-time university degree in property plus two years of profes-sional training
- a four-year sandwich degree (2 + 1 + 1) plus one year of professional training
- a six-year degree/diploma obtained as a part-time student while employed full time
- a university degree plus postgraduate diploma/degree plus two years of professional training

Candidates must register with the RICS or ISVA for periods of prequalification professional training. The work requirements for these periods of training are specified by the professional bodies and include a minimum number of days of supervised valuation work. Upon completion of their professional training, candidates must present themselves for a final assessment of their profes-sional competence.

Qualified valuers are required by their professional associations to undertake regular continuing professional development (CPD) throughout their working careers and may be called to account for their CPD activities.

Qualified valuers are bound by their professional codes of ethics, and in their valuation work they must follow the minimum standards for appraisals and valuations approved by the professional bodies. In developing these stan-dards, the professional bodies liaise with:

- The British Bankers Association
- The Council of Mortgage Lenders
- The accounting professions
- The Council of the Stock Exchange

Valuers appraising outside the United Kingdom are subject to the licensing and other requirements of the countries where they practice. Valuation work in Europe is normally in accordance with the standards recommended by The European Group of Valuers of Fixed Assets (TEGOVOFA); valuers working elsewhere follow the recommendations of the International Valuation Standards Committee (IVSC).

Valuation Practice

Following a major review of valuation practice in 1993-1994, revised standards of valuation and appraisal practice are being developed by the RICS. The principal aims of these standards are to:

1. Encourage valuers to carefully establish and understand at the outset their clients' needs and requirements, and to satisfy themselves that they are equipped to meet them to a satisfactory standard;

2. Promote the consistent use of bases and assumptions upon which valuations are provided and the selection on each occasion of the basis which will meet the clients' proper needs;

3. Help valuers to achieve high standards of professional competence in the preparation of valuations and appraisals;

4. Promote the provision of unambiguous and readily comprehensible valuation and appraisal reports which provide the advice and information which their readers need and should have; and

5. Ensure that published reference to valuations include clear, accurate and sufficient information which is not misleading.[2]

The standards provide detailed coverage of a number of key elements of the valuation process, including:

*   Confirmation of instructions

*   Bases and definition of value

*   Valuation reports

*   Guidance relating to specific valuation work such as

    -   valuations for secured loans

    -   valuation for asset valuation purposes, such as company accounts, stock market quotations, mergers, and takeovers

Confirmation of Instructions

Valuers must specify in writing the terms and conditions relating to their instruction (assignment). This requirement would cover:

*   The purpose

---

2. *RICS Appraisal and Valuation Manual,* Introduction, page 1, AS (1995).

- The subject of the valuation and the property interest
- The basis or bases of the valuation, i.e., open market value or other
- Assumptions
- Date of valuation
- Currency (£)
- Plant and machinery on hire purchase (paid for in installments) or in trust
- Dies, moulds, special tooling, or computer software
- Restrictions on the valuer's work
- Caveats relating to nonpublication
- Limitation on third-party liability
- Information to be provided by the client or his advisers
- The use of consultants, e.g., to investigate contamination and remedial costs[3]

Basis of Valuation

The normal basis for valuation work in the United Kingdom is open market value or estimated realisation price. Open market value is defined as follows:

> Open market value is the best price at which the sale of an interest in property would have been completed unconditionally for cash consideration on the date of valuation, assuming:
>
> (a) a willing seller;
>
> (b) that, prior to the date of valuation, there had been a reasonable period (having regard to the nature of the property and the state of the market) for the proper marketing of the interest, for the agreement of the price and terms and for the completion of the sale;
>
> (c) that the state of the market, level of values and other circumstances were, on any earlier assumed date of exchange of contracts, the same as on the date of valuation;
>
> (d) that no account is taken of any additional bid by a prospective purchaser with a special interest; and
>
> (e) that both parties to the transaction had acted knowledgeably, prudently and without compulsion.[4]

---

3. *RICS Appraisal and Valuation Manual,* Practice Statement 2, Conditions of Engagement, PS 2.2 (1995).
4. *RICS Appraisal and Valuation Manual,* Practice Statement 4.2.1 (1995).

This is subject to careful definition of the terms used and may be restricted to "open market value for the existing use" or extended to "open market value for alternative use."

Estimated realisation price (ERP) is defined as:

> The amount of cash consideration before deduction of costs of sale which the valuer considers, on the date of valuation, can reasonably be expected to be obtained on future completion of an unconditional sale of the interest in the subject property assuming:
>
> (a) a willing seller;
>
> (b) that completion will take place on a future date specified by the valuer to allow a reasonable period for proper marketing (having regard to the nature of the property and the state of the market);
>
> (c) that no account is taken of any additional bid by a prospective purchaser with special interest; and
>
> (d) that both parties to the transaction will act knowledgeably, prudently and without compulsion.[5]

In the case of buildings for which there is no open market and hence no market comparability, such as specialised buildings (oil refineries, breweries) to be valued specifically for company accounts and similar purposes, the valuer will adopt the depreciated replacement cost (DRC) basis of valuation, defined as:

> The aggregate amount of the value of the land for the existing use or a notional replacement site in the same locality, and the gross re-placement cost of the buildings and other site works, from which appropriate deductions may then be made to allow for the age, condition, economic or functional obsolescence and environmental factors etc; all these might result in the existing property being worth less to the undertaking in occupation than would a new replacement.
>
> The cost to be estimated is not that to erect a building in the future but that to have the building available for occupation at the valuation date, the work having commenced at the appropriate time.[6]

The current definition of open market value is well established and under-stood in the United Kingdom to mean market value, but differs from that agreed upon by the International Valuation Standards Committee (IVSC). The

---

5. *RICS Appraisal and Valuation Manual,* Practice Statement 4.5 (1995).

6. *RICS Appraisal and Valuation Manual,* Practice Statement 4.8 and 4.8.2 (1995).

requirement placed on the valuer is deemed to be the same. The IVSC definition is as follows:

> Market value is the estimated amount for which an asset (property) should exchange on the date of valuation between a willing buyer and a willing seller in an arms-length transaction after proper marketing wherein the parties had each acted knowledgeably, prudently and without compulsion.[7]

The RICS/ISVA also have definitions for

- Open market value for the existing use (OMVEU)
- Open market value for an alternative use (AUV)
- Estimated restricted realisation price (ERRP)

For properties such as hotels, which are normally bought and sold as operational entireties, valuers are required to value on the basis of OMVEU and to adopt a methodology that reflects the market approach to such properties. This will often involve a consideration of profits and profitability.

The new RICS Statements of Valuation and Appraisal Practice became mandatory on January 1, 1996. They apply to almost every purpose for which a client may require a valuation, with the noted exception of those associated with guidance from an agent/broker on asking price and those covered by statute. Noncompliance by any member of the RICS will be a disciplinary offence.

Valuation Report

The form of a report is determined by agreement between the valuer and the client and will depend upon the purpose for which a valuation is required. Reports are prepared in prescribed formats in the following cases:

- Valuations for residential mortgage purposes under the Building Societies Act
- Valuations prepared as part of an RICS/ISVA Home Buyers Survey and Valuation

In other cases, a full report is required.

> The report must convey to the reader a clear understanding of the opinions being expressed by the valuer, the basis of valuation used and the assumptions and information on which it is based. A report would not be regarded as satisfactory if it were ambiguous or if it in any way misled the reader or created a false impression.[8]

---

7. The International Valuation Standards Committee.
8. *RICS Appraisal and Valuation Manual*, Practice Statement 7.1.1 (1995).

The RICS recommend that all reports should include the following items:[9]

- Addressee - address of the client (e.g., company directors, trustees of a trust, partners of a partnership)
- Special instructions and assumptions
- Purpose of valuation
- Assumed date of valuation
- Basis of valuation and its definition (OMV, ERP)
- Assumptions and caveats
- Address(es) and identification of the subject property
- Description of plant and machinery
- Sources, extents, and nondisclosure of information
- Details of tenure and lettings
- Date and extent of the inspection
- Opinion of value in words and figures
- Explanation as to VAT, capital gains tax, and costs of acquisition or realisation
- Exclusion of liability to third parties
- Conformity to requirements of RICS Practice Statements or rationale for departure
- Nonpublication clause
- Whether the valuer is internal (the valuer prepared the appraisal for internal use within a company), external, or independent
- Valuer's signature

The practice statement goes on to list a number of other matters which must or may need to be included. Where relevant, appropriate reference should be made to the practice statement.

Reporting requirements in the United Kingdom are very similar to those in the United States. It is customary to include data used to support the valuer's opinion. However, in England and Wales there is no right of access to the records of sales and lettings kept by the Valuation Office Agency. This is a privatised agency that undertakes all government valuation work and holds the records of all property transactions. Valuers must rely on the information available to them from the activity of their own firms in the market. In Scotland, the records are open to the public.

---

9. *RICS Appraisal and Valuation Manual,* Practice Statements 7.4.1-13 and 7.4.16-20 (1995).

Methods of Valuation

Valuers in the United Kingdom use five principal methods of valuation:

1. Comparison

2. Income or investment

3. Contractor's or cost (for properties not normally bought or sold)

4. Profits (for properties normally bought and sold as operational entireties)
    An operational entirety is a unit of a business conducted from one
    property.

5. Residual or development

Comparison

This method is sometimes referred to as the *market sales approach*. The
method can be broken down into four steps in which the valuer:

1. Selects market comparables.

2. Analyses comparable sales data.

3. Adjusts sale prices for differences in location, condition, accommodation
    and market movements.

4. Formulates an opinion of open market value for the subject property.

The key to this method lies in the availability and quality of information relating
to known sales of similar interests in similar properties in the same locality.

Comparison Process

The process begins with the selection of comparables. The aim is to find
matching pairs, i.e., to find a property that is as similar as possible to the
property to be valued and has been sold at or about the date of valuation. In
most cases, due to the heterogeneous nature of property, comparables will be
less than perfect and adjustments will have to be made to bring the evidence
into line with the subject property.

The sale prices of comparables must then be adjusted for differences in
location, size, condition, accommodation, sale conditions, and market
changes due to time differences. The comparison method is used for the
valuation of freehold residential properties, rental properties, some agricultural properties, and land available for residential development.

Income Approach

The method is used in one of two forms—income capitalisation and discounted cash flow (DCF) analysis. Application of these methods in the United

Kingdom and the United States is very similar, but does reflect differences in market conditions.

Income Capitalisation

Income capitalisation is the preferred market approach for all income-producing properties, given good market evidence of rents and sale prices. In its simplest form, *income* divided by *yield* (capitalisation rate) produces an expression of market value.

In this form, the yield, or all risks yield (ARY), rate is the market capitalisation rate derived from analysis of sales of comparable investment properties. The valuer will use market experience to adjust the ARY for differences between market evidence and the subject property.

Where the property is currently let at a rent below market rent, capitalisation is performed in two or more parts; the contracted rent and future reversionary benefit are treated as separate tranches of income. The rent is always adjusted for any outgoings (operational expenses) to be paid by the freeholder before capitalisation.

Four examples of typical valuations are provided below. All four relate to a 50,000-sq.-ft. (4,600 m²) office building in a good location in central London.

Example A

The property is occupied by an international corporation paying market rent of £2,500,000 per annum. The lease runs 10 years with a scheduled review to adjust to open market rental levels after five years. The tenant is responsible for the cost of all repairs, insurance, and services.

In this case, the income can be treated as net. The level of rent is supported by analysis of market comparables, and a capitalisation rate, or all risks yield (ARY) rate, is derived from comparable market sales. A typical capitalisation rate is 7%. The reciprocal of the yield (1/0.07) used to capitalise the rent is known to valuers in the United Kingdom as *year's purchase (YP)*.

Net income	£2,500,000
Year's purchase or capitalisation in perpetuity* at 7%	14.285714
	£35,714,285

* Year's purchase or capitalisation in perpetuity is the same as the present value of £1 per period when the total period extends in perpetuity.

The valuer's final opinion of value, based on market evidence, may be adjusted for the fees and stamp duty that would have to be paid by a typical purchaser. This sum would then be rounded.

Capitalised value	£35,714,285
Less 2.5% for stamp duty	
and acquisition costs	£35,714,285/1.025
	£34,843,204
Rounded value	£34,800,000

Example B

If the property were occupied on the basis of a non-net lease, the rent would be adjusted for annual expenditures that would have to be met by the free-holder (landlord). The market generally supports a higher level of rent for properties that are let on non-net terms.

Example C

If the property were let at a rent below current market levels, the valuation would customarily be split into two capitalisation procedures, following present value concepts such as those applied to annuities by practitioners in North America. Thus, for a property let at a net rent of £2,000,000 with an upward revision to £2,500,000 in two years based on a lease review, the valuer would follow the *term and reversion procedure* illustrated below:

Current net income	£2,000,000	
PV of £1 per period		
at 7% for two years	1.808018	
		£3,616,036
Reversion to net income of	£2,500,000	
Year's purchase or capitalisation		
in perpetuity at 7%	14.285714	
	£35,714,285	
PV of £1 in two years at 7%	0.873439	
		£31,194,249
Capitalised value		£34,810,285
Less 2.5% for stamp duty		
acquisition costs		£34,810,250/1.025
		£33,961,219
Rounded value		£33,960,000

Alternatively, some valuers and users of software packages split the income estimate into a continuing income and an additional income, applying a *hardcore* or *layer method.*

Current net income	£2,000,000	
Year's purchase or capitalisation		
at 7% in perpetuity	14.285714	
		£28,571,428
Additional income due in two		
years at present rents	£500,000	
In perpetuity at 7%	14.285714	
	£7,142,857	
PV of £1 in two years at 7%	0.873439	
		£6,238,850
		£34,810,278*

* This sum is within £7 of the capitalised value calculated above.

After an adjustment of 2.5% for fees and stamp duty, the rounded value comes to £33,960,000.

The two procedures shown above are called the *term and reversion method* and *the hardcore or layer method* by valuation books in the United Kingdom. A third approach to the same problem may be called the *shortfall method.* When this method is applied, the property is valued as if it were producing market rent at £35,714,285. From this figure is deducted the net present value of the rent not being received, namely £500,000 for two years:

	£35,714,285
£500,000 × 1.808081	− £904,040
	£34,810,245

All three methods, carried out to full decimal places, will produce the same results.

Example D

Currently, properties in London are overrented (i.e., passing or contract rent exceeds open market rent), and a typical approach is to "top slice" the income at risk. Thus, if the property considered above were let at £3,000,000, or £500,000 above the rent paid for comparable properties, the following procedure would be applied.

Continuing secure income	£2,500,000	
Capitalised at 7% in perpetuity	14.285714	
		£35,714,285
Top slice of additional income payable for seven years*	£500,000	
PV of £1 per period for seven years at 10% to reflect added risk	4.868419	
		£2,434,209
		£38,148,494

* In the United Kingdom, rent reviews generally produce only upward adjustments.

After an adjustment of 2.5% for fees and stamp duty, the rounded value comes to £37,218,000.

In the case of properties normally bought and sold as operational entireties, such as hotels, the income to be capitalised would be derived from an analysis of accounts to arrive at the *sustainable net profit*.

Discounted Cash Flow

The rapid advance of spreadsheet development has simplified the use of discounted cash flow (DCF) techniques for valuation and appraisal purposes.

In a good market, the income capitalisation method just described is expected to produce the best opinion of market value. In providing investment advice to prospective purchasers of income-producing property, however, it is normal practice to analyse the investment opportunity by means of a cash flow structured over a 10- to 15-year holding period with a reversion or future resale price. This form of analysis provides a clearer picture of net income and a better assessment of the internal rate of return (*IRR*). DCF makes allowances for the costs of negotiating rent reviews, voids (vacancies), and the costs of lease renewal or reletting.

Income capitalisation traditionally uses an all risks yield or capitalisation rate and capitalises contracted rents and reversionary benefits assessed in terms of the rents obtainable at the date of valuation. A DCF analysis can follow this practice, adopting a more accurate assessment of net income and the timing of net income receipts, or it can be developed to incorporate rental growth. These are seen as two distinct practices and the discount rates used in each approach will be quite different.

Valuers in the United Kingdom are reluctant to use DCF techniques for valuation work as these techniques are not thought to reflect market behaviour. Valuers are even more reluctant to use DCF analysis linked to future forecasts of rental income. Evidence over the last 10 years has illustrated how volatile the rental market can be over the critical first 10 years of the holding period.

For these reasons DCF analysis is primarily used as a tool of analysis, rather than a method of valuation.[10] When it is used to support market valuations of unusual income patterns, the rental forecasts are usually derived using an implied rental growth model based on principles established by Myron J. Gordon.

DCF techniques are used more extensively when development opportunities are being valued. The British Association of Hotel Accountants has also recommended the use of DCF analysis for the valuation of major international hotels.

A DCF analysis performed in the United Kingdom is not dissimilar to one conducted in the United States, but it would reflect the income patterns associated with lease structures and the statutory issues in the United Kingdom arising from the Landlord and Tenant Act of 1954.

Cost Approach

In the United Kingdom, the cost approach is regarded as a method of last resort because cost rarely equates with value. It is used only for properties that are not normally bought or sold, such as oil refineries. In these cases it is seen as the only defensible method of valuation. However, its use is extremely problematic.

There are considerable problems in determining land value with the cost approach, particularly when the property is of a nonconforming nature, such as a hospital in a town centre location. Difficulties also arise in accurately assessing the allowance to be made for physical, economic, functional, and environmental obsolescence.

Profits Method

The profits method is used with properties that are sold as operational entireties, e.g., hotels, restaurants, pubs, theatres, cinemas, petrol filling stations, golf clubs, race courses, and caravan parks (trailer camps). The valuer reviews accounts of the business conducted on the premises. All annual costs, such as working expenses, costs of borrowed capital, and depreciation, are deducted from the total earnings. The balance is then

---

10. See A. Baum and N. Crosby, *Property Investment Analysis* (London and New York: Routledge, 1995).

divided between the tenant's share (or tenant's profits) and the rent, which is subsequently capitalized using the investment method.

Residual Method

The residual method of valuation is used to assess the value of land or land and buildings with latent development value. The steps of the method follow. The valuer:

1. Assesses the highest and best use for the site within the economic, legal, and planning framework.

2. Assesses the gross development value of the scheme (plan).

3. Assesses all the costs of development, including finance charges.

4. Makes an allowance for developer's profit.

5. Calculates the residual sum, which represents the value of the land based on the assumptions underlying points 1 through 4 above.

The final figure will generally be compared to available market evidence of sites sold for similar development purposes. As previously stated, this calculation is likely to be set out as a cash flow.

Applicability of Valuation Methods

Each method of valuation is seen as having specific uses within defined market segments. These uses are listed below:

Comparison	Residential
	Agricultural land
	Rental property
Income capitalisation and DCF analysis	Investment property
Cost, contractor's or depreciated replacement cost	Properties not normally bought or sold
Profits	Properties sold as operational entireties
Residual	Property with development potential

Residential Property

Residential property bought and sold for owner occupancy is valued by means of the comparison method (direct sales). This differs little from North

American practice, but this method's accuracy relies very much on the experience of the valuer operating within a defined market area. In the United Kingdom, statistical techniques have consistently failed to provide a viable alternative to market knowledge. This is partly due to the nature of the residential market in the United Kingdom, where values can vary dramatically within short distances for reasons that may have little or nothing to do with easily observable differences of size and condition, but a lot to do with factors that narrowly define an area or neighbourhood.

Formal valuations supported by comparables are undertaken for mortgages and loans, statutory compliance, and matrimonial purposes. In these cases, a form report or a full report will be produced. Advice on asking prices is not formulated in this way, although the basic methodology will be the same.

The residential investment market is complicated by legislation and it is essential to identify the nature of the tenants occupying the property in order to value it. Tenanted properties can be broadly classified as those held on short leases and those held on long leases of more than 21 years. Laws in the United Kingdom give qualified occupying tenants with long leases the *rights to enfranchise,* which require either extensions to their leases or sale of the freehold to the occupying tenants. These complications have created a specialised market segment serviced by a few valuers who have the necessary market and legal expertise.

Data Sources

Considerable demographic and economic data are collected centrally and at the local government level. Information is available from local and specialised libraries, particularly those run by property schools in universities and by The Royal Institution of Chartered Surveyors. Major property consultants in the United Kingdom hold much of the data in their own libraries and increasingly these data are available on the Internet.

The two, key professional bodies in the United Kingdom can be contacted at the following addresses:

The Royal Institution of
   Chartered Surveyors
12 Great George Street
Westminster
London SW1

The Incorporated Society of
   Valuers and Auctioneers
Cadogan Gate
London

Bibliography

Baum, A. and N. Crosby. *Property Investment Analysis.* 2d ed. London: Routledge, 1995.

Baum, A. and D. Mackmin. *The Income Approach to Property Valuation.* 3d ed. London: Routledge, 1989.

Baum, A. and G. Sams. *Statutory Valuations.* 2d ed. London: Routledge, 1991.

Britton, W. K. Davies and T. Johnson. *Modern Methods of Valuation.* 8th ed. London: Estates Gazette, 1989.

Crosby, Neil. Chapter 16 "The United Kingdom" in *European Valuation Practice.* London: E & FN Spon (an imprint of Chapman & Hall), 1996

Mackmin, D. *The Valuation and Sale of Residential Property.* 2d ed. London: Routledge, 1994

Royal Institution of Chartered Surveyors. *RICS Appraisal and Valuation Manual.* London: RICS, 1995, amended 1996.

3

Canada

Douglas L. Mendel, AACI

Douglas L. Mendel, AACI, has been involved for over 30 years in various aspects of the real estate industry in Canada, including municipal assessment, real estate development and management, appraisal, and counseling. He has served on the governing council of the Appraisal Institute of Canada and as a lecturer in the AIC education program. He is currently a fee appraiser with Grover, Elliott & Co. Ltd. in Vancouver, British Columbia.

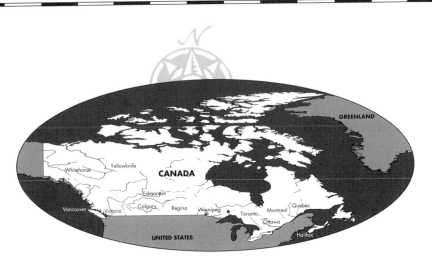

With the exception of the Maritime or Atlantic Provinces, most of Canada is a vast plain, bordered by the Western Cordillera (the Rockies and Coast Mountains), the worn-down Appalachian range, and the sparsely settled, but mineral-rich Canadian Shield (the Hudson Bay lowlands). The northernmost parts of Canada consist of permafrost tundra or coniferous forest. To the south and east lie the Ontario Peninsula (bordering the Great Lakes) and the fertile Saint Lawrence valley, Canada's urban and industrial heartland. Three prairie provinces make up the central part of the country. The principal cities of Canada are Toronto, Montreal, Vancouver, Ottawa-Hull, Edmonton, Calgary, Winnipeg, Quebec, and Hamilton.

Political Structure

Canada's origins date back to 1608 when a settlement was established on the present site of Quebec City. Although the colonization of Canada during the seventeenth century was mainly French (Quebec and Nova Scotia), the British took control of Canada between 1713 and 1763. During the American Revolution, many British loyalists from the colonies resettled in Upper Canada (Ontario). The provinces of Ontario, Quebec, Nova Scotia and New Brunswick were united under the British North America Act of 1867. British Columbia, the westernmost province, entered the confederation in 1871 when the federal government extended a transcontinental railway to the west coast. The prairie provinces and northern territories were added later. In 1949, Newfoundland and Labrador abandoned crown colony status to join the federation and become Canada's tenth province. Modern Canada's boundaries extend from the Atlantic to the Pacific and north to the Arctic Ocean.

Canada's government is patterned after the British parliamentary tradition. The federal Bill of Rights dates back to the 1960s; Canada's Constitution and Charter of Rights and Freedoms are embodied in the Constitution Act of 1982, which replaced the historic British North America Act.

The powers of the federal government are divided among legislative, executive, and judicial branches. The governor general is the formal head of state. The Cabinet is made up of the prime minister, who is the leader of the majority party, and ministers chosen from elected members of the House of Commons. A Senate, or upper house, made up of appointed members must pass, amend, or defeat bills approved in the House of Commons.

Parliamentary elections must be held at least every five years and can be called at any time if the confidence of the majority of elected members is lost. In practice, federal elections are held at least every four years.

The government is divided among federal, provincial, and municipal jurisdictions. The provinces are responsible for education, health and welfare, and the administration of civil law, which covers real estate. Municipal governments only exercise the powers granted by the provinces. Provincial legislation provides for statutory control over real property, including assessment and taxation, zoning, expropriation, and land titles procedures. Administration of most of these functions is carried out at the municipal level.

The Province of Quebec is governed by a civil code developed from French law, rather than from British common law.

The Supreme Court of Canada, the highest court in the country, is made up of a chief justice and eight junior justices, who are appointed by the governor general in council.

Canada's current population is 29.4 million. The most populous of its 10 provinces is Ontario, with 11 million people, followed by Quebec with 7.3 million. English and French are the two official languages of Canada.

Property Rights

Legislative power over property rights is the preserve of the provinces. Property law for all provinces except Quebec follows the British common law tradition; general property law may only be enacted by the provincial legislatures. Through its power to tax and expropriate property, the federal parliament may affect property rights.

Property rights are not specifically protected under the Canadian Charter of Rights and Freedoms. Such rights are recognized under common law and are therefore protected by statute law.

The ownership of real property in Canada is subject to the government powers of taxation, eminent domain, police power, and escheat. The *bundle of rights* theory applies in all Canadian jurisdictions, and the terms *fee simple, leased fee estate,* and *leasehold estate* have the same meaning in Canada as in the United States.

Registration of Land and Land Titles[1]

In Canada there are two systems of recording title to land. The registry system, which originated in the United States, and the land title or Torrens title system, which was developed in Australia. The registry system is used in the parts of Canada settled earlier. It is the only system in use in the four Atlantic provinces of Canada (New Brunswick, Newfoundland, Nova Scotia, and Prince Edward Island). The registry system coexists with the land title system in Manitoba and Ontario. Land titles are used exclusively in British Columbia, Alberta, and Saskatchewan and in parts of Manitoba and northern Ontario.

The Registry System

The registry system is a method of registering title documents and recording each transfer of land or any written interest therein. The registry system provides for the registration of legal instruments in those jurisdictions covered by provincial registry statutes. The effect of registration under the registry system is to give public notice of an interest or claim in land. Registration is the means by which priority over subsequently registered documents is achieved. The validity of registered documents is not guaranteed by the registry office. Rather, those who rely on the registered documents must judge

---

1. This section on land registration systems in Canada was developed by Larry O. Dybvig, AACI, MAI.

whether the documents constitute a valid claim or title, or evidence of true ownership of the land. Registered documents, including plans and instruments, provide the appraiser with a wealth of knowledge about the subject and comparable properties. Land area, rights appraised, easements, mortgages, restrictions, and other information can be discovered through a careful search and reading of the documents. In some provinces, the consideration involved in the transfer of an interest must also be shown. Sale prices, sale terms, mortgages, and rental terms/rates can thereby be accurately ascertained.

The Land Title System

The land title system was conceived and drafted by an Australian, Sir Robert Torrens, and by this name it is known. Torrens maintained that a land registry system should be reliable, simple, inexpensive, speedy, and suitable. The land title system was first introduced in 1858 in the Real Property Act of South Australia. The first areas in Canada to adopt the modern land title system were the present-day provinces of Alberta and Saskatchewan and the Northwest Territories. Here the old registry system had not yet become entrenched. Subsequently, the system was also adopted by British Columbia and parts of Manitoba and Ontario. Under the Torrens title system, a government office has custody of all original land titles and all original documents registered against these titles. Government staff examine and register the documents and issue titles. The accuracy of the titles is then guaranteed by the government. In Canada, the principles upon which the Torrens title system is based include:

1. The *mirror principle.* The register or certificate of title is supposed to reflect the current facts about the title in an accurate and complete manner.

2. The *curtain principle.* The current certificate of title should contain all information about the title.

3. The *insurance principle.* This principle provides compensation for the loss of rights. The register is supposed to reflect the correct status of the land and any flaw through human error which causes a party to suffer loss is to be made right insofar as money can compensate such loss.

Language

Canada has two official languages: English and French. The British North America Act of 1867 established the two languages in federal institutions and institutions of Quebec Province. It also provided for denominational schools, which were closely aligned with Anglophone and Francophone cultural traditions.

The Canadian Charter of Rights and Freedoms ensures the availability of bilingual services in federal institutions and safeguards minority language education rights in Canada.

French (joual) is spoken by the majority of citizens of Quebec; English is the predominant language in most other areas of the country.

Currency

The Canadian dollar is the only form of legal tender in Canada. All domestic real estate transactions are conducted in Canadian dollars, expressed as $1.00.

The Bank of Canada controls the growth of the money supply and each chartered bank is required to maintain cash reserves with the central bank based on a percentage of its deposits. The Bank of Canada, which is actually a private corporation owned by the federal government, is the lender of last resort.

Units of Measure

The British imperial system of measurement has been used historically, notwithstanding legalization of the metric system in Canada in 1871. The metric system was formally adopted by an Act of Parliament in 1971. Subdivision plans and architectural drawings are prepared in metric measurements and residential units are usually measured in metres. However, office and retail space is often described in imperial measure, and the value of development sites is usually described in dollars per square foot. Agricultural land continues to be described in acreage rather than hectares, the metric unit.

Inflation

Inflation in Canada is measured by the Consumer Price Index (CPI). The rate of inflation reflects the percentage increase in price levels and is expressed as an annual or monthly rate. At the time of publication, the base year used for this purpose was 1986 (stated as 100). The inflation rates cited by the CPI for subsequent years were

1987	104.4
1988	108.6
1989	114.0
1990	119.5
1991	126.2
1992	128.1
1993	130.4
1994	131.6

The federal government attempts to control inflation through fiscal and monetary policy, i.e., by reducing government expenditures or raising taxes and by restricting the growth of the money supply. Periodically, more drastic steps are taken, such as the introduction of wage and price controls. During times of low inflation, there is no need for government intervention.

Typical Lease Structure

Office leases are typically *triple net,* with an annual rate expressed in dollars per square foot and rents payable monthly. Under triple net leases, tenants pay a proportionate share of common area charges, property taxes, and insurance. In recessionary periods, landlords often offer incentives to prospective tenants, such as free rent, tenant improvement allowances, and other inducements. As a result, appraisers must be aware of both *face rates* (the rate per square foot stated in the lease) and *net effective rates* (the equivalent net rate after deducting the cost of landlord inducements). Office leases are typically for five years or more, with rent reviews built into leases with terms of 10 years or more. Gross leases are also found in the Canadian market, particularly in the case of government leases, but the net lease predominates.

Office space is measured using BOMA (Building Owners and Managers Association) standards of measurement, with usable floor space adjusted upward to reflect leasable area, thereby taking into account the proportionate share of common areas in partial floor leases. Most retail leases are also triple net, based on a dollar rate per square foot with tenants assuming responsibility for common area maintenance, taxes, and insurance in addition to rent. Shopping centre leases often include percentage rent and tenants are obliged to contribute to the marketing and promotion expenses of the centre.

Common area maintenance (CAM) expenses for both offices and retail space usually include a management fee expressed as a percentage of operating costs. Capital items may be written off as expenses over their expected lifespan. Structural maintenance is usually excluded from common area charges.

Landlord expenses such as leasing fees, depreciation, and debt service are not included in common area maintenance. Leasing commissions are usually based on a percentage of the rent achieved, but they may also be calculated based on dollars per square foot of space leased or as a negotiated lump sum.

Industrial buildings are typically leased on a triple net basis at a rate per square foot of gross floor area. Rental rates may reflect a blended rate for warehouse or shop space and office and showroom space. A recent phenomenon in some industrial markets is the advent of *flex space,* which incorporates office, retail/showroom, and traditional warehouse development into a flexible building design.

Tenant improvements (TIs) are considered to be the responsibility of office and retail space tenants, although basic TI allowances are common. In periods of recession, landlords often underwrite total TI costs in order to attract tenants (through leases referred to as *turnkey leases*).

Valuation Standards

Founded in 1938, the Appraisal Institute of Canada is the professional institute of real estate appraisers in Canada. The institute is a signatory member of the Appraisal Standards Board and has formally adopted the Uniform Standards of Professional Appraisal Practice (USPAP).

Licensing/Certification

The Appraisal Institute of Canada awards two appraisal designations. AACI (Accredited Appraiser Canadian Institute) signifies fully accredited membership in the institute. CRA (Canadian Residential Appraiser) designates individuals qualified to appraise dwellings containing not more than four, self-contained family housing units. Candidates must complete a rigorous course of study in all aspects of real estate valuation and apprentice under a qualified member for a specified period.

The Appraisal Institute of Canada conducts a comprehensive education program through its provincial associations and chapters, and certain colleges and universities offer a full curriculum of appraisal and related courses. AACI candidates must pass comprehensive exams, receive a passing grade on two demonstration appraisal reports, serve an articling period (apprenticeship), and attend a Standards of Professional Appraisal Practice seminar. Members of the institute are governed by a code of ethics, rules of professional conduct, and standards of appraisal practice. As noted, the Appraisal Institute of Canada has adopted the Uniform Standards of Professional Appraisal Practice (USPAP) and is a signatory member of the Appraisal Standards Board.

The Appraisal Institute of Canada maintains a mandatory recertification program and members must include a statement as to their recertification status in their appraisal reports.

Government control of appraisers is in effect in two provinces. To appraise real estate legally in the Province of New Brunswick, registration with the New Brunswick Association of Real Estate Appraisers is mandatory for all practitioners except provincial government tax assessors. The association is affiliated with the Appraisal Institute of Canada and has adopted the institute's regulations regarding education and professional standards, which include USPAP. Residency in New Brunswick is not a requirement for registration.

In the Province of Quebec, l'Ordre des Evaluateurs agrées du Quebec sets the educational requirements and confers three professional designations: Chartered Appraiser (C.App), Articling Appraiser, and student member. In French, these categories are Évaluateur agréé (EA), Évaluateur stagiaire, and membre étudiant. The corporation's founding members belonged to the Association of Municipal Assessors of Quebec, the American Right of Way Association, the Association of Condemnation Appraisers of Quebec, and the Appraisal Institute of Canada. EA members must have a university degree and complete an articling period (apprenticeship) under the tutorship of a chartered appraiser.

The Appraisal Institute of Canada has an affiliation agreement with l'Ordre des Evaluateurs agrées du Quebec.

Appraisal Reporting Requirements

There are several professional organizations in Canada that qualify their members in valuation matters. However, only the Appraisal Institute of Canada has adopted minimum standards under the Uniform Standards of Professional Appraisal Practice (USPAP), which require the inclusion of certain essential elements in appraisal reports. Section 1 of the standards is the Canadian supplement, which is issued twice a year by the institute. Section 2 is the core document, which is prescribed by The Appraisal Foundation. It includes ethics, competency, and departure provisions. Under USPAP, in addition to meeting competency requirements, an appraiser must describe the extent to which he or she was involved in collecting, confirming, and reporting data, with explanations for omissions if the appraisal is limited in scope.

Additionally, the Appraisal Institute of Canada publishes the *Handbook of Guidelines for the Valuation of Investment Properties,* which is the responsibility of the AIC Investment Property Valuation Committee. This committee was formed "to liaise with the commercial property investment industry, allowing for a higher level of understanding and consistency in the analysis and valuation of this property type."[2]

Users of appraisals in Canada have come to expect well-documented and clearly defined appraisal reports, particularly with respect to narrative appraisals dealing with investment and revenue-producing properties. Guidelines on the content of real estate appraisals are recognized by various financial and regulatory institutions, including Canada Deposit Insurance Corporation, the Office of the Superintendent of Financial Institutions, and

---

2. Appraisal Institute of Canada/Institut Canadien des Evaluateurs, *Handbook of Guidelines for the Valuation of Investment Properties* (Winnipeg: Appraisal Institute of Canada, 1994), introductory page.

the provincial securities commissions. The Appraisal Institute of Canada's textbook, *The Appraisal of Real Estate,* Canadian edition, sets out the same, four-part criteria for the content of appraisals presented in the U.S. edition.

Definition of Market Value

The USPAP 1995 Canadian supplement defines *market value* as:

> The most probable price which a property should bring in a competitive and open market under all conditions requisite to a fair sale, the buyer and seller each acting prudently and knowledgeably, and assuming the price is not affected by undue stimulus. Implicit in this definition is the consummation of a sale as of a specified date and the passing of title from seller to buyer under conditions whereby:
>
> 1. buyer and seller are typically motivated;
> 2. both parties are well informed or well advised, and acting in what they consider their best interests;
> 3. a reasonable time is allowed for exposure in the open market;
> 4. payment is made in terms of cash in Canadian dollars or in terms of financial arrangements comparable thereto; and
> 5. the price represents the normal considerations for the property sold unaffected by special or creative financing or sales concessions granted by anyone associated with the sale.

Income Approach

Income-producing properties are bought and sold in Canada on the basis of their actual or potential net earnings. Future earning potential is converted into an expression of market value by one of two valuation methods. The direct capitalization method is used when future net earnings are predicted to be relatively stable. The discounted cash flow (DCF) method is employed when future cash flows are expected to vary over the projected investment period. Both methods are market-derived and many appraisals include both direct capitalization and the DCF method.

In the direct capitalization method of valuation, a single year's income (or income expectancy) is converted into an expression of value in one direct step, by dividing the annual net income by an overall capitalization rate. The rate selected for the purpose of capitalization is derived from sales of similar properties and represents the relationship between net annual income and selling price.

The discounted cash flow method requires that certain assumptions be made with regard to market attitudes and expectations. Projected future net earnings are converted into present value through the application of a series of discount factors, the magnitude of which reflect all of the positive and negative features of the property being appraised. The DCF method requires that a definitive investment horizon or holding period be assumed. A 10-year period is typically adopted and the present worth of the reversionary value of the real estate at the end of the term is calculated based of the income forecast in the eleventh year. The present worth of all cash receipts projected over the holding period together with the value of the reversion represents the present value of the investment property. Discount factors used in the DCF method represent future expectations of investors and are not derived directly from sales, as is the case with capitalization rates. The DCF method is often required in appraisals prepared for pension funds, life insurance, and trust companies, which require periodic reappraisals during the period an investment property is held.

Direct Comparison Approach

The direct comparison approach is a traditional method of valuation in Canada and is included in most appraisal reports. It is the approach most easily understood and applied when comparable market evidence is available. The approach is applicable to all types of real estate when there are sufficient recent, reliable transactions for analysis. It is rarely applied to special-purpose properties such as manufacturing plants or mills because comparable sales are usually not available. The approach is most applicable to the valuation of single-family housing and non-income properties. Vacant land is normally valued by direct comparison.

Sources of data for the direct comparison approach include real estate boards, municipal records, private reporting services, and Realtors.®

All comparative data are historic. Changes in economic conditions can quickly impact local markets, rendering even recent sales unreliable without appropriate adjustment. Similarly, changes in planning legislation affecting specific properties may impact surrounding real estate values differently. The selection of comparable sales in these circumstances must be conducted with caution.

Units of comparison vary depending on the type of property being appraised. In the case of urban development land, value is typically quoted per square foot or per square metre. Agricultural land is valued on a per-acre basis. Apartment buildings are often measured on a per-unit basis and commercial space on a per-square-foot basis.

Cost Approach

The cost approach is routinely included in appraisals, but rarely relied upon for the final estimate of value. Sources of cost data include cost manuals and local contractors and builders. The approach can produce accurate results when improvements are new and represent the highest and best use of the property. When applied to older buildings or buildings that do not meet the test of highest and best use, however, the validity of the approach is suspect for a number of reasons.

The approach requires an estimate of depreciation, which may be highly subjective. Thus, although the replacement cost new of a structure may be accurately and painstakingly determined, its contributory value after deducting estimated depreciation often becomes a matter of judgment. Although appraisal theory includes various techniques for estimating depreciation through analysis of comparable sales in the market, for all practical purposes depreciation is extremely difficult to identify this way. Part of the problem is that the market does not identify depreciation in any particular way, often contradicting traditional appraisal theory which suggests that older properties should be worth less than new ones.

Another element of the cost approach that is often overlooked is entrepreneurial or developer's profit. Developer's profit is not an intrinsic cost and will vary with the market. It can amount to more than 25% of value, but it is the market that determines developer's profit, not the other way around.

Clients such as lending institutions insist that the cost approach be included in appraisal reports, even though many market participants pay no heed to cost in buying and selling real estate. The approach is most applicable in appraising properties which normally are not sold in the market and for which market evidence is not available. Properties such as churches, schools, and manufacturing plants are often valued by the cost approach simply because there is no other way to appraise them.

Reconciliation

The reconciliation section of an appraisal report summarizes the appraisal methodologies used in the report and discusses their relative strengths and weaknesses in regard to the specific appraisal. In addition to summarizing the appraisal process, this section of the report explains the reasoning that led to the final value conclusion.

Availability of Data

Sources of real estate data are listed below.

Demographic and Economic Data
- Provincial government offices—municipal affairs departments, assessment authorities, statistical bureaus, and land title or registry offices

- Municipal offices—land and property departments, planning agencies, statistical bureaus, and engineering services
- Chambers of commerce or boards of trade
- Libraries
- Real estate subscription services and local newspapers

Real Estate Market Data (Market Size, Occupancy Rates, Rent Levels)

- Real estate agents and property management and appraisal offices
- Quarterly reports published by major real estate brokerage firms in large urban centres dealing with office and retail rents, vacancies, and related information
- Appraisal Institute of Canada library in Winnipeg, Manitoba, and association libraries in most provinces
- International Council of Shopping Centres, New York, and Urban Land Institute, Washington, D.C.
- *Canadian Directory of Shopping Centres* (Monday report on retailers)
- Local real estate boards (Normally some form of membership such as affiliate membership is required.)

Rent and Sale Comparables

The availability of data varies from province to province and is, to some extent, dependent on the size of the market area in which the appraiser is employed. For example, in some of the larger centres, private reporting services provide land title information on a fee basis and regular monthly reports by subscription. Most appraisers have access to listings and sales through their local real estate boards, both on line and in hard copy form. Many appraisers subscribe to planning bulletins provided by their local municipal planning departments or regional planning authorities. It is essential to maintain good relations with real estate agents and salespeople in all market areas.

Appraisal Organizations

The addresses of the principal appraisal organizations in Canada are shown below.

Appraisal Institute of Canada
1111 Portage Avenue
Winnipeg, Manitoba
R3G 0S8

Real Estate Institute of Canada
305, 2200 Lakeshore Boulevard West
Toronto, Ontario
M8V 1A4

New Brunswick Association of Real Estate Appraisers
403 Regent Street - 2nd Floor
Fredericton, New Brunswick
E3B 3X6

l'Ordre des Evaluateurs agrées du Quebec
5303, rue Sherbrooke Est.
bureau 101
Montreal, Quebec
H1 1B3

Key Variances in Practice Between Canadian and U.S. Appraisers

The approaches, techniques, and terminology employed by Canadian appraisers most closely reflect those endorsed by the Appraisal Institute. Included among the textbooks used in Canada are those of the American Society of Real Estate Appraisers and the American Institute of Real Estate Appraisers (now the Appraisal Institute). In some cases, Canadian editions of U.S. texts exist. Most of the variances in practice between Canadian and U.S. appraisers, which are itemized below, stem from regulatory matters and British common law.[3]

- The appraisal profession is less regulated in Canada than in the United States.

- The vast majority of Canadian appraisers belong to a single professional organization, the Appraisal Institute of Canada. This organization accredits residential appraisers (CRA) and senior appraisers (AACI) and mandates articling (apprenticeship), continuing education, and professional liability insurance for all members. New members pursuing the AACI designation must have university degrees.

- In Canada, financial institutions are less regulated. There are fewer banks and each has a larger share of the market.

- Retail banking is dominated by five institutions. Failure on the part of financial institutions is uncommon, and regulatory audits of banks place emphasis on the institution's overall financial performance rather than a review of

---

3. This section on variances in practice was developed by Larry O. Dybvig, AACI, MAI.

individual loan files. Consequently, lenders rarely need to commission independent appraisal reviews.

- Canadian title registration systems are centralized and comprehensive. On-line title searches may be done in several provinces.

- Lending institutions regulated by the federal government of Canada are required to compound interest on a semiannual basis; special financial tables must be used.

- Short-term mortgages are the norm. For residential properties, renewal periods of six months to three years are common; for nonresidential proper-ties, five-year intervals are typical. The effect of financing in the market, therefore, tends to be less significant than in jurisdictions where 15- to 30-year terms are the norm.

- The payment of points, i.e., cash charges associated with mortgage loans, is uncommon, so adjusting for financing terms is simpler.

- Reserves for replacement are neither allowable under the tax code nor considered by the real estate industry. They are seldom, if ever, estimated in appraisals.

- Markets are smaller than in the United Kingdom or the United States. Invest-ment fund levels are lower and markets are characterized by less volatility.

- The quality and quantity of data available through commercial and coopera-tive data systems vary considerably. Market data is more limited and, except in the largest cities, greater economies of scale have not been achieved by commercial data systems.

Bibliography

Achour, Dominique. *Real Estate Analysis and Appraisal.* Quebec: Les Presses de l'Universite Laval, 1987.

Appraisal Institute of Canada/Institut Canadien des Evaluateurs. *Basics of Real Estate Appraising.* Winnipeg, 1991.

Appraisal Institute of Canada/Institut Canadien des Evaluateurs. *The Cana-dian Appraiser/L'Evaluateur Canadien.* Quarterly publication. Winnipeg.

Appraisal Institute of Canada/Institut Canadien des Evaluateurs. *Handbook of Guidelines for the Valuation of Investment Properties.* Winnipeg, 1994.

Appraisal Institute of Canada/Institut Canadien des Evaluateurs. *Real Estate Appraising in Canada.* 3d ed. Winnipeg, 1987.

Eger, Albert F. *Canadian Real Estate Finance: A Typical Transaction.* Montreal: Ad Valorem Press Inc., 1990.

Institute of Municipal Assessors of Ontario. *Assessor's Review.* Quarterly publication. Toronto.

Klaasen, Romain L. *Practising Real Estate Appraisal.* Winnipeg: Pennex Publications, 1977.

Reiter, Barry J. *Real Estate Law.* Toronto: Edmond Montgomery, 1979.

Watts, Peter D. *Real Estate Practitioner's Guide.* 4th ed. Vancouver: Butterworth and Co., 1979.

Willes, John A. *Contemporary Canadian Business Law.* 2d ed. Toronto: McGraw-Hill, Ryerson Limited, 1986.

Young, Frederick S.C. *Fundamentals of Real Estate Investment Analysis and Feasibility Studies.* Winnipeg: Appraisal Institute of Canada, 1991.

4

Australia

Lynne Armitage, FVLE, FRICS

Lynne A. Armitage holds a diploma in surveying, a master's degree in environmental planning, and a FRICS designation (general practice/valuation division) as well as two designations from the Australian Institute of Valuers and Land Economists—FVLE (Econ.) and FVLE (Val.). Armitage is a registered valuer in New South Wales and Queensland. She is an acting senior lecturer in property economics on the faculty of Built Environment and Engineering at Queensland University of Technology.

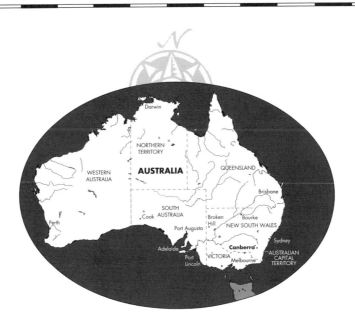

More than one-half of the continent of Australia is a flat plain (shield) extending west from the northeast. The Dividing Range sets off the humid eastern coast; two-thirds of the continent (the outback) is semiarid or desert. The Great Barrier Reef lies along the northeast coast (Queensland), which is covered by a rain forest. Australia's principal cities are Sydney, Melbourne, Brisbane, Adelaide, and Perth.

Political Stucture

Australia is an independent and democratic country with a population of more than 17.6 million. It is highly urbanised with about 70% of the population living in the 10 largest cities. Most of the population is concentrated along the eastern seaboard, especially on the southeastern corner of the continent.

European settlement in Australia began in 1788 when a British penal colony was founded on the east coast of the continent. Over the following 70 years, free settlers established six British colonies. In 1901 these colonies joined into a federation to form the Commonwealth of Australia. In the twentieth century, Australia has become increasingly independent of Britain.

Australia's political institutions and practices follow the western democratic tradition, reflecting British and North American experience.

The Australian federation is based on a three-tier system of government comprising federal, state, and local levels. The Australian Parliament (the legislature) and government (the executive and judicial branches) are responsible for all matters of national interest. Six state governments and legislatures, plus the similarly responsible and largely self-governing Australian Capital Territory (ACT) and Northern Territory, complement the activities of the national government. The third tier of local government comprises about 900 authorities at the city, town, municipal, and shire (county) level.

The powers of the Australian Parliament are defined in a written constitution which took effect on January 1, 1901, when the six colonies federated to form the Commonwealth of Australia. Queen Elizabeth II is Queen of Australia and head of state. Her representatives in Australia are the governor-general and the six state governors.

The Australian Constitution provides for the judicial power of the Australian federal government to be vested in the High Court of Australia and other courts created by the federal parliament. All six states, the ACT, and the Northern Territory have their own court systems. In some areas, the state courts are vested with federal jurisdiction.

The Australian Parliament is bicameral. The membership of the House of Representatives, which is set by the constitution, is about twice that of the Senate. The House of Representatives has 147 seats, divided among the states and mainland territories based on population. Elections for the House of Representatives are held at least every three years. The Senate has 12 senators from each of the six states and two each from the ACT and Northern Territory. Senators from the states serve six-year terms, with half retiring every three years. Senators from the territories serve a maximum of three years, coinciding with the terms of members of the House of Representatives.

The Cabinet is part of the executive branch of the Australian government and it is the major policy-making agency. Led by the prime minister, the Cabinet comprises about half the full ministry and meets both informally and in private. The effect of law is conferred upon Cabinet decisions by the Executive Council, a formal body presided over by the governor-general and normally attended by two or three ministers, though all ministers are members.

Australia has six states: New South Wales, Victoria, Queensland, South Australia, Western Australia, and Tasmania. The mainland territories are the Australian Capital Territory (ACT), where the national capital of Canberra is located, and the Northern Territory. Australia also administers seven external territories.

With the exception of Queensland, the ACT, and the Northern Territory, all the state parliaments are bicameral. In general, government authority not specifically delegated to the federal government is reserved for the states. Much of the regulation of property activity is the responsibility of the states, and thus various approaches have developed within a broad, common framework.

Local government is established by state government statute. Hence, the powers and responsibilities of local government vary among states. The bulk of these powers and responsibilities relate to land and property, including construction and maintenance of infrastructure, town planning, land use development and control, building regulations, and public health. The degree of legislative control over land use and development is essentially proportionate to the level of urbanisation throughout the country.

Among the principal sources of revenue for most developed local government areas are the rates (assessments) levied on real property. The value of property is assessed at the state level and the local authorities generate the rates required for their revenue purposes. Most state governments also levy land taxes. Except for property-related income tax or capital gains tax liabilities, no property taxes are paid to the federal government.

Property Rights

As is common in countries that follow the tradition of British law, the ownership of land in Australia is not considered absolute. It is only possible to hold *estates* in land because, theoretically, all lands are held under tenure from the Crown. For all practical purposes, however, the holder of a fee simple estate enjoys the benefits of absolute ownership. A fee simple estate is the highest form of ownership. It is a freehold estate that is inheritable and, in unrestricted form, carries unconditional rights of possession, use, and alienation (the right to transfer title to property).

In most cases, rights of use and alienation of land held under freehold or leasehold tenure are to some degree restricted by law. Restrictions, which are contained in the title or imposed externally by statute, may reserve mineral rights for the Crown or identify easements, rights of way, or other restrictive covenants.

Estimates indicate that about 80% of the privately occupied land in Australia is held under some form of lease or licence from the Crown; a little more than 2% of the remaining freehold land is held under lease from freeholders to lessees. From a valuation perspective, however, virtually all land in urbanised areas (except government land) is held in freehold title (fee simple) and much of the prime commercial, industrial, and retail property is leased, income-generating property.

As legally defined, land includes the ground, any building improvements on it, and everything attached thereto, whether above or below the surface. For purposes of ownership and use, land is divided into parcels, which are mostly delineated by vertical lines extending from the earth's centre to infinity. In certain circumstances, a parcel may be defined by vertical and horizontal boundaries to form a stratum. A stratum may be created below the surface to define a mineral deposit, the title to which is deemed separate from the title to the surface land. When the horizontal and vertical divisions are above the surface, they may be defined by a building or part thereof and be held under strata title freehold. Similarly, a stratum of vacant "land" may be created. For example, a railway authority may grant a lease to air space for the development of a building which will be erected on columns embedded in railway land.

There are two title systems for freehold lands in Australia: Torrens title and common law or old systems title. The Torrens system was established on the principle that title to land depends upon registration and certification, not on deeds. The title to land held under the Torrens system, which is guaranteed by the government, has essentially replaced the old system. Computerisation of land titles and property transactions establishes reliable public records which are easily accessible.

There are a number of forms of tenure which define the kind of title or right by which land is held. As noted, the individual fee simple estate (freehold) is the highest form of ownership, but there are a variety of lesser interests in the fee simple, such as joint tenancy, tenancy in common, and a life estate. Land may also be held under a lease granted by the Crown or some other owner.

While leases of Crown land apply mainly to rural holdings, leases of freehold land are normally negotiated in urban areas. Leases for three years or more are registered on the property title, but agreements for shorter periods need not be. Except in the case of ground or development leases, land and improvements are normally leased together to a sole tenant; when properties are leased to multiple tenants, a defined part of the building is leased to a tenant. Subleases and assignments may be generated, and options for renewal or sale and leaseback arrangements are commonly applied to investment-grade property.

Prior to federation in 1901, the ownership of all land in Australia was vested in the individual states. Hence, when land is acquired by the states under compulsory powers (eminent domain), it is said to be "resumed" from the current owner since the state is considered the original owner. Individual states and territories have legislation to provide for just terms of compensation. For federal purposes, land may also be compulsorily acquired under separate legislation, again on just terms.

Native Title

In late 1993, the Australian government introduced legislation into Parliament to give effect to its policy on native title to land. The legislation was designed to deal with the implications of a judgement by the High Court of Australia in June 1992 in what has become known as the Mabo case.

The High Court judgement rejected the notion of *terra nullius,* the concept that the Australian continent was unoccupied when European settlement began. For the first time, an Australian court recognised that aboriginal and Torres Strait islander peoples may still hold common law *native title* to land, which has not been lost through valid acts of government or the loss of a traditional connection with the land.

The aim of the legislation is twofold: 1) To preserve the integrity and certainty of Australia's land management system and thereby ensure continuing economic development, and 2) to provide a measure of justice for aboriginal and Torres Strait islander peoples.

Language and Culture

Australia's official language is English by common usage rather than legislative fiat. Australian English does not differ significantly from other forms of English.

The Australian lifestyle reflects its mainly western origins. However, Australia is also a multicultural society which has been enriched by nearly five million settlers from almost 200 nations. Four out of 10 Australians are either migrants or the first-generation children of migrants, half of whom are from non-English-speaking backgrounds. In 1991-1992 East Asia contributed 41% of settler arrivals.

Currency

The unit of currency is the Australian dollar. All domestic real property transactions are expressed in Australian dollars, AUD$1.00. There are 100 cents to the dollar.

Units of Measurement

Australia officially adopted the metric system (SI)[1] of measurement in 1972. Property income and expenditure are normally quoted in dollars per square metre per annum. However, it is not uncommon for people to refer to land prices using imperial measures, such as price per acre or per perch (equal to 30 ¼ sq. yds.), rather than price per square metre or per hectare. Metric measurements are used in all documentation.

Inflation

After peaking at 10% in 1982-1983, inflation in Australia has declined gradually from an average of 8% during the 1980s to an annual rate of 1.9% in 1993-1994. The Consumer Price Index (CPI), the most commonly used measure of inflation, reflects changes in the price of a fixed basket of specified goods as measured by the Australian Bureau of Statistics.

Australia is not subject to extreme inflation. The current low level of inflation reflects subdued demand, but has provided a significant stimulus to Australia's international competitiveness.

An awareness of the level and direction of inflation is important in the valuation of properties when discounted cash flow (DCF) analysis techniques are used because forecasts of anticipated inflation must be factored into the projections. (Further discussion of DCF analyses is presented in a subsequent section.)

Typical Lease Structure

Office

With the exception of major lettings of whole buildings, leases for office space normally run for terms of three to five years, often with annual or mid-term reviews to adjust rents to market levels or to the Consumer Price Index for inflation. Whole building lettings are normally for a longer term, again with periodic reviews.

Rents are typically net rents expressed in dollars per square metre per annum with tenants held responsible for all outgoings (expenses) relating to the

---

1. SI stands for Système internationale d'unités (standardised metric units).

building, including repairs, maintenance, cleaning, utility costs, property management, council rates (assessments), land tax, other statutory charges, and building insurance. Tenant liability for outgoings is based on the leased floor space plus a share of outgoings for common areas as a proportion of the tenant's leased area to total leased area. Tenants are not normally responsible for structural repairs, replacement of capital items, or capital improvements required by statute (e.g., new fire stairs); debt service (mortgage payments); or non-cash items such as depreciation.

Costs associated with leasing are normally borne by each party. Leasing commissions are calculated as a percentage of the first year's rent (normally 10%) and are paid at the start of the lease.

New prime space will normally be finished to a standard which includes fitted carpet, painted plastered wall panels, suspended ceilings, recessed fluorescent lights, ducted air conditioning, and sufficient power outlets. Depending on the state of the market, the tenant's fitout (finish) costs may be borne by the tenant or by the landlord as an incentive. Given the costs of relocating tenant fittings, it is often advantageous to tenants and landlords to leave a fitout (tenant finish) in situ (in place) at the end of a tenancy since tax advantages may accrue. A variety of lease incentives are used during periods of oversupply to maintain the face rent (or rent level specified in leases). These include rent-free periods, which may peak at one year of free rent in a three-year lease. Incentives are less common now than they were a few years ago in most of the larger cities in Australia.

Retail

Shopping centre leases follow a pattern similar to leases for commercial office space, but they tend to be less influenced by variations in the supply of retail space. Leases for specialty stores commonly run three to five years plus options, frequently with annual reviews and/or mid-term reviews to adjust rents to market levels. Terms for anchor tenants are of much longer duration—e.g., 10, 15, 20, or 40 years, depending on the size of the anchor—and are frequently held on very favourable conditions.

Retail properties are generally leased on a net basis, with the tenant responsible for a percentage share of the nominated outgoings (specified expenses) of the centre based on the proportion of the tenant's area to the net lettable area of the centre. The tenant's liability for outgoings (expenses) is essentially similar to that of office tenants, although specific items such as promotional levies or obligatory merchants' association fees may vary. Historically, the anchor tenants in many centres have received favourable treatment in respect to outgoings. However, the practice of loading speciality tenants with outgoings has been generally outlawed.

In shopping centres, space is frequently leased as a shell, with or without a shop front. The tenant is responsible for the full fitout (finish out), often closely supervised by centre management.

Percentage or turnover rents are paid by some retail tenants. Such rents vary with the type of trade as does the breakeven point beyond which the turnover rent is applicable. The virtual (total) rent paid by a tenant may thus comprise base rent, turnover rent, and outgoings (expenses), including levies.

Industrial

Industrial and warehouse premises are generally held under net leases. In addition to the rent for the premises, the tenant is responsible for all outgoings (expenses) including management, but excluding capital expenditures (principally structural repairs).

The length of the lease varies with the size of the property. Terms of three, five, or 10 years are typical with mid-term reviews to adjust rents to market levels or for inflation (CPI) above the minimum base. The normal option period is equivalent to two original terms of the lease. For example, leases for large premises may have a five-year term plus two, five-year options, each with a mid-term review to adjust rents to market levels.

Valuation Standards

Australia is currently in the process of establishing a more uniform approach to valuation standards. In the past individual states have developed their own, broadly similar practice standards.

The Australian Valuation Standards Board (AVSB) was established in June 1994 under the initiative of the Australian Institute of Valuers and Land Economists (AIVLE), the national professional body. The board is concerned with defining policy issues and the position of valuation standards within the context of relevant state and federal legislation, particularly the national corporation laws and Australian accounting standards. Conformity with international standards and guidance notes is also envisioned. To date, 21 practice standards have been identified, four have been approved by the AVSB, and drafts of five standards on additional topics have been released for discussion. Other topics proposed include project evaluation, the valuation of plants and equipment, and the valuation of rural property.

The AIVLE is also developing a series of model instructions, valuation guidelines, and valuation practice standards for residential, industrial, commercial, and retail property; valuations for mortgage purposes; and a practice standard for contaminated land. Property Development Management Guidelines were published in October 1995 and Due Diligence Guidelines for Commercial Office Acquisition Processes were released in January 1996.

Education and Registration

The AIVLE awards membership in its valuation strand (line) to applicants who satisfy rigorous membership criteria. These criteria include: graduation from an approved undergraduate degree program, completion of not less than two years' appropriate professional practice, maintenance of a satisfactory record of continuing professional development, and approval by an interview panel. The designation FVLE (Val.) or AVLE (Val.) represents membership in the valuation strand (line) at the level of fellow or associate, respectively. Elevation to the higher grade is based on demonstrated merit and interviews. The institute has some 7,000 members in Australia.

The AIVLE no longer offers educational programs except for short professional courses. It does, however, accredit and recognise undergraduate degrees presented by seven universities around the country as evidence of academic qualification.

All AIVLE members must undertake an approved program of continuing professional development. A strong code of ethics is enforced to maintain public confidence in designated members. Many leases stipulate that disputes be referred to the president of the institute (or a nominee) for resolution. Institutional lenders will normally specify that AIVLE members be included on their panels.

Over the last 25 years, individual states have established valuers' registration boards, which provide a statutory framework to control entry to the profession and recognise various levels of expertise. At the time of this writing, valuer registration is in flux. Three states, Victoria, Tasmania and South Australia, have abolished registration, and the remaining states are considering whether government regulation, industry regulation, or no regulation is preferable.

Appraisal Reporting Requirements

At the present, no reporting requirements are prescribed in Australia, either by law or by custom. Reports vary from simple, one-page, pro forma valuations of residential property for mortgage purposes (see pages 82-83) to fully documented valuation reports of 50 pages or more for more complex properties. The extent of documentation is determined by the type of property and the purpose of the valuation. Whether the report is concise or extensive, the same criteria of professionalism and competence apply. A Due Diligence Practice Standard for commercial property was published by the AIVLE in January 1996 and is likely to be adopted progressively by the profession in the immediate future.

The valuation report itself should be easy to read, relevant, comprehensive, and self-contained. Professional and industry bodies as well as the principal textbooks recommend coverage of the following items in an appraisal report :[2]

1. Report summary
   - property identification
   - reason for the valuation
   - interest being valued
   - opinion of value

2. Land and title
   - title reference
   - name of registered proprietor(s)
   - encumbrances (easements, covenants, etc.)
   - identification of registered leases

3. Location
   - description of the locality and situation
   - surrounding and adjoining development
   - proximity to amenities

4. Site description and services
   - land dimensions, area
   - access, shape, slope
   - services
   - special facilities or site problems, e.g., drainage, flooding, contamination
   - improvement(s) to the site/land

5. Town planning
   - current zoning
   - current land use and conformity to planning scheme
   - development controls affecting the land

---

2. BOMA, 1994; AIVLE, Due Diligence Practice Standard, 1996

- heritage controls (historic districts)
- environmental issues and controls (where applicable)

6. Statutory assessment (not always included)

- current statutory valuations of land for rating (assessment) and taxation purposes

7. Improvements

- description of improvements, including materials used in the structure, floors, walls, external cladding (siding), windows, roof, building core
- internal finishes (walls, ceilings, floors, doors)
- arrangement of accommodation for use, including toilets and tea rooms (breakfast rooms)
- commentary on age and condition of improvements and building services, including air-conditioning, lifts (elevators), fire alarms and escapes, security systems, etc.
- analysis of floor areas—gross and/or net, as required
- overview of the building's advantages and disadvantages

8. Tenancy details

- description of all tenancies and leases, including epitome (summary) of leases, date of commencement, name of lessee, demised premises (leased space), use, term/options, current rent, rent review frequency and conditions, lessee's obligations and liabilities for outgoings (expenses)
- comparison of passing (contract) and market rentals
- estimates of vacancies, letting up (lease-up) allowances, leasing costs, reversionary potential
- comments on rental arrears, financial position of tenants, tenant mix

9. Market overview

- general market overview—current and likely
- overviews of the specific locality or region in which the property is located and the property type
- overviews of supply and demand situation—vacancy factors and patterns, rental movements, micro- and macro-market trends
- analysis of where the property being valued fits into the overall market

10. Valuation approach

- basis of the valuation
- rationale for the valuation method(s) selected
- discussion, analytical review, and synthesis of market evidence, including explicit statement of assumptions
- valuation calculations (possibly in appendix, if extensive)
- sensitivity analyses and discussion
- reconciliation of the various valuation approaches

11. Valuation

- opinion of value, date, interest being valued
- signature and qualifications of valuer
- other assumptions and disclaimers as required by the valuer's professional indemnity insurer

12. Appendices

The following supporting documents should be included in numbered appendices in the sequence in which they are presented in the report and cross-referenced to the report.

- location plan, site plan/cadastral map, title documents, planning documents, building plans
- leases and/or summaries, schedules of tenancies and outgoings (expenses)
- analyses of comparable transactions
- valuation calculations
- photographs of the property
- additional materials, as appropriate

The increased clarity of valuation reports over the past 20 years has helped readers follow the logical evolution of the valuer's opinion. The increased intelligibility of reports has been paralleled, however, by the need for higher levels of professional indemnity insurance as the courts have extended valuers' liability for their professional opinions.

Definition of Market Value

The International Valuation Standards Committee (IVSC) definition of market value, which appears below, has been adopted by the AIVLE for use in Australia:

the estimated amount for which an asset should exchange on the date of valuation between a willing buyer and a willing seller in an arm's length transaction after proper marketing wherein the parties each had acted knowledgeably, prudently and without compulsion.

For assets held in property trusts, Australian Securities Commission (ASC) Schedule 7.12.15(5)(d) of the *Corporations Law* requires use of the following definition of market value:

the price at which the property might be reasonably expected to be sold at the date of valuation, assuming:

a) a willing, but not anxious, buyer and seller; and

b) a reasonable period within which to negotiate the sale, having regard to the nature and situation of the property and the state of the market for property of the same kind; and

c) that the property was reasonably exposed to the market; and

d) that no account is taken of the value or other advantage or benefit, additional to market value, to the buyer incidental to ownership of the property being valued; and

e) that the trust had sufficient resources to allow a reasonable period for the exposure of the property for sale; and

f) that the trust had sufficient resources to negotiate an agreement for the sale of the property.

The AIVLE/IVSC definition and the ASC definition of market value should produce the same opinion of value if prepared for a property by a single valuer.

It is important to clarify whether the opinion of market value to be reported is that of the property in its existing use or highest and best use. While in some circumstances the market value under the existing use and the highest and best use may be the same, the existing use value (mainly required for financial reporting purposes) is likely to be lower than the value under the highest and best use, which is the customary basis for valuation. In highest and best use analysis, the property's potential use and value must be assessed as well as its current worth.

Statutory Value and Compulsory Acquisition

A particular interest in property has only one market value at a given time, but a variety of other values may be ascribed to property components for different purposes or interests. Statutory values used for rating (assessment) and taxation purposes are determined in Australia by legislation in the individual state or territory. One of the following bases is used:

- land (or site) value—the value of the site, less the value of any improvements
- unimproved value—the value of the land, assuming it is in its original state (prior to European settlement)
- improved value—the value of the land including the improvements
- assessed annual value—the value based on the land's rental worth

When land is taken by a state, such compulsory acquisition for government purposes is termed "resumption," as the states theoretically hold all land and have granted title to it to freeholders. Hence, the states use their compulsory powers to take back (or resume) the land. Theoretically, the federal (commonwealth) government has no land-granting power since it was created by the federation of the states. Thus, land acquired by the federal government is referred to as a compulsory acquisition or compulsory purchase (taking). Essentially, the value in such a case is estimated as what the dispossessed owner would have been prepared to pay for the property rather than lose it. A "before and after" method is the most common approach to valuation. In exceptional cases, some jurisdictions allow a *solatium* (additional compensation) to be paid to the dispossessed owner, over and above the value of the land, to compensate for a nonfinancial loss. *Solatia* are neither usual nor large.

Methods of Valuation

Valuation practice in Australia has drawn upon two principal sources: the methods used in the United Kingdom and those applied in the United States. These methods have been modified and adapted to local conditions. In addition to the statutory approaches previously noted, five methods of valuation are recognised:

1. comparison approach
2. contractor's, cost, or summation approach
3. residual method or developer's test
4. profits method
5. income or investment approach, including direct capitalisation and discounted cash flow analysis.

The choice of method(s) depends on the use of the property, the interest being valued, the purpose of the valuation, and the data available.

Comparison Approach

The comparison approach, also called the *market value approach,* is the most frequently used method of valuation. Comparative analysis is generally applied even when other valuation methods are used.

The comparison method involves obtaining information on other transactions involving comparable properties, i.e., sales or lettings, and using the analysed information to determine an opinion of value for the property being valued. The method requires the collection of reliable evidence, usually from the same or a similar locality, concerning properties with the same land use and, as far as possible, the same potential use. The comparable property should be of similar size and in similar condition, and the transaction date should be recent. The greater the disparity between any of these factors, the less reliable the evidence. Unusual or specialised properties may have few comparables. In this case, the practitioner must expertly interpret the transactions or consider the application of another valuation method.

As a stand-alone method, direct comparison is most appropriately used for owner-occupied properties for which comparable evidence is available. Where investment incomes are generated, comparative analysis of the market is generally used to derive components for the income approach, i.e., rents, outgoings (expenses), and capitalisation rates. The significance placed on the date the information is collected will relate to its reliability.

When considering evidence from other transactions, the judgement of the valuer will determine which information is to be relied upon and what monetary allowances (adjustments) will be made for noncomparability, e.g., differences in size, location, or transaction data.

Australian valuers are very fortunate in that data on the vast majority of property transactions are accessible to the public. With strong personal and professional contacts, valuers can minimise the inconvenience that may arise when transactional information is elusive. Aggregated statistics are compiled for major commercial and retail property submarkets, which cover operating costs in particular. Details of transactions are also reported in the property press and by major agents at regular intervals. On-line databases operated by state departments of land and several private companies are other sources of transaction data.

Units of comparison vary by property type. The principal ones are cited below:

- For investment-grade properties: rentals per square metre, usually of net lettable area

- For general development sites: sale price per square metre for small parcels of land and per hectare for large parcels
- For specific hospitality and residential properties: price per room for hotels, price per unit for apartments, and price per bedroom for residential developments

Leasing incentives for office properties have complicated many CBD (central business district) transactions in recent years, but those familiar with the local market have local sources for appropriate evidence. In analysing the sale price of major tenanted properties (shopping centres, office buildings), capital value per square metre of net lettable area would only be used as a general indicator of value.

As noted previously, the normal method of valuation for investment-grade properties is an income approach procedure, either direct capitalisation or DCF analysis.

Contractor's Method

Also called the *cost* or *summation approach,* the contractor's method is used for properties that are rarely sold in the market and for which there is not sufficient evidence of sales or rents to generate a reliable pattern of values. Such properties may have specialised uses (e.g., public buildings such as police stations, railway stations, schools) or be in very remote locations where no market exists.

The contractor's method is open to much misinterpretation and, except for the situations noted above, it is generally only used to check more direct approaches.

The contractor's method recognizes that cost and value are often not the same and produces an opinion of value based on the relationship between the two. While construction costs and land value may be accurately estimated, the allowances made for physical depreciation and functional and economic obsolescence in this method have generated much controversy in the profession.

An application of the method is shown below.

Value of the land	$ 250,000
Replacement cost new (RCN) of the building (including developer's profit)	750,000
	$1,000,000
Less allowance for depreciation,* say 15% of RCN	112,500
Value of property by the contractor's method	$ 887,500

* The use of a percentage allowance for depreciation is based on local practice.

Alternatively, a more direct procedure is to develop an estimate of depreciated replacement cost per square metre from an analysis of sales of comparable properties, to which an estimate of land value is added. This procedure is used by many residential valuers in conjunction with direct comparison.

Residual Method

The residual method, which is also called the *developer's test* or *hypothetical development approach*, is used for properties with development or redevelopment potential, where latent value can be realised through additional expenditure or new construction.

In essence, this approach is very simple and can be explained as follows: the value of the completed development less the total expenditure on improvement or development, including developer's profit, finance costs, etc., gives the residual value of the site or the property in its present condition.

The value of the completed development can be called *gross development value* or *gross realisation value*.

In contrast to the theoretical simplicity of this method, its application presents a number of problems. For market valuations, the residual method may be difficult to use or may prove to be inaccurate for a number of reasons, including:

1. It is necessary for the valuer to decide the best form of development suitable for the site or property.

2. The many costs of the improvement or development must be calculated accurately over a projected timetable.

3. Projections of future sale prices, rents, and capitalisation rates may be required.

4. Financing costs, builder's profit, and developer's profit must be estimated.

The residual method can provide valuable insights when the comparison approach can be used to check the value estimate. If transaction data are not available, the residual method may provide the best assessment of value limited, like all opinions of value, by the soundness of the appraiser's assumptions.

The Profits Method

The *profits*, or *accounts, method* is used to value properties where the specific use, i.e., business activity, contributes to the earning capacity of the property and there may be some element of monopoly (e.g., location). Though market transactions will provide some data for the analysis, such properties do not generally lend themselves to valuation by the comparison method.

Properties valued using this method include licensed premises (pubs), hotels, theatres, racecourses, and petrol filling stations.

The profits method assumes that the rent that could be changed for the property reflects its earning capacity under the existing use. The business accounts for several recent years of normal trading (business activity) are used to generate a rental value which is then capitalised at a rate that reflects the norm for that type of business, i.e., a rate derived from the income streams and sales prices of other, comparable enterprises.

The basic calculation is:

Gross earnings less purchases	= Gross profit
Gross profit less working (operating) expenses (except rent)	= Net profit
Net profit less tenant's wages and an allowance (adjustment) for risk and enterprise and for interest on the tenant's capital invested in the business (opportunity cost)	= Rent

Some problems are associated with the profits method. Application of the method requires access to reliable trading accounts for the business over several years. Skill is also needed to assess the trading pattern over this period and to establish whether the actual performance level of the business operator corresponds to what is normal or typical. A better-than-average or worse-than-average performance will skew the amount available for rent and not reflect market levels. For these reasons, valuers tend to specialise in the valuation of properties within a limited range of business types, frequently over an extensive geographic area.

The Income Approach

Also called the *investment method,* the income approach is used for properties which generate a rental income or, if owner-occupied, belong to a class of property for which comparable data on rents and sales are available. The income approach can be used for commercial office and retail properties, industrial properties, and residential investment properties.

A direct, or simple, capitalisation method and discounted cash flow analysis are the two main techniques used to value investment-grade property.

The general steps in the income approach are described below. The valuer:

1. Collects information on the property's income and outgoings (expenses) in the context of the lease(s).

2. Collects information on comparable rents and sales and other market characteristics.

3. Analyses the comparable evidence to establish the pattern or range of rents, outgoings (expenses), and yields.

4. Determines the appropriate market rent and yield (or target rate) for the property.

5. Applies the capitalisation formula or undertakes a discounted cash flow analysis, as appropriate.

Direct Capitalisation Method

Direct capitalisation is used to value properties when it may not be appropriate to project incomes, outgoings (expenses), or yields beyond the current market level.

The basic capitalisation formula is:

Capital value *(CV)* = Net income *(NI)* × year's purchase *(YP)*

Where

CV = the amount someone will pay to receive the benefits of the property permanently, or to buy it

NI = the rent or annual value that someone will pay for use of the property for one year. Net rent excludes outgoings, i.e., all costs incurred to operate the property

YP = a multiplier, the inverse of the capitalisation rate, which is the rate of return generated by a property's annual net income as a percentage of its capital value derived from the analysis of comparable property transactions.

Depending on the treatment of income before obtaining a market rent, the direct capitalisation method may be further distinguished by three techniques. The *term and reversion method* treats the income in blocks. The *hard core method* (variously known as the *layer* or *hardcore and topslice method*) deals with slices of income. The *shortfall method* deducts notational profit rent (the difference between rent from subtenants and/or rent for the space occupied by the lessee and the total rent payable to the landlord) from market rent and treats it as rent foregone. Each method will generally produce the same outcome, but the hardcore method is most effectively applied to multiple tenancies and thus is most closely aligned to discounted cash flow analysis.

The three techniques of direct capitalization are described and illustrated in the appendix to this chapter.

Discounted Cash Flow Analysis

DCF techniques have been used in Australia for many years to assess the market value of investment-grade properties or other properties with uneven cash flows and to develop feasibility and investment analyses. In many respects, the DFC method does not differ from direct capitalisation, but it does explicitly quantify and project cash flows over a selected holding period, generally of five to 10 years. These cash flows are then discounted and the terminal value at the end of the holding period is estimated. Sensitivity analyses performed under alternative assumptions are also included. A DCF analysis will often be supported by direct capitalisation (on an initial or equivalent yield/*IRR* basis) and, where appropriate, by reference to sales and market evidence.

DCF analysis has not yet been adequately tested before the court. Thus, the use of this method in Australia is not restricted by court precedent. The Australian Institute of Valuers and Land Economists (AIVLE), major property owners, and industry bodies all support more research and discussion about its use, particularly in determining appropriate discount rates (target yields and growth assumptions for various types of property).

Overview of the Income Approach or Investment Method

The income approach requires appropriate market data obtained from the comparison approach. It facilitates comparison of the return on an investment in property with the return on other forms of investment. The internal rate of return *(IRR)* generated by DCF analysis is particularly useful for this purpose. The approach may also be applied to owner-occupied property when sufficient market evidence of rents and sales of comparable properties is available.

Availability of Data

All Australian states and territories have a Torrens (registered) title system of land administration, and transactions such as sales, leases, mortgages, and encumbrances are recorded in public land title offices, normally within the Department of Lands. This information is available for public inspection for a fee. Factors such as leasing incentives may affect the reliability of this information, but the vast majority of transactions are accurately recorded.

Within the bounds of professional confidentiality, valuers will assist one another by sharing the details of public transactions. Real estate agents can also help by providing recent data that may not yet have been recorded in the public system. The operating costs of individual buildings will not normally be released, but accurate, comprehensive, aggregated data on the expenses of major commercial and retail property are issued regularly by industry organisations such as the The Property Council of Australia (PCA), which was formerly known as the Building Owners and Managers Association (BOMA).

Under licence agreement from state Departments of Lands, commercial computer data services also provide current transaction data on line to subscribers. This information is available by local authority jurisdiction and for a full range of other access parameters, e.g., land use, price, registered proprietor, title.

Principal sources of information are summarised below:

Demographic and Economic Data

- Australian Bureau of Statistics
- State or regional planning authorities
- Larger municipal councils
- Economic and planning consultants
- Bank reviews
- The economic and business press

Aggregated Property Market Data

- Annual (or more frequent) market reviews published by:
    - the valuation division of state and territory Departments of Lands
    - large real estate agencies, often through their research departments
    - state real estate institutes
    - industry organisations, e.g., PCA (BOMA), Housing Industry Association (HIA)
    - Urban Development Institute

Rent and Sales Comparables

- Discussions with valuers, agents, and property managers
- On-line databases from commercial or state systems
- Professional Organisations for Valuers

Australia's principal professional organisation for valuers can be contacted at the following address:

National Secretariat
Australian Institute of Valuers and Land Economists
6 Campion Street
Deakin ACT 2600
Tel: 06 282 2411
Fax: 06 285 2194

Residential Valuations

Purpose

Valuations of residential properties are principally prepared for mortgage purposes. Other circumstances requiring valuations include the establishment of a reserve for auction purposes (perhaps where a mortgagee is in possession); Family Court (divorce) proceedings; and stamp duty or capital gains tax purposes. The valuation of residential property for "resumption" or compulsory acquisition is not covered here since legislation varies among states.

Use of Pro Forma

When the client requires a full valuation report, its format follows that used for commercial property. However, to facilitate most residential mortgage appraisals, the Australian Institute of Valuers and Land Economists has issued *Mortgage Valuation Practice Standards* (AIVLE September 1993 and AIVLE May 1994), which includes a pro forma and supporting statement for guidance. In order to promote the use of the pro forma, the AIVLE has waived copyright. A copy of the pro forma is shown in Figure 1. One feature which assists lenders in reviewing the completed report is the Lending Cautions box. Here the valuer indicates possible problems with the property and provides marketability and quality ratings.

Supporting Memorandum

The supporting memorandum is designed to clarify the valuer's role by identifying for the lender which activities are and are not part of the normal inquiry and inspection process. Similarly, the memorandum includes some points of information requested by mortgage insurers and explains each section of the pro forma:

- Title details. Unless specifically requested, a title search is not carried out for a residential mortgage valuation, but title details supplied by the lender are checked by the valuer. The valuer should be advised about encumbrances or restrictions on the title.

- Town planning. Current zoning and the appropriate planning instrument should be noted. A zoning certificate, however, is not obtained by the valuer.

Figure 1. AIVLE Pro Forma

RESIDENTIAL MORTGAGE VALUATION
AIVLE PROVISIONAL WORKING DOCUMENT

AIVLE

LENDER/BRANCH: LOAN NO:

BORROWER: VALUER REF:

1. **SECURITY ADDRESS:**

2. **TITLE DETAILS:**
Encumbrances/Restrictions Considered:

3. **DIMENSIONS/AREA:** LGA:

4. **ZONING & PLANNING INSTRUMENT:**

   EFFECT:

5. **LOCATION/NEIGHBOURHOOD:**

6. **SITE DESCRIPTION & TOPOGRAPHY:**

   Services:
   Environmental Hazards (Flooding, landslip or other problems):

7. **MAIN BUILDING** Detached House ☐ or .... ☐ or TBE ☐ (Dwelling to be erected)
   Style & Street appeal:

   Built about: Additions about:

   Main walls and roof:

   Flooring: Interior linings

   Accommodation: Bedrooms ☐ plus

8. **OBSERVATIONS**
   PC Fixtures:

   Features (Heating, cooling, outdoor areas, basement etc):

   Interior Layout:

   External Condition:

   Internal Condition:

   Defects Observed: (Drainage, pests, dampness, fractures etc)

9. **CAR ACCOMMODATION:**
10. **ANCILLARY IMPROVEMENTS AND CONDITION:** (Fencing, paving, grounds etc)

11. **REPAIRS/REQUIREMENTS:**

    EST COST: $

    AREAS:
    Living Area: m² Verandahs: m² Garage/carport: m²

Figure 1. AIVLE Pro Forma (continued)

PROPERTY ADDRESS:

12. COMMENTS ON THE PROPERTY:

TBE: Tender Price: Date: Builder: Check Cost: $

13. SALES EVIDENCE:

    Address: Date: Price: Comments:

LENDING CAUTIONS:

VALUATION
Vacant Possession Basis

EXISTING PROPERTY:		TBE (*or at completion of repairs*)
Land Value:	$	$
Main Building:	$	$
Other	$	$
Market Value	$	$ *

*Subject to confirmation by final inspection on satisfactory completion

MARKETABILITY:

V Good   Average   Moderate   Poor
☐   ☐   ☐   ☐

QUALITY:

High   Average   Low
1☐   2☐   3☐   4☐   5☐

STRATA TITLE:

The Market Value of Unit ....in plan .... (unit entitlement ....out of ....) is assessed without knowledge of orders against the Body Corporate and without the benefit of a search of the Body Corporate records at $

INVESTMENT PROPERTY: The Market Value of the property subject to the long term lease detailed under heading 12 comments (with valuation calculations) is assessed at $. The market rental is considered to be $ per week.

INSURANCE ESTIMATE: $
An estimated amount for replacement and reinstatement insurance, including allowances for professional fees, anticipated costs movements and removal of debris.

I hereby certify that I have inspected the above property on ....and subject to the terms of the AIVLE Supporting Memorandum to this valuation report, I assess the Market Value of the property as above and recommend it for an appropriate mortgage advance. The valuation is for the use only of the party to which it is addressed and its mortgage insurers for mortgage purposes and is not to be used for any other purpose. No responsibility is accepted or undertaken to any third parties in relation to this valuation and report. The valuers inspection and report does not constitute a structural survey and is not intended as such.

VALUER/FIRM: DATE:

QUALIFICATIONS/REG NO: SIGNATURE:

ADDRESS/TELEPHONE:

SUPPORTING MEMORANDUM:
This valuation pro-forma is made in accordance with the Australian Institute of Valuers and Land Economists Supporting Memorandum dated 1 June 1994 and must be interpreted with that Memorandum.

FINANCIER'S OFFICE USE ONLY:

The valuer identifies the property's existing use and zoning conformity.

- Location/neighbourhood. The valuer notes surrounding development and local features which would benefit or detract from the property's marketability.

- Environmental hazards and features. Reasonable enquiries should be made regarding flooding, landslip (landslide), contaminated land, and other detrimental environmental characteristrics.

- Main building. The valuer should include mention of the style, "street appeal," main elements of construction, and details of the accommodation.

- Observations will be made regarding fixtures and fittings, the property's physical condition and standard of maintenance (internal and external), and significant defects observed during inspection.

- Lending cautions. The valuer should note adverse features significantly affecting value as well as any uncertainty about the property's suitability as security for mortgage purposes.

- Comments on the property. The valuer provides an overview of the property's appearance and finishes, special features, and negative attributes.

- Marketability. The valuer offers an opinion of the property's salability in relation to prevailing market conditions.

- Quality rating. The valuer provides an overall assessment of the property, choosing from five quality ratings. Properties rated in the lowest two groups are viewed as borderline or unacceptable as security.

- Comparable sales. Two or more indicative sales should be recorded, showing the address, date of sale, contract price, and basic descriptive details of building, e.g., 44 Armitage Avenue 8/95 $220,000 - BV/tile 4 B/rm Ens Dble Gar. (Ens = suite bathroom). Evidence should relate to recent transactions, with any sale older than six months incorporating a comment on the market activity in the intervening period. The subject property's sale price should be considered in relation to other market transactions. For properties in newly built estates or subdivisions, evidence from outside the development should also be considered and enquiries regarding any incentives offered by the developer should be noted.

- Photographs. Normally, at least one photograph is included to show the property and its surrounding development.

- Insurance figure. An estimate may be included for replacement and reinstatement insurance. This estimate should include allowances for professional fees, anticipated cost changes and the removal of debris.

- Loan-to-value ratio. The valuer should be advised by the lender of the proposed loan amount, but should not provide an opinion of the suggested loan percentage. Where adverse factors are evident, the valuer may indicate that a high loan-to-value ratio is not recommended. If the valuation is subject to repairs or other work being completed, the valuer may estimate the cost of this work.

- Valuer's signature. Only an appropriately qualified and (currently) registered valuer, who is a member of the lender's panel of valuers, may sign the report, after completing and inspecting the property.

- Selling period. Where normal selling periods exceed three or four months, an estimate of the likely selling period should be noted.

- Investment property. Vacant possession of value (units available for immediate occupancy at open market levels) and passing or contract rentals should also be included where longer leases exist.

- Strata title. If a number of strata title units are being valued, a clear indication must be made of the value either individually or in one line (i.e., severally or jointly).

The supporting statements also address notes for lenders, the definition of market value, responsibilities for titles and searches, the provision of information to the valuer, and special circumstances relating to dwellings to be erected or under construction, issues of contamination, the quality of the structures, and needed repairs. Lenders are advised to request comprehensive valuation reports where:

- the value is likely to exceed $500,000 in Sydney or $300,000 elsewhere, or

- there are special circumstances (e.g., a property with development potential)

The pro forma notifies the user that it is to be read in conjunction with the supporting memorandum.

Bibliography

Note: The acronym AIVLE stands for The Australian Institute of Valuers and Land Economists; the acronym BOMA stands for the Building Owners and Managers Association of Australia, Limited. Since mid-1996, the organisation previously known as BOMA is called the Property Council of Australia (PCA).

AIVLE. *Contaminated Land Practice Standard.* Canberra, February 1994.

AIVLE. *Due Diligence Standard.* (first draft). Canberra, 1994.

AIVLE. *Model Instructions to Valuers for Commercial and Industrial Property.*

Canberra, September 1993.

AIVLE. *Mortgage Valuation Practice Standard* Canberra, September 1993.

AIVLE. *Provisional Mortgage Valuation Practice Standard, Valuation of Commercial, Industrial and Retail Property for Mortgage Purposes.* Canberra, October 1994.

AIVLE. *Residential Valuation Pro Forma Supporting Statement.* Canberra, June 1994.

AIVLE. *Use of Discounted Cash Flow in Property Valuations.* Canberra, 1993.

AIVLE. *The Valuer & Land Economist.* vol. 33, no. 4. Canberra.

Armitage, Lynne A. *Valuation Principles and Practice.* Unpublished course notes. Brisbane: Queensland University of Technology, 1995.

BOMA. *Practice Note: An Owner's Guide to Briefing Valuers.* Sydney, 1994.

Millington A.F. *An Introduction to Property Valuation.* 3rd ed. London: Estates Gazette, 1988.

Scarrett, D. *Property Valuation: The Five Methods.* London: E & FN Spon, 1991.

Appendix

Direct Capitalisation: Term and Reversion, Hardcore, and Shortfall Methods

Explanatory diagrams of the three direct capitalisation techniques are shown below. Although the methods should produce the same answer, sometimes one method is more appropriate than the others.

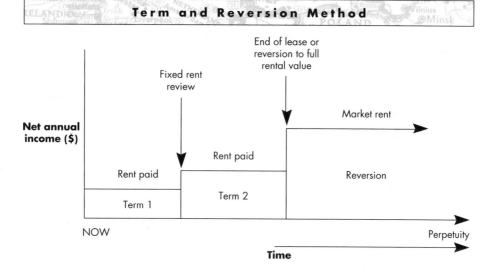

The capitalisation rate may be changed to reflect the varying security of each period of income, e.g., Term 1, Term 2, reversion

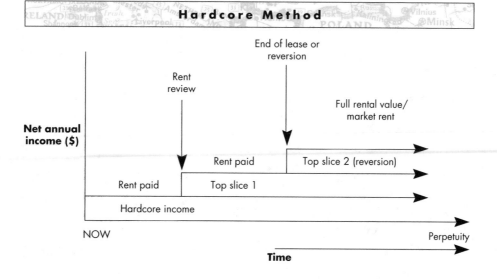

- In this method income is treated in horizontal slices.

- The income already received is the *core income,* which is most secure; the income received after future rent reviews is *top slice income,* which is less secure.

- This method is particularly useful when multiple tenancies are being valued, e.g., office buildings, shopping centres.

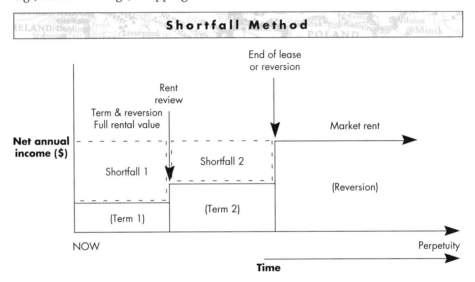

- Values the loss of income to the landlord, before market rent is received.

- Makes use of a modified term and reversion method.

- The value of the property is first calculated, assuming full rental value *(FRV)* is received now (i.e., *FRV × YP* perp*).

- The amounts that are not yet received, i.e., Shortfall 1 and 2, are then deducted.

Examples of Term and Reversion, Hardcore, and Shortfall Methods of Valuing Freeholds, Subject to Leases

The property is a 500 m² factory, leased for 15 years with nine years remaining and subject to reviews every five years. The rent paid now is $375,000 per annum and will increase by 40% at the next rent review.

Similar properties that are selling have 8.5% capitalisation rates and are renting for $1,500/m² nett (net).

---

*   *YP* perp. = Year's purchase in perpetuity

Term and Reversion Method

1. Draw a diagram.

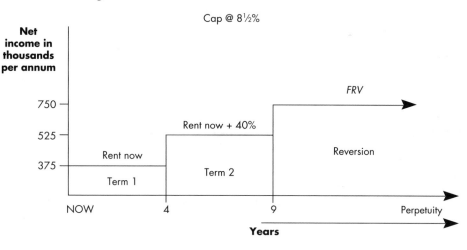

Cap @ 8½%

2. Calculate rents/analyse data.

Rent paid	$375,000 per annum nett	
Rent review	$375,000	
+ 40%	$150,000	
Rent after review		$525,000
Full rental value *(FRV)*:		
Area of factory	500 m²	
@ $1,5000/m² per annum		$750,000
Cap rate 8.5%		

3. Prepare valuation using term and reversion method.

   Next 4 years

Rent received:	375,000	
Cap @ 8.5% for 4 yrs.	3.2756 *(PV of $1 p.p.)*	
		1,228,349

   After fixed rent review

Rent received	525,000	
Cap @ 8.5% for 5 yrs.	3.9406 *(PV of $1 p.p.)*	
Deferred 4 yrs.	2,068,837	
PV of $1		
@ 8.5% after 4 yrs.	0.7216	
		1,492,819

At end of lease: rev. to FRV
Full rental value *(FRV)*   750,000
Cap @ 8.5% *YP* in perp.
   (100/8.5)   11.765
Deferred 9 yrs.   8,823,529
PV of $1 after 9 yrs. @8.5%   0.47988
                                                                                     4,234,235
                                                                                     6,955,403

Say $7.0 million

Hardcore Method

1. Draw a diagram

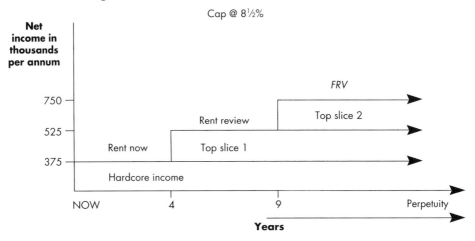

2. Calculate rents (see term and reversion method)

3. Prepare valuation using hardcore method

Capitalise hardcore income
Rent received   375,000
Cap. @ 8.5% *YP* in perp.
   (100/8.5)   11.765
                                                                                     4,411,765

After rent review
Rent increase (Top slice 1)   150,000
Cap @ 8.5% *YP* in perp.   11.765
Deferred 4 yrs.
PV of $1   11.765
@ 8.5% after 4 yrs.   0.7216
                                                            8.489
                                                 8.489 × 150,000   1,273,398

At end of lease: rev. to FRV
Rent increase (Top slice 2)   225,000
Cap @ 8.5% *YP* in perp.   11.765
Deferred 9 yrs   11.765
PV of $1 @ 8.5% after 9 yrs.   0.4799
                                                            5.646
                                                 5.646 × 225,000   1,270,260
                                                                          6,955,423

Say $7.0 million

Shortfall Method

1.   Draw a diagram.

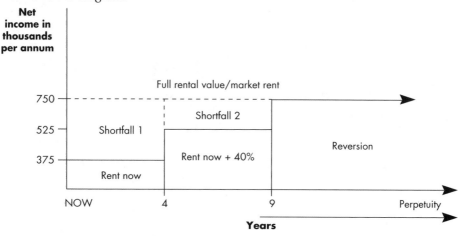

2.   Calculate rents/analyse data as above.

3. Prepare valuation using shorfall method
    Calculate unencumbered freehold value.
    (Assume market rent received now)

Full rental value *(FRV)*	750,000	
Cap @ 8.5% *YP* perp.		
(100/8.5)	11.765	
		8,823,529

Calculate Shortfall 1

Rent forgone	375,000	
(750,000 – 375,000)		
Cap @ 8.5% *YP* for 4 yrs.	3.2756 *(PV* of $1 p.p.)	
		1,228,349

Calculate Shortfall 2

Rent forgone	225,000	
(750,000 – 525,000)		
Cap @ 8.5% for 5 yrs.	3.9406 *(PV* of $1 p.p.)	
	886,635	
Deferred 4 yrs. @ 8.5%		
PV of $1 @ 8.5%		
after 4 yrs.	× 0.7216	
		639,795
		– 1,868,145
		6,955,384

Say $7.0 million

New Zealand

Richard Emary, ANZIV, ARICS

Richard Emary is a lecturer in the Department of Property at the University of Auckland in New Zealand. He is a member of the New Zealand Institute of Valuers and a state certified Registered Valuer. In addition to teaching valuation and financial economics, Mr. Emary is engaged in postgraduate research on residential property, pricing models, price index construction, efficiency measurement, and market analysis. He is also an Associate of the Royal Institution of Chartered Surveyors, and a member of both the American Real Estate and Urban Economics Association and the Pacific Rim Real Estate Society.

NEW ZEALAND

Auckland

Wellington

Christchurch

New Zealand consists of two main islands, the North Island and the South Island, separated by Cook Strait.

The islands are mountainous with fertile east coast plains, the largest lowland area being the Canterbury Plains on the South Island. New Zealand has a wet, subtropical climate. The center of the North Island is a volcanic plateau; there are glaciers on the South Island. The principal cities of New Zealand are Auckland, Wellington, and Christchurch.

Political Structure

New Zealand is a sovereign and independant state with a constitutional monarchy, an elected unicameral parliament, and a centralized administration. Queen Elizabeth II, the Queen of the United Kingdom of Great Britain and Northern Ireland, is also titular Queen of New Zealand. The Queen has a standing representative in New Zealand, the governor general, who is appointed by the Queen on the recommendation of the New Zealand parliament for a five-year term.

Like that of the United Kingdom, the constitution of New Zealand is unwritten. The constitution is based on a collection of statutes of the British parliament, including landmark constitutional acts such as the Magna Carta (1215) and Habeas Corpus Act (1679), as well as statutes of the New Zealand parliament and the conventions and principles of the rule of law.

The four principal branches of the government are: 1) the sovereign, represented by the governor general, 2) the executive branch, represented by the cabinet of the day, 3) the legislature or parliament of the day, known as the House of Representatives, and 4) the judiciary. While a separation of powers exists in theory, the executive branch and the parliament must often act in concert since they cannot legislate independently.

The Sovereign

The governor general exercises royal powers derived from statute and general law. The primary constitutional function of the governor general is to arrange for the majority party in parliament to form a government. An additional duty is to give assent to bills so that they can pass into law. The governor general is bound to follow the advice of the ministers of the elected government as laid down in the letters patent[1] (1983) although, at times, advice can be rejected if it is believed that the intent of the government is to breach the constitution.

The Executive Branch

The executive branch comprises the cabinet and the Executive Council. The cabinet is made up of ministers (all elected MPs) who are appointed by the governor general on the recommendation of the parliamentary prime minister. The cabinet is the policy-making body of parliament. It sets the legislative agenda for government and coordinates the work of the ministers. Cabinet proceedings are consensual, informal, and confidential. Traditionally, the cabinet makes decisions collectively and the entire body shares the responsi-

---

1. *Letters patent* refer to the official document conferring specific rights upon the ministers.

bility. In a multi-party cabinet, this consensus and collectivity may change. The Executive Council is separate but comprises all the cabinet ministers. Its functions, which are formal as opposed to those of the cabinet, relate to executing or validating decisions which have been made elsewhere.

The Legislature

The House of Representatives has traditionally been elected triennially on the basis of the "first-past-the-post" system, as evolved in the U.K. However, a new system modeled on the system used in Germany was adopted in 1996. Known as the "additional-member-system," it is based on proportional representation. In this system each voter has two votes—one for the local representative to parliament and the other for the national party favoured by the voter. The latter vote decides the total proportion of seats in parliament allotted among the registered parties. The minimum threshold for a party to secure a seat is 5% of the total vote. A party does not have to win an electorate (i.e., a local division—county, town, or district) to secure a seat in parliament.

There are 120 MPs, 64 of whom are electorate MPs (with three ministerial seats reserved for Maori voters) [2] and 56 of whom are elected from the party lists. The South Island is ensured a minimum of 16 electorate MPs.

If no party secures an outright majority of seats, the parties then need to establish a coalition prior to being asked by the governor general to form a government. Coalition agreements often result in cabinet posts being held by MPs of different parties.

The three Maori electorate MPs are elected by those choosing to vote on the Maori roll. If the option to vote on the Maori roll is not exercised, the voter is then registered on the general roll. There is not and will not be any requirement to prove eligibility for the Maori roll. Rather, the option is left to the individual. Any voter at any time may, on application, transfer to the Maori roll.

The Judiciary

The judiciary is independent of parliament. New Zealand law follows that of the United Kingdom and is therefore a mix of statutory and unwritten case law. Ancient legal principles that evolved in England relating to common law (i.e., property, contracts, and torts) are interpreted in light of case precedents, with priority being given to New Zealand case precedents. After these,

---

2. The Maoris, a Polynesian people who reached New Zealand in the 14th century, make up between 9% and 12% of the total population of 3,650,000. About three-quarters of the Maoris live on the North Island.

English case precedents and citations of English rulings are followed in turn. The higher the order of the court setting the precedent, the greater the weight given its judgments.

The court system in New Zealand is adversarial in nature and both the plaintiff/prosecution and the defendant are legally represented in all disputes or prosecutions by the state. A hierarchy of courts exists. District courts are presided over by panels of lay justices of the peace. High courts adjudicate through either a 12-man jury or a single judge. The New Zealand Court of Appeal is a panel of five judges who hear cases and adjudicate. Commercial disputes and cases are heard by the commercial division of the high court, which comprises panels of three judges.

Judges are former lawyers who are salaried officials of the Justice Department. Their task is to superintend court procedures, to advise the jury on points of law, and to pass sentence or make judgments and awards in civil disputes.

Barristers, as distinguished from solicitors, tend to monopolize court appearances in New Zealand because to practise in the high and appeal courts, one must be a qualified barrister-at-law. All lawyers may practise in the lower courts. The Privy Council[3] in London still has the status of the highest court in New Zealand, although various parties have stated a desire to eliminate the Privy Council from the New Zealand judicial system.

Various protocols and bodies exist to deal with land disputes, including the Maori Land Court, which adjudicates matters involving Maori-owned land. Planning tribunals and land valuation tribunals are quasi-legal entities which deal with planning and assessments/ratings.

The Arbitration Act of 1997 sets forth rules relating to the arbitration of disputes. The act closely follows the principle of the UNCITRAL (United Nations Commission on International Trade Law) Model Law of 1985, developed by a body working under the auspices of the United Nations. In essence, the act provides for the speedy and inexpensive resolution of disputes by a single arbitrator or panel. The arbitrator may act either as an umpire or an expert, whichever the arbitration agreement provides for. It is a private process which results in a binding decision subject only to review by higher courts on specified grounds or, alternatively, in circumstances where all parties seek a referral on a point of law prior to the umpire giving his determination.

---

3. The Privy Council is a committee of persons appointed by the Sovereign to advise on state affairs.

Property Rights

The origins of New Zealand land law lie in English land law. On February 6, 1840, the Maori tribal chiefs and Captain Hobson, the Crown representative, signed the Treaty of Waitangi, ceding New Zealand to British "sovereignty" in return for guarantees relating mainly to Maori land and traditional hunting and fishing rights.[4] The subsequent enactment of the English Laws Act (1858) recognized all English statutory and case law up to January 14, 1840, as the laws of New Zealand. Thus, New Zealand adopted the doctrine of tenure, which had evolved in England during the Middle Ages.

Fortunately for property professionals, New Zealand soon took advantage of the opportunity to sweep away the complexities of English law and develop a land law not dissimilar to that of South Australia. New Zealand also adopted the Torrens system of land registration, providing what is termed indefeasible title. Under this system, each parcel of land is accurately identified (almost 100% of the total land area of New Zealand has been surveyed) and all existing property rights to each parcel of land are recorded. Under the title registration system, the state guarantees the accuracy of the register and the land boundaries.

Compensation is paid by the state to those who suffer loss due to errors or those who have an adverse claim but are precluded from asserting it.[5]

Features of the title registration system of New Zealand are outlined below.

Information included in the title registration system:

- With regard to the parcels of land that form the recorded units, the boundaries of every unit that is uniquely identifiable are surveyed by the Department of Survey and Land Information,

- The rights and interests relating to the every parcel are recorded.

- The identity of the person or persons (individual or corporate entity) entitled to the particular interest are specified.

---

4. The treaty document is subject to different interpretations. There was an English version and a Maori version, the latter being signed by a majority of the participants. The Maori text has been widely accepted. The concept of *sovereignty* as defined in an authoritative English dictionary is not to be found in the Maori version.

5. A registered proprietor, who is a bona fide purchaser of property at value, but who may be a victim of a fraud perpetrated by a third party, has guaranteed title over and above the rightful owner. The common law remedy of returning the property to the rightful owner is overridden by the Land Transfer Act of 1952. In this instance, the rightful owner would be compensated by the government.

Transfer of title

- Transfer of title occurs only upon entry thereof into the *Journal Register* by the district land registrar of the Department of Justice, and not upon any prior contractual documentation or court order.

Working records

- Title Records are maintained in real time (i.e., immediately and continually), not in arrears.

- Records are open to public scrutiny and photocopies of titles are available.

- Title documents are held in duplicate and indexed on an electronic database for ease of access.

- Records and titles are revised to increase utility (e.g., converted to metric) and obsolete data is expunged.

National standardisation and quality control

- A government department, the Department of Justice, administers the district land registries.

- A state-owned enterprise, Land Information New Zealand, issues titles to property and maintains an accurate system for showing property, electoral, and census boundaries.

  A certificate of title is issued to all holders of estates in fee simple[6] and life estates. Leaseholders may also be issued a title if the registrar determines that the duration of registered leasehold interests (longer than 21 years) or their nature deems it necessary. All encumbrances are clearly noted on the certificate of title to indicate their priority. These include memorials (statements) of mortgages, easements, other encroachments, and miscellaneous interests such as notices of intent to a compulsory purchase (taking). There is also a provision for holders of equitable interests (a third party right or charge) to enter temporary caveats on the title to prevent transfer and to communicate to the public that clear title may not be available.

Types of Commercial Property Interests

Five types of interests are common to commercial property.

1. Freehold title. Ownership of the fee simple absolute interest in a property.

---

6. This includes unit titles as issued under the Unit Titles Act (1972), providing for "freehold" interests in defined, three-dimensional space. Unit title is discussed in the next section on interests in commercial property.

2. Unit title. The interest held by a registered proprietor of a unit in a scheme (development plan) in accordance with the Unit Titles Act of 1972. Devised to possess all the attributes of freehold title in the vertical plane (defined in three dimensions), the unit title is also referred to as a *strata title.*

3. Ground lease. A perpetually renewable property lease, usually for a fixed term of 21 years, on a fixed rental basis with the right of renewal in favour of the lessee; also known as a *Glasgow lease.* Rent is usually set by a formula relative to current land value and is renegotiated upon renewal. Some statutes (such as the Maori Housing Act) set a finite limit by determining the number of renewals to be exercised.

4. Cross-lease. A long, leasehold interest (usually 999 years) combined with an undivided share in the freehold for which composite title is provided. The cross-lease evolved as a means of providing a mortgageable, free-hold-like interest for occupancy.

5. Short, fixed-term leases with or without rights of renewal.

Language

There are two official languages in New Zealand: Maori and English. Almost all commercial and government business is conducted in English.

Currency

The currency is the New Zealand dollar (NZ$), which is divided into 100 cents.

Units of Measure

The official units of measure are metric. All land and building plans are measured linearly in metres and kilometres; areas are measured in square metres and hectares. Rents are stated in dollars per square metre per annum; commercial land values are often stated in dollars per hectare. In addition to metric units, real estate agents also use imperial linear and area units, such as feet and square feet.

A code of practice for measuring the net lettable (leasable) area of office, retail, and industrial buildings was devised by the Building Owners and Managers Association (BOMA) in conjunction with the Property Management Institute (PMI) in 1986. This code has been widely adopted in standard (BOMA/PMI) and nonstandard leases. Owners of new buildings often commission registered land surveyors to measure net lettable areas precisely. These measurements are then referenced in lease contracts.

Inflation

Figure 1. Quarterly Consumer Price Inflation: All Sectors

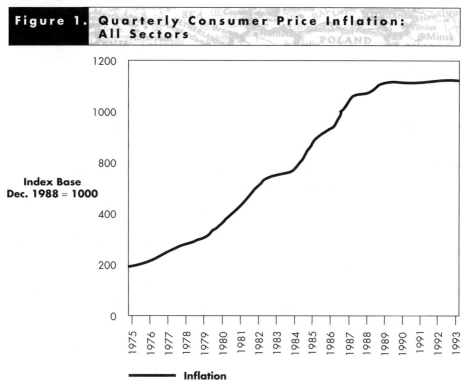

Index Base Dec. 1988 = 1000

Inflation

Source: Department of Statistics, Wellington, NZ.

Under legislation passed in 1990, the New Zealand Reserve Bank must keep inflation below 2% per annum. Thus, recent consumer price inflation has remained low. Although the opposition parties have indicated a desire to extend the range within which inflation may fluctuate and to add unemployment reduction as a primary target of reserve bank policy (currently excluded in the legislation), the medium-term inflation projection remains under 4%.

Historically, annual inflation has ranged from a high of 15%, in the boom years prior to the 1987 decline in global stock markets, to a low of about 0.6% in 1993. Although inflation control policy may be relaxed, the rate of inflation is expected to remain under 4% per annum for the foreseeable future.

Valuations relate to nominal rather than real dollars. Since a valuation based on discounted cash flows includes a forecast of future revenues and expenses, explicit estimates of inflation are usually incorporated into the cash flow forecasts.

Typical Lease Structure

Office

The length of lease terms varies from three years to 20 years or more. Longer lease terms usually involve tenants who are the sole occupants of the premises and who, in addition to a lease for accommodation, may secure the rights to name the building. Rents vary with the floor level (story) in the building, with the highest rents charged for the ground (street) and top levels. The rent for the rights to name a building is often based on a percentage of the rent applicable to the top floor.

The trend in the 1980s was toward net leases, which are common in the United Kingdom and Commonwealth countries. Under a net lease, the tenant is required to pay, in addition to rent (monthly, in advance), contributions towards the operating expenses of the property. These contributions are typically based on the previous year's expenses, appropriately adjusted for inflation. The Building Owners and Managers Association (BOMA) in conjunction with the Property Management Institute (PMI) (now called the Property and Land Economy Institute of New Zealand, or PLEINZ), devised a standard net lease. This net lease is known as the BOMA/PMI or BOMA/PLEINZ standard lease and has been widely adopted by landlords.

With the great demand for office accommodations during the boom years of the 1980s, the net lease became the accepted norm. It included among recoverable annual operating expenses or service charges, items of contention such as contributions to long-term maintenance funds, property manager's fees, and even the ground rent where the immediate landlord was a lessee. The characteristic net lease had an "upwards-only" rent review clause (or ratchet review clause) and the frequency of reviews was increased, in extreme cases to two or even three times a year. The aim of the net lease was to preserve the annual rent stated in the lease as revenue regardless of the effects of inflation on operating expenses. The BOMA/PMI or BOMA/PLEINZ standard lease came very close to achieving this goal.

Prior to the 1980s, leasehold accommodations to house government departments were centrally purchased, and mainly on a gross lease basis. These leases required the landlord to pay expenses out of the rental revenue. In common practice, however, increases in annual rates (local property taxes) over the rate at the commencement of the lease were passed on to the lessee. The civil servants purchasing the leasehold accommodations believed that the use of gross leases would encourage prudent management of the property. In reality, gross leases often motivated commercial property landlords to minimise maintenance expenditures in the pursuit of profit and to allow the building environment to deteriorate as essential work was deferred.

As the economy and overexpanded financial services industry began to contract in the period after 1987, a severe oversupply of office accommodations occurred in the three main cities of Auckland, Christchurch, and Wellington. With 30% of office stock in the prime CBD markets left vacant, incentives became widespread. These included rent-free periods (up to two years in some cases) and tenant fitouts (finish-out allowances) of accomodations, which were common between 1989 and 1991. Leases terms became very negotiable and many lessees would not accept the Standard BOMA/PMI net office lease. The "upwards-only" rent review became the exception rather than the norm in new leases. The rents in new leases fell dramatically below those being paid by existing tenants. Older buildings and buildings in less than prime locations were once again rented on a gross lease basis, with operating expenses either met by the landlord or capped and the existing lease liabilities of prospective lessees assumed by landlords.

By January 1995 the oversupply had been significantly reduced and this, combined with growth in the economy, helped decrease the need for incentives. The government is once again contracting nonnegotiable gross leases when taking accommodations from private sector landlords.

Commissions are usually paid to real estate agents who broker accommodations. Agents are typically self-employed and remunerated through commissions only. Tenants sometimes employ consultants to act as their procurement agents, but these individuals are often not registered valuers. Real estate agents usually earn their commission when a binding agreement to lease is signed, generally without recourse to lawyers; the commission often includes the agency authorisation and fee formula. Fees are taken from the purchaser's or lessee's deposit, which is held by the real estate firm as the stakeholder. Leasing fees typically range from 5% to 12% of the contract rent, depending on the length of the lease and the size of the accommodation; sales fees range up to 2.5% of the clearing price. Fees exclude marketing and promotion costs, which are recovered in addition to the fee. In the recent recession, fixed fees and promotional costs, including commission, have been offered by agency firms in an increasingly competitive market. Management fees traditionally have been high, up to 5% of total annual occupancy costs (TOC), but increasing competition has driven these fees down to more realistic levels.

Retail

The retail market can be divided into 1) CBD road frontage (strip commercial), 2) CBD mall accommodations, 3) suburban road frontage (strip commercial), 4) suburban malls, 5) regional shopping centres, and 6) new innovations, e.g., stand-alone retail warehouses and supermarkets.

Retail leases are often shorter than office leases with more frequent reviews, sometimes twice a year. The rents for retail units with CBD and suburban, strip or single-road frontage are based on annual market rents per square metre. Rent computation for comparable analysis is generally not standardised. The retail, frontage-to-depth ratio tables used in the U.S. and the zoning approach applied in Great Britain are understood, but not widely used in the retail industry, except by valuers in their analyses. However, raw computations of overall increments for *return frontages* (corner units) are regularly made.

Shopping centre and mall units are let (leased) at a base rent plus a percentage of turnover (volume of business), with an additional pro rata charge for operating expenses and a mall or centre marketing levy. This last sum is usually controlled to some extent by the tenants association. The percentage rent provides an incentive for the mall or centre owner to market the centre actively to maximise rental income. The standard BOMA/PMI or BOMA/PLEINZ retail lease, which is widely used, requires tenants to supply audited monthly turnover data (sales receipts) to the owner to monitor the volume of business and calculate percentage rent.

Large food stores and retail warehouses (a relatively new phenomenon) tend to be leased at base rent plus a percentage of turnover (volume of business). The leases are relatively long-term, extending up to 30 years with options to renew and periodic reviews of the base rent. The tenant takes on most of the operating and administrative costs; the landlord retains liability for maintaining the structure and external membrane (weatherproofing). A management fee is sometimes levied.

Industrial

Leases for industrial premises are renewable annually and based up gross external floor area measured in square metres.[7] Rents are periodically reviewed and adjusted to market levels. Typically, additional rent is apportioned for loading bays, office accommodation in excess of the 15% national norm, car parking spaces, and yard areas.

The tenant takes on most of the operating and administrative costs, while the landlord retains liability for maintaining the structure and external membrane. A management fee is sometimes levied.

---

7. Gross external (floor) area is defined in the glossary.

Valuation Standards

The New Zealand Institute of Valuers (NZIV) is a participating member of the International Valuation Standards Committee (IVSC). In 1986, the New Zealand Institute of Valuers published a set of asset valuation standards based on prevailing international standards. The asset valuation standards have been substantially revised and extended to incorporate additional standards besides those pertaining to annual reporting requirements.

In March 1995, the New Zealand Institute of Valuers issued a new set of standards incorporating the international revisions. The NZIV Standards Committee publishes periodic revisions on an ad hoc basis and engages in ongoing consultation with the Society of Chartered Accountants in New Zealand to ensure that the valuation standards and the Society's Statements of Standard Accounting Practice are complementary.

The institute also publishes statements of practice standards, guidance notes, and a code of ethics. Currently, these documents include:

Practice Standard No. 1: The Valuation of Residential Properties

Practice Standard No. 2: The Valuation of Residential Properties for Mortgage Purposes

Practice Standard No. 3: The Valuation of Rural Properties

Practice Standard No. 4: The Valuation of Suburban Commercial Properties

Guidance Note No. 1: Valuation and GST (Sales Tax on Goods and Services)

Guidance Note No. 2: Risk Assessment and the Valuer

Guidance Note No. 3: The Valuation of Contaminated Land (in preparation)

Guidance Note No. 4: The Use of DCF in Property Valuations

Guidance Note No. 5: Insurance Valuation Reports

Guidance Note No. 6: Letters of Engagement.

The institute also publishes the NZIV Information Series. The first five publications in this series were *The Building Act* (2d ed.); *The Privacy Act 1993; Title Searches under the Resource Management Act; Professional Practice, A Brief Guide; and Mortgage Recommendations.*

Licensing/Certification

Statutory licensing of valuers in New Zealand was laid down in the Valuers Act of 1948 (and subsequently amended). Valuers wishing to represent themselves to the public as qualified to conduct valuations of land for fees must be registered with the Valuers' Registration Board (VRB) and possess a current annual practising certificate. All registered valuers are required to be NZIV members. Although there are no restrictions on the type of property a valuer can appraise, valuers are required to abide by the rules and code of ethics of the institute. This means that valuers will only undertake instruction (an assignment) relating to properties they are competent to value. Thus, an informal distinction is drawn between specialisation in rural and urban valuation.

Complaints from the public about the improper, unethical, or incompetent conduct of registered valuers are referred to the register of the Valuers' Registration Board (VRB), an office established by the VRB chairman. If the valuer is found guilty of misconduct, the inquiry board can exercise its powers to levy fines and temporarily or permanently remove the individual from the list of registered valuers. Conduct likely to incur removal are conviction in court of an offence carrying a prison sentence of two years or more or conviction of any other offence likely to dishonour the valuer in the public esteem. The institute can only police its members through the Valuers Registration Board.

The requirements for earning the status of an associate of the New Zealand Institute of Valuers and registered valuer under the Valuers Act are summarised below:

> The candidate must be registered with the state Valuers' Registration Board for at least one calendar year and satisfy the local NZIV Branch Membership Subcommittee as to his or her range of expertise. Referees (references) in support of the candidate and documentary evidence of at least six valuations undertaken in the previous year must be provided. Candidates should be 25 years old.

To become a registered valuer, candidates must:

- Have a minimum of three calendar years' experience in valuation practice under the supervision of a registered valuer
- Present themselves before the board for interview
- Present documentary evidence in the minimum range of 60 valuations
- Present a log of the work undertaken over the three years in practice
- Hold a recognised tertiary qualification in property (e.g., brokerage, management)
- Have referees (references) who support the candidate's registration

Practising members, who hold practising certificates, must complete 20 hours of continuing professional development annually. The institute's code of ethics was recently amended to indicate that failure to fulfill the requirements constitutes a breech of the code of ethics, which is an offence worthy of an inquiry by the registration board.

Reciprocal agreements are in place with institutes overseas, including the Australian Institute of Valuers and Land Economists (AIVLE), the Royal Institution of Chartered Surveyors (RICS), and the Appraisal Institute of Canada (AIC). Each agreement sets specific conditions and requirements, but all provide that full practising members of the respective institute can, subject to an interview, obtain full associate membership in the New Zealand Institute of Valuers upon migration to New Zealand. The Valuer's Registration Board requires a minimum of one year of valuation practice, under the supervision of a registered valuer, and may require completion of a correspondence course on New Zealand property law.

Valuation Reporting Requirements

Lending institutions and other users of valuation reports on commercial properties have grown accustomed to reports that are well-researched and supported by comprehensive data. Commercial property valuation reports include all computations and property data, such as tenancy schedules, lease and rental summaries, and operating expense histories. Market and comparable data are generally supplied as appendices to the report.

Valuers apply a minimum of two, and usually three, traditional approaches to value. The report content was logically presented and includes an explicit statement of how the final value is derived. Also typically included are assumptions and limiting conditions, which qualify issues such as the availability of information, the definition of market value, technical matters beyond the reasonable skill of the valuer, and statements as to the valuer's independence and objectivity.

Valuation reports pursuant to a statutory instrument will clearly state so and will follow the prescriptions of the relevant statute, as appropriate. Statements of Standard Accounting Practice (SSAP) 17 and 28 of the Society of Chartered Accountants in New Zealand are applicable to annual property asset valuations and refer to the Standards of the New Zealand Institute of Valuers. The Financial Reporting Act of 1993 requires valuers to follow these two statements in certain situations.

Practice Standard No. 4, "The Valuation of Suburban Commercial Properties," lays down the de minimis content requirements for a commercial valuation report.

4.4 The following should be the minimum content of a written report.

4.4.1   A clear statement of the specific instructions or terms of reference upon which the valuation is to be performed.

4.4.2   A clear statement of the purposes and function of the valuation including any statutory criteria which may apply.

4.4.3   A clear statement of the total value of the estate or interest held in land that is subject to the valuation. Such a statement to include the valuers' certification and signature.

4.4.4   The effective date of the valuation.

4.4.5   The legal description and tenure, building tenure/tenancies, land tenure and postal address of the property.

4.4.6   A clear and reasonably complete description of the property including its ancillary improvements being valued together with its general state of repair.

4.4.7   A clear description of the existence and implication of zoning or any other resource management notation relating to the property including highest and best use scenarios.

4.4.8   A clear and reasonable summary of the data upon which the valuation is based including obvious conclusions of the evidence, market conditions and their application to the valuation databases.

4.4.9   A clear and reasonable presentation of the valuation method or methods adopted to arrive at the value.

4.4.10 A definitive synopsis of, or a specific reference to, all documents used in the valuation process which are germane to a proper understanding of the valuation report.

4.4.11 A clear statement of any assumptions and limiting conditions associated with the valuation conclusions.

Definition of Market Value

Another section of Practice Standard No. 4 sets forth the definition of market value to be adopted in a commercial valuation report.

4.0 The valuation

4.1 Market value is defined as:
The estimated amount for which an asset should exchange on the date of valuation between a willing buyer and a willing

seller in an arm's-length transaction after proper marketing wherein the parties had each acted knowledgeable, prudently and without compulsion.

4.2 Among the relevant factors to be taken into account in the valuation are:

4.2.1 Comparable sales evidence in support of the market value and land value opinions.

4.2.2 The tenure of the interest being valued and the terms of any tenancies to which that interest is subject.

4.2.3 The unencumbered rental value (supported by comparable rental evidence) of the property (subject to existing leases) and the resultant net cash flow of the entire property.

4.2.4 The economic/investment implications of vacant tenancies and/or accommodation and the implication of all rental deficiencies, including the unexpired intervals of existing rental review periods.

4.2.5 The consideration of necessary risk assessments in relation to assessed rental values and market yields and these implications upon the final market value assessment.

4.2.6 The assessment of extraordinary expenses associated with the refurbishment and leasing of vacant accommodation and the relevant effect of these costs on the market value of the property.

4.2.7 The age, type, accommodation, siting, amenities, building, services, fixtures and features of the property.

4.2.8 The construction and general state of repair of the improvements, including any defects which are obvious to the valuer in the course of the inspection.

4.2.9 The likelihood of the property being affected by subsidence flooding and other market and physical risks.

Capital Valuation Methodologies

The valuation profession in New Zealand evolved in large part from the government valuation (assessment) office now called Valuation New Zealand and from departments involved in the property market, i.e., the now defunct

Ministry of Works and Development, Housing Corporation, the Department of Lands and Survey, and the one-time State Advances Corporation.

The "annual values" methodologies for ratings (assessments for property taxation), which were initially adopted from the United Kingdom, were rejected as being too dependant on rents when most, if not all, property was owned as freeholds. In time, ratings based on the assessment of land value and, more recently, capital value were adopted as both equitable and viable. Due to the lack of transactions in many markets and a history of government intervention in the property market, the cost or depreciated replacement cost method (also known as the *replacement, summation,* or *contractor's approach*) was for many years a dominant valuation methodology.

Since the 1930s, contact with American appraisal practice and literature has resulted in a strong infusion of American appraisal methods and terms. This influence is reflected in the fact that two of the three university valuation courses offered are considered business courses and American appraisal texts are used along with standard New Zealand valuation texts (see bibliography).

Previously mentioned, three valuation approaches (or at least two) are customarily undertaken in a valuation assignment. The final value figure is attributed to the most appropriate approach, given the nature of the property and the market on the date of valuation. As in the United States, the averaging of different approaches based on fundamentally different value concepts is discouraged.

The approaches used in most valuation assignments are the income (both direct capitalisation and discounted cash flow analysis), cost, and sales comparison approaches.

Income Approach

Rational investors make investment decisions based on the present worth of future income streams. For investment properties, therefore, discounted cash flow analysis is usually undertaken alongside direct capitalisation, in which capitalisation rates are determined from recent comparable sales of investment properties.

Discounted Cash Flow Analysis[8]

A valuation based on cash flow analysis requires technical data and information on the physical characteristics of the accommodation, rents, operating expenses, and sale transactions for the subject property as well as information

---

8. The New Zealand Institute of Valuers publishes a monograph, *Discounted Cash Flow Valuation Techniques,* by R. L. Jeffries of Auckland University, on acceptable practice with regard to DCF models. It may be obtained from the NZIV in Wellington.

on closely comparable properties and the submarket as a whole. Utilising such data, the valuer develops a comprehensive understanding of the position of the property relative to other properties as of the date of valuation and into the future. The valuation is based on the application of objective reasoning to reliable quantitative data. Understanding the dynamics of the market for the accommodation, the market for investment property, and the critical interaction of the two is necessary to support the explicit projection required in the cash flow forecast.

Having selected an appropriate forecast period for the cash flow (usually between five and 10 years), the valuer prepares an estimate of rental incomes and expenses (both recoverable and nonrecoverable) to determine probable net cash flow (net operating income or *NOI*). A capitalisation rate is estimated and applied to the projected income for the eleventh year to establish the resale price (reversion) in Year 10. The net cash flow for each year together with the resale value in Year 10 is then discounted to determine the present value of the property.

The procedure for estimating the net cash flow may include the following steps. The valuer will:

1. Enter the contract rents for each tenancy, having verified that no current rental concessions exist. For any vacant accommodation, the valuer prescribes a period in which to lease and a rent that explicitly incorporates any incentives. On lease expiration, the valuer undertakes a similar exercise. A constant or variable per annum growth rate for rents is estimated and used to reassess market rents on periodic review, provided the leases have an "objective" review clause, i.e., to the prevailing market rent. Some leases from the 1970s have archaic review clauses calling for an equitable or subjective rent between the parties. In this case, the valuation may have to allow for added risk.

2. Identify other sources of revenue, such as separate partition rentals, building naming rights, hoarding (billboard) rentals, and income from annual car park licences.

3. Estimate and deduct nonrecoverable maintenance costs. If the lease is not a fully net BOMA/PMI or BOMA/PLEINZ standard lease, these costs may include ground rental, management fees, and long-term maintenance fund contributions.

4. Project the operating expenditures to increase in line with government treasury inflation projections.

5. Consider irregular expenses, such as expenses for vacant accommodations. The unpaid recoverable costs and unpaid rates (property taxes)

have to be deducted. Marketing, one-off (one-time) incentives to secure tenants, and leasing fees may also be deducted. The sale of the property in Year 10 is usually assumed to incur marketing, legal, and agency fees.

6. Determine the discount rate. The discount rate is generally a risk-adjusted rate built up incrementally from the rate currently available on government bonds, which represent the risk-free alternative. Increments are added to compensate for the risks associated with illiquidity, intensive management, tenant quality, and prospective functional and economic obsolescence. Some valuers attempt to analyse discount rates from comparable sales, but this approach is fraught with difficulties unless the valuer is actually privy to all the specific property data. Such information can only be obtained when one is acting for either the vendor (seller) or purchaser. Some economic consultants have attempted to determine required rates of return (applicable as discount rates) for classes of property assets using the capital asset pricing model (CAPM)[9] with an additional premium for the specific risk (location, structure, local market, etc.). Use of this model has not received widespread acceptance, however, by practitioners performing market valuations of individual properties.

Property Data for Valuation Examples

The property described below will be used to illustrate three valuation methodologies: discounted cash flow analysis, direct capitalisation (constant and variable income), and the cost approach. The values described will then be reconciled into a final value estimate.

Description of the Building

The subject property is a 10-level, reinforced concrete building with curtain-wall cladding of solar-reflecting, bronzed glass. Basement car parking is provided with access from the rear. The building is six years old.

Services Two automatic, 14-person passenger lifts (elevators) and two stairwells provide access to all building levels and the basement. Fire detection and a card-access security system has been installed throughout. Each floor has male and female toilets and a kitchenette. Limited power ducting is included in the floor slabs. The suspended ceilings have recessed fluorescent light fittings. Single-pipe, ceiling-void, mounted fan coil units with electric reheat provide for temperature control (heating and cooling). Six units are provided per floor.

---

9. There are equilibrium CAPMs, arbitrage pricing models, and hedonic pricing models. See Terrence M. Clauretie and James R. Webb, *The Theory and Practice of Real Estate Finance* published by the Dryden Press (Fort Worth, TX: HBJ College Division, 1993) and Arthur L. Schwartz and Stephen D. Kapplin, editors, *Alternative Ideas in Real Estate Investment,* American Real Estate Society, (Boston, MA: Kluwer Publications, 1995).

Fixtures and Fittings The floors are let (leased) carpeted and decorated in a shell state.

Tenancy Schedule

The building is fully let (leased) to an international computer company which occupies the building as its head office on a 12-year lease with a six-year right of renewal. The lease is a net, BOMA-style document (excluding the provision to levy a contribution for a long-term building fund) with reviews to market rents. The car parking is let (leased) on annual licenses and rents are reviewed each year.

Income Schedule

Location (Level)	Gr. Fl. Area	Net Lettable	Type	Rate $ Per Sq. Metre	Annual Rent	Op. Ex. Rate $ Per Sq. Metre		TOC Rate $ Per Sq. Metre
Basement	300	9 parking spaces	car	$35 per wk per parking space	16,380			16,380
Ground	300	260	retail	450	117,000	30	480	124,800
1	300	255	office	175	44,625	30	205	52,275
2	300	255	office	175	44,625	30	205	52,275
3	300	255	office	175	44,625	30	205	52,275
4	300	255	office	175	44,625	30	205	52,275
5	300	255	office	175	44,625	30	205	52,275
6	300	255	office	175	44,625	30	205	52,275
7	300	255	office	175	44,625	30	205	52,275
8	300	255	office	175	44,625	30	205	52,275
9	300	255	office	175	44,625	30	205	52,275
10	300	255	office	175	44,625	30	205	52,275
	3,600	2,810			579,630			663,930
Annual net rental income					579,630			
Less contribution to long-term repair and replacement fund					30,000			
Net rental income (NOI)					549,630			

Assume that the audit of operating expenditure charges indicates that all expenses are in line with what is typical for a building of the same size with similar services.

Example of Discounted Cash Flow Analysis

Assumptions

- Market total occupancy costs (TOC) for this type of property and location will continue in line with general inflation at 2% per annum for the foreseeable future. The Reserve Bank Act mandates that inflation is to be kept at less than 2% per annum.

- The tenant will be induced to exercise his right of renewal because the owner is spending $1.3 million on a refurbishment, thereby securing market TOCs and rents.

- The terminal capitalisation rate of 10.75% reflects the recent refurbishment, with disposal costs at 5% of the sale price.

- The rent review in Year 3 anticipates no growth in rents since the building services and common areas are substandard relative to market norms.

- The capitalisation rate reflects the status of the property as one in need of a substantial refurbishment with only two years remaining on the renewed lease.

The pro forma budget for the property is shown in Table 1. Discounting the building cash flows for Years 1 through 10 at rates of 12%, 13%, 14%, and 15% provides present values of:

$5,087,439	at 12%
$4,783,332	at 13%
$4,504,414	at 14%
$4,248,287	at 15%

If a 12% discount rate (after adjustment for the market risk typical of the type of property and the specific risk for the location) was felt to be appropriate, then a rounded value of $5,087,000 would be obtained.

Direct Capitalisation

Properties let (leased) at market rents may be valued by the application of a capitalisation rate (present value of $1 in perpetuity)[10] to the net income stream (net operating income or NOI). For properties that are wholly let (leased) at market rents and for which constant growth is a valid assumption, the use of a growth-implicit capitalisation rate (present value of $1 in perpetuity) is appropriate. In practice, the capitalisation rate is derived from an analysis of, and adjustment to, open market sales of comparable properties.

---

10. The present value of $1 in perpetuity is the present value of $1 per period when the the total period extends into perpetuity; it is the reciprocal of the capitalisation rate. In the example above, a 10.75% capitalisation rate is selected; therefore the present value of $1 in perpetuity is 1/0.1075 or 9.302325.

Table 1. Pro Forma Budget of Rents, Operating Expenditures, and Net Rental Income Streams

Years:	1	2	3	4	5	6	7	8	9	10	11
Office											
T.O.C.	536,250	538,050	539,886	541,759	543,669	545,617	617,708	619,735	621,803	663,614	
Esc. 2% OPEX (operating expenses)	90,000	91,800	93,636	95,509	97,419	99,367	101,355	103,382	105,449	107,558	
Net rent	446,250	446,250	446,250	446,250	446,250	446,250	516,353	516,353	516,353	556,056	556,056
Retail											
T.O.C.	39,000	124,236	126,721	129,255	131,840	134,477	137,167	139,910	142,708	145,562	
Esc. 2% OPEX	4,800	4,896	4,994	5,094	5,196	5,300	5,406	5,514	5,624	5,736	
Net rent	117,000	119,340	121,727	124,161	126,645	129,177	131,761	134,396	137,084	139,826	142,622
Car Parks											
T.O.C.	16,380	16,380	16,380	16,380	16,380	16,380	16,380	16,380	16,380	16,380	
Esc. 2% OPEX											
Net rent	16,380	16,708	17,042	17,383	17,730	18,085	18,447	18,815	19,192	19,576	19,967
Sum of net rents	579,630	582,298	585,019	587,794	590,625	593,512	666,561	669,565	672,629	715,457	718,645
Less provision for refurb.	5,000	5,000	5,000	5,000	5,000	1,305,000	5,000	5,000	5,000	5,000	5,000
Net cash flow (NOI)	574,630	577,298	580,019	582,794	585,625	-711,488	661,561	664,565	667,629	710,457	713,645
Terminal value										7,211,573	
Bldg. cash flow	574,630	577,298	580,019	582,794	585,625	-711,488	661,561	664,565	667,629	7,922,030	

Example One: Constant Income Growth

The office building described earlier can also be valued using direct capitalisation.

Analysis of sales of other office buildings indicates that current cash flow returns (capitalisation rates, initial yields) range between 10.5% and 11% per annum. A 10.75% overall capitalisation rate is selected and an investment value is calculated as follows.

Estimated maintainable cash flow (net cash flow or *NOI*):

$549,630 per annum capitalised at 10.75% = $5,112,837
Rounded: $5,112,500

To value properties with varying income streams, i.e., those with current rents under or above market rent which will revert to market levels at some known future time, a modified form of direct capitalisation is applied. First, the current annual net income or cash flow, as calculated from the current market rent, is capitalised in perpetuity. The annual shortfall, i.e., market rent less passing or contract rent, is calculated and this annuity is capitalised at the same rate for the number of years it takes to achieve market rent. This latter sum is then deducted from the former sum to obtain the capital value. In the case of overrented properties (properties above market rent), the inverse procedure is undertaken, with the capitalised annual overrent added to the capitalised market rent value to arrive at the end capital value.

The accepted practice is to use the same capitalisation rate for both the capitalisation of market rent in perpetuity and the annuity calculation. This rate is called the *equivalent yield (IRR)*. The use of *split* or adjusted rates, which is common practice in the United Kingdom, is described in certain New Zealand texts, but is used less frequently. In multi-use buildings, such as a city office tower with a ground-level shopping mall and basement car parking, some practitioners have proposed applying different capitalisation rates to the income streams from the different enterprises, citing differences in lease terms and rent review patterns as justification. The corollary in a DCF valuation would be to use different discount rates for each income stream.

Example Two: Varying Income Streams

Sales of other office buildings indicate current cash flow returns (capitalisation rates, initial yields) that range between 10.5% and 11% per annum. A 10.75% overall capitalisation rate is selected in the following equivalent yield valuation: Floors 1 to 10 of the property are let (leased) at $5 per square metre per annum below market levels; rent is anticipated to revert to market levels in Year 3.

Estimated maintainable cash flow (net cash flow, net income stream from units let at market rents)	$579,630
Less passing rent (below-market contract rent)	$566,880
Shortfall per annum	$12,750

Estimated maintainable cash flow (net cash flow or *NOI*):

$579,630 per annum capitalised at 10.75%	$5,112,837

Less the present value of the shortfall

$12,750 per annum (two years discounted at 10.75%)	$21,907
	$5,090,830
Rounded:	$5,091,000

Sales Comparison Approach

In the sales comparison approach, market value is estimated by comparing the subject property with similar properties that have recently been sold or are currently for sale in the market. While comparison may be undertaken on an overall price basis, usually unit prices are compared. This may be price per square metre of gross floor area or net lettable (leasable) area for commercial property or price per square metre or hectare for land. Residential and commercial land is commonly valued by comparing unit metre frontage (UMF), where the common unit is a one-metre-wide strip of land of standard depth. UMF is used in conjunction with a depth table that allows for variations in depth and establishes a nonlinear value gradient, assigning a high value to the land at the front and lower values to the land at the rear.

Once an appropriate unit metre frontage value has been determined from comparable analysis, e.g., $100 UMF, this figure is multiplied by the depth adjustment factor and the width. The depth adjustment factor may be obtained by means of the depth formula or from a table. For a site 18 metres wide and 35 metres deep, for example, the adjustment factor is 96% (18 metres is standard width, but standard depth is 40 metres). The calculation would be:

$100 UMF × 96% (depth adjustment factor) × 18 metres = $1,728.

For agricultural land and specialist (specialized) properties such as motels and hotels, the sale price may be expressed as price per stock unit, price per standard motel unit, or price per bedroom unit. Area measurements for office and commercial buildings may be misleading since the common areas are sometimes apportioned and ascribed to tenancies. Care must be taken to verify the accuracy of the areas by a standard method of measurement.

While most institutional investors and investment companies in New Zealand have given only passing regard to price per square metre of gross area, investors have recently become interested in this unit of comparison relative to current replacement cost per square metre. This change came about during the recent slump when CBD properties could be purchased at a substantial discount relative to their current replacement value, thus representing real bargains. New Zealand has also experienced a considerable flow of funds into commercial and agricultural property from overseas investors, especially those immigrating to New Zealand with surplus funds for speculative investments.

Cost Approach

As in North America, the use of the cost approach in New Zealand has diminished somewhat as the market for investment property has matured. The activities of institutional investors, such as life and mutual superannuation (pension) funds, and listed commercial property companies create a market in which values are determined largely by the present worth of future income streams, rather than by cost considerations. Some valuers follow appraisal practice in the United States and United Kingdom and add a sum for developer's risk and profit to building costs (BCs).

Example of Cost Approach

Building cost (BC) per square metre*

3,600 m² (gross area) x $1,400 per m²	$5,040,000
Add fees (for architect; structural, electrical, and mechanical engineers; the quantity surveyor; and the resource management consultant) @11.5%	579,600
	$5,619,600
Add goods and service tax (GST) @ 12.5%	630,000
Add margin for profit and risk, say 10% before tax costs	561,960
Estimate of current replacement cost (inclusive of GST)	$6,811,560
Less allowance for physical and economic obsolescense @ 2% per annum (straight line) for 6 years, or 12%	817,387
Estimate of depreciated replacement cost (inclusive of GST)	$5,994,173
Add land value, say	1,750,000
Value based on the cost appoach	$7,744,173
Rounded	$7,744,000

* From *Rawlinsons' New Zealand Construction Handbook*.

Rental Valuations (Estimating Market Rent)

Unlike UK practice, rental analysis in New Zealand is conducted from the tenants' perspective. Thus, comparison between properties are based on annual total occupancy cost (TOC), which includes the passing (contract) rent identified in the lease, the tenant's annual contribution to service charges (operating expenses), and the current rates (property taxes) payable on the tenancy. Thus, if the building for which market rent is being determined is 10% less efficient than comparable buildings in its services, then *ceteris paribus* (all other things being equal), the building's estimated market rent based on lease analysis will be 10% less, its total occupancy cost (TOC) having been established on the basis of the comparables. This approach is obviously more equitable than rental valuation (estimation of market rent) in the United Kingdom, where rates (property taxes) and service charges (operating expenses) have traditionally been ignored in determining market rentals.

Valuation Conclusion/Reconciliation

At the end of the valuation process, the registered valuer in New Zealand steps back from the analyses and objectively considers the appropriateness of the approaches employed to value the subject property. The valuer then selects a value, based upon what he or she believes to be the appropriate valuation methodology for the property under prevailing market conditions. The respective values for the subject office building, based on the three applications illustrated, are:

Value determined by DCF analysis	$5,087,000
Value determined by direct capitalisation	$5,112,500
Value determined by cost approach	$7,744,000

If the valuer is confident that an active investment market exists for the subject, he or she may select a value of $5,110,000, based on the indications derived in the DCF and direct capitalisation approaches. The justification might be that the valuer analysed sufficiently close comparables (in terms of sale dates and characteristics) and he or she was aware of the sensitivity of the discounted cash flow analysis to a few key parameters, e.g., the terminal value estimate, discount rate, and, in this case, the lease renewal.

Availability of Data

Transaction or price data is available in the public domain, but a fee is charged to recover the costs of accessing the data. Valuation New Zealand, the state assessment authority for property taxation, maintains a database of all transactions. Recorded data include:

- Gross sale price
- Net sale price (gross sale price less value of chattels sold with the property)
- Date of sale (date of transfer of title)
- Vendor (seller) name and address
- Purchaser name and address

Valuation New Zealand also maintains a nationwide database, known as the *valuation roll,* for every property falling under the Valuation of Land Act. In this database, 39 items of descriptive data are recorded for each property, including the property's unique identification number. Two final items of data are the land value and capital value, which the district valuer (assessment officer) ascribes to the property in accordance with the legislation in effect as of the last date of general revaluation for that district. Revaluations (reassessments) are generally undertaken every five years, but in some districts they are conducted every three years.

The assessed capital value is not an accurate indicator of current market value for several reasons. First, the assessed value excludes chattels, which are often a significant factor in pricing. Second, the descriptive data compiled in intermittent property inspections by assessors are necessarily historic. Third, revisions of residential assessments often utilise computer-aided valuation techniques (regression models), which by their very nature are sensitive to inaccuracies in the data. Thus, errors can easily be compounded.

Market data is generally obtainable in New Zealand. Valuers have a strong sense of professional camaraderie and a willingness to share data is the norm rather than the exception. In provincial centres, however, a donor will sometimes seek remuneration if a significant quantity of data has been supplied.

The requirements for client confidentiality have tended to slow the flow of information, especially about rents and operating expenses and tenant inducements to sign leases. Fortunately, the New Zealand Court of Appeal has recently upheld subpoenas issued to impel a landlord to disclose inducements given to secure tenancies, stating that confidentiality agreements could be overturned. In the words of one of the judges of the court of appeal, *"…..the overriding public interest is in as fair a fixation of market rents as possible."* Thus, if landlords can be compelled to reveal lease agreements, contracts binding valuers into confidentially may be seen as a futile exercise.

Useful sources are listed below.

Demographic and Economic Data

- The Statistics Department, 85 Molesworth Street, Private Bag 2922, Wellington, New Zealand.
  TEL: 09 495 4600; FAX: 09 472 9135
  http://www.snz.govt.nz.

- The Reserve Bank of New Zealand, http://www.rbnz.govt.nz.

- Local city councils (economic development units)

- Local chambers of commerce

- Libraries

Real Estate Data on Market Size, Occupancy, and Rental Rates

- Local valuers, real estate agents, and property managers
- National valuation firms that publish reports on markets throughout the country
- Property studies departments in universities that teach valuation and real estate

Building Costs, Rents, Property Taxes, Operating Expenses, and Depreciation

- The Editor, *Rawlinsons' New Zealand Construction Handbook,* PO Box 9804, Auckland, New Zealand.
  TEL: 09 525 0874; FAX: 09 524 4977

Rents, Operating Expenses, and Prices of Sales Comparables

- Sales and ratings/government assessments: The Research Officer, Valuation New Zealand, PO Box 5098, Wellington, New Zealand
  TEL: + 64 4473 8555; FAX: + 64 4473 8552

Sales and Market Indices

- Research Officer, The Real Estate Institute of New Zealand, PO Box 5663, Auckland, New Zealand.
  TEL: + 64 9 379 8008; FAX: + 64 9 379 8471
- Research Officer, The Building Owners and Managers Association of New Zealand, Inc., PO Box 1033, Auckland, New Zealand
  TEL: + 64 9303 0470; FAX: + 64 9379 0781
- Local registered valuers
- Local licensed real estate agents

  Property Internet New Zealand, Ltd. (PINZ) has some useful links to other New Zealand web pages relevant to property. Contact http://www.pinz.co.nz.

Professional Institutes

The two principal valuer organisations can be reached at the following addresses:

Chief Executive Officer, The New Zealand Institute of Valuers, PO Box 27 - 146, Wellington, New Zealand.
TEL: + 64 4385 8436; FAX: + 64 4382 921
http://www.nziv.wg.nz.; e-mail: ceo@nziv.org.nz.

President, Property and Land Economy Institute of New Zealand, Inc., Tower 1, Shortland Centre 51-53 Shortland Street, Auckland, New Zealand.
TEL: + 64 9358 9757; FAX: + 64 9358 9758
http://www.pleinz.org.nz.

Bibliography

Bell, R.A. *Investment Property Income Analysis and Appraisal.* 2d ed. Wellington: New Zealand Institute of Valuers, 1995.

Jeffries, R.L. *Urban Valuation in New Zealand.* vol. I. 2d ed. Wellington: New Zealand Institute of Valuers, 1991.

Jeffries, R.L., ed. *Urban Valuation in New Zealand.* vol. II. Wellington: New Zealand Institute of Valuers, 1990.

New Zealand Institute of Valuers. Asset Standards Committee. *Technical Handbook.* Wellington: New Zealand Institute of Valuers, 1995.

6

France

Simon Foxley, ARICS

For the last five years, Simon Foxley, a British chartered surveyor, has been responsible for international appraisal and consultancy services at Bourdais Expertises, S. A., a leading firm of French real estate agents and consultants and member of the ONCOR network. He is currently a property associate of General Electric Capital Corporation, with responsibilities for investment and financing.

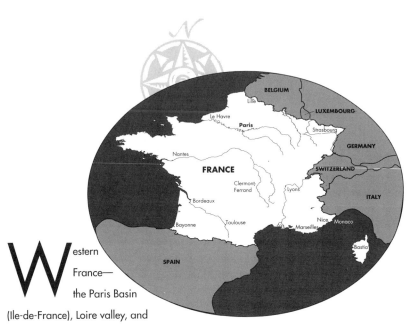

Western France— the Paris Basin (Ile-de-France), Loire valley, and Aquitaine—is an extension of the northern European plain. The peninsulas of Brittany and Normandy project from this lowland area. Mountains demarcate the southern border (Pyrenees) and much of the eastern border (the Alps and Jura); the south central area (Languedoc) is montainous plateau (the massif central). The northeast (Champagne, Burgundy, Lorraine) consists of rolling hills (escarpments) and the forested Vosges (Alsace). Most of France has a temperate marine climate, while the Riviera (Cote d'Azur) and Corsica are Mediterranean. Principal cities are Paris, Marseilles, Lyons, Toulouse, Nice, Strasbourg, Nantes, and Bordeaux.

Political and Administrative Structure

The present political system, the Fifth Republic, has been in existence since its creation by the 1958 constitution. Political power in France is shared by the executive (the French president and his ministers) and legislative branches (the parliament) of the government. The constitution provides for a political system based on the separation and balance of powers.

The French president is elected by universal suffrage for a term of seven years. He appoints the prime minister, who in turn recommends ministers for the government, who are appointed by the president. The president establishes policy guidelines and is responsible for the orderly functioning of the civil service.

Legislative power is vested in the parliament, which comprises two houses; the National Assembly (*Assemblée Nationale*) and the Senate (*Sénat*). Members of the National Assembly, known as *Députés*, are elected by universal suffrage for five-year terms. Members of the Senate, *Sénateurs*, are elected for nine-year terms by an electoral college.

A constitutional court (*Conseil Constitutionnel*) is responsible for the enforcement of the constitution and ensures that the laws passed by the parliament comply with the written constitution. The court is made up of nine independent members appointed by the President of the Republic, the President of the National Assembly, and the President of the Senate.

France was one of the original founding members of the European Community.

Metropolitan France[1] is divided into 22 regions and 96 departments (*départements*). The *départments* are themselves subdivided into 38,000 *communes*, two-thirds of which have less than 500 inhabitants.

Each *département* is administered by a *préfet*, appointed by the government, and a *conseil général* (general council). The members of the *conseil général* are elected locally. The *communes* are run by municipal councils, also elected locally, and a mayor, chosen from among the elected councillors.

Property Rights

The most widespread legal estate in France is absolute ownership known as *toute propriété* in the case of complete holdings, or *copropriété*, in the case of condominiums.

Both forms of ownership may be equated to a freehold or fee simple absolute, extending to everything above and below the ground level and held jointly in

---

1. The term *Metropolitan France* refers to France itself, exclusive of its overseas departments and territories.

the case of co-ownership. Owners' rights have become subject to various statutory controls over the years.

In the absence of long-term leasehold ownership, the practice of co-owner-ship is very widespread. Complex rules and regulations have evolved over the years and the relationship between co-owners is governed through both statutory law and jurisprudence. The authoritative source on the matter is the Co-ownership Code, which defines the different rights and liabilities of co-owners, especially in regard to the management of the co-ownership struc-ture. Co-owners generally prepare their own regulations, which must conform to certain aspects of the text of the Co-ownership Code.

Long-term ground leases which confer rights to build upon property are sometimes used by public authorities, often as part of the development process. It is common for all building improvements on a site to revert to the freeholder at the expiration of the contractual term.

Language

The national language is French.

Currency

The French currency is the franc. It is monitored and regulated by the central bank, the Banque de France, which has existed since 1848.

France belongs to the European Monetary System (EMS). This system, created in 1978, regulates the exchange rates of currencies of European Community nations within fixed limits to maintain currency stabilisation. When the exchange rate for the currency of one of the member countries fluctuates beyond a predefined limit (currently 15% above or below the level of parity), the monetary authority in that country must take the necessary steps to stabilise the currency.

The *franc zone* is another monetary system, which was created in 1945 and includes the overseas *départements* and territories as well as a number of African states, the majority of which are former French dependencies. Curren-cies are exchanged on a fixed basis.

Inflation

Until fairly recently, France experienced relatively high levels of inflation (over 13% at the start of the 1980s). Since the mid-1980s, however, the policy of the government and the central bank has been to maintain inflation at a low rate comparable to that of in Germany. Since 1992 the rate of inflation has remained below 3% and it is the stated aim of monetary authorities to see that this level is maintained.

Taxation

Sales of property are subject to either the VAT, or value-added tax (*taxe sur la valeur ajoutée*) or transfer taxes (*droits d'enregistrement*). The levels of taxation in France are among the highest in the world.

VAT is payable on the sale of land and the first sale of new buildings, provided the sale occurs within five years of completion of construction. The tax is recoverable by those companies who are registered under the VAT system. Individuals who purchase new residential property cannot recover this tax. The current rate of VAT is 20.6%. There are, moreover, a series of other nonrecoverable taxes or fees to be paid, including those of the notary (0.825% in addition to VAT), the mortgage office (0.1% in addition to VAT), and the property advertising tax (0.6%).

Sales not included in the VAT system are subject to transfer taxes, which are levied differently for residential and commercial property. Transfer taxes are made up of a series of taxes imposed by the different tiers of administration. The fees of the notary and the mortgage office and the property advertising tax are payable in the same percentages as under the VAT system. The following table shows the composition of taxes for both commercial and residential property in Paris:

	Commercial Property	Residential Property
State tax (*droit budgétaire perçu par l'etat*)	13.8%	2.6%
Additional departement tax (*taxe additionnelle départementale*)	1.6%	1.6%
Regional tax (*taxe régionale*)	1.6%	1.6%
Local tax (*taxe communale*)	1.2%	1.2%
Notary fees	0.825%	0.825%
Mortgage office fee	0.1%	0.1%
Property advertising tax	0.6%	0.6%
Total	19.725%	8.525%
	(excl. VAT)	(excl. VAT)

Regional and local taxes vary slightly across the country. A lower state tax is applied in a few areas which receive economic assistance (e.g., the island of Corsica and certain overseas territories). Apart from the VAT portion, these taxes are not recoverable.

Both VAT and transfer taxes are payable on either the purchase price or the open market value of the property, whichever is higher. If the tax authorities consider the purchase price to be less than the open market value, they will investigate and commission one of their own valuers to do a valuation. In the event of a dispute, the taxpayer has a right to appeal in court.

There is a separate tax system for property traders. Increasingly, property is being held in corporate structures which are potentially more tax efficient. In addition to VAT and transfer taxes, there are a number of taxes on properties occupied by enterprises and properties in development.

Town and Country Planning

Development control is essentially achieved through local land use plans (*plans d'occupation des sols*), which each *commune* is expected to prepare. These plans set out zoning strategies and plot ratios and identify major public projects. They are constantly under review.

Overall planning strategies are contained within large-scale plans *(schémas directeurs d'aménagement),* which all urban areas with more than 10,000 inhabitants are required to prepare. Special development plans are prepared for areas designated for development or redevelopment.

Floor Area Measurement

The metric system is used in France. Areas are measured in square metres, expressed m². Properties are measured differently for different purposes. Some of the most common area measurements are defined below:

- The *surface hors œuvre brute,*[2] as defined by the planning code, is the total floor area measured from the external walls and including everything therein, e.g., stairs, lift (elevator) shafts, plus accessible balconies and terraces, basements, and accommodation within the roof space. This floor area must be quoted in planning applications and is used for the calculation of building costs and quantities.

- The *surface hors œuvre nette* is defined by the planning code as the total floor area, subject to the following deductions: roof space accommodation with a clear height of less than 1.8 m. and a floor loading capacity inferior to 250 kg/ m², basement areas with a clear height of less than 1.8 m., balconies and terraces, including non-enclosed areas at ground floor level and car parking spaces within the building. This floor area must be quoted in planning applications and also used for the calculation of plot ratios and some development taxes.

- The *surface habitable,* as defined by the Habitation and Construction Code, is liveable floor area. It is the floor area excluding the walls, partitions, steps, staircases, and the arcs formed by the opening of doors and windows. This

---

2. The terms *surface hors œuvre brute* and *surface hors œurve nette,* which are defined in the administrative code, may not exactly correspond to *gross external area* and *net internal area* as they are used in the United Kingdom. See the glossary for RICS definitions.

definition is used in transactions and valuations involving residential property.

For commercial property transactions and valuations, there is no official area which must be used. However, the majority of the industry has adopted *surface utile* (usable area) which is defined as:

> the floor area measured from the interior side of the external walls, excluding columns, load-bearing walls, means of vertical circulation (stairs and lifts [elevators]), ventilation shafts and conduits.

It includes lobbies, landings, corridors, and toilet areas.

A weighted area (*surface ponderée*) measure might be used in certain cases, e.g., traditional retail units, where the overall floor area is expressed in terms of the relative value of its various sections. This is similar to the system of zoning in the UK. For example, the weighted area of a shop with 100 m² of retail space that faces onto the street, a 75 m² rear sales area, an 80 m² first-floor showroom, and a 150 m² basement storage area might be expressed as follows:

Area	Net Area	Coefficient	Weighted Area
Front shop	100 m²	1	100 m²
Rear sales area	75 m²	0.75	56.25 m²
First floor showroom	80 m²	0.5	40 m²
Basement storage area	150 m²	0.3	45 m²
Totals	405 m²		approx. 240 m²

Valuers rarely measure property. The only people who may certify floor areas for official uses are land surveyors (*géometre-experts*) and architects.

Typical Lease Structures

Most French commercial and residential leases are governed by the Civil Code, to which individual contracts are referenced. This keeps most lease documents relatively simple.

Commercial Leases

Commercial leases fall under the Decree of the 30th September 1953, which provides that leases should be granted for a minimum term of nine years with three-year break options in the tenant's favour. There has been a gradual evolution in the interpretation of break clauses over recent years and increasingly their inclusion depends on negotiations between the individual parties.

Tenants benefit from security of tenure provisions and have the statutory right to assign their lease in the event of a sale of their business.

Expressed in terms of "francs per annum, excluding service charges and taxes," rents for commercial properties are negotiated freely at the outset of the lease. It is customary for rents then to be indexed, either annually or at the end of every third year, to the movements in one of the official indices published by the national statistical office, *Institut National des Statistiques et des Études Économiques* (INSEE). The index that is most commonly chosen measures changes in the cost of building construction.

For offices and single-use properties (e.g., hotels), there is a review of the rent obtainable under open market value (see the subsequent definitions section) at the end of the nine-year term. For all other commercial properties, rents continue to be indexed even on renewal, except if the lease was granted for an initial term exceeding nine years or a nine-year lease has not been renewed within three years after the expiration of the contractual term.

Retail Leases

Retail units located in shopping centres often have their rents tied to the level of the tenants' turnover (i.e., sales within a given period). Generally the tenant pays either the guaranteed base rent or a predetermined percentage of the turnover, whichever is higher. For standard units, the percentage varies between 5% and 7%.

Although the responsibility for repairs and insurance is entirely contractual, landlords do not usually contract out of responsibility for structural repairs and taxes. Inevitably, however, the apportionment of responsibility for such items is a matter of negotiation between the individual parties. It is normal practice in buildings with multiple tenants, such as office towers or shopping centres, for the cost of maintaining common areas, such as the entrance halls, the malls, the lifts (elevators), to be shared by the different occupants, usually in proportion to the amount of space that they occupy.

Residential Leases

There are relatively few statutory controls affecting private residential leases. Although there are still some tenancies subject to legislation entered in the statute book prior to 1948 when the former housing act was passed, these tenancies account for a relatively small proportion of the private rental sector and no new leases can be granted under this system.

The principal legislation relating to residential leases is now contained within the *Loi Malandien,* which was passed in 1989. Leases are to be granted for a minimum of three years (or six years if the landlord is a company). Although the rents are negotiated freely at the outset, increases during the contractual term are limited to variations in the cost of construction index published by INSEE.

At the end of the lease, the tenant has the right to remain in occupancy at the same rent, except under certain conditions. For example, the landlord may wish to sell the property (in which case the tenant has the right of first refusal); the landlord may wish to use the property for a member of his own family; or the tenant may have violated the terms of the lease. A landlord wishing to relet property after the departure of a tenant may only do so at the same level of rent.

Rents for residential property are expressed in "francs per annum, or per month, excluding service charges and taxes." The Civil Code sets out clearly which costs relating to the maintenance and upkeep of the building may be passed onto the tenants.

Valuation Standards

Licensing and Certification

The activities of only a small proportion of French valuers are covered by formal legislation. Agricultural and forestry valuers (*experts agricoles et fonciers*) and judicial valuers (*experts judiciaire*) are both regulated by the state under laws established in the early 1970s. Lists of both types of valuers are kept by the Ministry of Agriculture and the Ministry of the Interior.

Almost all other valuers operate independently, without any formal legal control. While the majority are employed in the private sector, working for firms of independent valuers, subsidiaries of banks, or property consultancies, there are a number who perform specific tasks in the public sector, including tax valuers employed by the Finance Ministry and *Experts de l'Administration des Domaines* or valuers within the civil service who work exclusively for the government.

Generally professional organisations or groupings are identified with specific property types. Most valuers of urban land and buildings belong to the *Federation Nationale des Agents Immobiliers* (FNAIM) and the *Institut Français de l'Expertise Immobilière* (IFEI). Although the former is essentially a group of estate agents (brokers), it has a special category for valuers. There are no minimum educational standards for entry into FNAIM and the only requirements relate to appropriate professional experience. Members benefit from a low-cost professional indemnity insurance plan. Membership can be revoked at any time.

IFEI has a much more restricted membership and, again, entry is subject to an appropriate level of professional experience. This association is exclusively devoted to matters of valuation and is responsible for the publication of the valuation guide, *Guide Méthodologique relatif à l'Évaluation des Actifs Immobiliers,* which is increasingly regarded as the authority on valuation in France. The committee that oversees management of the organisation has no regulatory powers, although it can withdraw the right of membership on certain grounds, notably for unprofessional conduct.

Valuation Reporting Requirements

Standardised reporting formats (form reports) are used only by French insurance companies and SCPIs (*Sociétés Civiles de Placement Immobilier*), which are property unit trusts similar to real estate investment trusts. These investments are not quoted on the stock exchange.

Insurance companies are required by the *Commission de Contrôle des Assurances*, the regulatory body for insurance companies active in France, to value their investment property portfolio independently every five years on a rolling programme (continual basis). The valuer's conclusions are to be provided in a standard, two-page report. This document presents only a very brief summary of the valuation and is often augmented by a more detailed report addressed to the client.

SCPIs are regulated by the *Commission des Opérations de Bourse* (COB), the French stock exchange commission. The COB requires SCPIs to undertake formal valuations of their properties every five years. Updated valuations are to be prepared in each intervening year, but inspections are only necessary if substantial modifications have been carried out.

Formal valuation reports are more detailed than those prepared for insurance companies and must contain substantial comments relating to instructions, the manner in which the valuation has been conducted, identification of the property, situation (siting), planning, title, lettings, a description of the valuation process, comparable evidence, and conclusions. The revaluations conducted in intervening years are much simpler and contain only the principal elements, i.e., instructions, procedure, description of the valuation process, and a summary of previous valuations. In the absence of any other formal guidelines, valuation reports may vary from one valuer to another. Nevertheless, the same headings are found in most reports.

A distinction, however, should be made between *certificates of valuation* and *valuation reports*. The former typically includes few details about the property apart from identifying it, commenting on any important details, and setting out the amount of value. The annual valuations prepared for insurance companies and the revaluations prepared for SCPIs are good examples of certificates of valuation.

As mentioned previously, formal valuation reports are detailed and generally contain information under the following headings:

Instructions:	bases of valuation, assumptions, information provided
Definitions:	explanation of the terms being used
Situation:	the property's location and environment
Description:	the physical layout of the property and its characteristics
Tenure:	the ownership of the property and the use
Town planning:	a summary of the provisions of the land use plan
Comparable evidence:	details of transactions used to support the amount of the valuation
Appreciation:	the valuer's opinion of the property in the market forecast
Valuation:	the calculations used to arrive at the amount of value
Conclusions:	a summary of the final amount of the valuation
Appendices:	location maps, site plans, photographs

French valuation reports are usually significantly less detailed than those prepared in North America to support DCF appraisals.

Definitions

There are no legal definitions for any of the principal concepts of value. However, the *Institut Français de l'Expertise Immobilière* and French accountants have produced a guide to property valuation in which the bases of valuation are defined. Various regulatory authorities and others involved in the valuation of property assets increasingly rely on this work.

The definition of open market value (valeur vénale) set forth below is generally in keeping with other international statements on the subject.

The price at which a property or an interest in a property, freely offered for sale, is reasonably expected to be sold at the time of the valuation, assuming that the following conditions have been satisfied:

- a willing seller,
- a suitable period for negotiations, taking into account the nature of the property and the state of the market,
- property values remaining stable during that period,

- normal marketing and advertising conditions,

- neither of the parties being motivated by any special personal factors.

Guidance notes in the valuation guide refer to several other terms in use which are synonyous with open market value.

Valuation Methods

There is no legal obligation to apply a specific method of valuation to a particular property. However, the use of market comparison methods for valuing income-producing, or potential incoming-producing properties is fairly widespread. Other approaches, such as the profits method and the depreciated replacement cost method, are used when comparable market evidence is absent or when such methodologies are commonly applied to value the specific property type (e.g., hotels). Comparative methods include the investment method and the sales comparison approach.

Investment method

The investment method is used for almost all commercial and some types of residential property, e.g., residential investment properties. It involves capital-ising the income from a property using an all-risks yield rate. The calculations are similar to the *hardcore* or *layer method* used in the UK (i.e., direct capitalisation of market rent with the resultant value adjusted for contract rents above or below market rent). First, an estimate is made of the open market rent the property can obtain. This estimate is developed by reference to lettings of comparable properties in the marketplace. Adjustments are made to the market transactions before the transactional data is compared to the subject property.

Once the open market rent has been established, usually on a gross basis without any deductions for non-recoverable expenditures, it is capitalised using an all-risks yield rate derived from sales of comparable property let at the open market rental rate. This amount is then adjusted to take into account the actual passing rent (current contract rent).

If the property is overrented, i.e., the passing rent is greater than the open market rent, the difference between the open market rent and the passing rent is discounted until the end of the lease term, or until the next opportunity for the rent to be renegotiated to market levels. This discounted amount is then added to the value calculated earlier.

If the property is underrented, i.e., the passing rent (current contract rent) is less than the open market rent, again the difference is discounted until the next opportunity for the rent to be increased to open market levels. (A landlord of commercial property does not have the right to increase the rent at the end of one of the intervening three-year periods and can do so only at the end of the lease for certain types of property.) This discounted amount is then deducted from the value calculated earlier.

In both cases the discount rate used reflects the opportunity cost of capital. It is supposed to correspond to the highest and relatively risk-free rate of return on offer (available) from other investment investments.

Two examples are presented below:

Consider a typical, overrented (contract rent exceeds market rent), 2,000 m² Paris office building with the following characteristics:

Open market rent	
(excluding service charges and taxes)	4,000,000 F per annum
Passing rent (excluding service charges and taxes)	5,500,000 F per annum
Unexpired lease term	3 years
Capitalisation rate	7%
Opportunity cost of capital rate	9%

The property's open market value is calculated as follows:

Open market rent	4,000,000 F	
Capitalisation rate	÷ 7%	
Capital value		57,142,857 F
Add overrent (open market rent less passing rent)	1,500,000 F	
times PV of 1 F per annum for 3 years @ 9%	× 2.5313	
		3,796,950 F
Open market value		60,939,807 F
Rounded:		61,000,000 F
Initial yield		9.02%

Now consider an underrented (contract rent is less than market rent), 5,000 m² warehouse building close to Paris with these characteristics:

Open market rent	
(excluding service charges and taxes)	1,500,000 F per annum
Passing rent (excluding service charges and taxes)	1,250,000 F per annum
Unexpired lease term	5 years
Capitalisation rate	11%
Opportunity cost of capital rate	9%

Open market value is calculated below:

Open market rent	1,500,000 F	
Capitalisation rate	÷ 11 %	
Capital value		13,636,363 F
Deduct "loss" of rent (open market rent less passing rent)	250,000 F	
times PV of 1 F per annum for 5 years @ 9%	× 3.8897	
		972,425 F
Open market value		12,663,938 F
Rounded:		12,700,000 F

Sales comparison

This method is almost always used for the valuation of residential properties. Its use for the valuation of commercial properties is also justified on the grounds that the demand for certain properties is dominated by owner-occupiers. Moreover, an owner-occupier competing for a particular property may be prepared to pay more than an investor, although there may be a fine distiction between this offered price and the value to a special purchaser.

To apply the method, transactions of similar comparable properties are analysed in terms of a standard unit of measure, typically per square metre of floor area for residential and commercial properties and per room for hotels.

Once the value per unit has been found, it can be applied to the subject property after appropriate adjustment.

Cost Approach

Although the cost approach was used up until quite recently in certain situations, it has increasingly lost favour with mainstream valuers. The use of the depreciated replacement cost method is now limited to specific properties for which there is no market (e.g., power stations).

Other Valuation Methods

Mention has been made of the *profits method,* which is typically used for valuations of hotels, cinemas, restaurants, and other leisure (recreational) property when reliable information is available about the accounts of the enterprise occupying the property. When this method is applied, rent is estimated by assuming that anyone trading from the premises would be prepared to give up a certain proportion of the turnover (the amount of sales within a given period) in return for the right to use the property. The open market rent estimated is then capitalised using an all-risks yield rate applicable to the type of property in question, which is usually derived from market transactions. This method assumes that reliable information about a company's accounts can be obtained and that the valuer has sufficient experience with the specific business enterprise to be able to interpret the accounts accurately.

Discounted cash flow (DCF) analysis, which is essentially a more detailed version of the investment method described earlier, has yet to find widespread favour. Its use is typically confined to United Kingdom and North American clients and valuers. However, as investment techniques become more sophisticated, DCF valuations are expected to increase. Indeed, for certain types of property assets, notably investment-grade, multi-let (multitenanted) office buildings and regional shopping centres, DCF valuations are becoming more common.

Reconciliation

Valuers normally use more than one method to estimate property value, whenever possible. In reconciliation, they stand back and make a judgment about the final value that should be concluded for the valuation.

VAT and Transfer Taxes

The treatment of VAT and transfer taxes is a vexing problem in France. The majority of valuers capitalise rental income on the basis of a yield which is considered to be net. This means that they are placing themselves in the position of a purchaser who requires a certain return from the investment. In the previous example of the overrented office building, a purchaser who requires a return of 9% will be prepared to pay out 61,000,000 F.

If the property is subject to VAT, a tax equal to 20.6% of the purchase price or the open market value, whichever is higher, will be payable. In this case, the tax would be approximately 12,566,000 F (20.6% of 61,000,000 F). Provided the purchaser is registered under the VAT system, this amount is recoverable and he can still receive a return of just over 9% on his investment.

The situation is different, however, if the property is subject to transfer taxes. Assuming that the purchaser still requires a return of 9%, he will still be prepared to pay only 61,000,000 F. He is not likely to be influenced by the fact that approximately 20% of the amount will be payable to the tax authorities, not the vendor (seller). All that will matter to him is obtaining his target return. Nevertheless, the vendor will only receive 48,800,000 F because 12,200,00 F (20% of 61,000,000) will go to the tax authorities.

Generally open market values are expressed excluding taxes so that the amount of the valuation is the amount that the vendor will receive from the purchaser.

With nonrecoverable taxes of 20%, the effect on values is substantial. Thus, a property bought today for 100,000,000 F will only be worth 83,000,000 F tomorrow, all other things being equal. This has a substantial adverse effect on the liquidity of the market, especially when conditions are poor, and is one principal reason many property owners place their assets in corporate structures to minimise their tax liabilities.

Availability of Data

Obtaining market information is generally difficult. As long as the market was relatively unsophisticated, this did not prove to be a serious handicap. Now, however, following the severe downturn since 1991, there is an increased awareness of the need to develop both a greater understanding of the property market and the economic forces that influence it. There has been a steady improvement in the research data which is available and this trend is likely to continue. A better understanding of the market should make it easier to produce more accurate valuations and thereby improve confidence in property investment in general.

A list of possible information sources is set out below.

Demographic and General Economic Data

- The national statistical office, INSEE (*Institut National des Statistiques et des Études Économiques*). INSEE publications can also be studied in local libraries and chambers of commerce.

- Business newspapers and reviews

General Property Market Information

- Market reports produced by leading independent property consultants

- The Institut Français de l'Épargne Immobilière et Foncière. for information on savings and loan institutions

- The Observatoire des loyers de l'Agglomération Parisienne (OLAP), for data on residential property rents in the Parisian metropolitan area

- The Groupe de Recherche sur l'Économie de la Construction et de l'Aménagement (GRECAM), for economic information on building and town planning

- The Observatoire Régionale de l'Immobilière d'Entreprise (ORIE), for data on commercial property

- The Direction Régionale de l'Équipement de l'Ile de France (DREIF), for information on furniture, fixtures, and equipment in the central region of France

- Banks and investment banks
- Specialized property publications

Comparable Evidence

- Specialized property publications
- Members of professional valuer organisations

Conclusions

Property valuation in France is similar to appraisal in other countries with sophisticated property markets. Despite the absence of a strong regulatory framework, the definitions, methods of calculation, and procedures used in France are similar to those employed in the UK and North America. However, discounted cash flow appraisals are less common and the level of investigation that valuers are required to undertake is not as great.

There is still a certain amount of confusion among French valuers and a lack of uniformity in their work. Some valuers still employ terms that have been discarded by mainstream practitioners or use floor area measurements which have become redundant. These deficiencies are probably due in part to the absence of a formal education system for valuers. Although this situation is improving, often through the work of the professional organisations referred to earlier, local valuation reports should be read attentively.

Valuers Organisations

Institut Français de l'Expertise Immobilière
3, rue Catulle Mendes
75017 Paris
Tel. (1) 45 62 51 32
Fax. (1) 49 53 03 14

Féderation Nationale des Agents Immobiliers
(Chambre des Experts)
129, rue du Faubourg Saint-Honoré
75008 Paris
Tel. (1) 53 76 03 52
Fax (1) 42 56 28 28

Bibliography

Bardouil, Sandrine and Philippe Malaquin. Chapter 7 "France" in *European Valuation Practice*. London: E & FN Spon (an imprint of Chapman & Hall), 1996.

Bourdais Expertises, S.A. (the Bordais Group). *bibliothèque des études immobilières* (real estate research library) 160, boulevard Haussmann, 75008, Paris.

Institut Français de l'Expertise Immobilière. *Guide Méthodologique relatif à l'Évaluation des Actifs Immobiliers*. Paris, 1993.

Federal Republic of Germany

Robert C. Moren, CCIM®, CPM®

Robert C. Moren, CCIM®, CPM® is a state certified general appraiser who was serving as senior real property appraiser for the U.S. Department of State's Foreign Buildings Office in Arlington, Virginia, when this chapter was written. Mr. Moren previously served for more than six years as manager of real estate field offices in Nürnberg and Frankfurt for the U.S. Forces in the Federal Republic of Germany. Mr. Moren has since returned to Europe, as senior real property appraiser for the U.S. Forces in the Federal Republic of Germany.

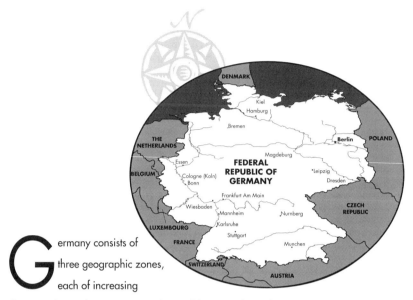

Germany consists of three geographic zones, each of increasing elevation: the northern European plain (Schleswig Holstein, lower Saxony [Hannover], the Ruhr, Mecklenburg, and Brandenburg), the middle uplands (the Saar, the Rhineland, Hessia, Thuringia, and Upper Saxony), and the mountainous south between the River Main and the Bavarian Alps (Franconia, Swabia, and Bavaria). Much of the country has a cool marine climate. Principal cities are Berlin, Hamburg, Munich, Cologne, Frankfurt, Essen, Dortmund, Stuttgart, Dusseldorf, Bremen, Duisberg, Leipzig, and Hannover.

Political Structure

After World War II ended in 1945, Germany was divided into four zones of occupation. The Federal Republic of Germany (FRG or West Germany) was established on May 23, 1949. The FRG included the former British, American, and French zones. The former Soviet zone was proclaimed the German Democratic Republic (GDR or East Germany) on October 7, 1949. West Germany and East Germany were reunified in October 1990. Britain, the United States, France, and the former Soviet Union formally relinquished any remaining powers six months later.

The government of the federal republic is divided into three branches: executive, legislative, and judicial. The executive branch is composed of the president (chief of state), the chancellor (head of the government), and the Cabinet, whose members are appointed by the president upon the recommendation of the chancellor. The legislative branch is bicameral. The lower house, or Federal Assembly (*Bundestag*), is elected by direct popular vote under a system combining direct and proportional representation; the upper house, or Federal Council (*Bundesrat*), consists of 68 representatives of the 16 states (*Länder*). The judicial branch, the Federal Constitutional Court (*Bundesverfassungsgericht*), provides judicial review of legislative acts.

Zoning or land use planning (*Flächenaufteilung/Bebauungsplan*) is prevalent throughout the Federal Republic of Germany. Through zoning, municipalities are able to regulate the type and density of real estate development.

Property taxes are assessed at the local level. No property taxes are paid to the federal government.

Property Rights

Types of Ownership

Property rights are clearly defined by law in the Federal Republic of Germany.

Absolute ownership (Eigentum) is very similar to the concept of *fee simple ownership* in common law. *Eigentum* is defined by §903 of the BGB (*Bürgerliches Gesetzbuch* or Civil Code). *Eigentum* implies absolute ownership, unencumbered by any other interest. Subject to the four powers of government detailed below, an *Eigentumer* (property owner) may sell, lease, bequeath, or give the property away.

Condominium ownership (Wohnungseigentum) is defined in § 1 of WEG (*Wohnungseigentumsgesetz* or Condominium Act) as ownership of a self-contained residential unit in a building. Part ownership *(Teileigentum),* which is also defined, applies to premises supporting nonresidential uses. In both cases, proportional ownership of common areas or components is specified, along with absolute ownership of the specified unit.

Hereditary building right (Erbbaurecht) is a legal estate in land similar to a leasehold and is defined by § 1 *ErbbauRVO (Erbbaurecht Verordnung* or Hereditary Building Right Ordinance). The owner of an *Erbbaurecht* has the right to build and use the building(s) on a particular site and may even control the entire site. However, the owner of the *Erbbaurecht* does not own the land. The *Erbbaurecht* may be for any length of time, but it often lasts 99 years or coincides with the life of the improvement. The *Erbbaurecht*, like an absolute ownership, may be mortgaged, bought, sold, or inherited, and easements *(Grunddienstbarkeiten)* or other restrictions may be placed on it. The owner of the land is usually paid ground rent *(Erbbauzins)* for the *Erbbaurecht* and may have the right of first refusal *(Vorkaufsrechte)* prior to disposal.

Long-term leases (Dauernutzungsrechte), with terms longer than 30 years, generally are recorded as land encumbrances *(Belastungen)* but may also be considered property interests similar to leaseholds. The Civil Code *(BGB - Bürgerliches Gesetzbuch)* recognizes short-term leases of less than 30 years, but these are not regarded as instruments that create leasehold interests. (See the subsequent section on lease structure.)

The Four Powers of Government

The illegal confiscation of property is not possible under the present government. Ownership of real property is subject to the four powers of government: taxation, eminent domain, police power, and escheat.

Taxation (Besteuerung) is the right of the government to raise revenue through assessments on goods, products, and rights.

Eminent domain (Enteignung) is the right of the government to take property for public use upon payment of just compensation.

Police power (Polizeigewalt/Staatsgewalt) is the right of government to protect public safety, health, morals, and general welfare.

Escheat (Heimfall) gives the state ownership of property when its owner dies without a will or ascertainable heirs.

Language

German *(Deutsch)* is spoken throughout the Federal Republic of Germany. Mastery of a second language is common, and many have a command of a third language as well.

Currency

The German mark *(deutsche Mark)* is the unit of monetary measure. One *deutsche Mark* equals 100 *Pfennige*. All domestic real estate transactions are priced in *deutsche mark*, expressed as DM. Along with the US dollar and the Japanese yen, the DM is one of the strongest currencies in the world. Because of its stability, many neighboring, newly developing countries in the former Soviet bloc use DM for real estate and other financial transactions. Germany belongs to the European Monetary System (EMS).

Units of Measure

The Federal Republic of Germany uses the metric system of measure. Real estate sizes are usually quoted in square meters (m^2). A square meter is approximately 10.764 square feet. The sizes of large parcels of land may be quoted in hectares (ha). A hectare is equal to 100 ares, 2.471 acres, or 10,000 m^2. For most real estate, income and expenses are typically quoted in DM per m^2 per month; for some industrial space, such as high-clearance warehousing, DM per cubic meter (m^3) is used.

Inflation

The rebuilding of West German industry after World War II resulted in the development of a powerful and highly successful economy. The Germans have kept an especially tight rein on inflation. In 1989 the annual inflation rate in consumer prices was 3% for West Germany and estimated to be 0.8% for East Germany. Reunification began a new chapter for Germany. Although the prospects seemed bright for quickly incorporating East Germany into the Federal Republic of Germany (West Germany), the modernization and integration of eastern Germany into the Federal Republic has been problematic.

The cost of reunification has been tremendous, with substantial sums of money being transferred to eastern Germany since 1990. This factor has contributed to the most severe recession since the end of World War II. In 1993 the inflation rate in consumer prices was 4.2% for western Germany and was estimated at 8.9% for eastern Germany. The Federal Bank *(Bundesbank)* has maintained high interest rates to offset the inflationary effects of continuing large government deficits. The economy continues to recover, with 1994 inflation rates between 3% and 4%.[1] The world-class companies in western Germany manufacture technologically advanced goods, helping to make this developed market economy a world leader in exports.

---

1. Preisindex 1988-1989: 3.2%; 1991-1992: 3.7%; 1993: 4.2%; 1994: 3.1%. From Federal Office for Statistics *(Statistisches Bundesamt)* in Wiesbaden

Because of this strong base, it is expected that inflation will continue to decline and price stability will return.

Inflation is most commonly measured by the change in the Consumer Price Index *(Lebenshaltungskostenindex)*. Annual rates of inflation are widely reported in the press and available to knowledgeable real estate professionals.

The discounted cash flow (DCF) technique *(Barwertkalkulationen)* is known in the Federal Republic of Germany, but has not yet been used widely in the valuation of property by the Appraiser's Committee *(Gutachterausschuss)*. (See the section on valuation standards.) However, property consultant firms do apply DCF analyses to major properties in larger cities throughout Germany.

Typical Lease Structure

In Germany, leases *(Mietverträge)* are regarded as contracts or tenancy agreements, rather than instruments that create estates in land. These contractual leases cannot cover periods of more than 30 years and are defined as short-term leases. Hereditary building rights *(Erbbaurechte)* and recorded leases *(Dauernutzungsrechte)* are the only property interests in Germany that are similar to leaseholds.

Dauernutzungsrechte are leases with terms of more than 30 years that are recorded as land encumbrances in the *Grundbuch* (land register). A lease may be concluded for a period longer than 30 years without being recorded, but certain statutes provide for the termination of a lease after 30 years, upon statutory notification.

Unless the parties have agreed to contrary terms, certain provisions of short-term leases *(Mietverträge)* are implicit in the Civil Code *(BGB - Bürgerliches Gesetzbuch)*. Some leases may be very brief. While brief leases are regarded as typical, the parties to such transactions are free to negotiate terms as they wish. Leases normally include a description of the property, specify the length of the lease and rental amount, and cover matters such as termination notices, lessor/lessee maintenance responsibilities, property use restrictions, insurance, security deposits, and payment requirements for rent, heating costs, and other expenses usually passed through to the tenant.

Length of Lease

Lease terms for commercial and industrial properties may be for any number of years, but terms of five, 10, or 20 years are common in large cities and shorter terms are common in smaller communities. Commercial and industrial leases are not governed by the stringent tenant protection laws that residential tenants enjoy, and therefore commercial and industrial tenants have no security for continued occupancy at the end of a lease term. However, leases commonly provide the tenant with an option to extend the lease for additional lease terms. Prudent lessors stipulate within the option provisions that the rental rate will be fixed at a specified rate or subject to negotiation upon extension of the lease term. Prudent lessees stipulate that the rent will be at the same rate as the initial lease term, fixed at a certain agreed-upon rate when the original lease was executed, or at least capped by the prevailing rental rates for comparable properties at the time the lease is extended.

Residential leases have relatively short terms, usually of one, three, or five years. The extension of these leases is virtually guaranteed, even when the lessor gives written notice of termination, by the so-called social clauses contained in § 556a-c BGB (*Bürgerliches Gesetzbuch* - Civil Code). However, if the lessor requires the apartment for his own use, a termination notice may be valid, but there may be extended delays before the premises are vacated.

Rental Rates

Rental rates are usually quoted in DM per m^2 and are payable monthly in advance. A security deposit *(Kaution)* in the form of a bank guarantee or a cash deposit equivalent to two or three months' rent is typical.

Rental rates for industrial space, may be based on building area in square meters or on building volume in cubic meters for buildings with high clear heights. Units with higher clearance are also sometimes priced at higher rates. Extra costs may be included for large parking, maneuvering areas, or other special features. For new retail space and retail space in larger cities, participation clauses (*Beteiligungsklauseln*) or percentage rent provisions allow for payment of additional rent over the basic rental rate to be paid, based on the lessee's sales.

In residential leases, rental rates are quoted in DM per square meter and are payable in advance on a monthly basis. A security deposit of two to three months rent is usually required.

Variation of Rental Rates

The basic rent called for in long-term commercial and industrial leases may vary during the initial term according to locally prevailing rents, as allowed by the lease or law. Lease rates may also vary by increments linked to an officially published index. The most commonly used index is the cost-of-living index *(Lebenshaltungskostenindex)*. Other indices of wages, salaries, fixed incomes, the trade of the tenant, or retail prices may be considered in special cases. Lease provisions commonly specify that rent adjustments must be justified and based on a certain percentage of change in a particular cost index. Adjustments are often linked to index changes of 5% to 10%, with the particular percentage selected through negotiation.

The automatic adjustment of rental rates is common in Germany, but some automatic rental rate adjustment clauses in commercial and industrial leases require the approval of the Central Bank of the State *(Landeszentralbank)* in which the property is located.[2] Automatic adjustment clauses are generally approved if the lease term is more than 10 years, the lessor is bound by the lease, and the adjustments are equitable to both parties. The adjustments, which may be upwards or downwards, are considered equitable if they do not allow percentage changes in rent that exceed the percentage changes in the cost-of-living index. Provisions for the automatic adjustment of rental rates need not be approved under three conditions: 1) if they call for adjusting rental rates to equal rental rates for comparable properties, 2) if the adjustment of rental rates is to be adjudicated by a neutral third party, or 3) if the adjustments are due to percentage rental lease clauses *(Beteiligungsklauseln)*.

For residential leases, the setting of rental rates is tightly controlled. Usurious rents are prohibited by the Penal Code *(StGB - Strafgesetzbuch)* and the Economic Offenses Act *(WiStG - Wirtschaftsstrafgesetz)* prohibits rental rates 20% higher than rents for comparable properties. Rental increases during the term of a residential lease are tightly controlled by the Law on Assessment of Rent *(MHG - Miethöhegesetz)*. Automatic increases according to indices are prohibited. Rental increases above the prevailing rentals for comparable properties in the locale and rental increases of more than 30% in three years are usually not permitted.[3] The increasing statutory protection of tenants that began in the mid-1970s greatly limits an owner's ability to set or adjust rents and to specify lease termination provisions. Buyers tend to be owner/users of one unit. Investment returns on residential property lag behind returns on alternative investments, and most investors avoid this market.

Because contract rental rates may not keep pace with market rental rates, the values of multi-family properties are lower than might be expected for properties in the United States.

Maintenance and Other Costs

Lease terms usually specify that the tenant is responsible for the maintenance and upkeep of the interior of the premises, and the landlord is responsible for the major structural maintenance and repairs *(Dach und Fach* - roof and

---

2. Rüdiger Volhard, Dolf Weber, and Wolfgang Usinger. *Real Property in Germany, Legal and Tax Aspects of Development and Investment,* 4th ed. (Frankfurt am Main: Fritz Knapp, 1991).

3. Ibid.

facade). The landlord recovers the costs of providing services by means of an accessory cost charge *(Nebenkosten)*, which is paid in advance on a monthly basis and is reconciled on an annual basis. In typical leases, all costs are passed through to the tenant via this service charge mechanism, which covers insurance, land tax, water, sewage, hot water, street cleaning, waste removal, antenna system, utility costs and common area costs, e.g., elevator mainte-nance, heating system maintenance, lighting, cleaning, lawn care, and chimney sweeping. Typical service charges range from 6 to 8 DM per m^2 for modern office buildings without air-conditioning and from 12 to 13 DM per m^2 for an air-conditioned office tower with full management services. How-ever, the landlord bears certain expenses, i.e., administrative and mainte-nance costs, that cannot be recovered. In new buildings, these expenses may range from 1% to 3% of the rent. In older buildings, these expenses may range up to 10%. This higher percentage reflects the higher maintenance costs typical of older structures, but also may be attributable to older lease contracts that do not allow property management fees to be recovered from tenants, a common provision in newer leases.

Most residential leases also pass all costs through to the tenant via the service charge mechanism. Again, this charge is paid in advance on a monthly basis and reconciled on an annual basis.

Tenant Improvements

Landlords do not usually fund initial improvements to suit a particular tenant prior to occupancy. Office space tenants usually find the premises fully outfitted with carpets, lighting, and services. Office space is typically not leased as a shell with the tenant finishing out the improvements.

In the industrial market, space is usually outfitted with lighting and heating for the typical tenant, the tenant is responsible for any other improvements. New retail space may be outfitted the same as office space. For existing retail premises, the space is usually leased as is, with the tenant responsible for any improvements.

In residential markets, a tenant usually rents a newly renovated space and is expected to return the premises to the same condition upon termination of the lease, although some wear and tear is accepted. The sizable security deposit of two, three, or more months rent helps to ensure compliance.

Rental Concessions

Depending on the strength of the market, lessors of retail, industrial, or office space may make certain concessions, such as periods of free rent or the payment of expenses usually borne by the tenant, as inducements to rent.

Valuation Standards

Value Determination Ordinance and Guidelines

Valuation standards are based on federal statutes and are specified in the Value Determination Ordinance (*Wertermittlungsverordnung*, 6 December 1988 - *WertV*), *BGB1.I S.2209*, and the Value Determination Guidelines (*Wertermittlungs-Richtlinien*, 11 June 1991- *WertR 91*). Preparation of the Value Determination Ordinance and Guidelines is the responsibility of the Federal Building Ministry *(Bundesbauministerium)*. *WertV* details the information to be gathered, the factors to be considered, and the framework and explanation of the appraisal process. *WertR 91* expands on *WertV* with discussions of different valuation problems, detailed forms, and examples of how to set up the appraisal report and how to perform the initial, intermediate, and final calculations required.

Publicly Appointed and Sworn Experts

The standards must be followed by publicly appointed and sworn experts *(öffentlich bestellten und vereidigten Sachverständiger)* in the preparation of all appraisals. All appraisals prepared for cases involving liquidation, inheritance, or other matters that may be presented in court must be prepared by a publicly appointed and sworn expert. Real estate brokers *(Makler)* and certain bank employees render value opinions that do not follow these guidelines.

Appraisal Fees

The minimum and maximum fees that may be charged for appraisals are set out in a special section of the *HOAI (Honorarordnung für Architekten und Ingenieure* - Fee Ordinance for Architects and Engineers) (See Table 1). For properties valued at less than 50,000 DM, fees may be negotiated as a lump sum or based on the time required to accomplish the work (up to the minimum fee allowed for a property valued at 50,000 DM). For properties valued at more than 50,000,000 DM, fees may be negotiated without restriction.

As the table illustrates, fees for appraisals of properties valued at 50,000 DM to 50,000,000 DM are based on the value of the property and the difficulty of the assignment. Maximum fees set the upper limits that may be indicated in a contract under usual circumstances, although less may be charged. If the fee for the appraisal is not specified in a written contract, the fee will be taken from the table of fees. Detailed instructions are furnished on types of assignments, clients, and other factors that may justify upward or downward adjustment of the fees specified in the table.

Although the setting of fees based on the final estimate of value would seem to be a conflict of interest for the appraiser, it is a workable system in Germany. The table of fees furnishes an initial framework of charges for a particular type and difficulty of assignment. Many adjustments to the fees specified in the table are possible and, in practice, the fees quoted in the bid process for an appraisal assignment may vary considerably from those specified in the tables.

In addition, most appraisers come from the fields of architecture or engineering; their qualifications for those fields also qualify them to perform appraisals. Appraisals are normally only a small part of the business of an architect or an engineer. Since fees for architects and engineers relate to the cost or value of the subject building or project, it is understandable that fees for appraisal work would follow the value of the property as well.

Table 1. Appraisal Fees

Property Value	Level: Normal Fees from	to	Level: Difficult Fees from	to
50,000 DM	420 DM	540 DM	520 DM	810 DM
500,000 DM	1,840 DM	2,250 DM	2,180 DM	3,070 DM
1,000,000 DM	2,480 DM	3,030 DM	2,930 DM	4,130 DM
10,000,000 DM	8,200 DM	10,000 DM	9,700 DM	13,700 DM
50,000,000 DM	25,500 DM	31,500 DM	30,500 DM	43,000 DM

Excerpted from the full table of fees listed in *Honorartafel (fee table) zu § 34 Abs. 1, HOAI,* for value increments of 50k to the 500k level; 100k increments to the 1 million level; 500k increments to the 5 million level; 1 million increments to the 10 million level; and 5 million increments to the 50 million level.

Appraiser's Committee

In 1960 the Federal Building Act *(BbauG - Bundesbaugesetz)* created a *Gutachterausschuss* (Appraiser's Committee) in each city and district. These committees are separate and independent from the taxing authorities. They have various responsibilities which include the gathering of sales data, property appraisals, the determination of valuation data such as price indices and interest rates, and the establishment of standard values. The *Gutachterausschuss* may conduct appraisals with its own appraisers (*Gutachter,* the literal meaning of which is expert) or may contract this work out to other valuation experts. The *Gutachterausschuss* publishes the *Bodenrichtwertkarte* (standard land value map) for its area of responsibility, usually a city, district, or county.

Standard Land Value Map

The *Bodenrichtwertkarte* is compiled from all sales of properties in the area of responsibility, but the sales information is one or two years old by the time the map is printed. The land values on the *Bodenrichtwertkarte* are averages for specific areas, often two or three square kilometers or larger, and do not take into account location, improvements, time of sale, unusual circumstances of sale, and other factors that would normally be considered in an adjustment grid if the information were known. The *Bodenrichtwertkarte* is available to the general public for purchase. A listing of sales information on which the standard land values are based can also be purchased for particular areas and parameters. However, because of strictly enforced privacy act laws, the information furnished is sketchy and it is impossible to identify the individual properties listed or to verify the sales information.

Property Consultant Firms

Within the last 20 years, property consultant firms and estate management firms have been established in Germany. They perform a full range of real estate services for the investor and developer. British chartered surveyors are often associated with these firms. The surveyors perform valuations and evaluations of properties, offer comprehensive advice to clients on financing, and provide other technical real estate services to clients. These activities are fostering subtle changes in the appraisal systems that underlie mortgage financing and property transactions.[4]

Licensing/Certification

As mentioned previously, most appraisers come from the fields of architecture or engineering. Others come from the following occupational fields: real estate brokerage, real property management, banking, forestry, land economics, and surveying. An individual who has a university degree in engineering or architecture, or sufficient knowledge of these fields, and is able to demonstrate ample experience, can be tested and sworn in at the local chamber of commerce *(IHK - Industrie und Handelskammer)* as a "publicly appointed and sworn expert" *(öffentlich bestellter und vereidigter Sachverständiger)*.

To become accepted as a publicly appointed and sworn expert, an applicant to the IHK must:

- Have a thorough knowledge of appraisal methods and their use

- Have a technical knowledge of construction materials and specifications

---

4. "The Dynamics of Real Estate Associated with the European Integration," *The Appraisal Journal* (July 1991).

- Have a knowledge of pertinent zoning and planning regulations
- Have a degree in architecture, construction engineering, surveying, or a similar field and five years of experience in economics and the technical and legal aspects of appraisal or 10 years of experience in one of these fields
- Submit a work sample to demonstrate the ability to write an appraisal report
- Pass a test given by the IHK

Appraisal Reporting Requirements

Users of appraisals in Germany, primarily lending institutions, businesses, and investors, do not require appraisal reports to be as well-documented as the narrative appraisals prepared in the United States. A complete appraisal report may be 30 or more pages long, but more than half of the report may consist of detailed descriptions of the type of construction and the condition of the improvements.

WertV and *WertR 91* dictate the requirements for appraisal reports. Set out below is a typical table of contents for an appraisal report on an improved property.

Part One - Introduction

Client identification

Purpose of the appraisal

Property owner

Land record reference

Legal description

Date of appraisal

Date of inspection

Regulation basis for the valuation

Part Two - Description of the Subject Property

A. Description of the land

Use/location description

Address, legal description, and size

Land register/recorded liens

Comments on condition

Status of development

Type and extent of construction use

Liens and other rights affecting value

Fees and taxes

Temporary or special use

Area transportation access

Area location

Adjacent properties

Property area

Property configuration

Soil condition

Environmental issues

Exterior grounds/facilities

Sewage systems

Paved areas

Lawn areas

B.   Description of improvements

Type and purpose of construction

Year of construction

Original life of improvements

Remaining life of improvements

Exterior improvements

Basic construction

Type of construction

Exterior walls

Interior walls

Floors

Stairwells

Insulation

Roof

Availability of utilities

Heating system

Floor covering

Interior finishing

Doors and windows

Technical systems

Part Three - Development of Value Estimate

Land value

Income approach to value

Cost approach to value

Sales comparison approach to value

Reconciliation of value indications into a final value estimate

Addenda

Plats, plans, calculations of interior space, survey, photos

Appraisers in Germany use published appraisal regulations and guidelines as models for the preparation of appraisal reports. Much, if not most, data used in analyses is drawn from the regulations or other published sources. Data from published sources include depreciation tables, construction cost indices, estimated building life tables, interest calculation tables, and schedules for management fees, maintenance costs, and operating costs. Values for land are often taken from the *Bodenrichtwertkarte* (standard land value map), which is developed by the local appraiser's committee by averaging land sales. The information is more than a year old when the map is printed, but more current market information (*Marktbericht*) can be obtained from the local appraiser's committee. Data is seldom obtained from original field research; data from published sources is widely accepted and seldom verified in the field. Because of this dependence on published sources, the typical appraisal includes little explanation of the analyses in the approaches to value.

While the German appraisal report is based on regulations and guidelines, its development into its present form reflects the expertise of its authors, the availability of data, and the level of demand for appraisals.

Appraisers with architectural backgrounds tend to include lengthy descriptions of the improvements and rely more on the cost approach to value; those with backgrounds in banking or land economics tend to focus on those aspects of the appraisal and may emphasize the income approach. Appraisers with legal backgrounds tend to stress the sales comparison approach since it seems most defensible in court.

Data for a comprehensive and convincing sales comparison approach is often unavailable. While there may be sufficient sales data in a market, data is often closely guarded and not easily obtainable by the appraiser because of strict enforcement of the privacy act. Any data that can be obtained from official sources will be minimal, without citation of exact addresses and contacts. With this scarcity of information, it is difficult to verify sales details and to inspect properties to determine which are truly comparable. Thus, appraisers deemphasize the sales comparison approach and depend more on the cost or income approaches to value.

Lending institutions tend to be conservative in Germany, with many loans restricted to 60% of value.[5] This restriction, along with other measures adopted to minimize risk and the expectation of future appreciation of value, lessens the need for comprehensive appraisal reports. Many clients would be unwilling to pay for more comprehensive reports.

Value Definitions

Fair Market Value

Fair market value *(Verkehrswert)* is officially defined in § *194 BauGB-Baugesetzbuch* (The Federal Building Act) 8 Dec 86/BGB 1.I S.2191 as the price for a property that would be achieved in a normal business transaction, in accordance with the legal interest and the actual characteristics of the property (e.g., condition and location), and in the absence of unusual or personal circumstances.

Assessed Value

Assessed value *(Einheitswert)* is often only 25% to 50% of the fair market value. The ratable assessed value and assessment base are calculated with a procedure set forth in the Tax Valuation Act *(Bewertungsgesetz)*.

Loan Value

Loan value *(Beleihungswert)* is a nonmarket value of property intended for use as collateral for a loan. It is usually based on the cost and income approaches to value. Since loan values in the past have varied considerably from fair market values, loans have been restricted to 60% of the loan value to minimize the risk to lending institutions. With the recent, well-publicized default of several large multiproperty real estate loans, lending institutions are formulating procedures and requirements to align the loan value more closely with the fair market value.

---

5. Rüdiger Volhard, Dolf Weber, and Wolfgang Usinger, *Real Property in Germany, Legal and Tax Aspects of Development and Investment,* 4th ed. (Frankfurt am Main: Fritz Knapp, 1991).

Land Valuation

The sales comparison approach is the commonly prescribed method of land valuation. Land values derived by sales comparison reflect the utilization potential of a land parcel. This approach is used most often in the appraisal of unimproved land, especially agricultural land. Some valuations of land, however, call for the application of the income approach or the land residual method.

In urban and suburban areas, land is generally valued using the standard land values developed by the appraiser's committee, rather than the sales comparison approach, although the *WertV* and *WertR 91* recommend use of standard values in limited cases only. The shortcomings of these standard land values have already been discussed.

The GRZ *(Grundflächenzahl)* is the ratio of building coverage to site area. The GFZ *(Geschossflächenzahl)* is the ratio of total building floor area to site area. These ratios are used in conjunction with height restrictions to calculate the development and income potential of a site, which is then compared to other sites. As is often the case, adjustments for time of sale, location, and other factors are usually made in a lump sum, rather than percentages. Little explanation of this lump-sum adjustment is provided.

The land residual technique is used when sufficient comparable land sales or standard land values are not available.

Income Approach

The income approach *(Ertragswertverfahren)* is used primarily in the valuation of multifamily and office buildings. While the income approach is occasionally used for retail and industrial space, the German appraiser still tends to use the technical method (cost approach) for these properties. Although the income approach is performed in much the same way as it is in the United States, there are several notable differences in the characteristics of income properties. A building life of 100 years is common and mortgage provisions impose hefty penalties for early repayment of loans. Mixed-use buildings are common. Owners tend to retain properties for long periods of time and are interested in long-range income.

Discounted cash flow techniques *(Barwertkalkulationen)* and other yield capitalization methods are known, but they are not used very often except for very large properties. Direct capitalization may be used, with capitalization rates derived from government sources. The appraiser may apply his or her knowledge of market rates to make lump-sum adjustments to the value estimate. The building residual technique is frequently employed. German appraisers use Inwood factors[6] to capitalize the income stream and reversion from a property into present value. It is noteworthy that the German appraiser tends to ignore the current rent in these calculations and instead uses the long-term achievable rent *(nachhaltig erzielbaren Mieten)*. For example, when office rents in Berlin increased markedly after the reunification of Germany, many German appraisers reasoned that the increases were of a relatively temporary nature and adjusted the rents used in calculations downward as a result.

Analysis of income and expenses to arrive at net operating income *(NOI)* is accomplished in a manner similar to that used in the United States, except that *WertV* and *WertR 91* recommend the use of actual (rather than market-derived) expense figures, when available. When actual data is not available, expense ratios are recommended.

In the income approach, the net operating income *(Nettoertrag/Netto-einkommen)* is apportioned between the land and buildings. For example, consider an improved property with an *NOI* of 500,000 DM per annum, a site size of 700 m², standard land value of 4,000 DM per m², and a building with a remaining life of 35 years. The land value is calculated at 2,800,000 DM (700 × 4,000 DM). If 6% is considered a reasonable return on the land, the land portion of *NOI* may be calculated at 168,000 DM (2,800,000 DM × 0.06). This leaves 332,000 DM of the *NOI* attributable to the building (500,000 DM less 168,000 DM). The present value of the 332,000 DM per annum for 35 years is calculated by applying an appropriate rate, often the same rate used for the land. An income of 332,000 DM per annum for 35 years at 6% has a present value of 4,813,336 DM (332,000 DM × 14.498), which represents the estimated value of the improvements. The estimated value of the improvements (4,813,336 DM) is then added to the value of the land based on standard land values (2,800,000 DM) to arrive a total value for the building and land of 7,613,336 DM by the income approach.

In Germany, the building life expectancies used in building residual techniques are often much longer than the building life expectancies used in the United States. Generally, lump-sum adjustments for building condition and market dynamics are also applied to the building residual value.

Sales Comparison Approach

The sales comparison approach *(Vergleichswertverfahren)* is used for the valuation of land and is recommended by *WertV* and *WertR 91* for valuations

---

6. An Inwood factor is a discount factor used to convert into present value a series of future level annuities of one per period for a specific number of periods at a specified interest rate.

of condominiums, rowhouses, and duplexes. It is also used to value properties in condemnation proceedings. *WertV* and *WertR 91* provide little guidance for the valuation of buildings by the sales comparison approach. German appraisers prefer the cost and income approaches over sales comparison. Difficulties cited by German appraisers in applying the sales comparison approach include possible errors in making adjustments for differences in buildings, the difficulty of obtaining and verifying sufficient income and sales data, and problems in confirming the circumstances of sales.

Cost Approach

Since most appraisers are architects or engineers, the cost approach (*Sachwertverfahren*) is the approach to value that is treated most comprehensively in Germany. Single-family dwellings and industrial facilities are valued almost exclusively by the cost approach.

The traditional formula of replacement cost, less depreciation, plus land cost is the basis for the cost approach. Construction costs are calculated using the construction cost guidelines quoted in DIN (*Deutsche Industrie-Normen*) 276, DIN 277, and DIN 283. *WertV* and *WertR 91* provide construction cost indices for different years of construction. These statutes provide average costs per m³, based on the particular use, design, and condition of the building. Construction cost indices are not provided for individual years. In the example of the cost approach that follows, the actual construction date of the building might have been 1942, but the basis year for construction cost used is 1936. Current factors based on DIN 276 are multiplied by the cost figure from *WertR 91* to arrive at the current construction cost. The factors are adjusted for regional cost differences in construction and are updated quarterly. The DIN applies to all of Germany, since standardized definitions, measurements, and construction methods are recognized throughout Germany, which represents an enviable achievement. Appraisers also rely heavily on the price index for construction costs (*Preisindex für Bauwerke*) published by the statistical office in each state to update the construction costs of buildings.

Cost Approach Example

Development of the Value of the Improvements

Description	Size
Villa	1,922 m³

Technical Depreciation

Normal life expectancy:	80 years
Age (effective):	55 years
Remaining life:	25 years
Depreciation from WertR91*	58%

Economic Depreciation

	Deduction
Damage/deterioration estimate:	189,000 DM
Total:	189,000 DM

Development of Building Value

Date of Inspection:	15 Nov 93
Construction price index:	2,343.7
Basis year:	1936

Description	Size	1936 Price	1993 Price	1993 Construction Costs
Villa	1,922 m³	39 DM	917 DM	1,762,269 DM
Total				1,762,269 DM
Construction cost on date of inspection				1,762,269 DM
Less depreciation for age 58.0%*				−1,022,116 DM
Less depreciation for damage/deterioration				− 189,000 DM
Cost approach value of villa				551,153 DM

Development of Value of Exterior Improvements

Building cost approach percentage for exterior improvements estimated at 8%	551,153 DM
Exterior improvements value	44,092 DM

* From *WertR 91*, derived by formula.

Development of the Value of the Property

Description	1993 Construction Costs	1993 Cost Approach
Villa	1,762,269 DM	551,153 DM
Exterior improvements		44,092 DM
Value of the construction	1,762,269 DM	595,245 DM
Land value		4,676,000 DM
Value of property by cost approach		5,271,245 DM

Depreciation

Depreciation *(Wertminderung)* is broken down into two forms—economic *(wirtschaftliche)* and technical *(technische)*. Economic depreciation is due to functional obsolescence, design deficiencies, or safety or health code inadequacies; technical depreciation is based on the age and condition of the improvements. Economic depreciation is observed and estimated by the German appraiser. Technical depreciation is calculated using a technical depreciation table in *WertR 91*, which considers the life expectancy and age of the structure. The table is based on the formula[7]

$$D\% = [1/2 \times (A^2/L^2 + A/L)] \times 100$$

where D% is the calculated percentage deduction for depreciation, A is the age of the structure, and L is the life expectancy of the structure.

The technical depreciation formula was originated by F.W. Ross, a master builder who lived in Hannover, Germany, in the late 19th century. Ross theorized that the depreciation in a structure that receives minimal periodic maintenance will be straight-line (column C in Table 2 and curve C in Figure 1), that is, 1% per year for a structure with a life expectancy of 100 years. In addition, he postulated that with normal (average) periodic maintenance (column B in Table 2 and curve B in Figure 1), the rate of depreciation will be slowed in the early years of the life of the structure. With superior periodic maintenance (column A in Table 2 and curve A in Figure 1) the rate of depreciation will be slowed even more during the early years of the life of the structure.

---

7. Ross, Brachmann, Holzner, *Ermittlung des Bauwertes von Gebäuden und des Verkehrswertes von Grundstücken (Determination of the Construction Value of Buildings and the Market Value of Real Estate),* 1993.

Table 2. Technical Depreciation (Ross formula)

Building Life Expectancy			Maintenance Level		
20 Yrs. Bldg. Age	60 Yrs. Bldg. Age	100 Yrs. Bldg. Age	Superior A	Normal B	Minimal C
				% Cost Deduction	
	3	5		3	5
2	6	10	1	6	10
	9	15	2	9	15
4	12	20	4	12	20
	15	25	6	16	25
6	18	30	9	20	30
	21	35	12	24	35
8	24	40	16	28	40
	27	45	20	33	45
10	30	50	25	38	50
	33	55	30	43	55
12	36	60	36	48	60
	39	65	42	54	65
14	42	70	49	60	70
	45	75	56	66	75
16	48	80	64	72	80
	51	85	72	79	85
18	54	90	81	86	90
	57	95	90	93	95
20	60	100	100	100	100

The *WertR 91* technical depreciation table is derived from the Ross formula, which estimates the percentage deduction for technical depreciation in a structure based on the life expectancy and age of the structure. The table provides the calculated percentage deductions for buildings with life expectancies of 20 to 100 years, in increments of 10 years, and building ages of one year to 100 years. However, only data for normal periodic maintenance (curve B) is given. Both Table 2 and Figure 1 indicate a 28% deduction for technical depreciation for a 40-year old building with a life expectancy of 100 years and normal periodic maintenance.

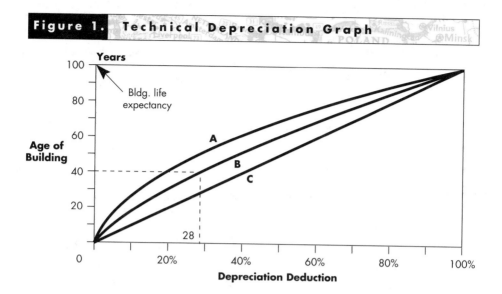

Figure 1. Technical Depreciation Graph

Reconciliation

In summary, the sales comparison approach is not often used in Germany and appraisers tend to rely on the value indications from the cost approach and the income approach. In the case of newly constructed improvements, it is normally conceded that the cost approach should yield a value relatively close to that obtained from the income approach. Thereafter, the value indications may diverge widely, due to different assumptions relating to the treatment of depreciation. Sometimes only one approach may be used, or a single approach may be emphasized to the exclusion of other indications in the final estimate of value. When more than a single approach is used or emphasized, the tendency may be to average the values to reach the final conclusion of value. However, *WertR 91* instructs German appraisers not to average the values.

Availability of Data

Data on completed sales is difficult to obtain in Germany. The privacy act is strictly enforced and consequently most data that can be obtained is insufficient to identify the properties or verify specific information. The properties, therefore, can seldom be examined for comparability to the subject property. Data can be gathered by the time-honored practice of knocking on doors and talking to property owners in the subject neighborhood, but, again partly due to the privacy act, this is seldom done. The difficulty of obtaining data leads to more dependence on, and acceptance of, official data and standard values than is the case in the United States.

Some information sources are listed below.

Demographic and Economic Data

- Offices at state *(Land)*, county *(Kreis)*, and city *(Stadt)* levels, e.g., the state and federal offices of statistics *(Statistisches Landesamt* and *Statistisches Bundesamt)*

- Local chamber of commerce *(Handelskammer)*

- Libraries

- Articles in business newspapers, both national and local

Real Estate Market Data (Market Size, Occupancy, Comparables, Rent Levels)

- Local appraiser's committees *(Gutachterausschüsse)*

- Offices at state *(Land)*, county, *(Kreis)*, and city *(Stadt)* levels, e.g., the housing office *(Wohnungsamt)*

- Local offices of German real estate brokers *(Immobilienmakler)*, property consultant firms (mostly British), and local appraisal practitioners

- *RDM (Ring Deutscher Makler/*Association of German Real Estate Brokers)

Appraisal Organizations

There are no national appraisal organizations in Germany comparable to the Appraisal Institute in the United States or the Royal Institution of Chartered Surveyors (RICS) in England. However, as of 1996, the newly founded German Association of Chartered Surveyors *(Deutscher Verband für Chartered Surveyors)* of RICS had more than 300 active members in Germany (fellows, professional associates, honorary members, probationers [candidates], and students). Other real estate organizations such as *RDM (Ring Deutscher Makler/*Association of German Real Estate Brokers) and FIABCI (The International Real Estate Federation) have appraisers among their members.

Publicly appointed and sworn appraisal experts can become members of the BVS *(Bundesverband der öffentlich bestellten und vereidigten Sachverständiger e.V. [eingetragener Verein]/*Association of Publicly Appointed and Sworn Experts, Inc. [Incorporated]), an association or federation for all expert fields (automobile manufacturing, construction, electrical, materials, etc.). Each state *(Land)* has a state federation connected to the BVS. The organizations publish directories of their members for public reference. The BVS is a member of the International Confederation of Associations of Experts and Consultants (CIDADEC - *Confederation internationale des associations d'experts et de conseils*, Rue Ten Bosch, 85-B-1050 Brussels).

Conclusion

While there are similarities in valuation practice in Germany and the United States, there are also variances. Many of these result from differences in appraisal education and training, the influence of government regulations and guidelines, the professionalization of the field, and the demand for appraisal services.

There are few formal opportunities specifically for appraisal education in Germany. Instead, the appraiser's preparation consists of a university education in an allied field and job experience. Although some appraisal courses are offered at the university level in certain fields of study, such as architecture or engineering, other appraisal training is usually limited to seminars offered by university departments, chambers of commerce, and construction societies.

The appraisal process and procedures are detailed in the regulations and guidelines, *WertV* and *WertR 91*, respectively, as published by the German federal government. Court-appointed experts adhere closely to the regulations and guidelines as do members of the appraiser's committee.

The demand for appraisal services in Germany is not as great as in the United States. Fewer real estate transactions take place in Germany due to a less mobile population, the tendancy for properties to remain in families, and the relatively high costs of property transfer.

Bibliography

Architektenkammer Baden-Württemberg. *Gebäudekosten 1993, Baupreistabellen zur überschlägigen Kostenermittlung, Baukostendatenbank. (Building Costs, 1993, Construction Cost Tables for Determination of Cost Estimates, Construction Cost Data Bank).*

Central Intelligence Agency. *The World Fact Book 1994.* 1994.

Downie, Mary Lou, Karl-Werner Schulte, and Matthias Thomas. Chapter 8 "Germany" in *European Valuation Practice.* London: E & FN Spon (an imprint of Chapman & Hall), 1996.

Federal Office for Statistics. *Preisindex 1994, Statistisches Bundesamt.* Wiesbaden, 1994.

(der) Gutachterausschuß für Grundstückswerte in der Stadt Bonn. *Bericht über die Entwicklung des Bonner Grundstücksmarktes im Jahre 1992 (Report on the Development of the Bonn Real Estate Market in 1992).*

Hines, M.A., PhD. "The Dynamics of Real Estate Associated with the European Integration." *The Appraisal Journal* (July 1991).

Jones Lang Wootten. *Quarterly Investment Report, Summer '94, European Property Market*. 1994.

Jones Lang Wootten. *European Retail Guide, Spring '94*. 1994.

(der) Obere Gutachterausschuß für Grundstückswerte in Land Nordrhein-Westfalen. *Grundstücksmarktbericht Nordrhein-Westfalen 1992* (*Real Estate Market Report [on the state of] North Rhine-Westphalia, 1992*)

Ross, Brachmann, Holzner. *Ermittlung des Bauwertes von Gebäuden und des Verkehrswertes von Grundstücken von. Ross, Brachmann, Holzner* (Determination of the Construction Value of Buildings and the Market Value of Real Estate). 1993.

Statistisches Landesamt. *Preisindex für den Neubau von Wohngebäuden 1994 (Price Index for the New Construction of Apartment Buildings)*. 1994.

Stauss, Dr. George and Steven Stauss. *Real Estate Appraisal in Continental Europe and West Germany, A Guide for the North American Appraiser and Investor*. October 1976.

Volhard, Rüdiger, Dolf Weber, and Wolfgang Usinger. *Real Property in Germany, Legal and Tax Aspects of Development and Investment*. 4th ed. (Frankfurt am Main: Fritz Knapp, 1991).

Wertermittlungsverordnung - WertV, Verordnung über Grundsätze für die Ermittlung der Verkehrswerte von Grundstücken Vom 6. Dezember 1988 (Ordinance of December 6, 1988 on the Principles of the Determination of the Fair Market Value of Real Estate).

Wertermittlungs-Richtlinien 1991 - WertR 91, Richtlinien für die Ermittlung der Verkehrswerte von Grundstücken Vom 11. Juni 1991. (Guidelines of July 11, 1991 on the Determination of the Fair Market Value of Real Estate)

8

Italy

Lynda M. Hinxman, B.Sc., ARICS
Marcello Allegri, MBA

Lynda Hinxman is a chartered surveyor and a senior lecturer in property management at Sheffield Hallam University. Prior to joining the university, Ms. Hinxman worked for Shell UK, the Costain Group, and Norwich Union as Property Fund Manager.

Marcello Allegri holds an M.B.A. from the Sheffield Business School. He is currently Account Manager for Multinational Market Intelligence Consultancy in London. He is responsible for handling consulting assignments involving real estate development in the Italian market.

The authors would like to thank Gianni Allegri and their other contacts at the Instituto Nazionale Assicurazioni (I.N.A.), the National Insurance Institute, for the assistance and materials they provided.

The backbone of the Italian peninsula is formed by the Appennines which branch off from the Alps above Genoa. The range is highly volcanic. The principal river, the Po, begins in the Alps and flows across the fertile plain of Lombardy to the Adriatic. Most of Italy has a Mediterranean climate. Important cities are Rome, Milan, Naples, Turin, Palermo, Genoa, Bologna, and Florence.

Introduction

The Italian property market and property valuation in Italy may be examined from two distinct perspectives: the official, legislative framework and practical valuation methodology based on actual sale and purchase activity. This chapter represents a starting point toward an understanding of Italian appraisal methods and market practices. As with any property matter in a foreign country, it is always advisable to seek professional help from registered valuers.

The Culture

Despite popular stereotypes of sumptuous culinary repasts, grand opera, magnificent countryside, and, of course, beautiful women, Italian culture is characterized in terms of attitudes toward the family.

The power, security and trust of the family are of paramount importance in Italian society. The concept of family may extend to trusted individuals whom one has grown to know very well. In many ways, property dealings are greatly affected by this principle. Although Italian culture is easily discernible, it has a depth to which no short introduction can do justice.

Political Framework

Since unification of the country in the 1860s, Italy has not enjoyed many periods of political stability. The country had a series of right-wing governments under the monarchy and Mussolini until the end of World War II, followed by 40 years of republican governments under Christian Democratic rule, and finally, the recent collapse of the scandal-ridden "Tangentopoli"[1] (Bribe-ville) regimes.

Being only 50 years old, the Italian republic is a relatively young state which reflects the administrative and cultural legacies of the former states that ruled the peninsula prior to unification. Geography also helps underscore differences between regions as disparate as the Piedmont and Lombardy (the Po valley), located at the foot of the Alps, Tuscany, the Mezzogiorno, and the islands of Sardinia and Sicily.

Against a backdrop of political instability, property and taxation have been subject to numerous acts of legislation, which must be fully understood to comfortably participate in the Italian property market.

---

1. From *tangenti* meaning kickback.

Language

Italian is spoken throughout Italy and there are several dialects, including Neapolitan, Milanese, Bolognese, Venetian, and Tuscan, which is the literary standard. English is widely known, especially in the larger communities and tourist areas. Italian schoolchildren study a second language, which is usually English, and often a third language, which may be French, German, or Spanish. In certain special status regions, there may be another official language, e.g., in Trentino-Alto Adige both German and Italian are spoken.

Currency

The Italian lira is the monetary unit. The lira is abbreviated as L. or Lit. Property market figures are usually expressed in Lit. 100,000,000 (hundreds of millions) or Lit. 1,000,000,000 (billions).

Inflation

Unsettled politics in Italy give rise to economic volatility. As a new government succeeds to power, policies often change dramatically and fluctuations in the economy and inflation follow.

After the recent change from a government controlled by the centre-right Forza Italia Party to a multiparty coalition government under the centre-left Olivo Party, the annual inflation rate as measured in consumer prices fell from 5.8% in October 1995 to 3.9% in July 1996.[2]

Inflation for 1997 is forecast by the government of Prime Minister Prodi at 2.5%. However, there is growing concern about the policies of the Prodi coalition government. Increasingly, politicians have expressed doubts about whether the economic forecasts are strong enough for Italy to meet the Maastricht criteria for joining the European currency union. Since this issue is likely to be the driving force behind Italian politics over the short term, another change in government can be expected in the not-too-distant future. The current volatility in the rate of inflation, therefore, will undoubtedly continue.

Units of Measure

Italy uses the metric system of measurement. Property is measured in a variety of ways, by the number of rooms or in square or cubic metres according to the purpose of the valuation.

---

2. *The Economist* (July 1996).

Legislation

Legislative Act 372 *(Legge No. 372)* issued in 1978 and all subsequent amendments deal with the relevant aspects of property rental, freehold ownership, contracts, and contract renewals. This legislation should be studied prior to undertaking any property valuation.

Leases

The usual term for lease contracts is six years. By law, the right of renewal for another six-year term is automatic. After 12 years, however, the contract cannot be automatically renewed and must be formally renegotiated. (For further discussion, the reader is directed to the section on valuation and sale of a property with a tenant in occupancy at the end of this chapter.)

With regard to alienation (the right to transfer property), a tenant may dispose of a lease only as part of the business, i.e., when the business is sold as a going concern.

General Property Concepts

The concept of market value is fundamental to property valuation in Italy. For historical and social reasons, there is a divergence between the market value and the actual value attributable to property.

The definition of market value in Italy is:

> The most likely price at which a property can be transferred from a willing vendor (seller) to a willing purchaser, both being fully aware of the possible uses and characteristics of the property after being put on a competitive market for a reasonable length of time, provided that all the conditions and prerequisites for a favourable transfer exist.

This definition of market value may vary according to the circumstances of the valuation.

Players in the Real Estate Market

In Italy, as in most continental countries, valuation of property may be carried out by practitioners of any of a number of disciplines. Typically, these practitioners are architects, engineers, lawyers, and entrepreneurs. There are, however, real estate agencies *(agenzie immobiliari)*, which deal with the sale, purchase, and letting (leasing) of commercial property. In large commercial cities such as Milan, British surveying or North American appraisal practices are followed by the *agenzie immobiliari*.

Several government offices and bodies are charged with the administration and control of real estate. The functions of these offices require some explanation because they are heavily involved in valuation matters through property registration and taxation. A brief description of relevant offices follows.

- The Italian real estate registry *(Conservatoria dei Registri Immobiliari)* logs and maintains all official records of property transactions. It has a central office and a small number of regional offices throughout the country. Real estate once registered has a certain date *(data certa)* which includes the official registry date and time. Without such a date, a transaction cannot be considered completed and this can have a severe influence on its ownership and valuation. For example, if a vendor has agreed to sell the same property concurrently to two or more buyers, the first buyer to secure a *data certa* becomes the official owner of the property. Any other purchaser, whose ownership position is not officially recognized, must then take the necessary legal action to recover purchase monies.

- The local branch of the Italian Ministry of Finance *(Ufficio del Registro)* is responsible for property and general business taxation. It is involved in property valuation and the establishment of standards relating to the property tax and property purchase tax. The *data certa* can also be provided here, but the property transaction is usually registered at the *conservatoria*.

- A *notaio* is a professional essential to all property transactions. *Notaios* may be private agents or hold public office. There is a regulated number of *notaios*, and all property transactions are channelled through them, whether directly or through a solicitor (lawyer). *Notaios* are responsible for holding all documents for property and business transactions, e.g., contacts, deeds, private wills. After checking their contents for validity, the *notaio* certifies that such documents are true and original and when required, will register documents at the *conservatoria*. All registrations must go through a *notaio* as this official is the only agent recognised by the *conservatoria*. The *notaio* may also release copies, abstracts, or certificates of held documents, which are considered legally valid and original unless proven otherwise in court.

- The government property register *(catasto)* holds all plans and descriptions for each individual property, i.e., it references and describes all the rooms as well as all structural and nonstructural partitions within a property. Property is classified according to five major groups based on the type of use, quality, or location. These groups are labeled A to E with subgroups within each category. Group A consists of residential and private offices. Group B includes public offices. Group C is commercial property (e.g., shops, stores, warehouses, laboratories, garages, stables). Group D covers special-use buildings (e.g., factories, hotels, banks, sports buildings), and Group E includes nontaxable buildings (e.g., churches, cemeteries, railway stations). The *catasto* is maintained by a number of technical tax officers *(uffici tecnici erariali)* who are also responsible for the valuation of property for tax purposes.

Taxes

Only those taxes that have a direct impact on property valuation are considered here. These taxes relate to the criteria for and purpose of property valuation. Although others taxes exist, they do not directly affect valuation.

Tax on Property Value

The major tax affecting the value of property is the council tax (assessment) on real property *(imposta communale sugli immobili,* ICI), which is a tax on the ownership of property. The ICI took effect on 1 January 1993 and is not a tax on property income, but rather a tax on the value of property in each tax year. Many consider it to be a "tax on wealth" although the government would certainly not acknowledge this idea. The ICI is charged in addition to any tax on the income from the property and is paid by the person in immediate possession of the property. When property is leased, however, the owner is responsible for paying the ICI and is therefore taxed twice on the same property (i.e., through both the tax on property income and the ICI).

To understand how to calculate the ICI, the components of the tax must be understood. The tax is based on a notional (nominal) income or rent recorded for the property in the *catasto.* To calculate the ICI, property group categories A through D are given ratios. Groups A, B, C (excluding A10 and C1) have a ratio of 100, D and A10 (offices) have a ratio of 50, and C1 (shops) has a ratio of 34.

A notional rent is attributed to a "basic unit," which may be either a building, part of a building, or land devoted to only one officially recognised use. The notional rent is calculated based on the total anticipated income and the number of rooms or square/cubic metres in the property. For example, the notional rent for an office unit is based on the number of rooms, while the notional rent for shops is calculated per square metre.

Each year the city council determines an ICI council (assessment) ratio which reflects the financial needs of the council. This rate varies from 0.4% to 0.6%.

The ICI notional value is calculated as follows:

Notional value = notional income × property category ratio (e.g., A10 = 50)

The ICI may be calculated as follows:

ICI = notional value × ICI council ratio (0.4% or 0.6%)

Sample ICI Tax Calculation

Property category A10 (office) with 6 rooms. Notional income of Lit. 1,025,000 per room.

$$\text{Total notional income} = 6 \text{ rooms} \times \text{Lit. } 1,025,000$$
$$= \text{Lit. } 6,150,000$$

$$\text{ICI notional value} = \text{Lit. } 6,150,000 \times 50$$
$$= \text{Lit. } 307,500,000$$

$$\text{ICI tax} = \text{Lit. } 307,500,000 \times .004$$
$$= \text{Lit. } 1,230,000$$

Source : Francesco Tamborrino, *How the ICI Is Applied (Como si Applica l'ICI)*, 1994

It should be noted that for tax purposes notional income and notional value are calculated according to invented parameters. In reality, the actual market income and value can be either greater or less than those recorded in the *catasto*. In such cases, a property owner may pay more or less tax than is actually owed. This is significant in the valuation of commercial property because values may be heavily influenced by the ICI tax requirement.[3]

Taxes on Property Purchase

Stamp duty *(tassa di bollo)* is a fixed sum which varies from year to year and from administration to administration. Since this tax has a number of variants, it is impossible to quote a general rule of thumb for its calculation. A *notaio* with access to all relevant information, laws, and local tax requirements does the calculation.

The value-added tax *(imposta sul valore aggiunto, IVA)* is a national levy which currently varies between 4% and 19% according to the type of transaction and property. The percentages cited apply to the tax year 1994-1995.[4]

The registration duty *(imposta di registro)* can either be a fixed fee or a percentage fee depending on the type and use of the property.[5]

---

3. For further reference the reader is directed to the ICI Act. *Decreto Legislativo No. 504/1992.*

4. Francisco Tamborrino, *How the ICI is Applied (Como si Applica l'ICI)*, 1994. For further reference the reader is directed to Act No. 243/1993, D.P.R. 643/1972 *et relata.*

5. For further information, the reader should refer to the legislation regarding the value added tax.

Tax on Property Sale

Another tax to be consdered is the tax on the increase in property values *(imposta sull'incremento di valore degli immobili, INVIM)*. Until January 1, 2003, whoever sells a property purchased or inherited before January 1, 1993 must pay the INVIM when signing the deed at the *notaio*. Only the vendor (seller) is liable for the INVIM. Exceptions, however, can be found in the relevant legislation. The INVIM is a tax on the difference between the purchase value and the value at the time of sale. The computation of INVIM, which is extremely complex, is usually performed by a *notiao*.

As with other taxes, such as the ICI, it is usual for the actual sale price of a property to be concealed in order to lower the taxes to be paid. This obviously adds to the difficulties of obtaining true market values for Italian commercial properties.[6]

Methods of Property Valuation

The formal methods of property valuation that characterize current practice in Italy are discussed below. This section should be read in conjunction with the section titled, "Other Matters for Consideration." The procedures described below may vary from region to region.

As the starting point in his 1992 book on valuation in Italy, *How the Value of Real Estate Is Calculated (Come si Calcola il Valore degli Immobili),* Francesco Tamborrino suggests that the logic of valuation take the following factors into account:

   a) general financial elements, e.g., ratios of average personal income to purchasing power or projected property income to development and building cost;

   b) the specific elements of the property, e.g., age, quality and location;

   c) income capitalisation;

   d) exceptional elements which may either be characteristics of the property (or parts thereof) differing from typical characteristics, or external factors such as rental legislation or planning regulations that apply to the property subject to the valuation;

   e) known elements such as the building costs for new properties and market estimates regularly published by official sources.

In Italy, as in other European countries and the U.S., three approaches to valuation (sales comparison, income capitalisation, and cost) are understood

---

6. For further reference, the reader is again directed to Act No. 243/1993.

and applied. Methodology, however, may be modified or adapted to the purpose of the property valuation or because of tax implications. The three approaches are briefly described here.

Sales Comparison Approach

As its name suggests, the sales comparison approach is based on a comparison of the property being valued and other, similar properties recently purchased or sold in the same market or in competitive markets. The application of the approach relies on the availability of comparable market data. Unfortunately, application of this method in Italy is seriously hampered by the lack of true market evidence due to the confidential nature of property transactions. This confidentiality stems from Italian culture, society, and fiscal considerations.

The following items must be considered in applying the sales comparison approach:

- comparative data
- type of transaction (conditions of sale)
- location of the properties
- physical condition of the properties
- use of the properties
- maintenance of the properties
- replacement cost[7]

In Italy, a large amount of data on property transactions is collected and made available through the national statistics office, ISTAT, and industry magazines such as *Consulente Immobiliare*. This information is processed and tabulated as market estimates and ratios, which are used as a preliminary means of valuing property. These market estimates are also used to make adjustments in the income capitalisation approach.

Income Capitalisation Approach

To apply the income capitalisation approach, anticipated cash flows from the operation of the property are capitalised. In simple terms, value is derived from either the capitalisation of net income or the application of a multiplier (obtained through comparison with similar properties or other investments) to net income. The method reflects the return of income on invested capital.

---

7. L. Civelli (1992).

Consideration of the following items is imperative in applying the income approach:

- net profit (future or historic)
- term of leases
- *IRR*
- initial yield
- growth rates for income and expenditures
- inflation
- end yield
- DCF analysis[8]

In Italy a multiplier of 20 is generally applied to net income before taxes. However, this simple approach may not indicate the "right value," i.e., the amount a purchaser would pay for the property, because income is often extremely variable and not necessarily related to the current market. To cite Francesco Tamborrino:

> it may occur, as the consequence of a block of flats (an apartment building) being put to alternative use either as residential or office space, that the resulting incomes to the property when let (leased) will differ. The resulting income to the building under the residential use may be Lit. 700,000 but under the office use, Lit. 4,000,000. The capitalisation of income under the former use will indicate a value of Lit. 14,000,000 but under the latter use, a value of Lit. 80,000,000. This indication is not an acceptable value .....

Whenever this method of income capitalisation is applied, the resulting value should be averaged with market estimates (discussed above) as follows:

(value indicated by income capitalisation + market estimates)/2

Cost Approach

The cost approach is based on the principle of substitution. It defines the maximum value of a property, which is the cost to develop a new property with similar utility to that of the property being valued.[9]

There are two main bases of calculation, namely replacement cost using the

---

8. Ibid.
9. In other words, the cost approach sets the upper limit of value.

same materials, design, and standards[10] and replacement cost using current technologies and materials.

The higher value indicated by these two cost calculation methods is selected, and deductions are made for depreciation, i.e., physical deterioration and functional obsolescence.

Consideration of the following items is imperative in applying the cost approach:

- replacement cost
- land value
- physical depreciation
- standard life and residual life[11]
- functional obsolescence (considering the costs of maintenance, energy, and replacements)
- economic obsolescence (the difference between net realised profit and net anticipated profit)[12]

As in the application of sales comparison and income capitalisation, the Italian valuer is able to refer to ISTAT and other industry tables for statistical information. Usually, cost approach valuations are based on such statistical data.

The practical application of cost approach methods is illustrated in the examples that follow. The logic for determining value may be set out in three steps:

- *First value.* Any previous value estimate that is available must be updated to current value. Updating may be done through the use of building cost indexes or ratios. The updated estimate may then be adjusted for the age, obsolescence, or rental characteristics of the property. Appropriate tables are available for reference.
- *Second value.* A current value may be calculated using replacement cost or residual life methods. The valuer refers to appropriate tables for the calculation of building costs, rental adjustments, etc.
- *Third value.* A market value is developed using appropriate market estimate statistical data and coefficients of variance from which an overall coefficient

---

10. In North American usage, this is equivalent to *reproduction cost.*
11. In North American usage, the equivalent terms are *total economic life expectancy* and *remaining economic life.*
12. L. Civelli (1992).

is developed, i.e., a coefficient to measure the overall variance from the average, characteristic property.

One or more of these methods may be applied, according to the circumstances of the valuation. If more than one method is applied, then the common practice is to divide the sum of the valuations by the number of values, in this case three, to achieve the estimated value.

Example 1

The property being valued is a workshop. The year of the valuation is 1991. The property is located on the outskirts of Turin. The building is 22 years old and classified as of average type, in satisfactory condition. The property was new when it was bought in 1969 for Lit. 16,000,000. The size is 200 m²/700 m³ (in theory, it could contain 7.777 rooms). It is located on the lower ground floor of a residential building and has its own entrance via a ramp. The property was vacant at the time of the valuation

First Value

The valuer refers to the index of residential building costs, the Residential Building Cost Rate (Table 3) and an Age Correction Coefficient (Table 4.2).

16,000,000/0.864 (building cost index for 1969)
× 14.43 (building cost index 1991)
× 0.80 (age coefficient for 22 yrs.) = Lit. 213,777,770

Second Value

The valuer estimates building value by a residual life method, referring to Building Cost (Table 4.1) and Residual Values of Residential Buildings (Table 4.2).

388,000 (building cost in 1991) × 700 m³
× 0.80 (Table 4.2, for 22 yrs.)   217,280,000
7.777 (number of rooms it could theoretically contain)
× 32,930,000 (Table 5, Theoretical Value of the
Developable Rooms)   256,096,610
Total 473,367,610 × 0.80 (coefficient for laboratories
and lower-ground floor workshops)   473,367,610

Lit. 378,694,088

Third Value

The valuer refers to Table 9 (Prices per m² in Council [assessment] Areas excluding Rome and Milan), Table 13 (Coefficients for Age, Quality, and Condition of Buildings Other Than Retail Shops), and Table 15 (Coefficients for Use and Location within a Building).

The overall coefficient of variance is determined by multipliying the two above-cited coefficients: 0.70 (for workshops 10 to 20 years old, of average type, and in satisfactory condition) × 0.80 (for lower ground floor with access via a ramp). The resulting overall coefficient is 0.56.

2,750,000 (from Table 9) × 1.07 (geographical correction)
× 200 m² × 0.56 (overall coefficient) = Lit. 329,560,000

Finally, the three value indications are averaged.

(213,777,770 + 378,694,088 + 329,560,000)/3 = Lit. 307,343,950

Example 2

The property being valued is office space in a block of flats (apartment building). The year of the valuation is 1991. The property is located on the outskirts of Burgamo, a town of between 100,000 and 250,000 inhabitants. The property is part of a luxury-quality block in good condition. It is 16 years old and was built in 1975 .The size is 150 m². No previous estimate of value or sale price is available. The property is located on the upper ground floor and was vacant at the time of the valuation.

First, the valuer calculates a global coefficient of variance.

0.80 (from Table 13 for office space in a 16-year old, luxury block in good condition) × 0.90 (from Table 15 for upper ground floor location) × 0.90 (also from Table 15 for an office in a peripheral location) = an overall coefficient of variance of 0.648

Value of the Office Space in 1991

1,800,000 (the 1991 estimate from Table 7, Council [assessment] Areas with Less Than 250,000 Inhabitants, of Average Importance, with Tourism) × 1.07 (for the geographical correction) × 150 m² × 0.648 = Lit. 187,207,200

The methods described and illustrated above are representative of practice in Italy, where value estimates are developed based on statistical data on costs, prices, and coefficients. However, there is a trend toward a more market-oriented valuation approach based on Anglo-Saxon methodology and experience. Some of the larger property companies and institutions are now using British property agents either to perform valuation assignments on their behalf or to advise them on appropriate methods of valuation.

Other Matters for Consideration

In Italy, it is difficult to value property without considering tax implications because the property tax system takes into account various criteria which are likely to affect any valuation. These tax implications govern the actual method and form of valuation.

Although the methods of valuation illustrated above are in common use, the four issues discussed below also require attention.

Market Value vs. Value for Tax Purposes

The market value of a property is usually not stated in contracts or official documentation so the owner can avoid tax liabilities. It is extremely difficult, therefore, for a property valuer to establish reliable sources as references.

The value quoted in a contract of sale may state the value at a much lower level than the true market value. The *Uffici del Registro,* however, is not unaware of this tactic to evade taxes, and local offices are empowered to serve notice on the parties to a sale, apprising them of the "true" calculated market value of the property and requesting further tax payment. If the difference between the value quoted in the contract and the market value is greater than 25%, a penalty or fine is charged to the parties to the transaction.

A further ploy to avoid official investigations may then make use of recommended valuation techniques/methods. For example, one means of preventing the *Ufficio del Registro* from checking contract valuations is to state a figure which is not less than the notional (nominal) value. Therefore, a shop (category C1) with a notional income of Lit. 10,000,000 multiplied by the ratio of 34 has a notional value of Lit. 340,000,000, even if the actual market value is Lit. 640,000,000. Assuming that the total purchase taxes account for 10% of the contract value, the *Ufficio del Registro* would expect a tax payment of not less that Lit. 34,000,000. It is recommended, therefore, that the contract value be stated as Lit. 340,000,000. Thus, the contract value bears no resemblance to the actual market value. Obviously this sort of valuation method cannot be used by purchasers who, for various reasons, must declare full values and are unable to hide part of the purchase price.

Valuation and Sale of a Property with a Tenant in Occupancy

If a property being valued for sale is occupied by a tenant, there is a legal requirement that the vendor (seller) inform the tenant of the terms and conditions of the sale, including the sale price. The tenant, thereupon, has the right of priority to purchase the property at that price or the equivalent market value. If the tenant refuses to exercise the right to purchase because the price is too high or for some other reason, and the vendor subsequently offers the property to a buyer at a lower figure and secures a sale, the tenant may step in and exercise his right to purchase.

Value in Vacant Possession (as Vacant) vs. Value with a Tenant in Occupancy

Although for tax purposes value in vacant possession and value with a tenant in occupancy will be virtually the same, in the market the value in vacant possession (as vacant) will invariably be higher. This may be peculiar to Italy where a large proportion of property is of mixed-use, i.e., residential and office units combined within the same block (apartment building). Retail shops are also highly integrated into blocks of flats. For tax purposes, it invariably benefits a business to form an association with a residential accommodation.

Rules Governing a Residential or Mixed-Use Block (*Regulamento di Condominio*)

A block of flats or, more generally, a building consisting of many property units as defined by the *catasto* and owned by a number of different individuals, is usually governed by a set of rules called *regulamento di condominio*. Such rules may prohibit the operation of certain businesses or determine the way in which a business is managed. These rules may either complement or override council planning regulations (municipal zoning) and may have an impact on property value and development potential. They should be investigated in depth.

Bibliography

Civelli, L. (1992).

Montagnana, Manfredo. Chapter 9 "Italy" in *European Valuation Practice.* London: E & FN Spon (an imprint of Chapman & Hall), 1996.

Tamborrino, Francesco. *Come si Calcola il Valore degli Immobili.* (Milan: Pirola, 1992).

Tamborrino, Francesco. *Como si Applica l'ICI.* (Milan: A. Giuffre, 1994).

Czech Republic

Jaromir Ryska, PhD
Martin R. Carr, AVLE (Val.)
Ivana Janovska, M.Sc.

Since 1975 Jaromir Ryska has been an official (sworn-in) appraiser of the Czech government. He holds an M.Sc. from the School of Civil Engineering of the Prague Technical University (1969) and a PhD from the Construction Research Institute in Prague (1973). In 1980 Ryska became an associate professor at the Prague Academy of Applied Art. He has been a Fulbright fellow at the University of Illinois (1991) and has served as Secretary General of the Czech Chamber of Appraisers (1993) and the Czech Committee of Valuers (1995). Ryska is currently the director of the Valuation Institute in Prague and on the faculty of the Prague University of Economics.

Martin R. Carr is the Director of Central and Eastern European Real Estate Services for Price Waterhouse in the Czech Republic. He holds a bachelor's degree from Auckland University in New Zealand (1989) and an advanced certificate in real estate from the Royal Melbourne Institute of Technology in Australia (1991). Carr is an associate member of the Australian Institute of Valuers.

Ivana Janovska is a property consultant with Price Waterhouse in the Czech Republic. She holds an M.Sc. from the Prague University of Economics (1992).

The Czech Republic consists of the Bohemian basin, drained by the Labe (Elbe) and Vltava (Moldau) rivers, the Bohemian and Moravian hill region, and the Morava valley. The country is ringed by mountains on the west (the Ore or Erz mountains) and the north/northeast (the Sudety [Sudeten] and Beskid ranges). Principal cities are Prague, Brno, Ostrava, Plzeň and Olomouc.

Political Structure

Prior to November 1989, the Czech Republic was part of the Czech and Slovak Federation of Czechoslovakia, which was under the control of a centralised communist government. Since the Velvet Revolution in November of 1989, there has been considerable political and economic change, including not only the election of a democratic government committed to the pursuit of capitalism, but also the split of the federation on January 1, 1993 into the Czech and Slovak Republics, two politically and increasingly economically separate countries.

The Czech Republic is a parliamentary democracy with a bicameral legislature known as the National Council *(Národná Rada)*. The lower house, the Chamber of Deputies *(Poslanecka Sněmovna),* has 200 members; the upper house, the Senate *(Senat),* has 81 members. Following the general elections held every four years, the presidium of the National Council appoints the prime minister and the Cabinet *(Vláda),* which wields the most power in the government. The president is elected by both chambers of Parliament.

The electoral system is based on a technically complicated form of proportional representation, with members of Parliament representing specific regions or districts.

Given the significant change in the form of government, there has been a major overhaul of most legislation. Although much of the new legislation has yet to be implemented, the increasing pace of legislative change is facilitated by the Supreme Court, which is responsible for uniform interpretation of Czech law.

Most laws governing real estate are formulated at the central government level, although local authorities assume primary responsibility for town planning and the imposition and policing of local bylaws.

Czech town planning is a well-developed system of land use regulation and control and is enforced throughout most of the republic. However, in light of the previously centralised policies of land management, the planning process in most major cities is now being reviewed or repealed.

Owners of real estate in the Czech Republic have not been subject to any direct taxation or rating (assessments) of their registered interests in real estate. However, according to legislation passed in 1995, which is to be implemented in 1997 (and every three years thereafter), all registered owners will be required to file a tax return on their real estate assets. The real estate tax will be paid on a quarterly basis, directly to the local governing authority.

Economic Overview

Following several years of negative growth and high levels of inflation, the Czech Republic has reassumed its position of economic leadership in Central and Eastern Europe. A combination of tightly managed, but well-selected, economic policies including privatisation has led to the gradual freeing up of local industry from centralised control, conciliation with the labour unions, improvement in labour efficiency, and a progressive increase in foreign investment. The development of the private sector, the growth in exports, relatively low inflation, and an undervalued currency have allowed the Czech Republic to register consecutive trade surpluses and upgrade its Standard and Poor's rating from BBB– to BBB+.

Improving macroeconomic conditions for the Czech real estate market have increased the amount of capital directed to the acquisition and redevelopment of green field (outlying) land and older buildings. The latter have been adapted into modern accommodations and commercial (warehouse and office) facilities. Capital investment and the restitution process, by which previously state-owned land is returned to the original (pre-1948) landowners, have established a firm foundation for the real estate market.

Owing to the patterns of corporate investment, this newly emerging real estate market is heavily localised in the capital city of Prague and the secondary cities. Even within these markets, however, there is at times little evidence of genuine transactional, rental, or development activity. It is difficult, therefore, to ascertain discernible market trends and parameters.

Nevertheless, over the course of the next 10 years, the confidence of foreign developers and investors in the leading local Czech markets is expected to improve dramatically, providing the necessary impetus for the development of a broader, more mature market nationwide.

Property Rights

During the rule of the Communist Party between 1948 and 1989, the right to use property, irrespective of property ownership, was introduced under various guises. For example, the Civil Code of 1950 permitted construction of a house (structure) on a plot of land belonging to someone else (e.g., the state), provided the right to use such a plot had been established.

The enactment of new laws and the amendment of existing legislation have brought a return to democratic principles and private ownership rights. Under the Constitutional Act of 1990, all rights inherent in ownership were again recognized. The corresponding part of the civil code was amended and Sections 123 and 124 now read: "An owner is entitled, within the bounds of the law, to hold (possess) the object of his ownership, to make use of it, to enjoy its fruits and profits, and to dispose of it. All owners have identical rights and duties (obligations) and are accorded equal legal protection."

There is no comprehensive act covering real estate. The civil code includes fundamental provisions on the acquisition of real estate ownership and on leases and subleases of flats (apartments) and nonresidential space (premises). Civil law involves private rights, property (things), and rights to property interests. Leases of flats and nonresidential space fall under civil law. Property may be personal (things movable) or real (immovable). Immovables include plots of land and structures attached to the land by a solid foundation. Ownership of property may be acquired under a purchase contract, a donative contract (gift), or other types of contracts; by inheritance; as the result of a ruling by a governmental authority (agency); or on the basis of other facts stipulated by law.

The Land Act, or Act on the Modification of Ownership Relationships for Land and Other Agricultural Property of 1993, covers the restitution of plots of land and other agricultural property. The ownership of real estate has been recorded in two different places: between April 1, 1964 and December 31, 1992, ownership was recorded in real estate registers kept by District Offices of Cartography and Geodesy; since January 1, 1993, ownership has been recorded in real estate cadastres. Entries in real estate cadastres may take the form of the registration or recording of ownership, a note recognizing ownership, or the deletion of registration upon transfer of ownership.

The restitution process, which was technically completed on December 31, 1993, has ensured settlement of those real estate assets that could be practically returned to private ownership and for which valid claims were made. Properties that could not be returned because of their inclusion as part of important public or private facilities were retained by the state (or private entity) with the original owner receiving either compensation or a suitable alternative.

Those involved in constructing a house or other building are required to follow the provisions of the Area Planning Act and Building Code. Obtaining planning and building permits is a lengthy process which can last more than a year. In addition, the following taxes are levied on real estate:

- The transfer tax on real estate paid by the seller upon sale of a property is fixed at 5% of the administrative value under the Ministry of Finance decree on prices (Decree No. 178/94 and the last edition of No. 295/95) or the market price agreed upon in the contract of sale between the buyer and seller, whichever is higher.

- The annual real estate tax is set at a very low rate. The base for computing this tax is the land or building area multiplied by the unit price for the land or building as set by the state. The tax is currently fixed at under 0.1% of the market price of the property. The tax is computed by the owner of the land and/or building.

Currently, a property law modeled upon that of Denmark is being drafted and is scheduled to be voted upon in the Chamber of Deputies in 1997 or early 1998. If passed, it would go into effect in 1999.

Language

Czech is the official language of the country. Most of the population is fluent in a second language, typically German or Russian, which was the compulsory second language during the period of Communist rule. French is less popular, but is still widely spoken in academic and cultural circles, particularly by the older generation.

English is becoming increasingly popular, especially among those under 30 years of age. While English is not likely to displace German, it is expected to become the second most widely spoken foreign language in the next two generations.

Currency

The Czech crown (*koruna*/Kč) is the monetary unit. The crown is divided into 100 heller *(haler)*. Most commercial real estate deals are transacted in German marks (DMs), while sales and valuations of residential and agricultural real estate are typically recorded in Czech crowns.

The long-term exchange rates for the German mark and the United States dollar to the Czech crown have been 1:17.5 and 1:28, respectively. With increasingly high levels of foreign reserves, there has been significant pressure to revalue the crown to prevent an increase in inflation. It is likely that a revaluation will take place.

Units of Measure

The Czech Republic uses the metric system. Real estate sizes are quoted in square metres, although appraisals often use cubic metres. The cubic metre is mainly used for cost approach appraisals, as required by Decrees No. 178/94 and No. 295/95.

Rental income and associated operating expenses are stated in German marks per square metre of lettable (leasable) floor area per month. Values and prices are quoted per square metre of net or gross building area (for improvements) or site area (for land).

Inflation

Inflation, which previously ran as high as 30%, has recently been reduced to near single-digit rates. Inflation was expected to stay at or around 10% during 1995-1996. Inflation rates below 10% are projected for the remainder of the 1990s, with a rate as low as 5% projected for 1998-2000.

Most rental contracts are indexed to the German cost of living index (*Lebenshaltungskostenindex*) or CPI since rents are linked to German mark equivalents. The German CPI is used to index rents in all the former socialist countries of Central and Eastern Europe.

Few, if any, valuations or development appraisals employ discounted cash flow (DCF) techniques, given future market and economic uncertainties. Inflation is rarely considered as a variable when undertaking assessments.

Typical Lease Structure

Office

Although larger tenancies are usually subject to longer leases, the average lease term ranges from three to seven years. Most leases have a three- or five-year initial term with several, two-year option terms thereafter.

All leases are drafted on a net basis. Tenants are liable for the payment of all apportioned operating costs, e.g., electricity, cleaning, insurance, security, and management. Such costs generally escalate in line with local inflation or contract prices.

Lease incentives are being offered in Prague due to a recent increase in the supply of available space. Typically, the incentives take the form of one- to three-month rent-free periods or, alternatively, fitting-out (finish-out) allowances limited to the cost of partitions and carpets. Incentives are unknown elsewhere in the Czech Republic.

Leasing commissions are calculated as a percentage of the first year's stipulated rent and are paid by the landlord upon lease commencement. Fees range from 12.5% to 15.0%.

Retail

As in the office market, the larger the retail unit, the longer the lease. Retail leases are usually no more than one to three years in duration, although five-year leases are becoming more common for prime locations in Prague.

There are no examples of modern shopping centres from which to assess anchor tenant lease terms, although the several centres that are under construction are demanding minimum terms of five to 10 years.

Again, all leases are drafted on a net basis, with tenants liable for apportioned operating costs, e.g., electricity, cleaning, insurance, security, water, and management. These costs generally keep pace with local inflation or contract prices.

Lease incentives are not offered on retail properties. Further, there is not enough data to estimate tenant turnover (volume of business) or the extent of percentage rental agreements.

As in the office market, leasing commissions on retail property are calculated as a percentage of the first year's rent and are paid by the landlord upon lease commencement. Fees range from 12.5% to 15.0%.

Industrial

There is no discernible rental market for industrial properties in the Czech Republic and there are no new or modern accommodations. Leases for existing, older buildings have generally been for one- to three-year terms with the tenant paying a net rent.

There are no lease incentives on industrial properties. Leasing charges are the same as in the office and retail markets.

Valuation Standards

In the Czech Republic, valuations are carried out by two types of practitioners: those who have qualified and are registered in a western country (typically, the United Kingdom, the United States, or Australia) and Czech valuers who qualify and are experienced locally.

Foreign valuers are generally guided by their own institutional codes of ethics and performance and respond to prevailing market expectations and demands. Most valuers adhere to the Code of Professional Conduct of the Royal Institution of Chartered Surveyors (RICS) or the comparable professional standards followed by German experts, who are registered with the German Industrial and Trade Chamber. All such standards stipulate minimum service requirements.

In regard to Czech valuers, however, there are two levels of professional regulation and control, and many Czech valuers are subject to both systems.

Most valuers are involved in the assessment of market value, as defined in international guidelines such as those prepared by the International Valuation Standards Committee (IVSC). All such valuers are associates of the Chamber of Sworn-in Valuers (Komora soudnich znalcù) in Prague, the Czech Committee of Valuers (Český komitét znalcù/CKZ) in Prague, the Czech Chamber of Appraisers (Česka komora odhadcù majetku/ČKOM) in Prague, or the Association of Sworn-in Valuers and Valuers (Asociace znalců a odhadců) in Brno. All of these groups have guidelines for conduct and codes of ethics and two are members of TEGOVA and IVSC.

The second level of regulation pertains to those valuers who are known as *court experts* (i.e., included in the list of experts kept by the Ministry of Justice). Court experts typically are the most experienced and qualified Czech valuers. When performing their duties as experts, they are bound to comply with the regulations set by the Ministry of Finance.

Licensing/Certification

Foreign valuers are usually fully experienced, qualified, and registered with a regulatory professional group in their home country. Many find it necessary to fulfill continued professional development requirements to satisfy technical and professional standards.

Sworn-in valuers, the first type of valuers discussed above, are appointed under Act No. 36/67. In order to be appointed, the valuer must be suitably educated (e.g., having completed postgraduate studies at the University of Economics in Prague or VÚT, the Technical University in Brno) and must demonstrate a high level of practical experience and integrity.

Valuers who wish to become members of ČKZ and ČKOM have to satisfy an expert committee by demonstrating that they are experienced in their chosen field and that they understand the ethical codes of ČKZ and ČKOM. The purpose of the examination is to test the applicant on his or her knowledge of acts and decrees concerning real estate, market/economic principles, and disciplines relating to construction technology. The ethical codes of ČKZ and ČKOM are similar to those of various foreign valuer associations. ČKZ and ČKOM are attempting to enforce the certification of valuers according to corresponding standards in the European Community.

Appraisal Reporting Requirements

There are no established institutional or legal requirements for valuers practising in the Czech Republic. Both foreign and local valuers adhere to the guidelines of professional institutes such as the RICS and/or to market demands.

Most appraisal reports will explain the nature of the assignment, review all salient physical and legal issues regarding the property in question, elaborate on the specific approach(es) to value used, and analyze the available data. Reports usually include supporting appendices as well as a statement of all necessary assumptions, limiting conditions, and disclaimers.

Approaches to Valuation

The Czech Republic has one of the oldest appraisal systems in the world, dating back to the 1860s. This system continued to develop during the interwar period up to the Munich agreement of 1938 and, subsequently, the establishment of the communist regime in 1948. During the ensuing 40 years, the valuation profession was progressively disbanded and, more importantly, the methodology and compilation of data required to determine market value were lost.

In 1939 the government issued Decree No. 269/39 which called for the creation of lists of sworn-in experts, including individuals appointed as asset valuers. These experts were mandated to prepare databases outlining the prices of real estate as of 1939 when *stop-prices* were declared.

The profession of sworn-in expert/valuer of assets was abolished by the communist regime in 1959. During this period of nationalisation, the need for asset valuers disappeared. Nevertheless, the state realised that it was impossible to determine the transfer fees on real estate exclusively on the basis of statements made by the seller and purchaser. Consequently, Decree No. 47/59 was issued to specify the obligation of local councils to calculate the price of transferred real estate. This decree established a standard procedure for calculating the value of property, although it must be noted that the unit price for improved land was determined on a centralised administrative basis. Since this decree imposed another uncompensated obligation on local councils, little interest was shown in carrying out valuations legally.

In 1967, Act No. 36/67 was passed to reestablish the profession of sworn-in experts/asset valuers. Experts appointed in accordance with this act were to guarantee that the administrative price of real estate would be exactly determined according to the then-existing decrees issued by the Ministry of Finance and that the state would not be cheated on the collection of transfer taxes.

The valuers appointed were usually graduates from universities or technical institutes (typically in civil engineering, water management, etc.). Their work consisted of assessing administrative values based on uniform, state-determined prices. It is worth noting that there was no difference between the price of a property in Prague and a similar property in a rural or regional location.

In the absence of free market forces, there was no identifiable marketplace and, consequently, valuers saw no need to challenge predetermined valuation methodologies or established limitations on prices and values. Over the past five years, however, there has been sufficient development in the economy and real estate markets at large to allow valuers to return to market-based principles.

Czech valuation experts, therefore, founded ČKOM and ČKZ to facilitate the application of universally accepted, market-based valuation principles to the newly emerging, albeit somewhat limited, Czech market.

The pace of change has been restrained by legislative backlogs and practitioners' inertia. Under current legal requirements, Czech valuers performing assignments for state authorities continue to use statutory valuation techniques which are purely technical and highly artificial approaches for determining value.

The following sections outline the valuation methods required under Czech law, describing their technical aspects and addressing practical concerns of their implementation. In light of the fact that valuation in the Czech Republic is practised on a broader basis by members of ČKOM and ČKZ and by foreign valuers, the most widely used market approaches are also discussed. In time, these approaches will most likely be adopted by all Czech valuers.

Methodology Used in Assessing Property for State Authorities

On 25 August 1994, the Ministry of Finance introduced Decree No. 178/94 regarding the valuation of improvements, land, and water and permanent growth areas (i.e., forests). The decree took effect on November 1, 1994.

The new decree applies to valuations undertaken for the purpose of tax assessments (e.g., inheritance tax, gift tax, real estate transfer tax, income tax, real estate tax), expropriation, and bankruptcy. The decree may also apply in cases where its application is not specifically stipulated by any regulations, typically in accordance with the decision of a government body (a court) or a financial or insurance institution.

The main valuation approaches are discussed below.

Valuation of Buildings

The most basic and widely practised method of valuing buildings is the replacement cost approach. The new decree also allows for valuation via an income or capitalisation approach, though this application is very limited.

Technically, the cost approach is based on unit prices of replacement cost. The new unit of measure is the cubic metre, by which the rate of replacement cost is multiplied. The decree stipulates prices, assuming a standard degree of finish and associated equipment. When the finish and equipment are non-standard, the price is adjusted by an appropriate ratio to obtain a more realistic estimate. Other details which may substantially influence the price of a building (e.g., location) must also be taken into account.

Past experience with the straight-line method of estimating wear and tear has led to the development of an analytical method for estimating deterioration. The new method is based on estimating the useful life of the individual components of the building.

The above methodology applies to production or commercial facilities. The new decree, together with collateral Act No. 72/94, addresses the valuation of apartments by regulating the ownership of apartments and nonresidential areas held in common. The accepted approach for valuing apartments is to determine the cost of the whole building within which the property is situated; the price of the property therefore is estimated as a share of the value of the whole building. This share corresponds to the proportion of floor area in the apartment or nonresidential space in relation to the total floor area of all the apartments and/or nonresidential areas in the building.

Valuation of Land

Land is valued according to its current use, and the decree stipulates that land prices be set in relation to the size of the municipality.

However, for valuing development sites (as opposed to other types of land), the decree provides for a more market-based approach making use of approved price maps which list transacted prices and prices analyzed by a comparative method.

Use, utility connections, and municipality size are decisive factors in analyzing prices via the comparative method. Price maps will continue to be issued by the municipalities as binding regulations and will be updated every year.

Agricultural land is valued in accordance with the productive capacity of the underlying soil, although location may also be significant.

Valuation of Water and Permanent Growth Areas

The method prescribed by the decree represents a new and independent approach to the valuation of water reservoirs, with the value being contingent upon the purpose of the reservoir, its size, and its economic importance.

The value of forest land is based upon the forest type. Value differentiation depends on the specific conditions of production relevant to the subject property, which is a factor closely linked to the soil type.

Permanent growth areas, in particular timber reserves, are valued using a procedure similar to the method employed in valuing forest land.

Internationally Recognised Valuation Methods

Most foreign valuers and members of ČKZ and ČKOM use approaches that have been developed in, and are widely used throughout, Western Europe, North America, and Australia. However, Czech real estate markets are highly localized and few commercial transactions ever occur outside of the capital and leading cities, so it is necessary to be selective in adopting an approach.

The main approaches to valuation are described below.

Given the inefficiencies of the Czech market, a reliable working definition of *market value* had to be adopted to serve as the basic premise for determining value. The definitions used in the Czech Republic are generally the same as those widely employed throughout Western Europe. The definition of value sets forth the key assumptions that the valuer considers when estimating value. While purists may argue that the adoption of these definitions can only lead to misinterpretation of the emerging market, or indeed constitutes an incorrect foundation upon which to estimate value in an economy that has not yet developed an identifiable and broad-based market, it is a practical necessity in conducting reliable and dependable valuations.

The definition typically used is that employed by TEGOVA and IVSC.

Market value is defined as the best price which might reasonably be expected to be obtained for the asset at the date of the valuation, assuming:

- A willing seller
- A reasonable period in which to negotiate a sale, taking into account the nature of the property and the state of the market
- That values will remain static during that period
- That the land and buildings will be freely exposed to the open market
- That no account will be taken of any higher price that might be paid by a purchaser or lessee with a special interest.

Capitalisation Approach

Most foreign and ČKZ- or ČKOM-affiliated valuers are involved in estimating the value of commercial development sites or existing income-producing properties. Valuation of these properties requires an approach that either directly or indirectly relates property value to the potential income of the property.

As elsewhere in the world, income-producing properties in the Czech Republic are bought and sold on the basis of their ability to generate revenue. Accordingly, their value represents the sum of future net benefits discounted to present value.

This valuation approach requires a good working knowledge of the property and the market within which it is physically and economically located. The valuer must accurately forecast income, expense allowances, and any necessary capital items.

In the capitalisation approach, the appraiser estimates the market rent for the income-producing property, from which any nonrecoverable but recurring expenses will be paid. Annual net income is capitalised at an appropriate discount rate to arrive at gross value. Adjustments are then made to the gross value for factors such as rent shortfalls or overage rent and for any necessary capital items. From adjusted gross value, the market value of the property is derived.

The capitalisation approach has shortcomings, particularly in rapidly changing markets where, even over a six-month period, significant fluctuations in rent or discount rates may occur and give rise to major variances in value. Elsewhere such fluctuations are taken into account by using a more explicit form of capitalisation such as discounted cash flow (DCF) analysis. Unfortunately, however, the very uncertainties of the Czech market can riddle a forecast with so many potential inaccuracies that the analysis becomes unreliable. Moreover, both investors and developers acknowledge that DCF analysis is an inappropriate technique for valuation in the Czech Republic.

Capitalisation Example

The following data relates to a newly built, fully leased property let (leased) at market rates. The tenants pay all outgoings (operating expenses) with 100% recovery being achieved. Valuations of commercial real estate such as this are normally calculated in Deutsche Marks (DMs).

Input data

Lettable (leasable) floor area

Offices	3,500 m²
Retail	650 m²
Subtotal	4,150 m²

Car parking

Number of spaces	65

Assumptions

Market rents

Offices	45 DMs per m² per month
Retail	65 DMs per m² per month
Car parking	200 DMs per space per month
Market yield	12.00% in perpetuity

Calculations

Rental income

Offices	1,890,000 DMs
Retail	507,000 DMs
Car parking	156,000 DMs
Total	2,553,000 DMs

Capitalised @ 12.00%

Value	21,275,000 DMs
Rounded	21,300,000 DMs

Sales or Direct Comparison Approach

The sales or direct comparison approach is best used to check the value estimate when income capitalisation has been the primary approach applied. Alternatively, sales comparison may be used as the primary approach to value income-producing property for which there is little or no data on rents and capitalisation rates. In addition, sales comparison is generally used to value non-revenue-producing real estate such as residential properties.

With this method a value is derived through comparison of the sale or asking prices for similar properties, typically expressed as unit prices, usually price per square metre of net or gross building area or, in the case of vacant land, per square metre of site area.

Adjustments must be made for differences between the subject property and the comparable sale properties. Differences to be adjusted for include location, building quality, the security of lease covenants and terms, development potential, and market trends.

In the Czech market, where the supply of reliable information is limited, it is often necessary to investigate critical data such as land or building areas, the date of sale, and the conditions of the sale more thoroughly. Without making extensive inquiries, the valuer may be unable to compare properties on a similar basis and the resultant value may be unreliable.

The accepted bases of measurement are net lettable (leasable) area for offices, gross lettable (leasable) area for retail space, and gross building area for warehouses. Development sites are valued on the basis of total site area.

Sales or Direct Comparison Example

The property is a regular parcel of level land with industrial zoning. Of the five comparables sales analyzed, three were undeveloped parcels with zoning for mixed retail/industrial uses in superior locations; the remaining two sales were partially improved, industrially zoned sites nearby that had been redeveloped for manufacturing purposes. Again, value is calculated in Deutsche Marks (DMs).

Input data

Land area	12,450 m²
Allowable floor area to land area ratio	0.45:1
Allowable floor area	5,602.5 m²

Assumptions

Value per m² of land area	1,000 DMs per m²
Value per m² of allowable floor area	2,300 DMs per m²

Calculations

Comparison per m² of land area	12,450 × 1000	12,450,000 DMs
Comparison per m² of allowable fl. area	5,602.5 × 2,300	12,885,750 DMs
Rounded		12,900,000 DMs
Concluded value		12,500,000 DMs

Depreciated Replacement Cost Approach

The depreciated replacement cost (DRC) approach is widely accepted as the best method to use in regional and rural markets where there have been few, if any, leasing or sales transactions. This method is appropriate when there is no market or the local market is too underdeveloped to warrant use of a more sophisticated, income-based approach.

In fact, it has only been over the last three years that this approach has been phased out for appraisals of commercial, income-producing properties in prime locations in Prague and secondary cities.

The DRC method has long been applied in the Czech Republic and is modeled on the methodology advocated by RICS. Value is determined by first estimating the cost to create a modern equivalent of the facility in question. This cost estimate is adjusted for physical (or technical) depreciation and economic and functional obsolescence to arrive at the depreciated replacement cost of the building. The value of the land is then added to the DRC to arrive at total property value.

This approach is highly technical and hypothetical. Implicit is the assumption that the property being valued is of value to the client or the user. When this assumption is untenable, the property will likely have little value to any other party, particularly if it is of highly specialized construction or, more typically, if it is located in a part of the country where neither a market for the facility nor any alternative use exists.

It is always necessary to assume that the property provides a level of economic utility to the going concern operated on the property. The tried-and-true test is whether the property adequately contributes to the continued profitability of the going concern. Clearly, the valuer is not an expert on the financial status of the occupying entity. Thus, to establish the premise necessary for the appraisal, the valuer must obtain a statement to this effect from the client.

Additionally, the valuer must ensure that complete and accurate records are obtained to calculate depreciated replacement cost correctly. Important facts include land and building areas, building specifications and ages, and the replacement costs and design/layout details of equivalent modern structures.

Depreciated Replacement Cost Example

The value of a large industrial property is calculated in Table 1. Industrial properties valued by the DRC approach are typically assessed in Czech crowns (Kč).

Table 1. Industrial Property Valuation

Value of Improvements

Description	Levels	Area (m²)	Replacement Cost (Kč per m²)	Gross Replacement Cost (Kč)	Date of Construction	Physical Depreciation	Economic and Functional Obsolescence	Depreciation (Kč)	Net Depreciated Replacement Cost (Kč)
Office building	2	800	20,000	16,000,000	1982	60%	40%	12,160,000*	3,840,000
Production hall	1	2,250	12,500	28,125,000	1893	100%	80%	28,125,000	Nil
Storage	1	2,500	12,500	31,250,000	1962	60%	60%	26,250,000	5,000,000
Production hall	1	800	12,500	10,000,000	1970	60%	60%	8,400,000	1,600,000
Production hall	1	600	12,500	7,500,000	1975	60%	60%	6,300,000	1,200,000
Production hall	1	450	12,500	5,625,000	1893	100%	80%	5,625,000	Nil
Production hall	2-4	900	12,500	11,250,000	1893	100%	80%	11,250,000	Nil
Boiler room	2	750	15,000	11,250,000	1973	60%	40%	8,550,000	2,700,000
Transformer station	1	120	15,000	1,800,000	1969	60%	20%	1,224,000	576,000
Porter's lodge	1	150	10,000	1,500,000	1962	80%	50%	1,350,000	150,000
Garage	1	800	7,500	6,000,000	1928	80%	20%	5,040,000	960,000
Purification plant	2	550	22,500	12,375,000	1971	60%	20%	8,415,000	3,960,000
Coal store	1	80	7,500	600,000	1976	80%	20%	504,000	96,000
Chemical store	1	90	20,000	1,800,000	1984	50%	30%	1,170,000	630,000
Subtotal		10,840		145,075,000				20,712,000	

Additional improvements (loading bays, ramps, shelters, etc.) @ 10% of total improvement value — Rounded to — 2,071,000

Subtotal for improvements — **22,783,000**

Land Value

Land 25,000 m² @ 250 Kč per m² — 6,250,000

Additional site improvements (roads, pavements, landscaping, etc.) @ 5% of land value — Rounded to — 315,000

Subtotal for land — **6,565,000**

Rounded to — **29,400,000**

* Physical depreciation is estimated at 60% of the Kč 16,000,000 replacement cost, i.e., Kč 9,600,000. Economic and functional obsolescence is estimated at 40% of the physically depreciated replacement cost of Kč 6,400,000, i.e., Kč 2,560,000. Thus, total depreciation (Kč 9,600,000 + Kč 2,560,000) comes to Kč 12,160,000.

Valuation of Residential Property

Generally, two methods are used for the valuation of residential property. The first is an administrative methodology outlined in the Decree on Prices of Buildings (Structures), Plots of Land, Perennial Vegetation, Compensation [to an Owner] for Granting a User the Right to Use Land, and Compensation [to an Owner] for the Temporary Use of Plots of Land. The most recent version of this decree (No. 295) was drafted by the Ministry of Finance in 1995. The administrative price, which is an artificial price, must be determined by a sworn-in valuer, and his or her report must be filed with the registration of new ownership in the cadastre. Administrative prices are estimated by the cost approach. The second method of residential valuation is sales comparison, which is based on the same principles applied in other developed countries. The sales comparison approach provides market value estimates. Market value appraisals are performed by valuers who are members of professional valuation associations.

Availability of Data

Information is difficult to obtain in the Czech Republic, be it rental or sales data, replacement cost information, building plans and areas, tenancy schedules, or title documentation. Two factors account for this scarcity. First, the market is characterised by great competitiveness, resulting in the generation of disinformation. Second, the records that have been kept are poor, particularly for older properties.

Nevertheless, an industrious valuer can obtain sufficient information to complete any assignment. A broader disclaimer may be used than is required in more developed and informed markets.

Sources of information are listed below.

Demographic and Economic Data

- Municipal offices
- Local and foreign chambers of commerce
- Embassies
- Local and regional publications, particularly guides written by economists

Real Estate Market Data

- Foreign and local brokerage and real estate agency firms
- Corporate tenants
- Other valuers
- Developers and investors

Appraisal Organizations

Prominent professional organizations include

- The Chamber of Sworn-in Valuers (Komora soudnich znalců) in Prague
- The Czech Committee of Valuers/CCV (Český komitét znalců/ČKZ) in Prague
- The Czech Chamber of Appraisers/CCA (Česka komora odhadců majetku/ČKOM) in Prague
- The Association of Sworn-in Valuers and Valuers (Asociace znalců a odhadců) in Brno

These magazines may prove useful:

- *Soudní Inženyrstvi (Forensic Engineering)*
- *Zpravodaj Znalců (Reporter of Sworn-in Valuers)* (Prague)
- *Bulletin ČKZ (Bulletin of the CCV)* (Prague)
- *Bulletin ČKOM (Bulletin of the CCA)* (Prague)

Poland

Krzysztof Grzesik, FRICS
Dorota Latkowska

Krzysztof Grzesik is a chartered surveyor (FRICS) and Polish licensed valuer. He is a Partner of Healey & Baker, International Real Estate Consultants.

Dorota Latkowska is a Polish licensed valuer and head of Research at Price Waterhouse Real Estate Services in Poland.

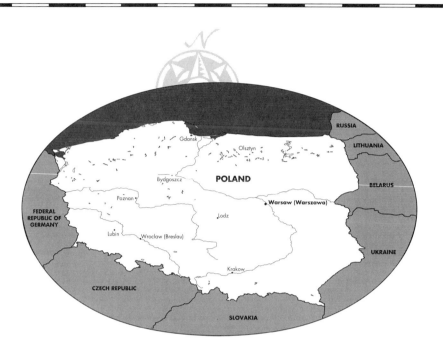

Poland is one of the larger countries in Central Europe and shares borders with Germany, the Czech Republic, Slovakia, Ukraine, Belorussia, Lithuania, and the Baltic enclave of Russia. Its northern border is formed by the Baltic Sea. Poland is part of the north European plain. The Sudety and Carpathian mountains run along the southern frontier, rising to nearly 2,500 metres (762 feet) near the town of Zakopane. Poland's largest rivers are the Vistula, Odra, Warta, and Bug, which provide the country with an ample supply of water. Poland also has an extensive lake district (Masuria) and the Baltic coast provides more than 500 kilometres (over 300 miles) of sandy beaches, bays, steep cliffs, and dunes. Poland has a moderate continental climate with a maritime influence along the Baltic coast. Winters can be severe. Principal cities are Warsaw, Łodź, Krakow, Wroclaw, Poznań, Gdansk, and Szczecin.

History and Economy

The history of Poland dates back to the sixth and seventh centuries when West Slavs emerged in the territory now constituting Poland. The first Polish state was founded in 966 AD when the Polanie tribe gained superiority over the surrounding Slavic tribes. Their leader, King Mieszko, married a Czech princess, adopted her Catholic religion, and thereby strengthened religious and cultural ties with Western Europe.

From the 14th to the 17th century, Poland was a great power. In 1385, Princess Jadwiga married the Duke of Lithuania, Jagiello, uniting the two countries under the Jagiellonian dynasty. Early in the 16th century, the monarch Zygmunt introduced the Renaissance to Poland. However, in 1572 the Jagiellonian dynasty became extinct and the parliament *(sejm)*, made up of the feudal nobility *(szlachta)* began to elect the monarch. This experiment with a "democratic" form of government resulted in the election of foreign kings, as competing neighbouring powers vied for influence. The right of veto *(liberum veto)* by any member of the nobility in the parliament rendered reform difficult and, after a series of wars with Sweden, Russia, Turkey, and the Cossacks in the 17th century, the kingdom declined.

In 1772 Poland was partitioned by Russia, Prussia, and Austria, who together took over nearly 30% of Poland's territory. The Polish government continued to function and attempts at genuine reform were begun. The Constitution of May 3 was adopted by the Parliament in 1791. It was the second written democratic constitution in the world, following that of the United States. However, a second partitioning of Poland occurred in 1793 and a third, in 1795, removed Poland completely from the map of Europe until 1918.

Polish independence was regained after World War I (November 11, 1918) and lasted until the outbreak of World War II (September 1, 1939), when the German army advanced into Poland. The Soviet Union proceeded to invade Poland from the east (September 17). Wartime destruction devastated Poland and some six million people, representing 22% of the population, were killed. The country lost 38% of its national wealth, 35% of its agricultural resources, and 32% of its capital goods (assets in industry, mining and the power resource sector). Warsaw was virtually destroyed following the 1944 uprising.

Churchill, Roosevelt, and Stalin drew the map of postwar Europe at the Yalta conference in February 1945. Poland was to become independent within the Soviet zone of influence. At the same time, it was decided that the borders of the country should be shifted approximately 300 kilometres (186 miles) to the west. After centuries of German rule, Silesia and the land east of the Odra and Nysa rivers were returned to Poland. The eastern territories occupied by the Soviets at the beginning of the war remained under their control.

The communist government began to rebuild the country and expand industrialization. Poland joined the Warsaw Pact and Council of Mutual Economic Assistance, both of which were dominated by the Soviet Union. Money to finance the industrial expansion was supplied by Western banks starting in the mid 1970s. By 1981 the country had accumulated a hard currency debt of $27 billion and, by the end of the decade, Poland was bankrupt. Living standards fell sharply, causing widespread labour unrest.

Growing opposition from industrial workers in the late 1970s culminated in the formation of the independent trade union, Solidarity, in 1980. Under the leadership of Lech Wałęsa, the Solidarity movement grew in popularity and began to challenge the government. General Jaruzelski reacted by imposing martial law at the end of 1981 and banning Solidarity. Strikes broke out again in 1988 when the government attempted to remove food subsidies. The government resigned and an interim Council of Ministers held serious round table talks with Solidarity, which was legalized again in 1989.

The first free democratic election in postwar Eastern Europe was held on June 4, 1989, with Solidarity candidates winning all the Sejm seats they were allowed to contest for as well as an overall majority in the Senate. Tadeusz Mazowiecki, the Solidarity nominee, became prime minister. In 1990, Lech Wałęsa was freely elected president.

The first Solidarity finance minister, Leszek Balcerowicz, introduced an economic plan on January 1, 1990, to transform Poland into a modern European country. The program successfully restrained hyperinflation, stabilized the currency, and encouraged foreign investment, albeit at great social cost. As a result, Poland has made considerable progress toward establishing a free market economy. A series of coalition governments has continued the program of reforms begun in 1989.

Poland's continuing transition from a centrally planned economy to a market economy should be viewed within the context of the "Strategy for Poland" programme introduced by Grzegorz Kołodko, finance minister over the last three years. In February 1997, Mr. Kołodko resigned his post and was replaced by Marek Belka. Strategy for Poland promotes balanced economic development on three priorities: rapid economic growth, macro-economic stabilisation, and improvement in the standard of living. In accordance with the plan, the gross domestic product was anticipated to rise by 5% per annum on average. In fact, the GDP rose by 3.8% in 1993, 5.2% in 1994, 7% in 1995, and 6% in 1996. Another positive factor has been growth in the level of foreign investment in Poland. During the first quarter of 1996, the influx of foreign capital into Poland amounted to $1,054,300,000 in U.S. dollars. This compares favourably with $2,511,400,000 in foreign investment for all of 1995.

Political System

Poland is a parliamentary republic. The national legislature consists of the Sejm (lower house) and the Senate. The Sejm votes on laws, establishes state policy, and supervises the activities of all other state bodies, including appointments to the Council of Ministers. Deputies to the Sejm, which has 460 seats, are elected during the national elections held every four years. The Senate, or upper house, was reinstituted in 1989 for the first time since the end of World War II. One hundred senators are elected for four-year terms.

Executive powers are entrusted to a prime minister and his Council of Ministers. The head of state is a nationally elected president, a position restored in 1989. The president plays an influential role in running the government, nominates the prime minister, and exercises other powers.

Poland is divided into regional authorities. Regional administration is effected through the province or *województwo* (voivodship), of which there are 49, and three municipal governments (Warsaw, Krakow and Łódź). Primary administrative power, however, is exercised by authorities at the town and commune (district) level. Local administrative functions are carried out by local town councils, whose members are elected in a similar manner to the election of deputies in the Sejm.

Legal System

The dismantling of the communist system has necessitated substantial changes in the constitution, which is currently being revised. The final draft will have a democratic tone not evident in the past. State entities will no longer have special advantages over other entities, and the legal framework will be more conducive to business activity, generally facilitating the transition to free enterprise. The principal sources of law are the constitution, statues passed by parliament, and subsequent decrees issued by the Council of Ministers or government ministers. Laws are grouped together under the civil code, commercial code, labour code, and civil procedure code. The Supreme Court supervises all courts to ensure uniform application of the law and hears appellate cases. A constitutional tribunal interprets laws and makes judgments as to their constitutionality.

Population

The population of Poland is approximately 38.3 million (1991 estimate), the seventh largest in Europe. The working age cohort accounts for 57.6% of the total population. A total of 23.7 million people live in urban areas and 14.6 million in rural areas.

The cities with the largest populations in 1990 were: Warsaw, 1,700,000; Łodź, 900,000; Krakow, 800,000; Wroclaw, 700,000; Poznań, 600,000; Gdansk, 500,000; and Szczecin, 450,000.

Language

Polish is the official language of the country. A sizeable German-speaking minority of approximately 350,000 resides along the Baltic coast and in Silesia. Approximately 350,000 Ukranians, 200,000 Belorussians, 30,000 Czechs and Slovaks, 25,000 Lithuanians, 25,000 Gypsies, and 15,000 Jews live in various parts of the country. Educated Poles often speak English or German and generally understand other Slavic languages, especially Russian.

Currency

The Polish currency is the złoty (zł), which is divided into 100 groszy. The złoty has been convertible within Poland since January 1990. In 1995 the new złoty (PLN) was introduced.

Units of Measure

Poland uses the metric system. All buildings are measured in square metres. Land is measured either in square metres or in hectares (10,000 square metres).

Inflation

Over the past three years, inflation has declined significantly, but it is still higher than anticipated. In 1991 the rate of inflation was 60.4%; by the end of 1996, it had dropped to 18.7%. The Ministry of Finance predicts a continuing decline to single-digit rates by the year 2000.

Property Rights

Individuals and corporate bodies may acquire and own real estate in Poland in various ways. While much urban land is owned by the state or local authorities, approximately 90% of agricultural land is in private hands. Foreign nationals or companies may acquire real estate with the permission of the Ministry of Interior through a standardised application process.

The highest form of title is freehold ownership, called *wlasność*. There are no limitations on the disposal of property held in *wlasność*, and the owner can do as he or she pleases with such property, subject only to building regulations and town planning restrictions. (The property must be used in accordance with the use designated in the zone of the local master plan.) Forty-five years of communism failed to destroy this fundamental form of land ownership in Poland, although much land held in freehold ownership in urban areas (especially Warsaw) belongs to the state or local municipalities. Most agricultural land is owned in *własność*.

There are several types of leasehold arrangements. The first is a perpetual lease involving land, called *użytkowanie wieczyste*. The term of a perpetual lease is generally 99 years. Such leases are created when the freehold owner is either the state or a local authority. Normally, the purchaser of a perpetual lease is required to make a down payment of 15% to 25% of the freehold value of the land, and thereafter pay an annual ground rent of 1% to 3% of the value. The perpetual tenant has the right to enjoy the use of the land and to dispose of it by sale, gift, or bequest. Thus, such a leasehold interest can be utilized effectively in development and investment situations.

A leasehold interest in property granted for an unlimited period of time or for a limited period not exceeding 30 years is called *dzierżawa*. In the former case, the owner may terminate the lease after giving six months' notice, or 12 months if the property is agricultural land. In return for the payment of rent, the lessee has the right to occupy and enjoy the benefits of the property for the duration of the *dzierżawa*. The lessee is obliged to maintain the property in good condition and may not sublet it to a third party without the permission of the owner. In the case of agricultural land held as *dzierżawa* for a fixed term of three or more years, or held for a duration exceeding 10 years, the lessee has the right of first refusal once the owner announces his intention to sell the freehold interest.

Another type of leasehold interest in property, which can be granted either for an unlimited period of time or for a fixed duration not longer than 10 years, is called a *najem*. If the lease is signed for an unlimited period, either side may generally terminate it upon three months' notice. The *najem* has become the typical form for occupational leases to units in new commercial developments. *Najem* leases are also used for the letting (leasing) of residential and industrial buildings.

Most *najem* leases have terms similar to those of standard leases in North America and Western Europe. The obligations of the landlord and tenant are set out in detail. Rents are quoted based on a monthly rate per square metre and are usually all-inclusive, i.e., service charges are included. In new commercial developments in town centres, leases normally run a minimum of five years for offices and 10 years for shops. Rents are quoted in U.S. dollars, but paid in złotys at the appropriate exchange rate. The tenant also must pay a separate service charge. The landlord is normally responsible for external repairs and the tenant pays for nonstructural internal repairs and the cost of insurance. Such generalisations may be misleading, however, since the occupational lease has yet to assume a standard form in the developing commercial real estate markets of Poland. Leases in new developments tend to follow the format used in the developer's native country. Because a growing number of American and British lawyers now work in Poland, there has been some tendency to follow American and British lease practice.

Development of a Valuation Profession

In December 1990 the Polish Parliament amended the law relating to land management and compensation by requiring the estimation of market value in property valuations for government purposes. Previously, land values were determined based on guidelines approved by an official committee, and buildings were assessed according to replacement cost. Following various legal and constitutional changes which dealt with land ownership and freed up the real estate market in Poland, this significant piece of legislation in 1990 marked the beginning of the rapid evolution of a Western-style Polish valuation profession.

In response to an overwhelming demand from practicing valuers and other real estate professionals (land surveyors, building engineers, architects, lawyers, and economists) and with the encouragement of the Ministry of Physical Planning and Construction, courses and postgraduate programmes in market-orientated valuation were organised throughout the country by universities, local valuers' associations, and private companies. In line with the recommendations of the ministry, most courses for specialists are at least 120 hours in duration. Postgraduate courses offered by universities tend to include more than 200 hours of coursework. It is likely that in the future emphasis will be placed on these postgraduate courses or on full-time university degree programmes.

The popularity of valuation courses stems from an appreciation of the future demand and employment prospects for real estate professionals in a newly developing market and from the introduction of a licensing system for government-approved valuers.

Licensing

In 1992 the Minister of Physical Planning and Construction appointed a qualifications commission to oversee the examination and registration of expert valuers. Under this licensing system, the following criteria must be met. Any person wishing to become registered as an expert in real estate valuation must:

- Obtain a degree or higher school certificate in science, economics, or law.
- Pass a ministry-approved specialist or postgraduate valuation course.
- Submit examples of completed valuations.
- Pass a written and verbal examination. To pass, a candidate must achieve a grade of at least 75% on the written examination.

The written examination comprises 15 standard questions plus one practical question. The standard questions are divided into the following subject groups:

- general legal principles (three questions)
- economic/financial principles (three questions)
- principles of urban property valuation (six questions)
- principles of valuation applying to rural and forest land (three questions)

Each question is worth a maximum of six points. The practical question, usually a valuation problem, has a maximum value of 10 points. Thus, a total of 100 possible points can be scored on the exam.

In order to proceed to the verbal part of the examination, a candidate must earn at least 75 points on the written part. During the interview, the candidate is normally asked to present one of the valuations he has submitted beforehand and to answer questions on any aspect of the valuation.

Since the introduction of the licensing system, examinations have been held throughout Poland every month. The examinations are difficult, with an average success rate of less than 50%. At the beginning of 1997, there were some 2,000 licensed valuers practising in Poland. There were also approximately 6,000 valuers entered on the lists maintained by each province. These valuers are authorized to perform official valuations in the *województwo* (province) to which the list pertains. However, the lists are unreliable because qualification criteria differ from region to region. These lists will be phased out as soon as there are enough qualified licensed valuers to service the needs of central and local governments.

It should be noted that a license is normally required under statutory law to carry out valuation work for central and local governments, but anyone (including foreign valuers) may perform privately commissioned valuation work in Poland. However, the license holder undoubtedly has an advantage when competing for private work. Due to the increase in the number of loans secured against property, many local banks and financial institutions have become major clients and most offer valuation work only to licensed valuers.

Valuers' Associations and Federation

The rapid development of a valuation profession in Poland over the last few years has coincided with the formation of local and regional valuers' associations throughout the country. There are now some 26 such associations with a total membership of more than 3,000 valuers. The associations have largely assumed the responsibility for running short educational courses for specialists, organising licensing examination sessions, publishing technical literature, and distributing information. More recently, they have begun to set up arbitration committees to deal with conflicting valuations and complaints against association members. Every year one of the associations is chosen to organise a National Conference of Polish Valuers.

At the National Conference of Polish Valuers held in Czestochowa in 1992, a motion was passed in favour of the establishment of a Polish Federation of Valuers' Associations (*Polska Federacja Stowarzyszeń Rzeczoznawców Majątkowych*/PFSRM) to represent the interests of Polish valuers at both national and international levels. With a founding membership of 16 regional and local associations, the federation was formally registered in 1994. The federation is led by an elected president and two vice presidents who hold three-year terms of office. The first elected president was Andrzej Kalus from Katowice; the vice presidents were Henryk Czajkowski and Mieczyslaw Prystupa. Most of the federation's decision-making powers are vested in the Federation Council, which includes a representative from each member association.

The federation has received much support from other organisations such as the Eastern European Real Property Foundation in Washington, the Royal Institution of Chartered Surveyors, The European Group of Valuers of Fixed Assets (TEGOVOFA), and the International Valuation Standards Committee (IVSC).

After becoming an associate member of TEGOVOFA in 1994, the federation drew up a set of standards for Polish valuers, which are consistent with both European valuation standards and the requirements of Polish law. A draft discussion document was published in September 1994, and the final *Professional Standards for Property Valuers* were approved by the Federation Council.

Valuation Standards

In 1995 the Ministry of Physical Planning and Construction issued regulations prescribing valuation practice, methodology, and terminology. The regulations clearly describe the process of valuation as the choice of a correct approach, method and technique. Four approaches are recognised: comparative, income, cost, and mixed. These are broken down into methods such as price comparison, investment, profits, depreciated replacement cost, and residual. The latter are, in turn, further divided into various techniques. For example, the investment method can be applied by means of either the simple income capitalisation technique or discounted cash flow technique.

In addition to endorsing the above methodology, the federation's *Professional Standards For Property Valuers* (also known as the *green book*) describes in detail the procedures to be followed in the valuation process and lays down a Code of Ethical Practice. The standards recognise only two bases of valuation—market value and depreciated replacement cost.

Market value is defined as

the most probable price which could be obtained in the market assuming:

a) an arm's-length transaction with each party acting in a rational manner and without special motivation

b) a willingness on both sides (i.e., a willing buyer and a willing seller)

c) that the parties are aware of all the existing circumstances affecting value

d) that the parties are acting without compulsion

e) passage of both the period necessary for exposure of the property on the market with appropriate publicity, and the required period within which to negotiate the sale, in view of the nature of the property and the state of the market.

The above definition is based on, and intended to be consistent with, the definition of market value adopted by both TEGOVOFA and IVSC ("... the estimated amount for which an asset should exchange between a willing buyer and willing seller in an arm's-length transaction after proper marketing wherein the parties have each acted knowledgeably, prudently, and without compulsion.")

Under the Polish standards, five categories of market value are identified:

- market value of a property under the existing use
- market value of a property under an alternative use
- market value of a property under the optimum use (highest and best use)
- market value of a property subject to forced sale
- market value of a property in a future sale

Market Value of a Property Under an Existing Use

The market value of a property under an existing use is understood to be the market value assuming that the property will remain under its existing use. This category excludes any anticipated value for an alternative use or any value increment resulting from development potential, except for development that is consistent with the existing use and does not impede the use of the property.

This market value of a property under an existing use is estimated on the assumption that the existing use is in accordance with the local master plan. The existing use does not have to be the actual use made of the subject; it is sufficient for an existing use to be consistent with the general nature of the activity conducted on the property. For example, similar industrial buildings will have similar values irrespective of the specific manufacturing activities carried out; shops in the same parade (thoroughfare) will have similar values irrespective of the nature of the goods sold.

A valuation of property under the existing use is especially relevant to properties occupied by a business entity, assuming that the business will contiue to operate in the foreseeable future.

Market Value of a Property Under an Alternative Use

The market value of a property under an alternative use reflects a prospective potential use of the property other than the existing use. If the value under the alternative use differs substantially from the value under the existing use, this should be clearly stated by the valuer in the valuation report.

In valuing a property that is occupied by a business entity that can be assumed to continue operation, an alternative use value posited upon liquidation or transfer of the business to other premises must be excluded. However, an estimate of an alternative use value could be important in arriving at the value of all the assets of the business, among which the real estate is but one component.

Land, buildings, and premises (rented space) that are treated as a source of income or are intended for future development should be valued under any potential alternative use(s).

In all cases, the value of a property under an alternative use should be based on concrete information and data supporting the feasibility of the potential alternative use. The valuer must not make unfounded or unrealistic assumptions.

Market Value of a Property Under the Optimum Use (Highest and Best Use)

The market value of a property under the optimum use is a specific variant of the market value under an alternative use. Optimum use value is based on the additional assumption that the property will be put to its most effective use, i.e., its highest and best use.

The market value of a property under the optimum use reflects the most effective and best use of the property that is legally permissible, physically possible, financially feasible, and results in the highest value.

An appraiser arrives at the market value of a property under the optimum use employing the above assumptions and the same principles followed to establish market value under an alternative use. This value concept is especially relevant to the valuation of land being considered for development. The valuer should disregard the present or anticipated use of the property if such use precludes the property from realizing its highest and best use.

The market value of a property under the optimum use should be based on credible data and research supporting the feasibility of the optimal potential use. The valuer must not make unfounded or unrealistic assumptions.

Market Value of a Property Pending a Forced Sale

The market value of a property pending a forced sale is based on the assumption that time and/or other restrictions will affect the sale of the property, which would otherwise sell after a reasonable period of time for marketing and negotiations.

In arriving at an estimate of forced sale value, the valuer must describe and substantiate in the valuation report any assumptions made that the valuer considered necessary or that arose from the client's instructions.

Market Value of a Property in a Future Sale

The market value of a property in a future sale is the value that can be anticipated at the time of a future sale. The market value in a future sale should only be determined in cases where the client has decided to put the property on the market immediately or wishes to know the price he or she may obtain at the end of the necessary marketing period.

The valuer must forecast the time required to market the subject property and negotiate the sale, and assess the market value of the property at the end of this period. In determining the market value in a future sale, the valuer should take into account all circumstances existing or anticipated at the time of the valuation.

Methodology

The *green book* prescribes two approaches to be used in arriving at the market value of a property, in accordance with the nature of the property and the purpose of the valuation. These are the comparative approach and the income approach. In the latter approach, the following methods and techniques should be applied:

- the investment method using the simple capitalisation technique or the discounted cash flow technique
- the profits method
- the residual method

The Poles have been successful in promoting the use of market-oriented valuation techniques. Whereas only five years ago, most valuations were carried out on a replacement cost basis, today Polish valuers are enthusiastically embracing price comparison and investment methods of valuation. The investment methods are generally applied as they are in Britain or the United States. The various training programmes of these two countries have had great influence on valuation methodology in Poland. Basic textbooks that present the methodology adopted in Poland include *The Appraisal of Real Estate* (11th edition, 1996) published by the Appraisal Institute, *Basic Principles of Property Valuation* (Polish edition, 1993) by Michael W. Green and David H. Mackmin, and *The Valuation of Property and Enterprises* (1994) by Andrzej Hopfer, Henryk Jędrzejewski, and Ryszard Żróbek.

The comparative approach is now most commonly applied in the valuation of residential property and agricultural, residential, and commercial sites. Although it is difficult, valuers can obtain market data through close observation, good detective work, and contact with friendly real estate brokers. Information about property sales is not otherwise available except to the revenue collector. A good valuer may have access to notarial deeds that specify the transaction prices of the properties sold, but such information is not always considered reliable.

Most valuations of residential property are carried out on the instructions of banks, which require valuations for loan security purposes. While long-term mortgages in Poland are still rare, there has been an increase in activity among banks extending short-term loans of five to 10 years on residential property. As a prerequisite, all banks now demand an open-market valuation on a comparative price basis.

Commercial (office, retail, and warehousing) and most industrial properties tend to be valued by the investment approach. Unfortunately, while data on the market rents being paid for office, shopping, and industrial properties is now available, there is as yet very little information about the sale prices of such properties. Thus, choosing a capitalisation rate to be applied in an investment method valuation is problematic. To derive rates, valuers have had to consider sale prices of investment-grade properties outside of Poland and the perceptions and expectations of potential future investors in Polish real estate. The valuation of a modern office building in the centre of Warsaw may be taken as an example. To arrive at its market value, a Polish valuer might apply a capitalisation rate in the range of 12% to 14%, based on known yield rates of 6% to 7% in less risky Western cities.

Discounted cash flow (DCF) analysis is now being recognised as a valid tool, but it is treated with caution because, in recent cases, huge differences were found in the value conclusions derived from DCF analysis in separately commissioned valuations of the same property. Current thinking seems to support the use of discounted cash flow techniques in more complex development appraisals.

Valuation Reporting Requirements

Valuers are encouraged to communicate their reports in writing, prepare them in a clear manner, and include all information needed to support the opinion of value. In accordance with Standard XIII of the *green book*, every valuation report should indicate:

1. *The purpose of the valuation*—i.e., the nature of the client's instructions, the use to be made of the valuation, the client's specific requirements regarding the valuation as well as any legal regulations governing the type of property to be valued

2. *The subject of the valuation*—a detailed description of the subject property indicating its location, physical characteristics, legal title and use. It is also recommended that plans, photographs, and other illustrative documents be appended to the valuation report.

3. *The date of valuation and date of inspection*—the value of the property set out in the valuation report is the value as of the date of the valuation. Unless otherwise apparent from the client's instructions or legal provision, the valuation should take into account the level of market values upon the date of valuation. The physical condition and legal status of the property, however, should be described as of the date of the inspection. Any departure from this principle should be clearly indicated in the valuation report.

In addition, the following matters should be addressed in the valuation certificate:

4. *The basis of valuation.* As a rule, the basis of the valuation will either be open market value or replacement cost value. The valuer must select the basis of valuation, in view of the purpose of the valuation and the statutory requirements. The

valuer should not be influenced by the client regarding the basis used. If the valuer chooses to adopt a basis of valuation other than those recommended above, he or she should substantiate the decision in detail. If the value under the existing use differs from the value under an alternative use, and the client is interested in the value estimated under such alternative use, the valuer should also estimate this value.

5. *Information and assumptions.* The valuer should disclose and describe the sources and nature of the information used in the valuation. Information may come from:

   (a) documents, such as entries in land and mortgage registers, geodetic documentation, judicial decisions, decisions of administrative bodies, and civil contracts relating to properties

   (b) property inspection, which should be described in detail and carried out personally by the valuer, upon the date shown in the report of value. The inspection should not be restricted to external observation, but should seek to determine the construction and depreciation of the building, plant, and any outbuildings on the site as well as the use of the property by its owner or occupant. The inspection of the property should result in the following:

   - a detailed description of the property,

   - an opinion of the optimal use of the property,

   - a comparison with other properties.

   The property inspection may be impossible to undertake or may be restricted in its extent because of the following reasons:

   (i) physical impossibility—e.g., the buildings have been demolished or altered, or the property is located abroad and inspection is out of the question

   (ii) legal obstacles—e.g., the owner refuses to give the valuer access to the property

   (iii) contractual provision, e.g., the agreement between the client and the valuer, foreseeing the impossibility of an inspection, has excluded it as a condition of the valuation.

   Each of these circumstances should be noted and described in detail in the valuation report. If the report of value is prepared by more than one valuer, the valuer who has carried out the property inspection should be identified and the date of inspection should be noted.

(c) information from third parties, e.g., information received from other valuers, public and self-governing bodies, and (real) estate agencies may be sources of the valuer's information. If information obtained by the valuer needs to be verified and the valuer is unable to do so himself, the report of value should include a clear statement to this effect.

6. *Physical condition.* If the subject of the valuation includes buildings, plant and premises, the valuer should describe their physical condition. The valuer should state whether a structural survey has been carried out, the results of such survey, and whether the valuer and his associates have carried out the survey. The valuer and his associates should also assess the condition and performance of the plant and installations. If wear and tear are detected in the physical condition of the property, appropriate deductions should be made and these must be clearly shown in the valuation report.

7. *Designation of the use of the property.* Prior to preparing the valuation, the valuer should determine whether the use of the property is in conformity with the local town plan, and indicate this in the report. On the client's instructions, the valuer should determine the highest and best use of the property consistent with the local town plan and economic feasibility.

8. *Summary report.* In certain situations arising from the need to abridge the valuation report or because of the client's instructions, the valuer can issue a summary report. Such a report should cover the basic conclusion of value as related to the various elements of a complete report. A summary report can only be based on a complete valuation report, of which it forms an integral part.

9. *Nonpublication clause.* The valuation report should include a clause stating that:

(a) the report may not be published, in whole or in part, in any document without the consent of the valuer and without the agreement of the valuer on the form and content of such publication,

(b) the valuation report must not be used for any purpose, other than that stated in the valuation report.

10. *Limitation of liability.* The valuation report may include additional clauses:

(a) altering the valuer's responsibility—in particular, clauses that may exclude any liability in relation to hidden defects which could not be detected during the property inspection or from technical and legal documentation,

(b) stating that any description in the report of the physical condition of the property does not amount to a structural survey.

11. *Signature of the valuer or valuers.* The signature(s) should not only indicate the full name of the valuer(s) but also the qualifications of the valuer(s). A qualified valuer should indicate his or her registration number. The valuer may also indicate the name of the association to which he or she belongs. The signature of the valuer should appear directly below the valuation.

Bibliography

Texts and Guides

Green, Michael W. and David H. Mackmin. *Podstawowe zasady wyceny nieruchomości* (*Basic Principles of Property Valuation*—the Polish translation of *Open Market Value and Methods of Valuation*). Warsaw: Korona Ltd., 1993.

Hopfer, Andrzej, Henryk Jędrzejewski, and Ryszard Żróbek. *Wycena nieruchomości i przedsiębiorstw (The Valuation of Property and Enterprises).* Warsaw: TWIGGER, S.A., 1994.

Polish Federation of Valuers' Associations (Polska Federacja Stowarzyszeń Rzeczoznawców Majątkowych/PFSRM). *Sztandardy Zawodowe Rzeczoznawców Majątkowych (Professional Standards for Property Valuers).* 1st ed. and updated 2d ed. Warsaw: Polish Federation of Valuers' Association, 1995, 1996.

Price Waterhouse World Firm Limited Company. "Price Waterhouse - Doing Business in Poland 1992." East European Services, Washington desk, 1801 K Street, Suite 1000, Washington, D.C.. Tel: (202) 833 7392 Fax: (202) 296 0830.

Periodicals

Rzeczoznawca Majątkowy (The Property Valuer). A quarterly magazine of the Polish Federation of Valuers' Associations (PFSRM). Available by contacting the Federation office at ul. Kopernika 30, pok 223, 00-95 Warszawa; tel/fax: 48 22 826 41 62.

11

Albania

David A. Allen, B.Sc., ARICS

David A. Allen, a chartered valuation surveyor, has worked both in private practice and for local government in the United Kingdom. In May 1992 he moved to Albania to establish a post-graduate programme in property valuation and management. Allen acts as a consultant to international organisations and advises senior members of the Albanian government on matters of valuation and land law. As a practising valuer, he is also a founder and executive secretary of the Albanian Society of Real Property Valuers and a member of the Valuers Licensing Commission. When conditions in Albania became unstable in March of 1997, Mr. Allen was evacuated from Durrës.

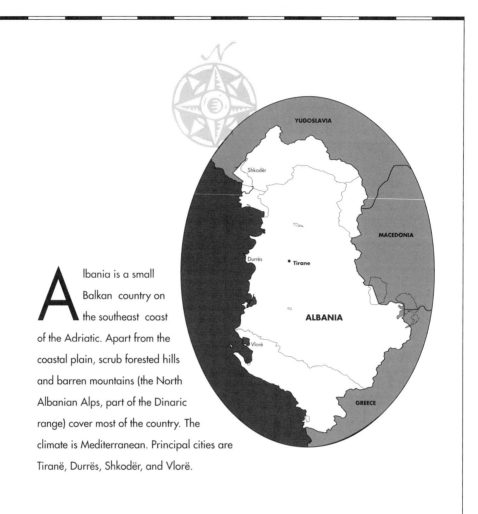

A
lbania is a small
Balkan country on
the southeast coast
of the Adriatic. Apart from the
coastal plain, scrub forested hills
and barren mountains (the North
Albanian Alps, part of the Dinaric
range) cover most of the country. The
climate is Mediterranean. Principal cities are
Tiranë, Durrës, Shkodër, and Vlorë.

Political Overview

In 1912, Albania proclaimed its independence after nearly five centuries of Ottoman rule. Ahmed Zogu, a conservative Moslem landlord, set himself up as King Zog I in 1928. Following the invasion by Italy in 1939, King Zog fled and the Italians took control of the country, which was subsequently occupied by the Germans. On November 28, 1944, communist guerrillas under Enver Hoxha[1] completed the liberation of Albania. As Communist Party secretary, Enver Hoxha established a hard-line Stalinist regime that exerted totalitarian control over all matters of life and effectively isolated Albania from the rest of the world. Upon Hoxha's death in 1985, Ramiz Alia succeeded as leader of the Communist Party and president.

The government of Ramiz Alia saw the collapse of the communist regimes across Central and Eastern Europe and realised that the time for major economic and political reform was at hand. In 1990, Ramiz Alia began talks on reform and permitted the formation of opposition political parties. Amid the collapse of public order and deteriorating economic conditions, the first democratic elections were held in March 1991. The new government, whose cabinet was monopolised by the reformed communists, only had time to adopt an interim constitution[2] before being replaced by a technocrat government in June 1991.

After winning the next election in March 1992 with a clear majority, the Democratic Party put forward a wide-ranging reform programme to ensure the transition to a market economy and to halt further deterioration in the economy and public order. Despite the many difficulties involved in such a major transition, particularly the political instability, the reform programme has been proceeding with success. During its term in office, the Democratic Party has had only one major setback, which occurred in November 1994 when a national referendum rejected the proposed new constitution.

In the general elections of May 1996, the Democratic Party won a resounding victory and thus continues to guide Albania in its transition. Some of the opposition parties, claiming irregularities in the elections, withdrew on the final day. Noting reports of irregularities, the Parliamentary Assembly of the Council of Europe[3] requested that all Albanian political parties gather to discuss a settlement that would restore confidence in Albanian democracy.

In January 1997 widespread demonstrations demanded the resignation of the government, which was tainted by an investment pyramid scheme in which

---

1. Pronounced en-ver hō-dja.
2. Law 7491, approved on April 29, 1991, as supplemented by Law 7692, approved on March 31, 1993.
3. Resolution 1095 of the Council of Europe Parliamentary Assembly, 1996.

many Albanians had lost their entire savings. In some towns, government buildings, court houses, and police stations were set afire. The opposition parties participated in these protests to try to engineer political changes. Failing to calm popular discontent, the Democratic Party majority government entered into a coalition with the Socialists in March of 1997. In the general election of July, the socialists won a two-thirds majority.

Political Structure

The People's Assembly (or parliament) is the highest state power and the only law-making body. Prior to approval, all laws must be presented to and discussed in the People's Assembly. This body defines the main internal and external policies of the state, adopting all laws and measures necessary for their implementation. It is made up of 250 deputies who are elected to four-year terms.

The People's Assembly elects from among its deputies a president, who is the head of state and symbol of national unity. The president remains in office for a period of five years and cannot be elected more than twice in succession. The president declares as law legislation decided upon in the assembly and has the right, among others, to ask the People's Assembly to re-examine laws. He selects the chairman (prime minister) of the Council of Ministers (cabinet) and, upon the proposal of the chairman, appoints and discharges members of the government and governmental institutions. It is clear both in the law and in practice that the president is not just a figurehead, but exercises considerable power and influence.

The Council of Ministers is a part of the executive branch, directing, guiding, and coordinating state policy. All laws are first examined by the Council, which must approve them before they can be passed on to the People's Assembly.

Although about 25 political parties are currently registered, three parties clearly predominate: the Democratic Party, the Alliance Party, and the Socialist Party (formerly, the communists).

Economic Overview

Since 1992 substantial progress has been made toward stabilising the crisis-ridden economy and bringing about significant structural reforms. The budget deficit is being brought under control and available figures[4] show macroeconomic improvement in the country. The relatively tight budget and restrictive credit policy have not only enhanced Albania's external position, but also

---

4. IMF/Albanian governmental sources.

have helped fight inflation. Greater availability of both domestic goods and imports has reduced the rate of inflation. The official inflation rate in 1994 and 1995 averaged about 1% per month.

Economic liberalisation has eliminated almost all price controls and brought the prices of subsidised goods up to cost levels. This programme has resulted in a complete privatisation of the retail sector and the emergence of private companies importing foodstuffs and home appliances. Coupled with this progress has been the development of the foodstuff industry; many domestically produced foodstuffs such as beer, soft drinks, yoghurt and sausages are now available. Mass privatisation by means of a voucher system is intended to complete the privatisation of medium- and large-scale industries.

Language

Albanian (Shqip) is based on extinct ancestral Indo-European languages of the Balkans (Illyrian, Thracian, Dacian). Its vocabulary has been enriched by borrowings from ancient Greek and Latin as well as from South Slavic, Turkish, modern Greek, and Italian. The decision to use the Latin alphabet was adopted at the Congress of Monastir in 1908. There are two dialects of Albanian: Geg, spoken in the north, and Tosk, spoken in the south. The Tosk dialect is the official language of the country. Italian and English are the most widely spoken foreign languages. Many young people speak at least one of these languages.

Currency

The Albanian Lek (Lekë in the plural) is the monetary unit, but the U.S. dollar is widely used, especially since the Lek is not fully convertible. The Lek has remained fairly stable since 1993 and in mid-1994 made strong gains on the U.S. dollar, going from 100 Lekë per $1 in January 1994 to 87 Lekë per $1 in August 1994. The exchange rate has since fallen to its previous level, apart from seasonal and political fluctuations.

Units of Measure

Albania uses the metric system. The English and American imperial system is unknown. Real property value is quoted in Lekë per square metre. Rentals are also usually quoted in Lekë per square metre per month.

Legislative Overview

Because the new constitution was not adopted in November 1994, all of Albania's laws still derive their ultimate authority from the interim constitution drawn up by the reformed communist government in April 1991. However, this has not prevented the adoption of laws requisite to the reform programme, i.e., laws allowing private commercial activity and foreign investment. Such laws include the civil code,[5] company law,[6] tax laws, accountancy law,[7] land laws, and foreign investment law.[8]

The civil code and other codes (a labour code and penal code) provide a foundation, often detailed, for all other laws, including those cited above. Some of these codes are detailed and others are very vague. The specific laws fill in the gaps and give clarity. The new civil code adopted in late 1994 addresses property matters, including property classification, ownership, inheritance, contracts, obligations, torts, and remedies.

One of the laws introduced a property tax.[9] This tax is administered through the offices of the Ministry of Finance at the local level, with revenues being divided between the central and local budgets. The property tax is levied on both agricultural land and buildings. The tax on agricultural land is based on the class of the land. The highest-yielding land is classed as Number 1 land; the poorest land is classed as Number 10 land. The amount payable is calculated by multiplying the appropriate rate by the area; if the land is not fully used for agricultural production, the amount payable increases tenfold. The building tax applies to all buildings throughout the country, even those in agricultural areas. The amount payable is based on the gross external area of the building and its use. The highest rate is levied on commercial buildings.

Property Law and Property Rights

The new civil code defines immovable property as "the land, water sources and running water, trees, and buildings and floating buildings (house boats), attached to the land as well as anything which is affixed permanently and continuously to the land or buildings."[10] Moreover, it states that "the right of ownership of land extends to the sky and down into the earth as may be profitable for use, under the conditions foreseen by the law."[11] The civil code explains in detail what constitutes ownership and the rights and obligations of owners.

Land in Albania is divided into two main categories: agricultural land *(toke)* and building land *(truall)*. Agricultural land is generally land outside the urban zone, which is defined by the "yellow line." Building land includes

---

5. Law 7850, approved on July 29, 1994.
6. Law 7638, approved on November 19, 1992.
7. Law 7661, approved on January 19, 1993.
8. Law 7764, approved on October 25, 1993.
9. Law 7805, approved on March 16, 1994.
10. Article 142 of the Civil Code.
11. Article 154 of the Civil Code.

land inside the "yellow line," land outside this line with a building on it (e.g., a house), and land that has been redesignated building land following a request, usually for development.

Under the distribution commissions, land formerly belonging to agricultural co-operatives has been distributed among the village families.[12] Some of the land assigned to the state farms has been given to the workers or, where such farms had been formed from co-operatives, to the village residents through the distribution commissions. Other state farms have been maintained as joint ventures. In some cases, individuals have occupied land on the basis of their previous ownership, and legislation is proceeding.

The land distributed falls into two categories: land held in ownership and land held in use. The former conveys ownership, whereas the latter only gives the right to use and clarifies the terms on which such a right is held. Following much discussion, the government has adopted a law to transfer such land to the ownership category.[13] The exact nature of the land is indicated within the title, i.e., whether the land is purely agricultural or nonagricultural (with a building on it or available for construction). The selling or buying of agricultural land is allowed only when a family follows a strict procedure, giving options to purchase it to direct-line ascendants, neighbours, or former owners.[14] Foreigners do not have the right to buy agricultural land, but may take out a lease for a maximum of 30 years.

Albanian nationals who were the owners of existing buildings of any kind have been ceded the ownership of the land on which the buildings stand, including the garden and yard.[15] In a few cases this is not valid because of an amendment made by the restitution law[16] (discussed below). Many owners of private houses in urban areas have become the owners of the land on which the houses stand.

Tenants of state housing have been given the right to privatise their apartments;[17] the land under the building and the common areas has been conveyed to the apartment tenants in joint ownership.[18] Condominium associations have been set up to handle relations among co-owners.

---

12. Law 7501, approved on July 19, 1991.
13. Law 8053, approved on December 21, 1995.
14. Law 7983, approved July 27, 1995.
15. Law 7512, approved on August 10, 1991.
16. Law 7698, approved on April 15, 1993.
17. Law 7652, approved on December 23, 1992.
18. Originally Law 7688 approved March 13, 1993, but superseded by the Civil Code.

Effective July 28, 1995, both nationals and foreigners have the right[19] to buy land on which buildings stand (building land) as well as the buildings themselves. However, a foreigner can only buy land under a building if the building has a value equal to three times the value of the land. In the case of development land, the foreigner must lease the land until the building is constructed.

Two laws deal with restitution and compensation for former owners of real property. Former owners of agricultural land[20] do not have the right to physical restitution of the property, only to compensation. The other restitution and compensation law (Law 7698) fully covers real property inside the "yellow line" and addresses all circumstances. The closing date for making a claim was August 31, 1994; real property is now being returned or compensation is being made.

The right of the government to expropriate real property for public purposes (eminent domain) has been guaranteed since the first laws were enacted, although it was not fully set out until 1994.[21] The law explains the circumstances for expropriation. Property may be expropriated for the construction of roads, schools, hospitals, and residential centres and for the protection of archaeological sites. In all cases, the owner is to be compensated for the full market value of the property at the date of expropriation, plus payments for any disturbance, injurious affection (diminution of value), and severance (damages resulting from the physical separation). Lease interests are also to be taken into account.

The registration system in Albania is undergoing a complete transformation. This transformation is expected to take a number of years but should produce a modern registry system.[22] The new system will bring together the agricultural land cadastre and the urban land registry office *(Hipotec)*. The system being adopted is parcel-based, so that an interested party will no longer have to find out the owner's name to obtain information about the property. All sale contracts, mortgages, rights to use, and similar documents linked to the legal interest in the property still must be registered in the land registry offices. Leases, however, will only be registered if the term exceeds nine years.

Permission must be obtained to build on a parcel of land.[23] The permission process has two stages. First, the general nature of the building—the use,

---

19. Law 7980, approved July 27, 1995.
20. Law 7699, approved on April 21, 1993.
21. Law 7848, approved on July 25, 1994.
22. Law 7843, approved on July 13, 1994.
23. Law 7693, approved on April 6, 1993.

height, and area—has to be approved. To apply for this approval, ownership of the land is proven and the investor must demonstrate that 10% of the development cost is available. Within six months of initial approval, detailed plans must be submitted to obtain a building permit. At the completion of construction, the building is checked to ensure that it is in accordance with the plans. When the land is state-owned, the investor must obtain permission to access the land and construct the building. Only at the end of the construction process is ownership of the land transferred to the investor.

Typical Lease Structure

The property market is still in the first stages of development and this is certainly reflected in the leases that have been drafted. Until the introduction of the civil code, no modern legislation addressed the rights and responsibilities of landlords and tenants. The new civil code limits the length of leases to 30 years (except for residential properties) and requires that all leases with terms longer than nine years be registered. At the end of the lease, the tenant has priority to a new lease, provided all covenants have been kept.

Responsibility for all but minor repairs rests with the landlord. The landlord must cure all defects in the property; even a prior agreement cannot remove this obligation. The tenant has the legal right to sublet, but cannot assign without the written consent of the landlord. In principle, when a landlord sells a property encumbered by a lease, the buyer must continue to honour any obligations specified in the lease.

In the market, standard leases prepared by agents are simple and contain few details relating to rights and responsibilities. Leases specify the names of the parties, the address of the property, the rent, and the payment schedule. A lease also includes an inventory of movables (personalty) and assigns liability for the payment of services to the tenant. As time progresses, additional points are being added to leases, usually in response to problems that have emerged or to restate provisions of the civil code. Lengthy European leases are usually regarded as too detailed and specific about matters that are standard practice. In the majority of cases, however, such leases will be accepted subject to minor amendments.

In the major cities, leases of commercial property (offices, retail shops, and warehouses) generally run for one to three years. Leasing agents have begun to advise their clients to let (lease) retail shops for a period of five years. This trend also applies to large warehouses and offices requiring alterations. Most leases include an automatic right to renew. In the suburbs, the leases may be much shorter, i.e., three to six months, due to the uncertain future prospects of the business.

Leases taken by nationals on smaller retail units generally run for shorter periods, while leases taken by foreign companies on larger, more centrally located units run for longer periods of three to five years. Many retail units in the major centres have already undergone some modernisation and only need fitting out (finishing out).

In the early 1990s, many of the residential properties being let (leased) as offices were in poor condition and required electrical and plumbing work, decoration, modification, or other improvement. In such cases, leases were granted for periods of three to five years to allow the tenant to recoup his investment through a lower rental. Options for renewal were commonplace. This trend is beginning to change as owners of properties in poor condition realise that it is to their benefit to make the necessary repairs and decorations at low cost before letting (leasing) and thus obtain higher rents.

In all circumstances, the tenant is only responsible for internal repairs and the landlord has the responsibility for all other repairs. There is some debate about who provides electricity, plumbing, and other services. Contributions for common expenses and maintenance funds have yet to be considered by most owners and tenants in Albania.

Rent is payable monthly in advance in U.S. dollars, although for legal reasons contracts express rent in Lekë. Some leases are beginning to specify that rental payments be made quarterly in advance. The payment of a deposit is also becoming common. Because leases have short terms and the prospects for renewal have not been fully considered, rent review provisions in leases are rare.

When a tenant undertakes alterations to the property, either a rent-free period is provided or, more commonly, the rent is reduced. While the calculation of this reduction is often very simple, the actual amount is typically not based on a calculation, but rather negotiated to determine the highest possible reduction the landlord would be willing to make.

Leasing commissions paid by a landlord vary from 40% to 100% of the first month's rent; leasing commissions paid by a tenant vary from 10% to 20% of the first month's rent (for contracts that run for more than a year).

Property Market and Valuation

Before the transition to a market economy, Albania was unlike many other communist countries in that no form of private land ownership was possible. Thus, a real property market did not exist. The market has had to develop from nothing. At the outset, most people had no real idea of possible market values. In addition, there was a perception that many foreigners were coming to Albania and, within the first few years, prices for buildings increased enormously. A few markets have already developed in Tiranë, the capital. Market levels have stabilised and the availability of comparables can provide the valuer with some idea of market values.

There have been special problems in developing the market for land because of the restitution and compensation laws, the re-opening of the old registration system in 1991, and uncertainties over the ownership of property. Furthermore, only since the introduction of the new civil code has it been possible to identify the rights attached to the ownership of a parcel of land.

Even now there is often confusion about what is being sold, i.e., the land, the buildings, or the land and buildings. In many privatisations, buildings subject to five-year leases have been sold. Since the rights to renewal after the term expires have not been clarified, the question arises, "What happens to the building ownership?" The government is making efforts to remove such doubts.

In many parts of the country, there is still no developed market and it is difficult to find evidence for comparables. Since the cost of replacement is used as the method of valuation and the general public's current need for valuation services is limited, the lack of comparable data presents no real problem. In privatisation, the government uses its own methods. Rent and sale indices provide one method for valuing land (as discussed at the end of this section) and other methods are used for valuing buildings. The government does not require open market valuations. However, as banks become more concerned about the security of their loans, they are beginning to insist that property valuations be undertaken on a market value basis with reliance on the cost approach to check the value indication.

There is still poor understanding of the need for market valuations, due primarily to the prevalence of the cost approach and the fact that opportunities to obtain a mortgage or loan are so limited. One situation in which an opinion of value is required is the sale of property, whereupon the agent will either provide advice regarding the general market environment—advice that is usually accepted by the buyer—or take the figure directly from the seller.

A valuation may also be required when a loan is requested from a bank, although such loans are rare. In these cases, a construction engineer undertakes a valuation based on cost, which can result in an estimate very different from the value in the market. Undertaking a cost-based valuation presents difficulties. Information on construction costs is unreliable since materials are difficult to obtain and their costs are continually rising. Finding land sales can be just as challenging as finding the information required to apply the sales comparison or income capitalisation approaches. Another problem is that many buildings are old and poorly constructed, so it is difficult to determine the level of depreciation. Inevitably, cost-based valuations are simple and have no direct bearing on the market.

As a consequence of the restitution law, many families have been able to take back possession of their property. These properties often had been owned by one person, i.e., the father. Now, however, his close relatives have inherited the property and the ownership is split into several parts. When disputes over the allocation occur, the parties may seek assistance from a court valuer. The court valuers now need valuation licences although until recently they were licensed engineers.

The government has very few recently trained property valuers (only three at this time). For this reason, indices have been compiled since 1992 citing values for land to be rented or sold or land for which the previous owners claim compensation. The most current rent/sale index for building land (*truall*) takes into account the size of the population of the town in which the land is situated, the location of the land according to municipal zone or accessibility to roads, and the structural possibilities for the land. The sale value of land is set at 10 times its rental value. This rent multiplier (called *year's purchase* elsewhere) has been adopted randomly, without regard to the market, and therefore does not reflect capitalisation rates. Real property to be privatised is subject to a specified method of valuation.

Investment Method or Income Capitalisation Approach

The investment method, one of the five principal methods of valuation, considers the possible future benefits of ownership and applies a capitalisation yield (cap rate) to the prospective income. The yield (rate) can be an initial yield (direct cap rate) taken from comparables in the market. This yield implicitly includes growth. Alternatively, an equated yield (internal rate of return) can be developed based on a long-term, risk-free investment, such as a treasury bond, with an adjustment added for the risk associated with the property. In the latter case, growth is explicitly added to the equated yield.

Even when it is possible to determine future benefits, i.e., the rental income from a property, the valuer must determine what yield (cap rate) to adopt and, when appropriate, what level of growth to assume. The yield used can greatly influence the valuation when the income is substantial and the initial yield is low (say 5%). It is therefore essential that good market information be obtained. With such a limited real property market in Albania at the present time, it is difficult to assess the initial yield and growth possibilities. Moreover, there is no investment market from which to extract the risk-free yield (rate) for developing the equated yield (internal rate of return). Therefore, investment method valuations are exceptionally difficult.

The Valuation Profession

As the property market has evolved, so has the need for professionals who understand the market and valuation based on market principles. To meet this need, a one-year postgraduate programme is now offered at the Polytechnic University of Tiranë. This programme seeks to provide students with a good theoretical and practical basis for undertaking valuations. Five areas are covered: valuation, management, law, planning, and economics. Those trained are generally architects, economists, engineers, planners, and lawyers interested in adding to their professional skills.

Through contact with valuation professionals across Europe and beyond, it soon became apparent that Albania would need an organization to represent its valuers and to establish and maintain educational and professional standards. Accordingly, the Albanian Society of Real Property Valuers[24] (Shoqëria e Vlerësuesve të Pasurive të Paluajtshme) was established on August 15, 1995. Albanian property valuation professionals understand the need to follow accepted standards and have agreed to abide by international and European standards of real property valuation.

Various levels of membership in the society allow for the involvement of those trained or interested in property valuation. To become a full member and obtain a government license, the society requires candidates to satisfy the following criteria: the attainment of a university degree, diploma, or comparable level of academic education; the completion of specialised training in real property valuation; and practical experience in real property valuation.

The society is committed to ensuring and assisting in the education of real property valuers. In addition to the one-year programme at the Polytechnic University curriculum planners envisage undergraduate course offerings that will become the nucleus of an undergraduate programme (major). This will provide the educational foundation for the future profession.

At the same time, short valuation courses are being offered to ensure that professionals in financial institutions and priority sectors of the economy gain a knowledge of property valuation. Such training courses have been established for employees at the major banks that extend loans with property as a guarantee.

---

24. To contact the society, write to the following address: Rruga Qemal Stafa, Nr. 219, Tirana, Albania; tel/fax: +355 42 24549. The e-mail address is: davidallen@xc.org

On May 26, 1996, the government approved the licensing of real property valuers.[25] This represents a great step forward in the development of an officially recognised profession. The granting of licensing commissions will be administered by the Albanian Society of Real Property Valuers. The society can maintain high professional standards by requiring those who seek licenses to fulfil its membership requirements and by monitoring the professional conduct of its members. The new valuation profession has many challenges to meet in this rapidly developing economy, but the opportunities and prospective rewards are substantial.

Bibliography

The Institute of Statistics (INSTAT) of the Government of Albania publishes monthly and yearly information sheets on economic data.

All the laws referenced in the footnotes can be found in the *Fletorja Zyrtare (Official Gazette)*.

The International Monetary Fund (IMF) publishes an annual country report which, unfortunately, is not available to the general public.

---

25. Decision No. 394

12

Russia

Olga Z. Kaganova, PhD, CRE
Ellen A. Avrutis, M.A.

Olga Z. Kaganova, PhD, CRE, and member of the RSA, joined the Urban Institute in Washington, D.C. in 1994 and is currently providing technical assistance on real estate reform in Russia for the Housing Sector Reform Project of the U.S. Agency for International Development (USAID). Dr. Kaganova was also the founding partner of a private real estate consulting firm in St. Petersburg (AUREC). An internationally recognized expert on the urban real estate market in Russia, she has been a consultant for such clients as USAID, the World Bank, the European Bank for Reconstruction and Development (EBRD), the USAID-funded East European Real Property Foundation, the Chicago Title Insurance Company, COWI-consult (Denmark), and private clients in St. Petersburg. Between 1989 and 1994, she was the real estate and land policy advisor to several Russian municipal administrations as well as governmental agencies of the Russian Federation (the State Property Committee [GKI] responsible for the privatization of enterprises and nonresidential property, the Ministry of Construction, and the Ministry of the Economy). Dr. Kaganova has also appraised sites in Russian cities that were slated for sale to private developers. A graduate of the Novosibirsk State University (1972), she received her PhD in applied mathematics from the Institute of Biophysics of the Academy of Sciences of the USSR (at Krasnoyarsk) in 1981. Dr. Kaganova has received training in a broad range of real estate issues at schools in Sweden, Germany, and the United States. She has published extensively in professional and academic journals on the emerging real estate market in Russia.

Ellen A. Avrutis has been Vice President of Appraisal and Technical Services at the Chase Manhattan Bank since 1992. As an appraiser and real estate consultant, she has served in various managerial and technical capacities at Lincoln Savings Bank, Laventhal and Horwath, the Realty Valuation Group/Touche Ross & Company, and Landauer Associates, Inc. Ms. Avrutis holds an M.A. in philology and linguistics from Leningrad University. Since coming to the United States in 1978, she has pursued studies in computer science and real estate at Manhattan Community College, Baruch University, and New York University.

The Russian Federation occupies the vast plain stretching across northeastern Europe and western Siberia, broken by the Ural Mountains, the divide between Europe and Asia. Siberia east of the Yenisei River is largely plateau or mountainous, except for the coastal lowland along the Arctic Sea. To the west, the Russian Federation borders Finland, the Baltic states, Belarus, and Ukraine; to the south, the Black Sea (Kuban), Caucasus, Caspian Sea, Kazakhstan, Mongolia, and China (Manchuria); and to the east, the Sea of Japan, the Sea of Okhotsk, and the Bering Sea. The climate is continental and winters can be severe. The northernmost arctic zone is tundra (permafrost). Zones of taiga (coniferous forest), mixed forest, and grassland extend across the country. Much of the black earth (chernozem) region (the steppe) and the industrial Donets Basin are now part of Ukraine. Two-thirds of the population live in European Russia. Siberia, the Urals, and Caucasus are rich in natural resources. Industry is concentrated in the Urals, Kuznetsk Basin (west Siberia), and the principal cities of Moscow, St. Petersburg, Novosibirsk (Siberia), Samara (Volga), Yekaterinburg (Urals), and Nizhny Novgorod (Volga).

Political Structure

The first stage in Russia's post-communist development began in December 1991 with the abolition of the Soviet Union. On March 31, 1992, representatives of 11 former Soviet republics initialed a treaty of federation. Thus, the Soviet Union was transformed from the most centralized state in Europe to a decentralized federation of 11 fully sovereign countries, the Commonwealth of Independent States (CIS). The former Russian Soviet Federated Socialist Republic (RSFSR) became the Russian Federation.

According to the new constitution, adopted in December 1993, the federal government of the Russian Federation is divided into three branches: 1) an executive branch, which includes the offices of the president and prime minister, the council of ministers, and the federal ministries, state committees, and agencies; 2) a judicial branch (not yet constituted); and 3) a legislative branch with two houses: an upper chamber, the Federation Council, with 178 seats and a lower chamber, the State Duma, with 450 seats.

The first *free* presidential election was held in 1996. The president of the Russian Federation is elected for a five-year term and can serve for no more than two subsequent terms. The president appoints a prime minister. Upon the recommendation of the prime minister, the president appoints ministers responsible for overseeing the ministries of the economy, finance, defense, internal affairs (police), public health, education, transportation, culture, and others.

In post-Soviet Russia, consistent reforms, including the privatization and transfer of government property to private hands, the liberalization of prices and trade, and government support and stimulation of the private sector, have reinforced the irreversibility of the country's transformation to a free market economy.

One of the most important shifts in Russia's transition to democracy and a market economy has been the delegation of many responsibilities and rights that were once prerogatives of the central (federal) government and legislature to regional and municipal government levels. As yet, this process is far from complete. In many areas related to real property, the distribution of power among the different levels of authority has not been settled.

Urban planning and land use regulation are expected to fall under regional or municipal governance, but the future division of responsibilities between these two levels of authority is not clear. The reform-oriented branch of the federal legislature seeks to establish legal zoning plans, which are similar to the American system in which the territory of a locality is divided into separate zones, each of which is subject to certain development parameters set out in a local regulation which has the force of law and is binding throughout the municipality. Currently, the old Soviet-era system of urban planning is in force, where one may develop or redevelop a land parcel only after the local authorities prescribe the exact type of land use and all the parameters for the improvements. Naturally, under the current system, it is impossible to employ the concept of "highest and best use" in land development.

The taxation system has undergone fundamental reform. The draft of the new tax code has reduced the number of taxes from 150 to 30. It has also introduced a new division of taxes at federal, regional, and local levels to replace the current practice of distributing revenues from each major tax among the three levels of government. Regions will have a right to introduce the joint property tax instead of the three, separate taxes that now exist (the land tax, the tax on property of natural persons, and the tax on property of legal entities). The current land tax is definitely not an *ad valorem* tax. Two other taxes on property have an *ad valorem* tax structure, but the taxable values are not market values, but bookkeeping values. The existing draft of the new tax code does not address the question of the institutional structure for, or the principles of, property assessment.

Property Rights

Russia is in the process of rapid transition to a political and economic system that recognizes and offers equal protection to private, municipal, federal, and other forms of property.

Private ownership of real estate was illegal until the county's first privatization law was passed in 1991. The concept of real estate as land and anything permanently affixed to the land was deleted from Soviet legislation in 1922; since then, even in the new laws of the 1990s, land and improvements have been treated separately.

Private ownership of buildings and structures is permitted by current legislation and is not questioned in Russian society. The cornerstone of debate is the concept of the private ownership of land. Both the constitution of the Russian Federation and the next most important body of law, the civil code, allow for private ownership of land. However, Special Chapter 17 of the civil code, which is devoted to land rights, can be implemented only after a special law, the land code, is passed by federal legislation. This law is to specify land rights and the procedures for transferring these rights.

The civil code contains a passage which reintroduces the notion of real (immovable) property as land with attachments, but this effort is quite contradictory. First, the permitted "bundle of rights" differs in part for land and improvements. Second, the rights for land and improvements may be transferred separately. In the case of a building transaction, a transfer of some rights to the underlying land is automatically assumed. Undoubtedly, implementing such a practice will create a very complicated combination of rights for land parcels and buildings that are being appraised.

The civil code recognizes four different types of private land property rights: fee simple *(pravo chastoi sobstvennosti)*, leased fee estate *(vladeniye nedvizhimim imushchestvom, vzyatim v arendu)*, inheritable lifetime possession *(pozhiznennoye nasleduyemoye vladeniye)*, and right of permanent use *(pravo postoyannovo pol'zovaniya)*.[1]

The condemnation of privately owned real property for municipal or state needs (eminent domain) is allowed only upon the payment of compensation for the market value of the property and any lost profit.

The civil code requires that all principal rights to real property, liens and easements on real property, and any transfer of such rights be registered in a unified state registry. The code also provides that all issues relating to registration be addressed in the special federal law on the registration of real property and property transactions. Such a law has not yet been passed, and a unified state registry is not expected to be set up any time soon.

Meanwhile, various regions and cities are in the process of creating their own title registration systems. It is quite common for localities to have separate agencies for the registration of different types of properties. For instance, residential transactions are registered separately.

In general, Russian real estate transactions are less regulated and less standardized than transactions in the United States.

Currently, authorities do not guarantee the quality of titles, even if they are registered in compliance with local regulations. This creates a number of problems in both leasing and purchasing. The most basic difficulty is verifying the right of a given landlord to sell or lease the space in question. While

---

1. The Russian word for lease is *arenda;* leasehold or leasehold estate is *pravo arendi.* The word for estate, *pomest'ye,* has pre-1917 connotations. Distinctive property relationships evolved in Russia over the course of its history. Peter the Great perpetuated the system of conditional land tenure and the "service gentry" *(dvorianye/pomeshchiki),* whose holding of an estate *(pomest'ye)* was contingent upon providing military or other service to the government. The *pomeshchiki* collected the government poll tax *(podushnaya podat',* literally soul tax) from the bond serfs *(krepostniye)* on their estates. After Peter, the gentry managed to expand its prerogatives—the word for property *(sobstvennost')* first appeared in Russian law in the late 18th century. The serfs were eventually emancipated by a reformist tsar in 1861, but had to indemnify the gentry for the land they worked. The promising development of a landed peasant class in the last decade of imperial Russia was brought to an end by the Soviets, who first nationalized industry and in the 1930s collectivized agriculture. See Richard Pipes, *Russia under the Old Regime* (New York: Charles Scribner's Sons, 1974), 120-121, 172-173 and George Vernadsky, *A History of Russia* (New Haven: Yale University Press, 1961), 174-178.

the official registration process for such transactions is far from perfect, the very existence of a property registry gives rise to hope that the issue can eventually be resolved. In large cities, there are several private companies that specialize in issuing title insurance.

The greatest risk in a buy-sell transaction is that the documentation provided may either misrepresent the true state of affairs or reflect only part of the picture. The seller of an apartment, for instance, may keep silent about a family member who holds an interest in the unit, or the seller may not even be aware that this interest exists. Upon purchase, the new owner can find that there is a claim against the property from another party. In other scenarios, a property may already have been seized in a dispute, or the owner and his enterprise may be attempting to evade a major public utilities obligation. It is also possible that temporary-use restrictions were imposed on a building at the time of privatization.

Scope of Privatization

Russia is making great strides in the privatization of real property and the development of the real estate market. This process, however, is very uneven across market subsectors.

The privatization program started with the transfer of the ownership of apartments to private hands. At the end of 1995, more than 50% of the residential units in urban Russia were privately owned. The turnover in the existing home market in large Russian cities approximates that of the U.S.

The extent of privatization for existing commercial and industrial buildings is not known. For example, different sources report that from 30% to 75% of such properties were privatized in St. Petersburg by the fall of 1995. Although the exact inventory of existing nonresidential buildings in St. Petersburg is not known, the number of privatized properties may range between 5,200 and 13,000.[2]

Urban land was not privatized until recently. The only exception was a small amount of land that had been allocated to families for single-family homes and garages, or privatized by families living in existing, single-family homes. In 1995, after three years of failed attempts, the privatization of the land underneath previously privatized enterprises finally began. By December of 1995, about 1,300 enterprises across Russia had completed purchases of such sites and another 2,300 enterprises had submitted applications.[3]

---

2. O. Kaganova, "Reconstruction in Central St. Petersburg," a report prepared for the World Bank Working Group, September 1995.

3. L. Limonov, "Land Buy-outs by Privatized Enterprises and Market Development in Russia," a paper submitted to the AREUEA International Real Estate Conference, May 1996.

Geographically, the privatization process is quite sporadic. A few cities and regions, such as St. Petersburg, Orenburg (the Urals), the Saratov Region (Volga), Krasnodar (Kuban), and the Primorsky Territories (Vladivostok), account for more than 50% of the total number of these transactions and applications. About 40% of federal entities (regional administrative units) have not even initiated land sales to enterprises. Moscow authorities consistently ignore the constitution and presidential decrees regarding land privatization. They allow only long-term land leases that run up to 49 years, sometimes with an option to renew for a second, 49-year term. The 17 other federal entities have adopted the same policy through local legislation.

Delays in the privatization of land have resulted in the absence of a private land market for development. Many cities have declared their intentions to develop a market for long-term leasehold rights to land rather than ownership rights. In particular, the Moscow government made efforts to create a legal and administrative framework for the development of a secondary market in leasehold rights to land. So far, very few such transactions have been registered.

Considering all these factors, identifying the property interest being appraised may be very complicated in Russia and should be addressed with special care.

Language

Russian is the official language spoken in the Russian Federation. Many European languages are taught in schools on a mandatory basis, including English, French, German, and Spanish. In general, the citizens of Russia are not bilingual; however, in some non-Russian families (e.g., Ukrainian, Belorussian, Estonian), the native language is preserved and spoken. The most popular foreign language is undoubtedly English.

Currency

As a direct legacy of the command economy, which had no need for real money or real banking, there are deep structural problems in the monetary system in post-Soviet Russia. The collapse of the ruble as a medium of exchange was precipitated, in part, by a more than five-fold increase in the money supply and a huge budget deficit. As a result, by mid-1991 the ruble's value had dropped sharply in the limited exchange auction, from 50 per $1 U.S. to more than 200 per $1 U.S.[4]

Although the Russian ruble is the monetary unit, the majority of domestic real estate transactions are quoted in U.S. dollars or a ruble equivalent of the

---

4. W. G. Lapidus, ed. *The New Russia, Troubled Transformation* (Boulder, CO: Westview Press, 1995).

U.S. dollar rate. As of July 1996, the average conversion rate was 5,125 rubles to $1 U.S.[5]

Units of Measure

Russia uses the metric system of measurement. Real estate dimensions are quoted in square meters, expressed m^2. Both income and expenses for commercial properties are typically expressed in a ruble equivalent of the U.S. dollar rate per square meter per year. Rental rates for residential properties are usually quoted on a monthly basis. One square foot equals 929.03 square centimeters and one square meter equals 10.75 square feet.

Inflation

After the disintegration of the Soviet Union, the sudden shift from a command economy to a modern market economy exposed deep structural problems in all spheres of the economy and gave rise to financial and monetary chaos. By the end of 1991, uncontrollable hyperinflation had reached about 20% per month.[6] As the developing money market, real estate market, and capital market get closer to the turning point in this inflationary cycle, the prospects for more manageable inflation become much brighter. In mid-year 1996, inflation was averaging an annual rate of 58.4%.[7] Still, wide and unpredictable changes in the consumer price index represent a great problem for the appraiser, especially in estimating growth rates for future revenues and expenses.

Typical Lease Structure

In spite of the rapid privatization of real estate, municipalities continue to be the largest landlords. Open, competitive markets for municipal leases do not really exist. Leasing municipal properties depends mainly upon personal connections. The terms, rates, and conditions of such leases are usually determined either by formula, as opposed to real demand, or by officials who are bargaining for personal interests. For these reasons we will limit our discussion to leases offered on the open market by private landlords.

In general, lease contracts in Russian cities are much simpler than in the United States. Typically, the terms and structure of leases do not differ with the type of space (office, retail, or industrial). Standard lease terms run up to three years with net rents. The tenant pays a stipulated base rent plus building expenses and a value-added tax (VAT) on both amounts. Currently, VAT

5. *Novoye Russkoye Slovo* (June 1996).
6. Lapidus.
7. *The Economist* (June-July 1996).

equals 20% of the total payment amount. Base rents are often negotiated in U.S. dollars per square meter per year, although in lease contracts base rents are specified as a ruble equivalent of the U.S. dollar rate. Commercial leases are most commonly based on a flat rental rate. Some landlords, especially foreign ones, include an annual rent increase at some fixed percentage or, less often, "in accordance with inflation," but without specifying a method to adjust for inflation .

As a rule, tenants pay rent in monthly installments. Some owners request a deposit or advance payments equal to three months' to three years' base rent.

Although the average rental rates for retail space do not usually exceed those for office space, in addition to the minimum or base rent, retail tenants are sometimes obligated to pay a share of their gross sales. This percentage rent clause is found, almost exclusively, in the leases signed for the most famous shopping centers in the downtown areas of Moscow and St. Petersburg. In Moscow, for instance, the tenant's payment can be as high as 20% of gross sales.

The building expenses paid by the tenant usually cover all utilities, maintenance, and repairs. As a rule, the owner is responsible for capital expenditures and management fees. In St. Petersburg, for example, operating expenses are typically about 20% of the base rent. Further, tenants pay the VAT on the base rate and their share of the building expenses, which may equal 20% of the total payment amount. Thus, in St. Petersburg the total occupancy cost is about 144% of the base rent.

A great number of leases in many Russian cities have two components. Accordingly, a landlord and a tenant each sign two contracts. One is "official" and usually covers a smaller part of the negotiated rent. Payments stipulated by this contract go through bank accounts and are subject to all taxes, including the aforementioned VAT. Under the second, "unofficial" contract, the balance of the total rent is paid in cash. This rental payment is not registered and, thus, allows the contracting parties to avoid the VAT. Moscow brokers think that up to 90% of commercial and industrial leases are of this double nature.

Leasing commissions typically equal a month's rent and are paid upon signing the lease contract. Incentives such as a tenant improvement allowance are extremely rare.

Office Market

The commercial market for office space has several major components with different characteristics. Four types of space can be identified: privately owned, Western-quality space; privately owned, local-quality space; municipally owned space leased to private tenants; and municipally owned space occupied by public institutions.

Privately owned office space that meets Western standards in building design, amenities, construction materials, and private property management is typically found within new or reconstructed buildings in major cities. The growing demand for Western-style space has been met, in part, by the construction of business centers offering such amenities as modern offices, hotels or residential units, telecommunication lines, and parking facilities. Leases for space in business centers are more clearly formulated and may have a more Western rent structure.

In the fall of 1995, annual rents for office space in the business centers of St. Petersburg ranged from $370 to $800 U.S. per square meter, with space located in the low-prestige areas priced at the lower end of the range. In the Moscow office market, space in business centers commands higher rents. As of January 1996, the average net rent in Moscow was about $825 U.S. per square meter, and the total occupancy cost was about $1,050 U.S., which makes the Russian capital the sixth most expensive office market in the world.[8]

Privately owned space of local quality is typical of office buildings built in the Soviet period. It is characterized by low-quality design, construction materials, and workmanship. Although privately owned by privatized enterprises and institutions, space of this type is often poorly managed and rarely renovated.

In St. Petersburg, average rental rates for renovated office space range from $190 to $370 U.S. per square meter per year (as of the fall of 1995). There is growing competition in the office market because the amount of both privately owned, Western-standard space and privately owned, local-quality space is expanding through privatization, new construction, and reconstruction.

A third type of space is found in municipally owned buildings and units within these buildings. Such office space may be leased to private tenants by municipal agencies.

Finally, office space in buildings and units within buildings owned by municipalities may be occupied by public institutions (e.g., state research institutions, state universities, defense agencies) which rent out space to obtain revenues. The legality of these lease transactions is often questionable.

---

8. Richard Ellis, *World Rental Levels: Offices* (January 1996).

Properties in these last two categories are very similar in quality and condition to privately owned space of local quality.

In all Russian cities, there is a gap between the supply of office space in desirable locations and the demand for such space. The effective demand for office space in major cities created by new businesses and foreign companies is very sensitive to location and strongly oriented toward prestigious districts. Many of the office buildings constructed during the Soviet era and currently offered for rent are located in undesirable areas such as industrial zones. The difficulty of obtaining sites for construction from the municipalities limits the ability of private developers to close this gap.

Retail Market

In contrast to more developed real estate markets where retail space is typically more expensive than office space, in most big cities in Russia (with the exception of Moscow) the average retail rents are equal to or less than the rents for office space. This is attributable to a combination of factors.[9] First, as a condition of privatization, long-term restrictions on permitted uses were imposed on many retail and service-sector properties. A typical example would be a ground-floor unit occupied by a bakery in a mixed-use building. This unit must retain the same retail profile for five years after privatization, even if its highest and best use changes. Second, the commercial real estate market is still a long way from achieving equilibrium in supply and demand. Demand for office space is much greater than demand for retail space. To a significant degree, demand for retail space is a function of overall purchasing power, which for a sizable segment of the population is currently rather low.

Industrial Market

As a result of privatization, many industrial buildings and warehouses in Russian cities are available for lease or purchase. Based on the available information, annual rental rates for industrial properties in St. Petersburg typically range from $30 to $60 U.S. per square meter.

Currently, two problems are likely to make this type of real estate an undesirable investment. First, the majority of these structures are in very poor condition. Second, the taxable value of these structures, based on depreciated replacement cost, is often higher than the market value. Consequently, market demand for this type of property is low.

---

9. D. Jaffe and O. Kaganova, "Real Estate Markets in Urban Russia," submitted to *EMERGO, A Journal of Transforming Economics and Societies* (Sweden, 1996).

Valuation Standards

The appraisal of real estate emerged as a profession in Russia in 1993 when the Russian Society of Appraisers (RSA) *(Rossiiskoye Obshchestvo Otsenshchikov)* was founded and the first courses in real estate appraisal were conducted in Moscow and St. Petersburg.

The RSA developed and approved a set of professional standards in 1994. These standards set forth requirements governing the activities of appraisers. They are incumbent upon all members of the RSA. The standards include basic appraisal terminology, a listing of the professional responsibilities of appraisers, a discussion of the valuation process and procedures an appraiser should follow, and the factors an appraiser should consider in performing an assignment. They also contain requirements governing the data an appraiser uses, requirements for appraisal reports, and two special chapters on the methods the RSA may use to control the quality of the performance of its members and to resolve conflict. Many ideas in these standards are drawn from the experience of U.S. appraisal organizations. The standards are available to the public and have been promulgated by the RSA.

Licensing/Certification

By the spring of 1996, about 10,000 people in Russia had gone through different valuation training courses. Every course issues some kind of certificate. The most respected certificates are those from courses held under the auspices of the RSA.

The RSA is in the process of designing and implementing a graded system for the certification of members according to their level of formal training and experience. There are two primary forms of membership in the RSA: designation as a "member of the RSA," which has no educational requirements, and designation as a "full member of the RSA," which may be received upon completion of specified training courses.

To obtain other, more advanced designations, such as "certified appraiser of the RSA," an applicant must submit a certain number of documented examples of professional practice and receive the approval of the certification commission of the RSA. The RSA also has a code of ethics.

There is a clear trend to introduce the state licensing of appraisers.[10] Some regional and municipal authorities have already implemented local systems certifying appraisers as eligible to appraise state or municipal properties.

---

10. The draft law on appraisal activity in Russia, passed as soon as it was introduced into the Russian Duma in May 1996, stipulates the compulsory licensing of appraisers. The largest professional organizations, such as the Russian Society of Appraisers and the Russian Guild of Realtors, have lobbied for the licensing of appraisers.

A number of American and international real estate organizations have played a consultative role in the development of a licensing program for appraisers in Russia. The regulatory system in many ways mirrors the criteria developed for state licensing and certification in the U.S.

Appraisal Reporting Requirements

The RSA has established requirements as to the content, format, and style of an appraisal report, which are obligatory for RSA members. These requirements are modeled on the standards of the Appraisal Institute (in the U.S.) and the international standards of the IVSC.

Definition of Market Value

The definition of market value given in the draft of the law on appraisal activity in Russia is set forth below.

Market value is understood as the most probable price for which the subject of the appraisal will be sold in an open market with competing sellers and buyers, where both parties are acting prudently and have all required information, and the price is not affected by special circumstances. This means that:

a) The seller and buyer are typically motivated;

b) Both parties are well informed and acting in their own best interest;

c) A reasonable time is allowed for exposure in the open market;

d) The price represents reasonable compensation for the property unaffected by any concession granted by anyone associated with the transaction;

e) Payment is made in cash or its equivalent.

Income Approach

As privatization in Russia continues, the private owners of office buildings, retail units, warehouses, industrial buildings, and residential units realize that they can enjoy the current and future earnings of a property plus the proceeds from resale of the property at the termination of the investment. Naturally, as the market matures, the need to value income-producing properties for various reasons will grow.

There are two fundamental problems that any appraiser will encounter in trying to value real property in Russian cities. First, there is a lack of available and reliable market data, which are essential to any appraisal of real property.

The second problem relates to the instability of the Russian economy, particularly its high inflation.

Direct Capitalization

The main obstacle in applying the direct capitalization method lies in the derivation of overall capitalization rates from market data. In a limited resale market such as Russia, it is extremely difficult to find a reasonable number of properties for which relevant information on sales, income, and expenses is available and from which the appraiser can extract capitalization rates.

Even in large cities, the market for certain types of properties is marginal, with just a few properties being sold in an open, competitive environment. Therefore, there is not enough information regarding market sales prices, particularly for office buildings. The resale market for retail space is fairly active. However, the sales prices of many retail units held under separate property title, but situated within mixed-use buildings, do not reflect free market prices due to specific use limitations prescribed at the time of their privatization. In addition, many retail units have been bought by the retailers themselves. While the sales prices can be obtained, rental data do not exist.

The reliability of the available data on the income of commercial properties is limited due to double nature leases, for which both official and non-official contracts are negotiated.

The most open segment of the market is represented by Western-quality properties in the business centers of cities. Typically, the tenants of these properties are foreign companies that avoid illegal business transactions. Unfortunately, this market niche is small and has such distinctive characteristics that the information derived from it is not applicable to the rest of the real estate market.

The most developed sector of the real estate market consists of sales and rentals of residential units. However, it is impossible to get substantial data on sold units for which both sales prices and rents are known. In the absence of direct data, an appraiser must use the sales and rental information derived from different properties. To estimate a capitalization rate (the ratio of income to sales price), one uses average income per square meter from one sample and an average sales price per square meter from another. For this kind of estimate, it is important to adjust average income to reflect the occupancy rate in the rental apartment market. The occupancy rate can be estimated as the ratio of the average lease term for rental apartments to the sum of the average listing time and the average lease term. Both the average listing time and the average lease term can be obtained from the databases of brokerage companies.

When gathering sample data on apartments to estimate an average income per square meter, the appraiser should carefully select units that are under the same type of rental arrangement. For example, if the owners of all the units in the data sample are responsible for making outside payments such as utilities, these estimated carrying costs should be deducted from gross rent when the net operating income for each apartment is calculated.

It is important to understand that the real estate market, money market, and capital market are not yet as strongly interrelated in Russia as they are in countries with a developed market economy. For instance, construction lending does not yet exist. Banks lend for construction very rarely and only to companies which they somehow control. Thus, the banks act more as holders of an equity position than as actual lenders. Even mortgage lending to home buyers is in an embryonic stage. In Russia only about 4,000 mortgages had been originated by the summer of 1996. This means that estimating a capitalization rate as a weighed average of debt and equity costs, a method commonly used in the U.S., is not applicable in Russia.

Discounted Cash Flow (DCF)

The instability of the Russian economy and its high inflation limit the applicability of discounted cash flow analysis. It is impossible to project with reasonable accuracy either future rental rates or many categories of operating expenses. Rental rates are very sensitive to the relationship between demand and supply, which is difficult to forecast in the growing and unstable real estate market of Russia. Further, many expenses, utility costs in particular, are increasing at rates that differ from those indicated in officially published indexes of inflation, such as the consumer price index. As a result, inflationary increases in operating expenses are difficult to forecast realistically. As a part of tax reform, the real estate tax rate is expected to be revised shortly. Moreover, the ground lease agreements for municipal land often do not specify future rent increases. All these factors increase the uncertainty of future earnings and expenses.

Discounted cash flow analysis is popular in Russia for the valuation of new construction and reconstruction projects. Sometimes the DCF technique is used by appraisers and consultants even when their clients do not think in terms of cash flow discounting or net present value, but instead formulate their return requirements in simple terms of annual profit. This is especially true of real estate developers. The general immaturity of real estate, money, and capital markets and the lack of available information further complicate the situation. This backdrop creates a situation in which there are different types of investors. Each looks at its own available investment opportunities and sets its required returns. As a result, the discount rates utilized in DCF analyses are based on investment requirements of different types of investors and vary considerably. The resulting value estimates are analogous to investment values rather than market values.

Sales Comparison Approach

As a secondary market for various types of privatized real property develops in Russian cities, the sales comparison approach is becoming more applicable and its popularity among Russian appraisers is increasing. In big cities, this approach is widely used for "quick and dirty" pricing of major types of real property, i.e., residential, office, retail, and industrial (including warehouses). As a rule, the unit of comparison is sales price per square meter of gross building area.

As the hospitality industry in Russia is quite young, very few, if any, hotels have changed hands. Comparable hotel sales data do not exist. In most cities there are no comparable data on sales of land under permitted uses other than gardening or single-family housing.

The sales comparison approach is commonly used for the appraisal of housing units; in the big cities, these are mainly apartments. Most brokerage companies use their own in-house models for residential appraisals. As a rule, such models consist of lists of adjustment factors or coefficients that are applied to the basic price of a standard housing unit of a particular type. Basic prices are usually mean prices taken from samples of transaction data on units of a similar type. For example, the units in a sample could be three-room apartments in a prefabricated concrete building constructed in Moscow between 1975 and 1980. Some appraisers also use mass appraisal models to estimate the market value of an apartment unit. Different adjustment factors are used in the various proprietary models, each of which is based on data compiled by an individual firm. The compatibility of these models is limited. Every company considers its program the best on the market and does not publicize the details of its appraisal models.

New product is constantly entering the rapidly growing real estate market in Russia. For example, there are now townhouses, which were practically unknown in Russian cities until recently, and luxury country homes of 300 square meters or more. Very few units have already gone through the sale cycle, and thus their market values have not yet been established. New construction is extremely risky for developers because the demand for innovative projects and future profits are not easily forecast.

Cost Approach

In Russia, the cost approach is very popular for estimating the market value of newly constructed improvements. It is also used to value existing properties, especially when comparable sales data are not readily available.

The applicability of this method in Russia has several unique characteristics and some limitations:

1. The cost approach principally considers the improvements. Land value often is not estimated because it is not clear who possesses the land rights. (Currently, municipalities are the landowners.)

2. The main data sources are construction cost indexes, which are published on a quarterly or monthly basis by specialized regional information centers. There is a great difference between published costs and cost data obtained directly from developers, which, to a large extent, may be a result of high inflation. It is preferable to get actual cost information on the property from either a building contractor or a developer.

3. There are no commonly accepted standards as to what components of direct and indirect costs should be included in the construction cost indexes. These indexes may mean different things in different regions. In one region, for instance, on-site landscaping or architectural and engineering fees may be included in construction costs, while in others some of these items may not be included. This can cause double-counting or the complete omission of important cost components.

4. Estimating entrepreneurial profit is yet another challenge for appraisers. The market is so far from equilibrium that the profit required by developers may vary greatly, perhaps from 30% to 60%.

5. There are not enough data to estimate the market's reaction to the different components of depreciation. Thus, when applying the cost approach to existing structures, the appraiser has to rely on his or her experience and intuition, rather than accepted industry practice, which has yet to be established.

Land Residual Technique

A market for land available for new development has only recently come into existence. Nevertheless, there is a continuing need to establish potential sales prices for sites, especially to acquire long-term rights to municipally owned parcels. In the absence of comparable data, the land residual technique is the only applicable method of valuing land. The underlying concept is that a purchaser of long-term land rights is going to construct something to be sold on the market. A feasible land price is determined by estimating the difference between the anticipated future proceeds from a sale and the cost of the project including the required profit. The formula for the land residual technique in this context is:

Sales proceeds – direct & indirect costs – entrepreneurial profit = estimated land value

To employ this formula, the appraiser has to rely upon conclusions obtained from both the sales comparison and cost approaches. Application of the land residual technique, therefore, involves the problematic areas of these two approaches which were previously discussed.

Sensitivity Analysis

All quantitative parameters of the Russian real estate market are highly volatile. Thus, a point estimate of market value or investment value cannot be considered reliable. Sensitivity analysis is required to test a value conclusion obtained by any method other than direct sales comparison. As the result, the appraiser should offer the client a range of value estimates rather than a single value estimate.

The simplest way to address volatility is to estimate appraised value as a function of key parameters. As the parameters change within ranges set by the appraiser's assumptions, the estimated value will fluctuate. The ranges for the value estimate can be wide but, as this is an undeniable feature of reality, the conclusions reached will be helpful and informative. Creating different sets of parameters, the appraiser explores the value of the real property under various scenarios, e.g., optimistic, worst case, or mid-range. Estimating value using several different scenarios may be a very useful tool to assist clients in their decision-making.[11]

Reconciliation

The report requirements of the Russian Society of Appraisers do not call for the formal inclusion of reconciliation in an appraisal. Because the real estate market is still immature and fragmented, it is practically impossible to employ all three approaches when valuing real property in Russia. To reach a reasonable value conclusion, the appraiser has to be cautious, yet innovative. Every possible effort must be made to compare the results obtained by the one or two applicable methods against others, even those that result in only rough estimates. Verification of data is extremely important in the appraisal of any type of property, and particularly in appraising new real estate products. If not tested against the prices of competitive products, the value conclusion can be very misleading.

---

11. Jaffe and Kaganova.

Availability of Data

Reliable market data are very difficult to obtain in Russia. There are three primary reasons for this.

1. The real estate market is so young that many of the elements in its institutional infrastructure have not yet been developed.

2. A remarkable number of real estate transactions and operations are carried out within the gray economy, which seeks to avoid any kind of public attention.

3. Even reliable data become obsolete quickly due to general economic instability and high inflation.

Because statistical information is released by municipal and state agencies only after great delay, it fails to reflect the rapid changes in both the political situation and the economy. Furthermore, the very structure of these statistics does not reflect new market realities. The data being published in real estate periodicals or available from brokerage companies usually relate to asking prices rather than consummated transaction prices and rental rates. Certain subsectors of the real estate market have not yet developed, so comparable sales simply do not exist. Property management is in an embryonic stage, and information on operating expenses, rent levels, and vacancy/occupancy rates, which is typically obtainable from property managers in more mature markets, is either not available or too fragmented. Other critical problems relating to inflation have already been mentioned.

The availability of local statistical data relating to real estate is quite uneven across Russia. The type of information published in a local weekly newspaper in one city may be treated as a "state secret" in another. Below are some suggested sources of data.

Economic and Demographic Data

- Regional and municipal departments of statistics
- Public libraries
- Periodical press (local, real estate, business)

Real Estate Market Data (Demand, Supply, Costs, Sale Prices, and Rents)

- Brokerage companies and property managers
- Local companies providing real estate consulting and market analysis
- Real estate periodicals
- Pricing in regional centers of construction

- Local organizations of real estate practitioners (i.e., local chapters of the Russian Guild of Realtors and the Russian Society of Appraisers, local independent associations). Membership may be required.

Appraisal Organizations

The Russian Society of Appraisers has more than 50 local chapters, a list of which is available from the central office of the RSA at 107078 Moscow, Novaya Basmannaya Street, 3 21-1. Phone/fax (095) 261 56 53 or (095) 263 01 00.

Bibliography

The Economist (June-July 1996).

Ellis, Richard. *World Rental Levels: Offices.* (January 1996). London: Richard Ellis.

Goldman, Marshall. *Lost Opportunities.* Norton Press, 1994.

Jaffe, D. and O. Kaganova. "Real Estates Markets in Urban Russia." Submitted to *EMERGO, A Journal of Transforming Economics and Societies.* Sweden, 1996.

Kaganova, O. "Appraising Undeveloped Land in Russian Cities." *The Appraisal Journal.* (July 1997).

Kaganova, O. "Reconstruction in Central St. Petersburg." Trip report prepared for World Bank Working Group, September 17-28, 1995. The Urban Institute, October 1995.

Lapidus, W. G., ed. *The New Russia, Troubled Transformation.* Boulder, CO: Westview Press, 1995.

Limonov, L. "Land Buy-outs by Privatized Enterprises and Property Market Development in Russia." Paper submitted to the AREUEA International Real Estate Conference, Orlando, Florida, May 23-25, 1996.

Matthews, Roderick J. "Russian Real Estate: Still in the Early Stages." *Urban Land* (May 1997), 7-8.

Novoye Russkoye Slovo. (June 1996).

13

Republic of India

David S. Elmo, M.A., M.S.

David S. Elmo is a real estate appraiser and asset management specialist for the United States Department of State in Washington, D.C. In this capacity, he contracts for, reviews, and performs appraisals and financial analyses in more than 180 locations worldwide. Mr. Elmo received an M.A. in management from Webster University in St. Louis, Missouri, and an M.S. in real estate development from Columbia University in New York City.

Mr. Elmo was assisted with this chapter by an Indian market expert, Kantilal K. Vikamsey. Mr. Vikamsey is a Mumbai (Bombay)-based appraiser specializing in all areas of real estate appraisal in India. He is a government registered architect and valuer, a chartered engineer, and a fellow member of the Institute of Valuers in India. Mr Vikamsey received an M.S. in foundation engineering from Marquette University in Milwaukee, Wisconsin.

The Indian sub-continent is formed by a triangular shield pushed up against the Himalayas. This mountain range acts as a barrier to the cold winter winds of central Asia. At the base of the Himalayas lies the densely-populated, alluvial Indo-Gangetic plain stretching to the Bay of Bengal. The Thar Desert makes up the central western part of the country along the border with Pakistan. The Deccan plateau, bordered by the ranges of the Western and Eastern Ghats, forms the center of the Indian shield. India's climate is shaped by the seasonal monsoon, which brings the subcontinent tropical rain-laden winds between May and September. Seventy-five percent of India's population is rural. Principal cities are Mumbai (Bombay), Calcutta, Delhi, Madras, Ahmadabad, Bangalore, and Kanpur.

Political Structure

India is the fifth largest economy in the world and home to more than 900 million people. After gaining independence from Great Britain in 1947, India became a republic under a constitution approved two years later. Its form of government is a federal republic, similar to that of the United States. The central government of India exercises great power over the 25 states. This government is generally patterned after the British parliamentary system.

The president and the vice president hold largely ceremonial positions and are elected for five-year terms. Elections to each position are staggered and the succession of the vice president is not automatic. Real executive power is centered in the Council of Ministers, to which the president appoints the prime minister. The president, under the advisement of the prime minister, then appoints the subordinate ministers. The governmental ministry most involved in India's real estate industry is the Ministry of Urban Development.

India's parliament is bicameral, consisting of the Rajya Sabha and the Lok Sabha. The Rajya Sabha, commonly referred to as the Council of States, has 240 members, each elected or nominated for six-year terms. The Lok Sabha, commonly referred to as the House of the People, has 544 members, each elected for five-year terms.

India's independent judicial system began under British rule. Judicial concepts and procedures resemble those of Anglo-Saxon countries. The Supreme Court has 26 appointed justices.

Governmental authority not expressly delegated to the central government is reserved for India's 25 states and six union territories. One of the governmental powers delegated to the local level is zoning.

Zoning (land use planning) is prevalent throughout India's 25 states and six union territories. Through zoning, municipalities implement appropriate land use planning by regulating the type and density of real estate development.[1]

Property taxes are assessed annually at the municipal level. These taxes represent charges for services provided by the municipal authority, e.g., water supply, sewage treatment, and road maintenance. Throughout India, taxes are typically based on a percentage of the value of the real estate.

---

1. For example, the Urban Land Ceiling and Rent Control Act of 1976 (ULCRA) is a national act that is amended and interpreted at the local municipal level. This act regulates allowable densities for real estate development and encourages rent control and other protections.

Property Rights

India has a long tradition of property rights protection. The classification of properties recognizes two major categories: freehold estates and leasehold estates.

The owner of a freehold estate holds an absolute and unencumbered ownership right. A freehold estate in India is similar to a fee simple estate in the United States. Because of its free transferability, the freehold estate is the most sought-after property right in India.

In India, a growing trend in freehold residential ownership is the condominium. Once only common in Mumbai (Bombay), condominium ownership is gaining popularity and widespread acceptance in many of India's major cities. Condominium ownership gives owners a combination of freehold title to an individual unit and an undivided fractional interest in common areas.

In a leasehold estate, the lessee or tenant leases the land from a lessor or landlord. The lessee has the right to use and occupy the structure until the expiration of the lease. Leasehold estates are very common throughout property sectors in India, especially in the larger metropolitan areas. In New Delhi, for example, more than 50% of all properties are held in leasehold. These properties include all of the plots and flats (apartments) assigned by the Delhi Development Authority (DDA) and the Land and Development Office (L + DO) of the Ministry of Urban Development.[2]

India is a land of small, family-worked agricultural plots.[3] Many historical, political, and economic factors have contributed to the development of the existing system of land tenure. The ownership, acquisition, disposition, and taxation of land fall, by provision of the constitution, under the jurisdiction of India's states. Although the central government issues general guidelines for land tenure, the states are responsible for their implementation. The operators of most agricultural plots possess rights to the land they farm, either as owners or protected tenants. The land tenure system developed from the

---

2. Leasehold estates are commonly conveyed by assignment. Government agencies (e.g., L+DO) and quasi-governmental agencies (e.g., DDA) generally use power of attorney to assign the right to occupy a property, subject to the ground lease. A power of attorney conveyance is also used by sellers to evade significant capital gains taxes. Capital gains would otherwise be taxed at 50% of profit, i.e., the difference between the original purchase price of the improvement and its current value would be taxed at 50%. When analyzing and comparing transactions, valuers must recognize the local nuances that affect the exchange of property "rights."

3. A recent survey of land use in India indicated that 55% of the land is arable, 1% is used to grow permanent crops, 4% is meadows and pastures, 23% is forest and woodlands, and 17% is under other uses. A breakdown of India's farms according to size shows that more than 50% contain less than one hectare, about 20% have between one and two hectares, 16% have between two and four hectares, and 11% contain 4 to 10 hectares.

zamindar tradition.[4] The absentee landlord system tended to result in the subdivision and, over time, the fragmentation of farms. A major fault in the system is that it lacked a formal agency for documenting evidence of land ownership and tenancy.

Toward the end of the twentieth century, most large absentee landlords had been eliminated through an extensive legislative process. By the 1970s, the rights to their agricultural holdings had been acquired by the state in exchange for cash and government bonds. By now, more than 20 million former zamindar tenants have acquired the occupancy rights to the land they work. While some tenants still rent from the state, most have acquired the right to purchase the property they till. Payments are spread out over 10 to 20 years.

Recent land reform legislation, passed by most of India's states, protects agricultural tenants from exorbitant rents by prescribing maximum rates. For example, the maximum rental rate might be fixed at 20% to 25% of the annual income associated with the farm's product. Several states have also taken steps to create a *panchayat,* or village assembly.[5] These assemblies, which have performed with mixed results, are typically charged with maintaining land records, managing government-owned plots, and collecting land revenues (taxes).

The government affects the real estate industry in India through the exercise of police power, the imposition of taxes, the enactment of special legislation, and the governance of succession law.

Police power gives local government the authority to establish rules governing land use, public safety, and welfare, e.g., city planning, zoning, and building or health codes.

Taxation gives local government the authority to collect annual assessments and fees for public services such as garbage collection, water, and mainte-

4. *Zamindar* originally meant landowner, but later came to refer to revenue collectors (often tax farmers) during the Mughal period (1526-1858). The British Permanent Settlement (Landlease) Act of 1793 served to transform the zamindars into a class of landlords, often absentee, who bought estates as financial speculations and paid the government fixed annual revenues. Peasant cultivators, who held traditional hereditary rights to their plots and were rarely dispossessed, became tenants at will of the zamindars. From Percival Spear, *A History of India,* vol. 2 (Baltimore: Penguin Books, 1973), 96-97.
5. A *panchayat* is typically a council of five or more members. It may also be an administrative grouping of villages under a constitutionally mandated elective council.

nance of the infrastructure. Additionally, all real estate sales transactions are taxed, based on regulations in India's Income Tax Act of 1961 (as amended).[6]

Special legislation gives local government the authority to enact rules that can influence property use and value, e.g., local rent control laws and other restrictions on real estate. One example of special legislation that is vested in the central or state government is the law providing for *acquisition in the public interest.* Like eminent domain law in the United States, acquisition in the public interest involves the right of the government to take private property after payment of just compensation. Acquisition in the public interest is governed by the Land Acquisition Act.

Right of succession to owned property is governed by the Indian Succession Act of 1925 and the law of India. The Indian Succession Act details the rights to the inheritance of immovable property, including all legal rights of family members and other interested parties. The Indian Succession Act further details rules of property distribution in cases where estate owners have died intestate.

Foreign Investment and Property Rights

Since the early 1990s, India has embarked on sweeping economic liberalization. Key components of this economic liberalization have been significant amendments to India's Foreign Exchange Regulation Act (FERA), especially as it relates to real estate. Beginning in 1994, the central government of India has given non-resident Indians (NRIs) and other overseas corporate bodies (OCBs) the right to acquire and/or develop real estate for residential or industrial purposes. Another amendment of FERA gave Indian companies, capitalised by foreign equity of more than 40%, the right to acquire real estate. These changes allowing foreign ownership of property are examples of the fundamental nature of India's economic liberalization.

---

6. Regulations on the taxation of real estate transactions have changed significantly since the early 1990s. In order to evade taxes, it was previously common practice for payment in sale transactions to be made both by check (which was the recorded, taxable basis of payment) and cash (which represented the unaccounted or unrecorded part of the payment). This unrecorded cash payment was known as *black money.* The prevalence of black money payments has been curbed with the introduction of section 37 (i) of India's Income Tax Act of 1986, which established the following procedures: a) all purchases of real estate with values greater than Rs 1 million need to be cleared first by the central government's Income Tax Department, b) if the Income Tax Department considers the recorded purchase price to be at least 15% below the property's value, it is authorized to acquire the property and auction it publicly. The sale must be transacted by a check (recordable) payment. Understanding the traditions and conventions of paying black money is extremely important, especially when analyzing or verifying the prior sales history of a property or comparable sales. Before the introduction of section 37 (i) into the Income Tax Act, real estate transactions were characterized by approximately 40% to 50% of property value being paid in black money. Since the enforcement of these rules, payment of black money has declined substantially—to levels as low as 5% to 10% of overall property value.

Language

More than 24 languages are officially recognized in India. While Hindi[7] is the national language and primary tongue of more than 50% of the population, English is the most important language for national, political, and business communication. An appraiser who speaks only English should not anticipate any communication problems while performing valuation services in India. Other major languages in order of the number of speakers include: Bengali, Punjabi, Telugu, Marathi, Tamil, Kannada, Gujarati, Malayalam, Oriya, Assamese, Sindhi, Kashmiri, Konkani, Nepali, and Manipuri.

Currency

The monetary unit of India is the rupee, expressed Re or, in the plural, Rs. One Indian rupee equals 100 paise. All domestic real estate transactions are priced in rupees.

In quoting large real estate values, it is important to understand notational conventions and two additional terms used for monetary measurement in India. First, the convention of placing a comma before every three digits is followed only for the first thousand, e.g., one thousand rupees is written Rs 1,000.00. After the first thousand, commas are placed at intervals of every two digits to the left, e.g., one hundred thousand rupees is written as Rs 1,00,000.00.

Second, two unique monetary terms will be found in most valuation reports: *lakh* and *crore*. One lakh is one hundred thousand rupees, written numerically as Rs 1,00,000.00. In a valuation report or print media, this amount will most likely be expressed as Rs 1 lakh. One crore is one hundred lakh or ten million rupees. One crore is written numerically as Rs 1,00,00,000.00. In a valuation report or print media, this amount will most likely be expresses as Rs 1 crore. For example, the number Rs 4,50,53,705.00 is read as Rupees Four Crore, Fifty Lakhs, Fifty Three Thousand, Seven Hundred and Five only.

The short notation for lakh and crore values is typically expressed in the decimal point system. For example, as indicated in Table 1 near the end of this chapter, a value of Rs 11.22 lakhs equals Rs 1,22,000.

---

7. The Constitution of India mentions 18 principal languages. Hindi and Urdu (the most widely spoken language in Pakistan) essentially represent overlapping languages, sometimes called Hindustani. Hindi is written in the Devanagari script; Urdu, in the Arabo-Persian script. Linguists sometimes separately classify two other languages of eastern Hindustan that overlap with Hindi, i.e., Awadhi (Lucknow area) and Bhojpuri (Bihar). Sanskrit is the classical language of Hindu and Vedic literature.

Units of Measurement

The Republic of India uses both the English and metric systems of measurement. Typical units of measurement in the English system include the square foot (sq. ft.) and square yard (sq. yd.). The typical unit of measure in the metric system is the square meter (m²). In less urbanized areas, land is commonly measured in either acres (one acre = 4,840 square yards) or metric hectares (one ha = 10,000 m²). Sometimes government agencies quote prevailing land rates[8] as the value of land in *grounds* (one ground = 223 m² or 2,400 sq. ft.).

Another important area measurement in India is the *plinth*. Plinth area, as defined by Indian Standard 3861-1975, includes "the built-up covered area at the floor level of the basement or of any story."[9] Plinth area includes walls and columns, internal shafts, stairways, machine rooms, and porches, but excludes areas such as balconies, lofts, terraces on the first floor, and spiral staircases. A full understanding of plinth measurement is especially important to the valuer because it is needed to apply the cost approach.

Inflation

Between 1980 and 1991, the average annual rate of inflation in India was 8.2%. Approximate annual estimates of inflation were 10% for 1992, 8% for 1993, and 10% for 1994.

Inflation is measured over time (per year) as the percentage change in consumer prices. Inflation rates are widely reported in the press and are readily available to knowledgeable real estate professionals.

The Reserve Bank of India also publishes an inflation index. The base year for this index is 1981. Thus, in 1981 the inflation index for India was 100. In 1994, the Reserve Bank of India reported an inflation index of 259. Inflation statistics can also be researched in publications such as the *Financial Statistics Yearbook* of the International Monetary Fund (IMF) and in reports published by the World Bank.

India's sustained 8%+ rate of inflation is most likely attributable to the following factors: the devaluation of the rupee against other international currencies, the rapid increase in foreign exchange assets, government borrowing from the Reserve Bank of India (monetised deficit), rapidly growing portfolio investments by foreign institutional investors, increases in direct

---

8. The term *land rate* is explained in the discussion of land valuation in the subsequent section on the sales comparison approach.

9. *Practical Valuation* by B. Kanaga Sabpathy (Tiruchirappalli, India: Ezhilarasi Kanagasabathy, 1994).

foreign investment, and borrowing by Indian companies through global depository receipts.

Inflation statistics are especially important in conducting discounted cash flow analysis. While present value theory is understood by many valuers in India, discounted cash flow analysis, which relies on annual inflation statistics and other forecast assumptions, is not usually applied in real estate valuations.

Typical Lease Structure

While ground leasing is a widespread practice throughout the Indian real estate market, premises are not generally leased. Occupant ownership of office, retail, and residential property is typical throughout India. The ownership interest is especially prevalent in the larger metropolitan areas.[10]

Office and Commercial (Retail)[11] Leases

Only a small percentage of the total supply of office and commercial space in India is available for leasing. Approximately 90% of all office and commercial facilities are owned by the occupants, leaving only 10% available for leasing.[12]

The typical office or commercial lease runs between three and nine years. Leases are negotiated on a gross square foot basis, with payments made at the beginning of each month. It is a common practice for the lessor to request and receive up to one year's rent as a security deposit. This deposit is usually refundable, without interest, after the tenancy period expires.

Escalation clauses are written into office and commercial lease agreements. Typical, annual escalation increases may be tied to the consumer price index or set at a certain percentage, e.g., 10% to 15% per year or 20% every two years. Most leases specify renewal terms and conditions. Upon termination of

---

10. In analyzing Indian leases, valuers must be aware of both the official and unofficial details of transactions. When leases are drawn up, some of the rental money may not be accounted for. Specifically, the value of the leases may be underrecorded. In order to evade taxes, lessors and lessees typically underreport the agreed-upon rent. A recorded amount is written into the lease (and typically paid by check), and an unrecorded component is paid in cash. Through underreporting, the taxes paid by the lessor and the lessee are reduced. This practice, similar to black money in sales transactions, is being curbed through the efforts of government tax regulators.

11. In India, the term *commercial* corresponds to *retail* in North American usage. There is no distinction between the structure of leases for office and commercial (retail) buildings.

12. In India, most office space is purchased or reserved after the developer has determined the property design. Typically, each floor has several ownership units, each consisting of a few hundred square feet. Many of those who take purchase options on space are speculating on future price increases in rentable office space. Tenants who want additional space must rent or purchase it from other owners and reorganize the partitioned areas into a customized office. Sometimes companies with large space needs, such as foreign firms recently established in India, are forced to negotiate with up to a dozen owners in order to assemble a sufficient amount of contiguous office space.

the lease, renewals usually require the consent of the lessor, unless the tenant is specifically protected by an applicable rent control act. Rental rates for renewals are generally set at the prevailing market rate. Because demand greatly exceeds supply, rental concessions and other discounts or benefits are not typically offered to tenants in India.

Most office or commercial leases are not assignable. If a property is being considered for sale, it is common practice for the right of first refusal to be reserved for the lessee.

Unless otherwise specified in the office or commercial lease agreement, the tenant bears practically all operational costs, including tenant improvements, utilities, maintenance, cleaning, repairs, management, and taxes.

Residential Leases

Only a small percentage of the total supply of residential units in India[13] is available for leasing. Approximately 90% to 95% of all residential units are owned by the occupants, with the remaining 5% to 10% available for leasing. One reason residential leases are uncommon is because of strict rental controls, as codified in the various rent control acts. These rental controls significantly favor the tenant, from both a financial and a legal perspective.

A typical residential lessee could be an employee of a multinational firm, a diplomat, or an Indian national (business executive with family) on temporary assignment. Residential leases are for three years. Like leases in the office sector, residential leases are based on gross square footage and payments are made at the beginning of each month. It is a common practice for the lessor to request and receive up to one year's rent as a security deposit, often refundable without interest after the tenancy period expires.

Escalation clauses may be written into residential lease agreements and most leases specify renewal terms and conditions. Upon termination of the lease, renewals usually require the consent of the lessor, unless the tenant is specifically protected by an applicable rent control act. Lease rates at renewal are typically set

---

13. This section only discusses residential units available to the middle and upper classes of Indian society, which constitute 30% of India's population. The weakest societal tiers in India, which account for approximately 70% of the population, do not own real estate. Indian society consists of an extremely wealthy class (about 1% of the population), a middle class (29%), a lower class (30%) of the population, and a very poor class (the remaining 40%). The population is approximately 75% rural and 25% urban.
    Increasing the housing stock has not been a priority of the Indian government, and housing shortages exist in both urban and rural areas. Analysts believe that one-third of the population of India's larger cities live in areas officially regarded as slums, i.e., large shantytowns built of scrap or natural material on any space available (even sidewalks). Such dwellings lack running water, sewage lines, and electricity. The government has attempted to build housing facilities and utility connections for urban developments, but its efforts have fallen far short of demand. Administrative controls exercised by the government have discouraged many private investors from constructing housing units.

at the prevailing market rate. Like office leases, residential leases are not generally assignable. If the property is being considered for sale, it is common practice for the right of first refusal to be reserved for the lessee. Unless otherwise specified in the lease agreement, the lessee bears practically all operational costs, including utilities, maintenance, repairs, management, and taxes.

Industrial Leases

Approximately 80% of all industrial concerns in India hold ground leases, while the remaining 20% own the land on which the plant stands. Industrialists pay for and develop their own improvements. To encourage industrial development, the Indian government targets specific zones for industrial leasing and pursues policies to promote industrialization.

The typical length of an industrial ground lease is between 30 and 99 years. Ground leases are measured on a gross square meter basis. Typically, an initial rental premium is paid at the onset of the lease to the state authority that established the industrial zone. This one-time initial premium, which is based on the prevailing rate for land rent per square meter, represents most of the rental payment over the life of the lease. Initial industrial lease premiums can range anywhere from Rs 50 per square meter in underdeveloped, less desirable sections of the country to Rs 1,500 per square meter in industrialized areas in great demand. Annual lease payments are made, but these payments are usually quite nominal, at times as low as Re 1 per year.

The lessee of industrial ground bears practically all costs for the development of facilities, maintenance, utilities, repairs, management, and taxes. Renewals for ground leases are set at the prevailing market rate upon termination of the lease.

Valuation Standards

Comprehensive valuation standards have not yet been established in India and, as discussed later, there are many different formats for valuation reports. Although comprehensive standards do not exist, some aspects of the valuation process have been standardized through the efforts of the central, state, and local governments. This standardization especially applies to the procedures in the cost approach. For example, many jurisdictions publish construction costs for specific types and sizes of properties. Further, the same jurisdictions may publish and document standardized land prices for certain land types and parcel sizes. Frequently these standardized price levels are used as benchmark costs for a given locality. They may also be used to assess tax values.

Licensing/Certification

In India, there are two types of valuers of immovable property: approved valuers and registered valuers. Approved valuers are recognized by the

Institution of Valuers, a trade organization headquartered in New Delhi. The scope of assignments an approved valuer can undertake is limited to appraisals for purposes of taxation, unless the approved valuer is also a registered valuer. Registered valuers are registered with India's Income Tax Department (Central Board of Direct Taxes, or CBDT). They can do valuations for all purposes.

Requirements for recognition as an approved valuer include:

- An undergraduate degree in architecture or civil, mechanical, electrical, automobile, or mining engineering
- Membership in, or possession of, a diploma from a recognized institution of chartered engineers, architects, or surveyors or from a school of mines
- Practical valuation experience for not less than 10 years
- Application to, and acceptance by, the Institution of Valuers

Requirements for recognition as a registered valuer include:

- An undergraduate degree in civil engineering, architecture, or town planning or evidence of similar qualifications
- Former employment in a government post as a gazetted officer (i.e., the appointment has been published in a government list), or in a post under any other employer receiving a renumeration of not less than Rs 2,000 per month, or as a professor in any institution preparing students for degrees in civil engineering, architecture, or town planning
- Practical experience in consulting engineering, surveying, or architecture for not less than 10 years and work in the valuation of buildings and land, quantity surveying, architectural/structural design, town planning, or land development
- Application to, and acceptance by, the state Chief Commissioner of Income Tax

No formal program of continuing professional education is mandated for either the approved or registered valuer designations. For self-improvement and skill development, Indian valuers can avail themselves of annual conferences and seminars on valuation issues.

The written body of knowledge on the Indian valuation profession is growing. *Indian Valuer,* the professional journal of the Institution of Valuers, publishes informed articles on appraisal practices and procedures. In 1994, a textbook focusing on the valuation of immovable property was published.[14]

---

14. This textbook, *Practical Valuation,* is a comprehensive outline of the practical procedures required to perform valuations in India. B. Kanaga Sabapathy, *Practical Valuation* (Tiruchirappalli, India: K. Ezhilarasi Kanagasabathy, 1994).

Appraisal Reporting Requirements

Valuation reports in India are tailored to meet client needs and to satisfy state/bank requirements. Valuations are used to support business decisions (acquisition/disposition), analyze feasibility, manage portfolios, administer taxes, and plan estate inheritances. Report formats vary, based on use as well as the wishes and requirements of the client. Indian valuations are significantly less detailed and voluminous than the narrative appraisals prepared in the United States.[15] Reports over 30 pages long are uncommon.

Most Indian valuations are questionnaires or forms supplemented by analysis.[16] Valuers define the appraisal problem by answering basic questions, such as, What is the address of the property? What is the use of the property? and Does the property have commercial potential? These questions are usually included on a preprinted form. Once much of the basic, factual data has been established, written analysis and interpretation follow. A value is reported after the preliminary questions have been answered, the analysis has been developed, and the interpretation has been provided. While no standard format is prescribed for Indian valuations, many share similar features. One common format is illustrated in the following outline of a typical table of contents of a valuation report for a bank.

Part One—Introduction

Title page

Letter of transmittal

Overall summary (valuation certification in which the valuer declares that the value estimate is correct)

Part Two—Factual Data

Questionnaire:

> Forty to 50 preprinted questions (on Form O-1) that establish all the terms and details of the appraisal assignment. Areas covered by the questionnaire include identification of the property to be appraised, property

---

15. Many Indian valuers are aware of the requirements for narrative appraisals specified by appraisal standards and can fully meet these specifications.

16. The standardized questionnaire for Indian valuations is Form O-1. This form was prescribed by the central government for income tax purposes, pursuant to the Wealth Tax Act of 1957. The "O" in "O-1" refers to the official purpose of the valuation. The "1" in O-1 signifies that it is the first type of valuation recognized by the central government, the valuation of immovable property. Valuations of other types of assets, such as agricultural or mining enterprises, have different numerical suffixes, i.e., O-2 or O-3.

description, land description (and details), improvements description (and details), discussion of rents, discussion of comparable sales, and costs of construction. Most questions require short answers that can appear as annotations next to the questions. Typical questions and answers follow.

Typical Question	**Typical Answer**
Purpose for which the valuation is being undertaken:	To assess the fair market value of the property.
Brief description of the property:	Address, block, lot
Boundaries of the property:	North ...
	East ...
	South ...
	West ...
Type of use to which the property (as though vacant) can be put?	Residential
Accessibility to public amenities such as schools, hospitals, markets, etc.:	Moderate distance
Commercial potential of the property?	None

Part Three—Valuation

By the cost approach:

Land: Analysis includes the size of the plot and current market rates, concluding with the estimated value of the plot. The analysis can be presented in paragraph form or as an answer to statements in a questionnaire.

Building: Analysis includes details of the plinth area and general construction as well as replacement costs and depreciation estimates. This analysis can be presented in paragraph or answer form.

Extra items: Comments on and analysis of any extra items (e.g., an overhead water tank) or other significant improvements can also be presented in paragraph or answer form.

Amenities: Comments on and analysis of amenities, e.g., interior decorations, architectural details, air conditioners, etc., can also be presented in paragraph or answer form.

Services/miscellaneous: Comments on and analysis of services provided, outdoor amenities (trees, gardening), or separate buildings can be presented in paragraph or answer form.

By the rental or capitalisation method (if desired by the client)

By the open market value method (sales comparison approach)

Part Four—Conclusions

A recapitulation of the previously recorded values is provided. A typical format is illustrated below.

By the cost approach:

Component	Rs Indicated Value
Building	18,00,000
+ Amenities	2,00,000
+ Services	1,00,000
+ Miscellaneous	50,000
+ Land	12,00,000
= Total Rs:	33,50,000

By the capitalisation of rent:

Net Annual Rental Income	Divided by Capitalisation Rate	Equals Indicated Value
Rs 4,00,000	/ 12%	= Rs. 33,33,333

Values by other approaches, such as the open market value method (sales comparison approach), may be provided as requested by the client.

Remarks

Includes a verbal restatement of the value, other certifications such as the date the valuer inspected the property, and the valuer's signature.

Annexure (Addenda)

Includes items such as sketches, photographs, and other documents (deeds, surveys).

Definition of Market Value

In India it is universally accepted that value is a function of the time, place, and purpose of the valuation. The Indian appraiser or valuer considers market value to be one of the most important appraisal concepts. A commonly accepted definition of market value is "the sum of money that a property would fetch if it is sold on the open market."[17]

---

17. B. Kanaga Sabapathy, *Practical Valuation* (Tiruchirappalli, India: Ezhilarasi Kanagasabathy, 1994). In valuation reports, the terms *market value*, *fair market value*, and *open market value* are used interchangeably.

Other Commonly Reported Values[18]

Understanding the nuances of the different values reported in Indian valuation reports is critical. In India, there are many commonly reported values. While some of these terms have similar connotations in appraisal practice in other countries, other terms have a different meaning in India. For example, the term *present value* is used in India to mean cost less depreciation, which is significantly different from its definition in the United States of America.

Below are definitions of some of the more common types of values.

Replacement value. The cost of replacement of a similar building with comparable specifications at the current market price on the date of the valuation. In India, this term is interchangeable with *reproduction* or *reinstatement value.*

Present value. The replacement value less depreciation value (see the following definition).[19]

Depreciation value. The reduction in value of the property due to age, deterioration, lack of maintenance, obsolescence, decay, or wear and tear. Depreciation value depends on the age of the property and its future life.

Earning value. The present value of a property which will start to yield an income in the future. Also called *investment value.*

Guideline value. The value of the land which is recorded in the local registrar's office and used for the purpose of determining stamp duty at the time the property transfer documents are registered.

Monopoly value. In a developed area, the value of a vacant plot continues to increase as the number of available plots decreases. The premium price asked by the vendor (seller) for the remaining plot (or final group of plots) is known as the monopoly value.

Fancy value. When it is absolutely necessary for a purchaser to have a specific property (for various reasons), the purchaser will be prepared to pay more for it in comparison to others. Also known as *desired value.*

---

18. Ibid.

19. In contrast, the *Dictionary of Real Estate Appraisal,* 3d ed. (Chicago: Appraisal Institute, 1993) defines present value as "the value of a future payment or series of future payments discounted to the current date or time period zero."

Income Approach

The two principal methods traditionally employed in the income approach to value include direct capitalisation and discounted cash flow analysis. In the income approach, the valuer analyzes a property's capacity to generate benefits and capitalises these benefits into an indication of value. This approach can also be used to estimate investment or earning value. In India, the most frequently used income technique is direct capitalisation, commonly referred to as the *rental or capitalisation method.*

Direct Capitalisation (Rental or Capitalisation Method)

In this approach to valuation, a single year's flow of cash (or a single year's income expectancy) from a property is estimated and converted into an indication of value using a capitalisation rate or factor. In India the net annual rental income *(NARI)* is capitalised at an appropriate rate of interest or capitalisation. Net annual rental income equals the gross annual rental income *(GARI)* minus any specified expenses. While it is typical practice for the lessee to bear most of the expenses of a lease, some lease agreements may contain clauses whereby the lessor pays some expenses, such as property taxes, repairs, maintenance, service charges, insurance, rent collections, and management charges.

Capitalisation rates can be derived from government sources or the market. When the capitalisation rate is derived from government sources, it must be consistent with the rates published in Schedule III of India's Wealth Tax Act of 1957, as amended in 1989. The typical capitalisation rates suggested in Schedule III range between 8% and 12%. If an appropriate capitalisation rate is derived from the market, the valuer is strongly encouraged to document and discuss the logic used in selecting the rate.

Direct capitalization is the most prevalent income technique among Indian valuers because it is simple and less sensitive to dramatic changes in market conditions. Given the uncertainty of market conditions and the difficulty predicting future trends, estimating appreciation rates, and developing other assumptions, evaluators are reluctant to use discounted cash flow analysis.

Discounted Cash Flow (DCF) Analysis, Yield Capitalisation

While present value theory is well understood and can be applied by many valuers in India, few rely on discounted cash flow (DCF) techniques in valuing real property. In yield capitalisation future benefits are converted into investment or earning value by discounting each future benefit at an appropriate yield rate. DCF theory is based on assumptions about future income and property value. One reason DCF analysis is not commonly used in India is that it is difficult to predict a future income stream. In addition, DCF analysis is not used because 1) strict rent control laws add to the owner's risk and therefore discourage long-term real estate investment; and 2) the tax structure discourages the purchase and resale of investment property—assumptions that are key to DCF analysis. In those rare situations in which discounted cash flow projections are analyzed, typical forecasts run 10 to 11 years. Critical assumptions should be validated by the best possible market evidence and trends as to the residual (reversionary) value, discount rates, appreciation rates/escalators, and operational costs.

Open Market Value Method (Sales Comparison Approach)

In India the sales comparison approach is called the *open market value method.* Using this approach, market value is estimated by comparing the subject property to similar properties that have recently sold, are listed for sale, or are under contract. For property types that are bought and sold regularly, the open market value method can provide a supportable indication of market value. However, the approach is not used in India to the extent or with the degree of rigor that it is applied in the United States.[20] While the principles of the open market value method apply to the valuation of land as discussed below, Indian valuation reports rarely make an extensive study of comparables. When the open market value method is applied, analysis of comparables, field verification, and on-the-spot enquiries are conducted to obtain data indicating trends in value.

Although sales comparison is not typically included in Indian valuation reports, many valuers maintain personal databases on sales of specific property types in their local area. Based in their exposure to the market, some valuers are able to generate a list of comparable sales upon request. For example, an office valuer in Mumbai (Bombay) would typically maintain a list of recent office sales in his subject area. The appraiser would sort out properties on the list by considering factors that influence value, e.g., date/type of sale, price per unit of measure, location, size, amenities. For a demanding client who may want rigorous evidence, a tabulation of sales can be used to develop an appraisal based on sales comparison.

---

20. Indian valuation reports do not treat comparable sales in a format and style similar to that used for narrative appraisals in the United States. Unless specifically requested, an Indian valuer will not take a photo of the comparable sale and will not report the transaction details of each comparable property on a separate page as is common in the United States. Indian valuations rarely include paired data analysis in support of the open market value method.

Land Valuation and the Open Market Value Method

The open market value method is used for land valuation. The valuer analyzes recent sales of parcels of land that are similar in terms of location, size, intended use, zoning, and configuration. The most critical element in the comparison is the degree of similarity among the parcels of land involved in the transactions.

After analyzing sales transactions of comparable parcels, the appraiser can develop an estimate of unit value, which is known in India as the prevailing market rate. Once the rate is established, it can be applied to the area of the plot to provide an overall indication of land value.

The valuer may check the prevailing market rate developed against traditional benchmarks of land value, such as guideline rates, prices fixed by the development authorities for their plots, and enquiries from real estate agents and brokers. Periodically updated government reports of land value are widely used to establish a basis for land value. Sample land value data is shown in Table 1.

Table 1. Land Rates in Madras (Mylapore) During 1991		
Period	**Location**	**Rate per Ground***
January 1991	Warren Rd.	Rs 11.22 Lakhs
January 1991	Royapettah High Rd.	Rs 10.90 Lakhs
February 1991	Kutchery Road	Rs 6.04 Lakhs
June 1991	East Abiramapuram	Rs 9.77 Lakhs

* 1 Ground = 223 m² or 2,400 sq. ft.

Based on official land rates in Madras, as published in the *Indian Valuer* (March 1992).

Cost Approach

The cost approach is the most widely applied valuation approach in India. The traditional formula for the cost approach is: estimated replacement cost[21] for the subject property less depreciation plus land value. The cost approach is also used to estimate the value of proposed construction, additions, renovations, and special-use properties. There are many reasons why the cost approach is favored by Indian valuers.

---

21. In India, no distinction is made among the terms *replacement cost, reproduction cost,* and *reinstatement cost.*

1. Indian valuers often have backgrounds in architecture and engineering, which are fields that rely heavily on cost approach techniques.

2. The government (Income Tax and Public Works Department) promotes standardization of the information required to perform a cost approach analysis. Standardized data are available for:

   • Local land prices

   • Depreciation schedules

   • Costs of construction for various types of improvements on a plinth-area basis (periodically updated). These costs are published either by India's Central Public Works Department or by state-wide jurisdictions. Table 2 provides an example of construction cost data.

Table 2. **Plinth Area Rates of Buildings in Tamil Nadu (Madras), 1989-1990 in Rupees per m²**

Classification	Floors	Load Bearing Wall Structure	Framed Structure
Residential buildings	Ground floor	Rs. 1,650	Rs. 2,060
Nonresidential buildings	First floor and above	Rs. 1,440	Rs. 1,870

Based on official construction costs in the State of Tamil Nadu, as published in the *Indian Valuer* (April 1990).

A summary of a cost approach appraisal is shown in Table 3. This example assumes that, in a previous section of the valuation report, the valuer has established the land value and the reinstatement value (replacement cost new) and depreciated value of each building component using standard plinth areas and government-reported cost calculations.

Reconciliation

Reconciliation presents a brief summary of the applicability, reliability, and relative merits of the various appraisal approaches used by the valuer in the valuation report. Reconciliation typically appears at the end of the report before the final value is concluded. While a formal process of reconciliation is expected in reports prepared by appraisers in the U.S., reconciliation is uncommon in Indian valuation reports.

At the conclusion of the valuation, an Indian valuer typically restates the pertinent values derived in the report. Like appraisers of the United States, the Indian valuer does not average indications. In reporting the final values, it is a convention for the valuer to report the values both numerically and in written form, i.e., Rs. 4,50,53,705.00, which reads as "Rupees Four Crore, Fifty Lakhs, Fifty Three Thousand Seven Hundred and Five only."

Table 3.	Cost Approach, Tabular Summary (For the Valuation of a Factory Complex)	
Component	Reinstatement Value (Replacement Cost New in Rs)	Depreciated Value in Rs
Security structure	95,000	91,400
Office building	3,18,150	2,85,400
Porch	55,950	50,200
Toilet block	1,34,500	1,20,600
Boiler house	1,25,500	1,12,550
Compressor room	1,27,900	1,14,700
Main factory bldg.	3,57,71,750	3,20,90,900
Substation	2,57,200	2,30,700
Miscellaneous	5,00,000	5,00,000
Plus land value	76,67,800	76,67,800
Indicated value	4,50,53,750	4,12,64,250

Availability of Market Data

Accurate and verifiable market data on real estate transactions is significantly more difficult to obtain in India than in the U.S. With effort, however, valuable market data can be researched and reported. A valuer who insists that market data does not exist probably does not have the requisite understanding of the property under valuation. Further, the valuer who relies solely on published rates, standard values, and official formulas will probably not be able to provide the client with a market-based valuation.

While confidentiality and privacy are real concerns that hinder the collection of specific market data, the valuer's challenge is to identify trends in the real estate market. The difficulty of developing and maintaining accurate market knowledge in specialized areas (e.g., square meter prices of office sales in Mumbai [Bombay]) should not be used as an excuse for not collecting such data.

Market research may test the valuer's investigative skills, but real estate market data is available from a wide variety of sources. Some obvious sources of information are listed below.

Demographic and Economic Data

- Government offices (state, county, municipal)
- Local chambers of commerce
- Libraries
- Articles in local and national newspapers

Real Estate Market Data (Market Size, Occupancy Rates, Rent Levels)

- Real estate appraisal, brokerage, management, and construction firms
- Government offices (state, county, municipal)
- Appraisal trade journals such as the *Indian Valuer*
- Articles in local and national newspapers

Rent and Sale Comparables

- Appraisers
- Brokers
- Other individuals who know about specific sale transactions (i.e., buyers, sellers, and real estate lawyers)

Appraisal Organizations

India's principal appraisal organization can be contacted at the following address:

The Institution of Valuers
Anand Parbat
Opp. Police Station
New Delhi - 1100 005
Tel. 011-91-11-572-5854

Conclusion

Although there are similarities in the valuation techniques used in India and the United States of America, there are also many differences. The reasons for these differences are varied. The uses and intentions of valuation reports differ as do the histories and traditions of land use. The education and professional training of Indian and U.S. appraisers are different as well. The influence of taxation and government regulations also account for divergence.

In the United States, appraisal education is well developed. Courses are taught within college programs and are offered by professional trade organizations such as the Appraisal Institute. In India, the absence of a valuation curriculum at the college level makes it necessary for valuers to seek professional development through workshops, seminars, and conferences sponsored by a variety of organizations. The demand for these seminars continues to grow as does the level of valuation expertise and sophistication.

The valuation profession in India is a demanding and dynamic field. As is true throughout the world, developing a value opinion requires a thorough understanding of property value, practical experience in the profession, an ability to communicate clearly both verbally and in writing, and well-honed analytical skills and judgment. Indian valuers follow ethical guidelines, demonstrate professionalism, and maintain high levels of technical competency. Internationally oriented valuers can adapt their findings to more rigorous report formats such as the narrative appraisals used in the United States. Many Indian valuers uphold and even exceed international valuation standards.

Bibliography

The Institution of Valuers. *Indian Valuer.* New Delhi. Published monthly.

Sabapathy, B. Kanaga. *Practical Valuation.* Tiruchirappalli: Ezhilarasi Kanagasabapathy, 1994.

14

Japan

Hiroshi Yoshida, Licensed Real Estate Appraiser,
Japan Real Estate Institute
Kazuhiko Fujiki, Licensed Real Estate Appraiser,
Japan Real Estate Institute

Hiroshi Yoshida has worked for the Japan Real Estate Institute (JREI) since 1966 and is currently a member of the JREI senior advisory staff for appraising. Mr. Yoshida became a licensed real estate appraiser in 1970 and has remained an active practitioner. Until September 1994, he led the Income Approach Working Group of the Land Appraisal Committee at the National Land Agency, and he currently serves as chairperson of the Income Approach Development Subcommittee within the Ad Hoc Committee on Income Approach Applications of the Japanese Association of Real Estate Appraisal. This subcommittee makes recommendations on improving current income approach methods. Mr. Yoshida translated the income approach chapters of the sixth edition of *The Appraisal of Real Estate* into Japanese. He holds a bachelor of commerce degree from Waseda University in Tokyo and is a real estate counsellor certified by the Japanese Association of Real Estate Appraisal.

Kazuhiko Fujiki is the North American liaison for the Japan Real Estate Institute. He is also affiliated with Richard Ellis Cumberland in Vancouver, Canada. Mr. Fujiki was a research associate at the Japan Real Estate

Institute before immigrating to Canada. He holds a bachelor of business administration degree from Ritsumeikan University and a master of science in business administration (urban land economics) from the University of British Columbia. Mr. Fujiki is a licensed real estate appraiser in Japan and a candidate member of the Appraisal Institute of Canada.

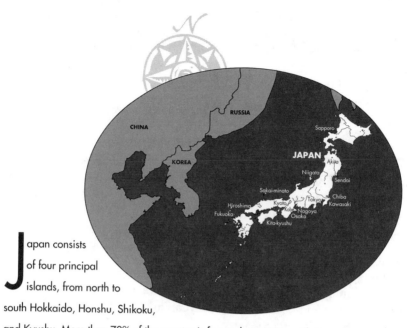

Japan consists of four principal islands, from north to south Hokkaido, Honshu, Shikoku, and Kyushu. More than 70% of the country is forested mountains with several active volcanos. The islands are prone to earthquakes. Rich coastal plains (e.g., the Kanto plain on Honshu) constitute the arable land. The moist climate is influenced by the warm south-to-north Kuroshio current, the cold north-to-south Oyashio current, and the monsoon. Principal cities are Tokyo, Yokohama, Osaka, Nagoya, Sapporo, Kobe, and Kyoto.

Political Structure

The government of Japan is a constitutional monarchy with independent legislative, executive, and judicial branches. The Emperor does not take any direct part in government, but as the head of state he performs diplomatic and ceremonial functions. For example, he formally appoints the prime minister and the chief justice of the Supreme Court. He also receives important guests from abroad.

The legislative branch, the Diet or Parliament, claims the supreme power in the political structure. It consists of the House of Representatives and the House of Councilors. The lower house contains 500 members, each elected for a term of four years. The upper house is composed of 252 members, each elected for a term of six years. Half of the members are elected every three years. The Liberal Democratic Party (Jiyu minshuto), the majority party between 1955 and 1993, is still the largest single party.

The Diet elects the prime minister from its membership. The prime minister appoints about 20 Cabinet members. At least two-thirds of the Cabinet members must be members of the Diet. There are 12 ministries and various other agencies and committees. Each Cabinet member usually heads a ministry or an important agency.

The chief justice of the Supreme Court is appointed by the Emperor based on the Cabinet's recommendation. The other 14 justices on the Supreme Court are appointed by the Cabinet. Every judge on the Supreme Court can hold his or her office until the age of 70, provided he or she is not rejected in a national ballot held every 10 years.

Japan is divided into 47 prefectures *(ken)*. The area of a prefecture can include cities and counties. A county generally consists of more than one town or village.

Compared to other countries with a federal system, government power in Japan is fairly concentrated in the national government. The centralization of authority is also reflected in the field of real estate. Most regulations affecting real estate are enacted by the national government. For example, the framework for zoning is stipulated in specific laws and regulations prepared by the central government. A municipality decides on its zoning within this framework.

Property taxes are assessed and levied by municipalities. However, in 1992 the national government introduced land value taxes. The national government also levies another category of property taxes on certain types of land.

Property Rights

The ownership of property gives owners the right to do as they please with the property, subject to laws and regulations. An owner of real property can reside in the property, build on the site, lease the property, or tear down the existing improvements. The scope of ownership rights, however, is limited in various ways. Condemnation represents the strongest limitation on property ownership. Land use and building regulations also restrict ownership rights.

The prefectural governors and the mayors of major cities monitor land transactions in regions where an unusual jump in land value is expected. In these regions, the parties to a sale of a land parcel that exceeds a certain size must report the agreed-upon sale price and the intended land use to the governor or the mayor, who may recommend that the parties revise the actual sale price.

Ownership of real property is registered at the local real estate registry office. In Japan, land and improvements are recorded separately in two different registers. Unlike the Torrens System employed in countries such as Australia and Canada, the Japanese registration system does not protect innocent purchasers from losing ownership to a legitimate owner who has been unlawfully deprived of his or her property rights.

Tenant rights are safeguarded in Japan. The old Ground Lease Act and old Building Lease Act, both of which were originally enacted in April 1921 and are still binding for lease contracts signed before July 1992, protected tenants by giving them automatic renewal after expiration of the lease contract unless the landlord has rightful cause to terminate the contract. Under an automatic renewal, rent is negotiated between the landlord and the tenant. Due to recent amendments to the Ground Lease and Building Lease Act,[1] ground lease contracts containing no option for renewal have been valid since 1992.

Language

Japanese is spoken throughout Japan. The Japanese writing system is composed of Chinese ideographic characters (kanji) and Japanese phonetic characters (kana). English is taught as a second language at public high schools beginning in grade seven.

Currency

The Yen (¥) is the unit of currency in Japan. There are three kinds of bills, in denominations of ¥1,000, ¥5,000, and ¥10,000. There are also coins in the amounts of ¥500, ¥100, ¥50, ¥10, ¥5, and ¥1.

---

1. The Ground Lease Act and the Building Lease Act were consolidated into the Ground Lease and Building Lease Act in 1992.

Units of Measure

The metric system is used in Japan. Areas are usually measured in square meters. Larger tracts of land, especially farmland, are often measured in hectares. Traditional units of area measurement, such as the *tsubo, tan, choh,* and *joh,* are sometimes preferred to square meters. One *tsubo* is equal to 3.3 square meters (35.5 square feet); one tan equals 300 *tsubo;* one *choh* equals 3,000 *tsubo;* and one *joh* is one-half a *tsubo.* The *tan* and *choh* are used for measuring farmland, whereas the *joh* is used to measure room size in residential properties.

Inflation

Over the last 15 years, prices have been generally stable in Japan. During this period, annual inflation as measured by the Consumer Price Index ranged between 0.0% and 3.9%. In contrast to consumer prices, land values experienced a sharp upswing and downswing during the same period, especially in metropolitan areas. According to a survey compiled by the Japan Real Estate Institute, the urban land value index for six major cities in 1980 was 24.5. Within 10 years, it surged up to 105.1, but by 1994 had plummeted down to 63.2.

Inflation is an important factor to consider in the appraisal of real estate, especially in the estimation of net operating income for use in the income approach. The Consumer Price Index is prepared by the Management and Coordination Agency. Statistics on land values have long been available from the National Land Agency. Several private real estate research firms also publish data.

Typical Commercial Lease Structure

Lease terms for office or retail space usually run less than five years. Most commonly, office leases run from two to three years. In contrast, a landlord and tenant negotiating a lease for a large-scale retail store sometimes agree to a contract term of 20 years. Under the provisions of the civil code and the Ground Lease and Building Lease Act, a lease with a term of less than one year is considered to be a contract without a specific term; a lease term of more than 20 years is automatically reduced to 20 years. A lease without a specific term can be terminated six months after notification is given by the landlord, provided there is reasonable cause. The period is reduced to three months when the tenant wishes to move.

Rent reviews usually take place every two to three years. Rent can be revised either upward or downward. However, most leases include a clause that makes any upward revision by the landlord contingent upon certain economic conditions.

A retail tenant usually pays percentage rent above base rent. Rent concessions such as free rent are not characteristic of Japanese commercial rental markets thus far.

Under a lease, the lessee is required to make a lump-sum payment both before and at the commencement of the lease. There are three kinds of deposits paid by the lessee. The first is known as *shiki kin,* a refundable security deposit. Usually the equivalent of six months' to one year's rent is paid as *shiki kin* to the landlord at the beginning of the lease.

The second kind of deposit, called *hoshō kin,* is also refundable. The literal translation of *hoshō kin* is earnest money. The amount of *hoshō kin* ranges from several months' to several years' rent. The landlord receives *hoshō kin* before the beginning of the lease. There are two types of *hoshō kin.* One type, like *shiki kin,* is paid back at the end of the lease. The repayment of the other type of *hoshō kin* starts during the lease term.

The third type of deposit is called *kenri kin.* It is nonrefundable and is paid at the beginning of the lease contract. The concept of *kenri kin* is similar to that of "key money," which might be required to rent a house or an apartment. Between two months' and six months' rent is usually required as *kenri kin.*

The interest income from both refundable and nonrefundable deposits plus the amortized amount of nonrefundable deposits are included among the income line items for appraisal purposes.

Triple net leases are not popular in Japan. A commercial tenant often pays both the utility charges for the leased area and a pro rata share of certain expense items for the common area. These expense items include building HVAC, building utilities, cleaning, security, and insurance.

Valuation Standards

The valuation standards for Japanese appraisers were developed and revised by an agency of the national government. The Land Appraisal Committee of the National Land Agency introduced the revised *Standards of Real Estate Appraisal* in 1990. The standards are considered the uniform principles for real estate appraisers. Article 1 of the Code of Ethics of the Japanese Association of Real Estate Appraisal stipulates that a member of the association must follow the *Standards of Real Estate Appraisal* when he or she appraises real property.

Licensing of Real Estate Appraisers

The National Land Agency licenses real estate appraisers. There are two categories of real estate appraisers, i.e., licensed real estate appraisers *(fudōsan kanteishi)* and licensed assistant real estate appraisers *(fudōsan kanteishi ho)*. Unlike their counterparts in North America, both categories of appraisers in Japan are qualified to appraise any kind of property. However, licensed assistant real estate appraisers almost always work under the supervision of licensed real estate appraisers.

The requirements for licensure as an assistant real estate appraiser include

- Two years of full-time appraisal experience
- Passing grades on the two levels of national examinations
- Registration with the National Land Agency

The first level of the national examination covers three subjects: Japanese, mathematics, and essay writing. This level can be waived for a candidate who holds an undergraduate degree. At the second examination level, a candidate is tested on the following five subjects: 1) the civil code, 2) laws on urban/rural planning and real estates taxes, 3) economics, 4) accounting, and 5) real estate appraisal theory.

To be licensed as a real estate appraiser, the following requirements must be met:

- Being a licensed assistant real estate appraiser or meeting the qualifications to become a licensed assistant real estate appraiser
- Attendance at a 160-hour appraisal course offered by the Japanese Association of Real Estate Appraisal
- Seven months of full-time appraisal experience with a designated appraisal firm
- Completion of at least 22 appraisal reports on various types of properties within the seven-month period
- A passing score on a comprehensive examination
- Registration with the National Land Agency

Seminars are frequently offered to help appraisers expand their professional knowledge.

Licensing of Real Estate Appraisal Firms

The Minister of State for the National Land Agency or the governor of a prefecture licenses real estate appraisal firms. An appraisal firm that has offices in more than one prefecture must obtain a license from the National Land Agency, whereas a firm with one office applies for a license to the governor of the prefecture where the office is located. For an applicant to be licensed, each office must have at least one, full-time licensed real estate appraiser. Without a license, no one can practice for a fee. However, unlike the licensing system in the United States, a firm with only one office can undertake assignments in any prefecture of Japan.

Appraisal Reporting Requirements

Article 39 of the Real Estate Appraisal Act and other relevant regulations require an appraiser to include the following items in an appraisal report:

1. The appraised value and the type of value.[2]

2. Identification of the subject property and the description of the rights pertaining to the subject.

3. The purpose of and critical assumptions underlying the appraisal.

4. The effective date of the appraisal and the date upon which the value was concluded.

5. A summary of the process by which the value was estimated. This includes, but is not limited to:

    a. A description of the neighborhood and the subject property;

    b. Judgment as to the highest and best use;

    c. Application of the approaches to value;

    d. Comparison of the value of the subject site to the officially publicized value of the typical lot in the area; and

    e. Comment on any points particularly significant to the appraisal.

6. Any conflict of interest and/or relationship with the client or to the subject property.

7. The names of the licensed real estate appraiser(s) and/or licensed assistant real estate appraiser(s) responsible for the appraisal. A signature and name stamp are required.

---

2. There are three types of value an appraiser may be asked to estimate. The first type, *market value*, is defined in the next section. The second category of value is called *limited market value (gentei kakaku)*. For example, when a building owner who is leasing the land upon which the building stands purchases the building site, or when two or more sites are combined (plottage), the appraiser may seek to estimate this type of value. The last type of value is called *unique value (tokutei kakaku)*. This value would apply to an old religious building with no planned change in its use. Since this type of building cannot ever be marketed, a value must be estimated without consideration of any market exposure.

If necessary, maps, plans, photographs, and other information about the subject property and its neighborhood may be attached to the appraisal report. Market data can also be included in the report.

Generally, the main body of an appraisal report is between 15 and 20 pages long. An appraiser must retain a copy of each appraisal report and relevant materials for at least five years.

Definition of Market Value

In the *Standards of Real Estate Appraisal,* market value translates as normal value *(seijō kakaku).* The definition of *normal value* according to the standards is:

> a real property's fair value, representing the value it can attain in a competitive market, where buyers and sellers enjoy an open market operating under no restraints and acting without any special motivations.

This definition implies the following points:

1. To qualify as fair value, the market value must be acceptable to both buyers and sellers.

2. In a competitive market, buyers and sellers have extensive knowledge about the market.

3. Buyers and sellers are typically motivated, and properties are exposed to all potential buyers for a reasonable period of time.

Typical Approaches to Value

In estimating the market value of a real property, an appraiser usually employs the cost approach. The sales comparison approach is not applied to a whole property, i.e., both land and building components, except in the appraisal of condominiums. The income approach is used for appraising income-producing properties only when applicable.

In the cost approach, land value is initially estimated by means of one or more of the three approaches to value, i.e., the cost approach,[3] market comparison approach, or income approach. The current value of the improvements is next calculated by deducting accrued depreciation from their reproduction or replacement cost. Finally, the value of the whole property is calculated by adding the building value to the land value.

---

3. The use of the cost approach to value land developed as subdivisions or reclaimed from the sea is discussed in a later section.

The popularity of the cost approach in Japan may be attributed to the prevalent thinking that real estate is a dichotomy of land and improvements. Each is a legally severable component of the property and each is registered separately, even when the whole property has a single owner. Market participants normally attach more importance to land value than building value because land represents a far greater contribution to the overall value. The land portion is so important that a client often asks the appraiser to ignore the existing improvements and to value the property as if it were vacant.

Use of the Income Approach to Estimate Land Value (Under a Proposed Building)

In the income approach, a land residual technique is used to estimate land value. In applying this technique, the appraiser assumes that the building to be constructed represents the highest and best use of the site.

The first step is to calculate the net operating income after depreciation *(NOIAD)* for the whole property. To estimate the *NOIAD* for the proposed building and its site, total property expenses are deducted from total income. Total expenses include real estate taxes, depreciation, repairs, maintenance and management, insurance, and vacancy and collection losses. Total income includes rent, interest on the deposits and the amortized amount of the nonrefundable deposits, and other income.

The residual income to the land is then estimated by deducting the income required to support the investment in the building from the total *NOIAD* of the property. The income to be allocated to the building is derived by multiplying the building value (based on its hypothetical cost) by a building capitalization rate.

The land value may be estimated by capitalizing the residual income using a land capitalization rate.

The land residual technique is illustrated in the following example.

Sample Application

Land size:	1,368 square meters
Assumed building:	Steel-framed, reinforced concrete, 12-story retail/office building with basement
Total floor area:	9,922 square meters
Building value:	¥2,780,000,000 (¥280,000 per square meter)

Land value is estimated as follows:

Income

Rent	416,313,000
Interest on the deposits and amortized amount of nonrefundable deposits	34,827,000
Other income	33,165,000
Total income	¥484,305,000

Expenses

Real estate taxes	47,430,000
Depreciation	74,133,000
Repairs	27,800,000
Maintenance and management	13,480,000
Insurance	2,780,000
Vacancy and collection losses	22,466,000
Total expenses	¥188,089,000
Income less expenses	296,216,000
Building value × R_B (2,780,000,000 x 0.06)	– 166,800,000
Residual income to land	¥129,416,000
Land value	
Income to land, capitalized by R_L of 0.04	¥3,235,400,000
	or ¥2,365,000 per square meter

The Land Appraisal Committee of the National Land Agency recently adopted a new land residual method which explicitly considers the change in net operating income to be a constant ratio.[4] In this method, both total income and total expenses are assumed to change at the same constant rate. Also, an indefinite holding period for the real property is postulated. This reflects the behavior of typical Japanese real estate investors, who anticipate that at the end of its economic life, a building will be demolished and a new building will be constructed on the site. This process is considered to continue indefinitely.

The constant-ratio change model for the land residual method can be expressed in the three following equations:

---

4. This constant-ratio growth model is a variation of a technique popularized by Myron J. Gordon in the 1960s for the analysis and valuation of financial securities. In North America, the technique is mainly encountered in appraisals of regulated public utilities. See Marcus Jackson, "The Gordon Growth Model and the Income Approach to Value," *The Appraisal Journal* (January 1994). The first equation appearing in footnote 9 on page 540 of *The Appraisal of Real Estate*, 11th edition, can be rewritten as $NOI/(r - g)$ where *n* is assumed to be an infinite period.

$$V_L = \frac{NOI_L \times a}{r - g}$$

$$V_L = \frac{(NOI_O - NOI_B) \times a}{r - g}$$

$$V_L = \frac{\left\{NOI_O - V_B \times \overline{1 - \left(\frac{1+g}{1+r}\right)^n} \times (r - g)\right\} \times a}{r - g}$$

where:

V_L = land value

NOI_L = net operating income attributable to the land

a = adjustment factor for zero income during the construction

r = yield rate

g = compound growth rate

NOI_O = total net operating income of the property[5]

NOI_B = net operating income attributable to the building

V_B = building value

n = economic life of the building (in years)

In the first equation, the *NOI* attributable to the land is adjusted for the period of no income during construction. Then, the adjusted *NOI* attributable to the land is capitalized by $(r - g)$. Because a constant-ratio change is assumed for NOI, the compound growth rate (g) is subtracted from the yield rate (r).

The second equation shows that the *NOI* attributable to the land is calculated by subtracting the *NOI* attributable to the building from the *NOI* of the whole property.

As indicated in the third equation, the *NOI* attributable to the building is calculated as follows:

$$NOI_B = V_B \times \overline{1 - \left(\frac{1+g}{1+r}\right)^n} \times (r - g)$$

---

5. Unlike the traditional land residual technique used in Japan, the new method excludes depreciation charges from the expense items when the total net operating income of the property is calculated.

This formula can be derived from the following equation, which shows the present value *(PV)* of an annuity that starts at $1 and grows at a constant rate *(g)* for a certain period *(n)*:

$$PV = \frac{1 - (1 + g)^n/(1 + r)^n}{r - g}$$

Use of the Sales Comparison Approach to Estimate Land Value

In the sales comparison approach, an appraiser must select appropriate comparables to arrive at an indication of market value. *The Standards of Real Estate Appraisal* require the following four criteria to be met in choosing comparables:

1. The comparable property must be located either in the same neighborhood as the subject property or in an area with similar locational characteristics.

2. The conditions of the sale must be normal or adjustable to equivalent conditions for an arm's-length transaction.

3. A time adjustment to the comparable must be practicable.

4. The property from which transactional data are taken must be comparable to the subject property in regard to the other elements of comparison.

The standards, which were revised in 1990, emphasize that appraisers must not include data from speculative transactions among their comparables.

Use of the Cost Approach to Estimate the Value of Land (Recently Developed into Subdivisions or Reclaimed from the Sea)

The cost approach is only applied to estimate the land value of newly developed land subdivisions and reclaimed land. A value indication is derived by adding the costs of purchasing raw land to the engineering fees and soft costs of development. In the case of reclaimed land, a fee for the reclamation license and the compensation for fishery losses are used instead of the costs of raw land. The cost approach cannot be used to estimate the land value of developed land.

Reconciliation

Before reaching a final conclusion of value, an appraiser must reconcile value indications derived from more than one appraisal method. In reconciliation, an appraiser considers the characteristics of both the approaches to value and the data employed in the assignment. The appraiser must also review each step of the appraisal process objectively. If the subject property is located within a city planning zone, the appraiser is required to adjust the typical land value published by the National Land Agency or the prefecture for market conditions, location, physical characteristics, or other factors. The adjusted price is then compared to the appraised land value of the subject.

Availability of Data

The availability of market data is relatively limited in Japan compared to the situation in North America. People are more conservative about disclosing information. In addition, due to the absence of multiple listing services and other differences in practice, sales data are not readily available. Two other factors contribute to this situation. First, the real estate transfer tax and registration tax are levied on the basis of the assessed value of the property. Thus, when recording a sale price with the tax authority, a real estate buyer tends to file a lesser amount than the actual transaction price. Second, because of the conservative nature of market practices in Japan, sales contracts are seldom open to third parties, including appraisers.

However, extensive data on sale and rent comparables are compiled from the data collected by appraisers for government land value surveys. These data are shared by appraisers in each prefecture. The following list provides some suggested data sources.

Demographic and Economic Data
- Government offices (municipal, prefectural, national)
- Libraries
- Economic magazines and newspapers

Real Estate Market Data (Market Size, Occupancy, Rent Levels)
- The Real Estate Economic Research Institute
- Real estate agencies that specialize in renting offices
- Real estate magazines and newspapers

Rent and Sale Comparables
- Japanese Association of Real Estate Appraisal (10 regional offices and 47 chapter offices)
- Tokyo Kantei (Appraisal) Co., Ltd.
- *Atto Hohmu* rent information
- Appraisers
- Local realtors

Appraisal Organizations

The Japanese Association of Real Estate Appraisal is an organization of real estate appraisers and appraisal firms. Its address is:

SVAX TT Building
3-11-15 Toranomon, Minato-Ku
Tokyo 105
Japan
Tel. 81 3 3434 2301
Fax 81 3 3436 6450

The Japan Real Estate Institute is a nonprofit organization of real estate research, appraisal, and consulting professionals. The Japan Real Estate Institute employs more than 600 people in its Tokyo headquarters and 53 branch offices throughout Japan. About half of the employees are licensed appraisers. The Institute itself and all of its employees who hold an appraisal license are members of the Japanese Association of Real Estate Appraisal. The address of the Japan Real Estate Institute is:

Kangin-Fujiya Building
1-3-2 Toranomon, Minato-Ku
Tokyo 105
Japan
Tel. 81 3 3503 5335
Fax 81 3 3597 8063

Addendum

This chapter has cited examples of differences between Japanese practice and appraisal in North America, both in regard to the application of techniques and the disclosure of transactional data. As one of the world's economic powerhouses, Japan has played a vital role in investing in real estate markets overseas. Between 1985 and 1992, the Japanese became major investors in U.S. real estate. The fallout from the banking crisis that Japan experienced during the early and mid-1990s revealed that overinflated real estate values accounted for a substantial portion of bank investment. In the wake of the crisis, major Japanese banks have written down bad loans,[6] restructured other troubled loans, and, since 1993, have been selling overseas properties targeted for disinvestment. The need to rebuild Kobe, which suffered a major earthquake in January 1995, has also played a role in the repatriation of Japanese capital.

---

6. In June of 1995, the Finance Ministry reported that Japanese banks had $500 billion in nonperforming loans.

Bibliography

In English

Hines, Mary Alice. "Appraising Japanese Real Estate." *The Appraisal Journal* (January 1992).

Hines, Mary Alice. "Investing in Japanese Real Estate." Westport, CT: Quorum Books, 1987.

Ohkochi, Kazuo. "The Growth of Japanese Real Estate Appraisal." *The Appraisal Journal* (October 1982).

In Japanese

Japan Real Estate Institute. *Fudōsan Kantei Hyōka Nyumon (Real Estate Appraisal Primer)*. Tokyo, 1996.

Hiroshi Takase, *Shū-eki Kangen Hō No Riron To Jitsumu (Theory and Applications of the Income Approach)*. Tokyo: Seibun Sha, 1996.

Isao Tsukamoto. *Shū-eki Kangen Hō [DCF Hō] Nyumon (The Income Approach [DCF Analysis] Primer)*. Tokyo: Toyo Keizai Shimpo Sha, 1996.

Kazuo Uno. *Shintei Reikai Fudōsan Kenteisho No Yomikata (How to Read A Real Estate Appraisal Report)*. 3d ed. Tokyo: Seibun Sha, 1995.

Kantei Hyōka Riron Kenkyu Kai (Appraisal Theory Study Group). *Yohsetsu Fudosan Kantei Hyoka Kijun (Annotated Real Estate Appraisal Standards)*. Tokyo: Jutaku Shimpo Sha, 1991.

Thailand

Pichet Arriyavat, PhD

Dr. Pichet Arriyavat is Chairman of the Board of the Sirida Group, a real estate consultancy, management, and appraisal firm in Bangkok. A graduate of Chulalongkom University (Bangkok), Dr. Arriyavat holds an M.S. degree and a PhD in civil engineering from Purdue University, with a specialization in structural engineering. He is a registered engineer in Thailand and in two states of the United States (California and Illinois). He has designed buildings in the United States, Korea, and Singapore. In addition to membership in several engineering institutes and societies, Dr. Arriyavat is also a member of the Valuers Association of Thailand and the Thai Property Valuation Standards Association. He was an advisor to the president of the National Assembly of Thailand in 1994 and to Thailand's Minister of Energy Policy in 1996.

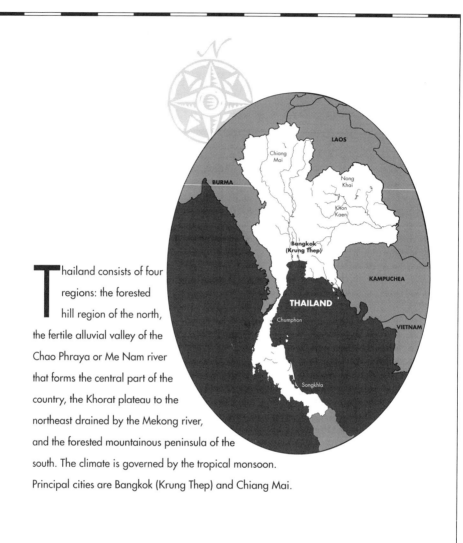

Thailand consists of four regions: the forested hill region of the north, the fertile alluvial valley of the Chao Phraya or Me Nam river that forms the central part of the country, the Khorat plateau to the northeast drained by the Mekong river, and the forested mountainous peninsula of the south. The climate is governed by the tropical monsoon. Principal cities are Bangkok (Krung Thep) and Chiang Mai.

Political Structure

Unlike other countries in Southeast Asia, Thailand never fell under colonial rule. The country did, however, lose some territory in the nineteenth and twentieth centuries. Thailand, which was formerly known to westerners as Siam, has a long history of rule by kings. The last seven centuries have seen the succession of four dynastic periods named after the respective capitals, i.e., Sukhothai (mid 13th century-1438), Ayutthaya (1350-1767), Thonburi[1] (1772-1782), and Rattanakosin[2] (under the Chakkri dynastry, 1782 to the present). Eighty percent of the population is Buddhist; the remaining twenty percent belong to other religions such as Christianity or Islam. The population of Thailand is fairly uniform although there are small minority groups (Chinese, Malays, Indians, and hill peoples) who live in harmony with the Thais.

In 1932 King Rama VII granted democratic rule to the people of Thailand. Since then the government has often been controlled by military generals who maintain semi-democratic rule. For more than 60 years the country has had military and civilian governments. The King and his family are considered essential under the constitution. The Thai people love and respect the King and his family, who symbolize national unity.

The development of democracy in Thailand over the past 60 years has been based on the following principles:

1. The people are considered the highest authority. The people exercise power through Parliament, whose members are elected to four-year terms.

2. The highest law is the constitution, which guarantees the rights and liberties of the people.

3. A balance of power exists among the three independent branches of government: the legislative, administrative [executive], and judicial branches.

The National Assembly consists of senators and representatives who act on behalf of the Thai people and in accordance with the constitution, exercise legislative and administrative powers, and decide many important matters. Normally, the party that gains a majority of the seats in the Parliament forms the government, headed by a prime minister who serves a four-year term.

The judicial power comprises three courts.

---

1. Thonburi is located across the Chao Phraya from present-day Bangkok.
2. The royal palace of the kings of Thailand is located on Rattanakosin Island in Bangkok.

1. The civil court and the criminal court. The civil court has unlimited original jurisdiction over civil and bankrupcy cases. It acts as the court of first instance for all civil and bankruptcy cases. The criminal court also has unlimited original jurisdiction over criminal cases. It acts as the court of first instance for criminal cases.

2. The court of appeal. The court of appeal has appellate jurisdiction over all civil, bankruptcy, and criminal matters. Appeals from all courts of first instance throughout the country proceed to the court of appeal.

3. The Supreme Court. The Supreme Court is the final court of appeals in all civil, bankruptcy, and criminal cases. The Supreme Court consists of the chief justice and 21 judges.

Three judges are normally sufficient to constitute a quorum in the Supreme Court. The majority opinion prevails and a single judgment is delivered.

Zoning

At present, zoning is determined by the town planning offices in each of the provinces of Thailand. The town planning offices play an especially important role in the zoning of urban areas. In accordance with the bylaws of the Ministry of the Interior, master land use plans include the following colour-coded categories:

Yellow	low-density residential areas
Orange	medium-density residential areas
Brown	high-density residential areas
Red	business areas
Purple	industrial and warehouse areas
Light yellow	warehouse areas
Light purple	specialized industrial areas
Green	rural and agriculturul areas
Light green	open land for recreation and environmental preservation
Olive green	educational institutions
White with border and diagonal green line	rural and agricultural areas
Light brown	preserves for Thai art and culture
Light grey	religious institutions
Blue	civil and public service facilities and public utilities.

Zoning is designed to direct the growth of the country in an orderly manner. Sometimes changes in zoning occur as the result of an adjustment to the municipal master plan.

Property Rights

In accordance with the real estate law issued in 1954, Thai citizens can own and exploit land held in fee simple, a property right on which there are no legal limitations or restrictions. They may dispose of the land by sale or exchange, or may will it to whomever they please. Foreigners may also own real property in fee simple under special conditions. Foreigners may acquire real property through special procedures approved by the Minister of the Interior. A percentage has been set as the maximum limit on foreign ownership of condominium buildings. In the past there were legal limitations on the amount of land a person could own, but these laws have been abrogated. Ownership of real property is normally subject to the powers of government, i.e., taxation, expropriation or eminent domain (exercised by the Ministry of the Interior which oversees the Department of Land) and escheat.

Taxes on real property are normally paid to the government when title to the ownership of land (the deed) is transferred or when the land is leased or mortgaged. There are three types of taxes: 1) a tax on property income, 2) a sale or transfer tax, and 3) a stamp and duty fee. Property not used for residential purposes is subject to annual taxation.

Property income taxes are calculated on the basis of sale price or appraised value, less a deduction for allowable expenses to a maximum of 50% of the price/value, depending on the number of years the property has been held. The net taxable income is then calculated based on a progressive tax rate on property income. The transfer fee is calculated at 2% of the sale price. The stamp and duty fee is set at 0.5% of the sale price.

In expropriations, landowners are compensated for the property value estimated by government appraisers. If the landowners are not satisfied with the appraised amount, they may appeal to the court.

The real estate law stipulates that the government may exercise the power of escheat to regain property ownership when a property has no owner.

Land transactions that involve the sale, leasing, or realization of any profit are subject to the approval of the Ministry of the Interior in accordance with the conditions stipulated in the Ministry bylaws. Thirty-year leases are permissible and can be secured by registration with the Department of Land. Many government agencies, such as the Railway Authority of Thailand, the Crown Property Bureau, and the Treasury Department offer leases to private individuals and companies. Various prime locations in Bangkok are occupied by properties either under long-term leases or owned as freeholds.

Language

Thai, a tonal language, is spoken throughout Thailand. It is written in a script that derives from Devanagari. English can also be used in most areas. Many international schools teach English at both primary and secondary levels.

Currency

The Thai baht (B) is the monetary unit. All domestic real estate transactions are priced in baht. Approximately 25 baht equal one U.S. dollar.

Units of Measure

Thailand uses metric and Thai systems of measure. Real estate prices are quoted in baht per square meter of building area and in baht per square *wah*, per square *ngarn,* or square *rai* of land. The symbols for these are sq.m. (m²) and sq. wah. One square *rai* (1,600 square meters) equals four square *ngarn* or 400 square *wah.* Both income and expenses are typically quoted in baht per month or per year, depending on the contract.

Inflation

Seven years of rapid economic growth have increased the purchasing power of Thai consumers. Private consumption grew 37% between 1988 and 1992 and continues to surge. Inflation is most commonly measured by the change in the Consumer Price Index (CPI), a measure of the average increase or decrease in the price paid for a fixed market basket of goods and services tracked by banking and financial institutes. The average rate of inflation from July 1993 to July 1994 increased from 3.3% to 4.3%. Inflation in the price of food and drink increased to 5.2%, while inflation in the price of non-food items declined to 3.7%. The average annual inflation rate for 1994 was 5%.

Typical Lease Structure

Office Properties

Lease terms for office space range from three to 30 years, but most contracts are written for three-year terms. Office leases are typically net, meaning the tenant is obligated to pay a base rent, expressed in baht per square meter per month or year. Base rent may be fixed or may increase annually over the lease term.

In 1995, base rents varied between 350 and 600 baht per square meter for office space in prime locations. The rate was fairly negotiable during that period due to the oversupply of office buildings.

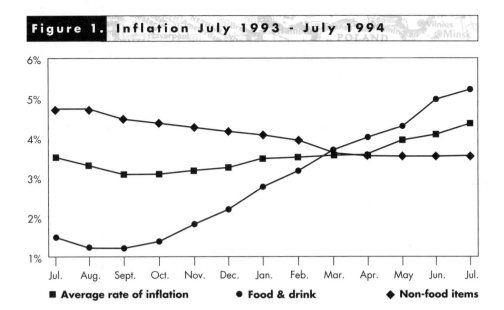

Figure 1. Inflation July 1993 - July 1994

■ Average rate of inflation　　● Food & drink　　◆ Non-food items

Retail Properties

Lease terms for shopping centres are usually longer than those for offices, commonly extending for five, seven, 10, or more years. Leases for anchor or major tenants are usually signed for 20 to 30 years and sometimes longer.

Like office buildings, retail properties are usually let (leased) on a net basis, with the tenant agreeing to pay a stipulated base rent plus a full pro rata share of the shopping centre expenses.

The expenses for the maintenance of common areas, such as hallways, elevators, surrounding areas, and the building envelope, are shared by the tenants and managed by the landlord. The maintenace expense is charged normally in proportion to the square meters of area leased to the tenant. The electricity, water, and telephone charges are additional bills. In 1995 mainte- nance expenses ranged between 20 and 40 baht per square meter of leased area. Rents for retail space have increased considerably and vary among individual shopping centres. In a good location with proper management, a lease can go up threefold within a few years. New shopping centres on the outskirts of an urban area may suffer a decline in rental rates due to oversup- ply and competition for particular locations. Many tenants demand that their landlord increase budgetary expenditures for advertising the retail facility. In 1994 many newly opened retail shops lost business; in 1995, retail businesses in many shopping centres began to improve.

Industrial Properties

Industrial properties in Thailand are normally built by the owners of the land. The building construction costs for industrial properties range between 5,000 and 6,000 baht per square meter. In 1995 the price of land sold in various industrial zones ranged between 700,000 baht per *rai* to 2,000,000 baht per *rai*. Lot sizes range from three to 10 *rai*. When a factory is offered for sale, the transaction price represents a price negotiated between the seller and the buyer. The appraised value may be used only as a basis for reference. There are well-equipped properties in the industrial sector with complete basic infrastructure such as roadways, electricity, water, and waste water treatment plants in place. The Industrial Estate Authority of Thailand (IEAT) operates many industrial properties and grants many privileges to industrialists, e.g., tax and import duty exemptions. The Thai government has granted special privileges to industrial properties located in the export processing zones (EPZs), where businesses can import parts and export their products without any impediments. These measures are part of Thai government policies to help the Thai export industry.

Valuation Standards

There are two valuation associations in Thailand: the Valuers Association of Thailand, founded in 1986, and the Thai Property Valuation Standards Association, founded in 1993. These associations share some committee members and ordinary members, including members of committees working on valuation standards. The members of the Valuers Association of Thailand are individual valuers, whereas the members of the Thai Property Valuation Standards Association are valuation companies. All valuation reports in Thailand are issued by companies and signed by their principal valuers.

In 1992 representatives of the independent valuation companies formed a working committee on behalf of the Valuers Association of Thailand to draft a valuation standard on assets. This was submitted to the Securities and Exchange Commission and the Stock Exchange of Thailand to provide guidance to those concerned with asset valuation. International standards of practice from Europe, the U.S., and Malaysia were studied and modified to suit valuation practice in Thailand.

Topics discussed in the draft standard included the following:

- Asset valuers
- Classification of assets
- Principles to be observed in preparing asset valuations in Thailand
- Asset valuation standards

- Standard format for valuation summaries
- Minimum information required of valuers in preparing asset valuations
- Definitions and guidance notes for open market value and other bases of valuations
- Conditions of engagement
- Notes on unacceptable valuation practices

At present, the draft of the valuation standard is under review by the Securities and Exchange Commission (SEC) in communication with the above-mentioned societies.

Some of the guide notes on unacceptable valuation practices being discussed are cited below:

Responsibility to the Public

- A valuer shall not accept any valuation assignment for which the value is "predetermined."
- A valuer shall not accept any compensation other than the professional valuation fee.
- A valuer shall not change a valuation report upon the client's request.

Reponsibility to Other Valuers

- The valuer and valuation company shall not bid on the valuation fee against another known valuer.
- A valuer shall not discredit another valuer by circulating misleading or false information.
- The valuer and valuation company shall not propose any other commission besides the professional valuation fee.

Responsibility to Associations

- A valuer shall not behave in such a manner as to discredit professional valuation practitioners or associations.
- The valuer and valuation company shall report to the professional societies any unethical valuation practice which reliable evidence corroborates.

Licensing and Certification

In Thailand a *qualified valuer* refers to a member of an independent valuation company with the following qualifications:

- The company shall have at least two principal qualified valuers available to certify the valuation report prepared by the company.

- The company and its management shall have no interest, direct or indirect, in the valued asset.

- Individual qualified valuers shall be approved by the Valuers Association of Thailand.

To ensure the maintenance of valuation standards by member companies, the Thai Property Valuation Standards Association holds monthly meetings to discuss the performance of member companies, their responsibilities to clients, the conditions under which companies are engaged by various clients, report formats, the minimum information requirements for purposes of valuation, the circulation of information on unacceptable valuation practices, and the behavior of clients who may try to abuse an appraiser's value conclusion. The association also promotes an exchange of information with the Securities and Exchange Commission and the Bank of Thailand.

Various educational institutes in both the government and private sectors issue certification for property valuation. Government schools such as Thammasart University and Ramkamhaeng University have begun to offer courses in property valuation. The Rajamongola Instutute of Technology and the Bangkok Technical College have a three-year program and award students a vocational certificate upon completion. Among private schools, the Sirida School of Real Estate Appraisal offers courses in valuation practice for students who hold a bachelor's degree. The four government institutions cited above all award certificates to those who pass the courses.

The laws of Thailand do not yet require valuers to hold a license. However, there are lists of qualified individual valuers who work for valuation companies. The Bank of Thailand issues a list of qualified valuation companies, and the Securities and Exchange Commision plans to compile a list of qualified valuers.

Appraisal Reporting Requirements

Generally, valuers preparing asset valuations for the public are required to provide certain minimum information. Supplementary information may or may not be included in the report. The minimum information required includes a background check by the professional valuer on the description of the property being valued. The required information is based on a standard which professional valuers are obliged to follow. The information shall consist of

- An examination of the ownership documents

- A survey and inspection of the actual asset

- An investigation of the circumstances, where expropriation (eminent domain) is involved

- A review of the information necessary to form a judgment and conclude the valuation

The above information and the content of the appraisal report shall only be disclosed to the client or persons authorized by the client and shall be kept on file for five years.

In practice, there are various types of reports for different clients. An example of the table of contents for a valuation report is shown below.

Table of Contents

- Cover letter
- Summary
- Limiting conditions
- Value definition
- Property description
- Regional and neighbourhood data
- Site data
- Improvement(s) on the property
- Property development status
- Statement of highest and best use
- Cost approach to value
- Market approach to value
- Income approach to value
- Reconciliation and final value conclusion
- Comments
- Photos of the property
- Map of the location and vicinity
- Site plan
- Floor plan
- Title deeds

Definition of Market Value

The term *market value* of a property, i.e., of the land and existing buildings (if any), as used in a report is defined as the price for which the property may reasonably be expected to sell in an open market transaction between a willing seller and a willing buyer, neither of whom is under duress. In addition, the following assumptions must be valid:

1. The price applies upon the date of valuation.

2. The sale is transacted in cash or on an equivalent basis.

3. All information regarding the property is equally available to both the buyer and the seller.

4. The title rights to the property of the seller are valid and transferable.

5. The price has remained stable during a reasonable period for negotiation between the buyer and the seller.

Income Approach

The income approach to real estate valuation produces reasonable value indications only for income-producing properties such as hospitals, hotels, office buildings, and apartment buildings. Application of the income approach is based on information collection techniques which require considerable expertise relating to the particular type of business and building being appraised. Data on monthly or annual revenues and expenses are collected. The difference between revenues and expenses, i.e., net operating income, is used to derive the property value either by direct capitalization or discounted cash flow analysis. Both methods require not only an understanding of business accounts, but also a forecast of the net operating income for the subject property over a period of at least eight years.

It has been very difficult to apply the income approach in Thailand during the past few years (1992-1995) because of the great fluctuation in rents and land prices. A more sophisticated technique that correlates increases in income and expenses with the business cycle should be used to forecast net operating income. Other factors that may significantly influence the future operations of an income-producing property are the property's location, its management team, and market demand.

Many apartment buildings and retail centres that are in good locations, but use the wrong pricing strategies, have accrued losses. To revitalize their businesses and restore profitability, the owners have either had to sell their properties off or replace the existing managment team with new management. The income approach may have greater applicability for valuing income-producing properties that are pending acquisition.

Discounted Cash Flow (DCF) Anaylsis

A sample appraisal of an apartment building by the income approach is provided below. The general steps applied in the valuation procedure are listed as follows:

Step 1. Data are collected from the current tenants and management. Data collection includes:

- An examination of the lease contracts of the individul tenants
- The compilation of a computer table detailing the base rents for each unit, expiration dates, escalation rent clauses, and notes on any special conditions, e.g., security deposits and advance payments
- A summary of income from base rent
- An examination of accounts for other sources of income, e.g., electricity and water collection bills, rents for furniture and household items, rents from beauty shops and laundries, rents from restaurants, membership fees from fitness clubs, parking revenue, etc.
- Note of vacant units and losses from other causes
- Calculation of business expenses, including monthly salaries, maintenance reserves, leasing commissions, etc.

Step 2. A forecast of income and expenses is made, taking into consideration the business climate and property location.

Step 3. A reasonable discount rate is applied to the net operating income forecast (generally 10 years) to calculate the net present value of the property, including a residual value (resale value).

Raumsirimitre Apartment Appraisal by the Income Approach

Raumsirimitre Apartment is a 12-storey, reinforced concrete building with two elevators and two fire escapes. The total floor area is 11,403 m² with the following allocation:

Central hall area	2,490 m²
Car parking	2,280 m²
Apartment area	6,633 m²

From the data survey, it was concluded that rents for furnished apartments ranged as follow:

65 m² apartment	11,500 Baht per month
60 m² apartment	10,500 Baht per month
46 m² apartment	8,000 Baht per month
26 m² apartment	6,000 Baht per month

The average rent is 240 Baht per square meter per month. Estimated revenue is tabulated in the following table.

Estimated Revenue Table

No.	Year	Occupancy Rate (%)	Discount Factor (%)	Rent Increase (%)	Rental Revenue	Other Revenue
1	1995	70	5	0	12,417,000.–	86,000.–
2	1996	90	5	0	16,238,000.–	113,000.–
3	1997	100	5	10	20,052,000.–	139,000.–
4	1998	100	5	0	20,052,000.–	139,000.–
5	1999	100	5	0	20,052,000.–	139,000.–
6	2000	100	5	10	22,058,000.–	151,000.–
7	2001	100	5	0	22,058,000.–	151,000.–
8	2002	100	5	0	22,058,000.–	151,000.–
9	2003	100	5	10	24,264,000.–	168,000.–
10	2004	100	5	0	24,264,000.–	168,000.–
11	2005	100	5	0	24,264,000.–	168,000.–

Notes

The estimated discount factor reflects losses due to tenant turnover.

The building should be able to achieve an occupancy rate of 100 % within three years because of its good location and the high demand in the area. It is very close to a train depot planned for the Mor Chit Area.

Rental increases are calculated at a conservative estimate of 3.33% per annum, or 10 % every three years.

Other revenue, i..e, the revenue from business operations, water and electricity billings, shops, and restaurants was estimated conservatively because the management team is new.

The estimated annual expenses of the apartment may be categorized as follows:

Estimated Expenses

Salaries

Maids	2 × 4,000 Baht × 12	= 96,000.– Baht
Guards	2 × 5,000 Baht × 12	= 120,000.– Baht
Operators	2 × 4,000 Baht × 12	= 96,000.– Baht
Manager	1 × 20,000 Baht × 12	= 240,000.– Baht
Cleaners	2 × 5,000 Baht × 12	= 120,000.– Baht
Total		672,000.– Baht

Insurance	814,000.– Baht
Maintenance	120,000.– Baht
Taxes	436,000.– Baht
Total	2,042,000.– Baht

It is assumed that expenses will increase by 5% annually.

Estimated Net Operating Income

No.	Year	Total Revenue (in Baht)	Total Expense (in Baht)	Net Income
1	1995	12,503,000.–	2,042,000.–	10,461,000.–
2	1996	16,351,000.–	2,144,000.–	14,207,000.–
3	1997	20,191,000.–	2,251,000.–	17,940,000.–
4	1998	20,191,000.–	2,364,000.–	17,827,000.–
5	1999	20,191,000.–	2,482,000.–	17,709,000.–
6	2000	22,209,000.–	2,606,000.–	19,603,000.–
7	2001	22,209,000.–	2,736,000.–	19,473,000.–
8	2002	22,209,000.–	2,873,000.–	19,336,000.–
9	2003	24,432,000.–	3,017,000.–	21,415,000.–
10	2004	24,432,000.–	3,167,000.–	21,265,000.–
11	2005	24,432,000.–	3,326,000.–	21,106,000.–

Estimated Residual Value in Year 11

Value by cost approach = Land value + building cost
= 30,000,000 + 110,000,000.– Baht
= 140,000,000.– Baht

In 11 years, the residual value will equal the future value less depreciation (assuming that the property appreciates 5% annually for 10 years and depreciates 20% within the same 10-year period).

$$= 140,000,000 \ (1.05)^{10} - 110,000,000 \ (0.2)$$
$$= 228,000,000 - 22,000,000$$
$$= 206,000,000 \ \text{Baht}$$

	Present Values	
Year	Net Operating Income	Present Value*
1	10,461,000	9,686,000
2	14,207,000	12,180,000
3	17,940,000	14,241,000
4	17,827,000	13,103,000
5	17,709,000	12,052,000
6	19,603,000	12,353,000
7	19,473,000	11,362,000
8	19,336,000	10,447,000
9	21,415,000	10,713,000
10	21,265,000	9,850,000
11	206,000,000	88,350,000
Total		204,338,000

*Assuming an 8% discount rate

Appraised value by discounted cash flow analysis = 204,338,000.– Baht

Appraised value by direct capitalization[3]   = 10,461,000.– Baht /0.08
                                                           = 130,762,500.– Baht

Direct Capitalization

Direct capitalization is used when only a single-year estimate of revenues and expenses is available. It is based on the simpler assumption of uniform revenue and expenses or an average income-generating capability. In the apartment building example, an 8% capitalization rate was applied.

Sales Comparison Approach

The sales comparison approach is used extensively in Thailand. The market value of the subject property is estimated by comparing the subject to similar properties that are currently being offered for sale or have recently been sold in the market. In practice, there is always some confusion between the prices

---

3. The overall capitalization rate applied in direct capitalization should reflect the cost of money in the market, i.e., the interest rate. In reconciliation, however, a Thai appraiser may conclude that the value indication derived from direct capitalization is too rough an estimate for valuation purposes.

of sold properties and offers-to-purchase. Our guide to valuation standards has adopted the following comments on open market value:

- The valuer makes the assumption that the assets will be sold on the valuation date and elaborates any additional assumptions pertaining to the sale.[4]

- The "best price" and open market value are considered equivalent to the highest price expected to be received in the market on the valuation date (not taking into account offers to purchase from buyers with special interest in the property, nor the fair price, the average price, or the price the seller expects to receive).

- "Hope value" and "marriage value." A "hope value" component (if any) is already included in the market value since the market recognizes that the asset may be used differently than it is currently used. In practice, "hope value" may be an incentive offered to purchasers in the market (not taking into account purchasers with special interest in the property). A "marriage value" component (if any) would result from assemblage with other assets or the combination of individual rights to occupy the same asset.

- The date of completed sale represents the date of valuation, which may be the same date as the date specified in the appraisal report (i.e., the delivery date) or a previous date, but not a future date.

- "A willing seller" is the seller who holds legal title to the property, who is neither overly eager nor unwilling to sell, nor under compulsion to sell at any price. A willing seller is, therefore, not a person having financial problems, not an anxious lender, and not a person who will hold out to sell only when a buyer meets the asking price. In other words, a willing seller will sell at the best price he receives in the market after an appropriate marketing period, regardless of what that price is.

Cost Approach

When the cost approach is applied, the value of the appraised property is based on the value of a similar property built to replace the subject property, less the depreciation the subject has accrued. The value estimate derived from this approach reflects the depreciated replacement cost. The application of the cost approach to older buildings with special stylistic or historic value may be fairly subjective, but the approach is very applicable to newly constructed properties.

There are normally three ways to apply the cost approach:

4. Including the five assumptions specified in the definition of market value.

- An estimate based on the unit cost of construction per square meter
- An estimate based on the construction cost of components
- An estimate based on the unit cost of materials and labour (quantity survey method)

A brief example of a cost approach valuation based on the unit cost of construction per square meter follows. The subject property in the example is the same 11,403 m^2 apartment building used to illustrate the income approach.

Replacement cost 11,403 @ 9,646	110,000,000 Baht
less one year's depreciation @ 2%	− 2,200,000 Baht
	107,800,000 Baht
plus land value	+ 30,000,000 Baht
Total value	= 137,800,000 Baht

Reconciliation

After all three approaches have been applied, the valuer examines the values derived and uses his expertise to judge the best indication and conclude the most appropriate value. The valuer considers various factors, such as the property type, the existing use of the property, any future alternative use of the property, and the purpose of the valuation. After considering these factors, the valuer applies judgment and decides on the most appropriate value for the subject property.

Availability of Data

In Thailand, data on real estate can be obtained more easily today than in the past. There is more coverage of real property in newspapers, magazines, and publications of the Department of Land.

Sources of Demographic and Economic Data

- The Bank of Thailand
- Various commercial banks
- The National Economic and Social Development Board
- Libraries
- Articles in newspapers and magazines

Sources of Real Estate Market Data

- Real estate brokerage, real estate management, and appraisal firms
- The Thai Property Valuation Standards Association
- The Valuers Association of Thailand

Sources of Rent and Sale Comparables

* Locally based real estate brokers

Appraisal Organizations

Thai Property Valuation Standards Association
410/135-136 Rajchadapisek Road
Bangkok 10310
Tel. 662 - 541 - 5408 to 13
Fax. 662 - 541 - 5414

The Valuers Association of Thailand
Central Valuation Authority
Charansanidwong Road, Bangkok Noi,
Bangkok 10700
Tel. 662 - 424 - 6808, 424 - 0139
Fax. 662 - 424 - 6808

Bibliography

Appraisal Institute. *The Appraisal of Real Estate.* 11th ed. (Chicago: Appraisal Institute, 1996).

Arriyavat, Dr. Pichet. *The Effect of Environmental Impact Concerns on Property Appraisal.* A technical paper submitted to the Asian Valuation Seminar in Indonesia. 1994.

The International Valuation Standards Committee (IVSC). *Guide Notes and Background Papers on the Valuation of Fixed Assets.*

Office of the Secretary of the National Assembly of Thailand. *The National Assembly, 1993-1994*

Thai Ministry of the Interior. *A Description of Thai Real Estate Law with the Bylaws and Regulations of the National Land Division Committee.*

Valuation Standards Working Committee. *Guide Notes on Asset Valuations in Thailand* (draft copy).

16

Singapore

Dr. Shi-Ming Yu
and
Mrs. Amy Lee

Dr. Shi-Ming Yu is a senior lecturer in valuation and management and Deputy Head of Estate Management of the School of Building and Estate Management at the National University of Singapore. Dr. Yu is also President of the Singapore Institute of Surveyors and Valuers.

Amy Lee is a lecturer in valuation and finance at the National University of Singapore. Mrs. Lee is also Deputy Director of the Centre for Real Estate Studies and Vice President and Chair of the Valuation and General Practice Division of the Singapore Institute of Surveyors and Valuers.

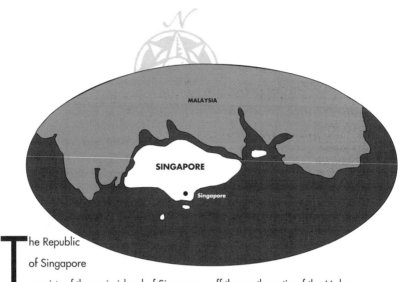

The Republic of Singapore consists of the main island of Singapore, off the southern tip of the Malay Peninsula, and 58 nearby islands. Singapore's position along the straits that link the Indian Ocean and South China Sea gives it a significant commercial advantage. Founded in 1819, Singapore formed part of the former British Straits Settlements colony until 1946. Full self-rule was attained in 1959. Between 1968 and 1970, the British withdrew from the large naval base they had maintained on the island. The climate is tropical and monsoonal, and mangrove swamps are found along many coastal inlets.

Introduction

Geography and Population

Singapore is a small island republic with a total land area of about 640 km² (247 square miles) and a population of about three million. Having celebrated its thirtieth year of independence in 1995, Singapore has a relatively short history among developing nations. The republic is a multiracial, secular state comprising four main ethnic groups: Chinese (78%), Malays (14%), Indians and Pakistanis (7%), and Eurasians and Europeans (1%). There is also a large expatriate community working in Singapore.

Languages and Currency

Four principal languages are used in Singapore: Chinese (Mandarin), Malay, Tamil, and English. Malay is the national language, while English is the language of administration and business. The currency in use is the Singapore dollar (S$).

Economy

Despite the limitations of size and a lack of natural resources, other than the skilled labour of its people, Singapore is by far the most important centre of commerce and industry in Southeast Asia. It is an important growth centre in the Asia-Pacific region, which is becoming the hub of the world economy. Indeed, the rate of growth and development in Singapore over the last 30 years has been remarkable. The economy has enjoyed rapid and continuous annual growth, except for the brief recession of 1986 when negative growth was experienced for the first time. The success of Singapore's economy hinges on its strategic location, well-developed infrastructure, skilled labour force, and the government policy of industrialisation and economic diversification. In recent years, the application of high technology and the development of skill-intensive and capital-intensive industries have been emphasized. These policies have also encouraged more Singaporean investors to venture into neighbouring countries and capitalise on the rapid economic growth of Malaysia, Indonesia, Thailand, and China.

Planned Development

Concomitant with the rapid growth of Singapore's economy is a heavy investment in the development of infrastructure, which comprises a large number of residential, commercial, and industrial buildings. In this regard, Singapore is a city-state in which every development is centrally guided by a master plan. The plan clearly spells out the type and density of use for each parcel of land. Various government ministries and statutory boards, headed by the Ministry of National Development, are responsible for creating and implementing the master plan.

Government

In terms of political structure, Singapore is governed by a unicameral parliamentary system. The 81 members of Parliament are democratically elected; each represents an electoral division or constituency for a five-year term unless Parliament is dissolved before the term expires. The Cabinet, headed by the prime minister and made up of 13 ministers, wields executive power in running the state. The head of state is the president, who is vested with some custodial and executive powers. The president is elected by the people for a six-year term.

The Real Estate Market in Singapore

Tenure and Ownership System

As a former British colony, Singapore has a system of landholding which is based on English common law. In the United Kingdom, all the land is vested in the Crown. In Singapore, all land ultimately belongs to the state. Thus, what a person "owns" is not the land itself, but an "estate" in land. The two kinds of title to property in Singapore are freehold and leasehold estates.

Freehold Estates

The owner of a freehold estate holds the land in perpetuity, subject only to the state's right to acquire land compulsorily. Freehold estates in Singapore include the fee simple estate and the estate in perpetuity. The fee simple estate, called a *grant in fee simple (GFS), grant,* or *indenture,* is an absolute freehold estate without any obligation upon the owner to pay any rent except statutory charges such as the property tax. The estate in perpetuity, called the *state land grant (SLG),* is subject to payment of a nominal ground rent or quit rent[1] of S$12 per annum as well as fulfillment of various implied terms, covenants, and conditions under the State Lands Act. Since January 1, 1992, payment of ground rent or quit rent has been waived indefinitely. In general, freehold estates are no longer granted by the state except in cases involving the surrender and reissue of one or more titles to land for subdivision and/or development. Leasehold estates, generally of a 99-year duration, are now more commonly issued by the state. Hence, the proportion of freehold to leasehold properties in Singapore is small.

Leasehold Estates

Leasehold estates have a definite duration. The most common lease term is 99 years, but leases with longer terms exist, e.g., 999 years or even 999,999 years. Such leases may be contracted either between private parties or with

---

1. *Quit rent* refers to the payment a freeholder once made to the lord of the manor to be released from obligatory labour or military service. Quit rents were abolished in the United Kingdom in 1936.

the state. Long-term leases are now rare because the State Lands Rules (subsidiary legislation to the State Lands Act) stipulate that, apart from certain exceptions, no other leases issued by the state may exceed 99 years.

The typical lease term for commercial and residential sites sold by the state through the Urban Redevelopment Authority (URA) and the Housing and Development Board (HDB) is 99 years. Leases with shorter terms of 60 years, 30 years, or 21 years are also issued by statutory bodies such as the Jurong Town Corporation (JTC), Sentosa Development Corporation (SDC), Housing and Development Board, and Urban Redevelopment Authority for various industrial, commercial, and recreational uses. Sixty-year leases on land have been issued recently by the Urban Redevelopment Authority for residential developments, mainly to house foreign workers.

Tenancies and Short-Term Leases

Typically, commercial leases of office and shop units have three- to five-year terms with the right of renewal for another term of equal duration. For residential properties, tenancies are even shorter, usually one to three years. Because the law does not require leases of less than seven years to be registered, short-term leases are prevalent in the leasing market. However, cyclical movements in property subsectors do influence the terms of leases and rights of renewal.

To some extent, lease terms and conditions are also influenced by the condition of the market. For instance, in a down market, rent-free periods of up to three months can be expected. However, the property market in Singapore has yet to witness a prolonged recession which would substantially change typical lease terms and conditions. Rents in commercial and industrial leases are commonly quoted per square foot of lettable (leasable) space per month, while rents for residential properties are usually quoted at a monthly rate for the unit (house or flat). Rents are payable monthly in advance. Landlords are responsible for the payment of property tax and for long-term maintenance and management of their property. Tenants and lessees usually have to pay a monthly service charge for routine maintenance and management.

Land Registration

Land registration in Singapore is currently based on the Torrens system. Under this system, titles are recorded with the Land Titles Registry. However, a Registry of Deeds also exists concurrently to administer the old system of land registration under common law or deed title. The policy of the state is to systematically and gradually convert all titles to land held under the common law or deed system to the new Torrens system. Hence, all land in Singapore will ultimately be registered under the Torrens system.

Real Estate Submarkets

The property market in Singapore broadly comprises residential, office, retail, industrial, and hotel submarkets. Except for the entirely private hotel sector, all the submarkets include both private and public sector space. The residential sector has the highest proportion of public to private housing. Currently some 87% of Singapore's total population lives in public housing, built mainly by the Housing and Development Board (HDB), with the remaining 13% in private housing. The industrial sector, which comprises factory and warehouse space, is also dominated by the government. Public sector owners of industrial space in Singapore include the Jurong Town Corporation (JTC), the Housing and Development Board (HDB), and the Port of Singapore Authority (PSA). At present, the JTC is the largest developer of industrial land, with some 30 industrial estates (properties) including the established Jurong Industrial Estate. The other two sectors of the property market, the office and retail markets, also include a significant amount of public sector space. As of September 1994, some 24% of office space and 40% of retail space was owned by the public sector.

The following discussion of the residential subsector highlights the owner-occupied residential market in Singapore.

The Housing and Development Board (HDB) was initially established by the government to cater to the housing needs of lower- and middle-income citizens. The prices of flats (apartments) sold by the HDB are generally subsidised so that they are set at only a fraction of the prices of private apartments with similar floor area in a similar location. To further encourage home ownership, the government has allowed central provident funds (CPF), a compulsory provident (pension) fund to which all employers and their employees contribute monthly, to be used for the purchase of residential properties, including HDB flats. As a result, more than 90% of the people in Singapore own their own homes.

Currently only Singapore citizens whose monthly gross household income falls below an established ceiling and who satisfy other conditions imposed by the board are able to purchase newly completed HDB flats on a 99-year lease. Such flat owners are not allowed to own any other private dwelling premises. However, since last year, both citizens and permanent residents are allowed to purchase HDB flats offered in the market for resale by the original owners five years after acquisition. There is no income ceiling imposed on purchasers of resale HDB flats and they are also allowed to own other private dwellings. Hence, there is currently an active and sizeable market for resale HDB apartments. Depending on the location and time of purchase and on the extent of renovations undertaken, the price of a HDB resale flat may be as much as 100% higher than its original price.

Private sector residential properties are generally considered "landed" properties and apartments. Landed properties are houses that sit on privately owned parcels of land. Privately owned apartments are usually condominium developments which provide common facilities such as a swimming pool and game courts. Foreigners are only allowed to purchase private residential properties that are approved as condominium developments or are located in buildings with more than than six storeys.

The Valuation Profession in Singapore

Valuation Firms

The real estate profession in general, and the valuation profession in particular, are relatively small in Singapore in comparison with other major professions such as accounting, law, and engineering. The structure of the profession is not unlike that of the real estate industry in other countries such as the U.K., Australia, and the U.S.

Valuations in Singapore are usually performed by a valuer who works for a real estate consultancy firm. By and large, such firms provide many, if not all, real estate services, including valuation, property management, and investment counselling. There are currently some 60 real estate consultancy firms in Singapore. In larger consultancy firms, different services are normally handled by separate departments, while in smaller firms the valuer frequently performs other functions.

Another category of valuers are those employed by private organisations such as banks and development companies or by government or quasi-governmental bodies such as the Urban Redevelopment Authority (URA) and the Inland Revenue Authority of Singapore (IRAS). These valuers are largely responsible for the assets of the organisation and/or its property transactions only; they handle no external clients.

Legislation and Licensing

The real estate profession in Singapore is currently governed by the Auctioneers Licences Act of 1906. This act is administered by the Inland Revenue Authority of Singapore (IRAS). Under the act, those wishing to practise as valuers, auctioneers, and estate agents are required to obtain a licence. Licences to practise as valuers are only issued to applicants who have acquired the relevant experience while affiliated with a licensed valuer and possess a recognised degree or professional qualification.

Under the act, valuers who are employed by organisations such as government bodies and banks are not required to be licensed. However, they are only permitted to undertake valuations for the organisations that employ them; they can have no external clientele and cannot charge fees for their valuation work. They may apply for a licence if they wish to do so.

Presently, there are some 500 valuers in Singapore. Based on Singapore's total population of 3,016,400 as of June 1990, this represents approximately one valuer per 6,000 persons. In 1980 there were some 160 valuers and a total population of 2,413,900, approximately one valuer per 15,000 persons. Hence, there has been a marked increase in the number of valuers serving the population.

All licensed valuers possess a relevant degree, such as a B.Sc. degree in estate management from the National University of Singapore, a similar degree from a recognised overseas university, or equivalent professional qualifications from the Royal Institution of Chartered Surveyors (RICS). They should also have at least one year of postgraduate experience in valuation work acquired locally while affiliated with a licensed valuer.

Professional Institution

The Singapore Institute of Surveyors and Valuers (SISV) is the only national body in Singapore representing land surveyors, quantity surveyors, project managers, valuers, auctioneers, estate agents, and property managers. The Singapore Institute dates back to 1937 when the Malaya branch of the Royal Institution of Chartered Surveyors (RICS), the original professional institution for land surveyors, quantity surveyors, and valuers, was formed. In 1957 when Malaya gained independence from Great Britain, the local RICS branch was split into the Singapore branch and the Malaya branch. The Singapore branch was phased out in 1968 and, in its place, the Singapore Institute of Surveyors (SIS) was formed the same year.

Another professional organisation, the Real Estate Valuers' Association (Singapore), which included valuers, auctioneers, and estate agents, was established in 1963. This association was reconstituted as the Singapore Institute of Valuers (SIV) in 1977. The Singapore Institute of Surveyors (SIS) and the Singapore Institute of Valuers (SIV) subsequently merged into the Singapore Institute of Surveyors and Valuers (SISV) in 1982. Upon merger, the institute had some 500 members within three divisions, namely, the land surveying division, the quantity surveying division, and the valuation and general practice division.

Thus, the valuation profession in Singapore has a 60-year history, beginning with the formation of the Malaya branch of the Royal Institution of Chartered Surveyors in 1937. As of October 1994, the institute had about 1,097 members, of which more than half (583) are members of the valuation and general practice division.

Membership Categories

The categories of membership in the SISV include student members, probationers (candidates), members, fellows, and honorary fellows. Of these, member and fellow are the two main professional membership categories conferred by the institute. To qualify as a member of the institute, the applicant must possess an acceptable degree or professional qualifications and have acquired at least two years of relevant postgraduate experience locally. Since 1989, applicants must keep a diary and log of their experience for two years from the date of conditional approval of their application. During this probationary period, an applicant is to be supervised by a senior member of the institute who is either a fellow of the institute or a member with at least seven years of postgraduate experience. The applicant must submit his or her diary and log for inspection every six months. At the end of two years, the applicant has to attend an assessment of professional competence (APC), which involves an interview. Upon successful completion of the interview, the applicant becomes eligible for membership. A member may apply to be upgraded to a fellow if he or she is at least 35 years old, has at least five years of professional experience in a senior executive position, has been an SISV member for at least two years, and has completed a minimum of two years of recognised service with the institute.

Code of Conduct and Ethics

All members of the SISV are obliged to follow a code of conduct and ethics prescribed under the institute's by-laws. The by-laws prohibit conduct which is fraudulent or misleading, define the confidential nature of the agent-client relationship, and specify the proper means of publicity and promotion. Members who are alleged to have breached any part of the code of conduct and ethics under the by-laws are subject to disciplinary action. If found guilty, the member may be reprimanded, suspended, or expelled.

As part of its objectives to promote and enhance professionalism, SISV disseminates information about developments in the industry to its members through a newsletter and journal publications and organises various conferences, seminars, and talks. One of the most important services the institute provides its members is a subscription for data on all real estate transactions through SISV Services Pte. (Private) Ltd., a wholly owned subsidiary of SISV. SISV Services was set up in 1990 to spearhead the institute's efforts to improve the efficiency and standards of the profession through the application of information technology in the real estate service industry. In addition to this computerised sales data service, SISV Services also runs the Multiple Listing System, which is Singapore's first and currently only computerised listing service.

Training and Education

In Singapore, most practising property valuers hold B.Sc. degrees in estate management from the School of Building and Estate Management (S.B.E.M.) of the National University of Singapore (N.U.S.). The B.Sc. programme in estate management is one of two undergraduate degree programmes offered by the School of Building and Estate Management. The other undergraduate degree programme is the B.Sc. in building programme. Both degree programmes, which have been offered by the university since 1968, are now accredited by the Royal Institution of Chartered Surveyors (RICS) and recognised by the Singapore Institute of Surveyors and Valuers as well as by the Commonwealth Association of Surveying and Land Economy (CASLE). The linkage with RICS is important in that a substantial number of practising valuers in Singapore acquired their professional qualifications through RICS.

Valuation Practices in Singapore

Overview of Valuation Work

Valuation firms vary in size and in the number of appraisals carried out annually. The number of appraisals completed in a year may range from fewer than 100 to nearly 5,000.

Valuation firms generally maintain some type of guidelines for valuation work. These guidelines are considered especially useful when new graduates perform work on behalf of the company. Although there is no standard version of such guidelines, they generally specify the procedures to follow in undertaking a valuation. Most firms also use the criterion of assignment size, as measured by the value of the property, to determine who should perform the work. More experienced staff are usually entrusted with the higher value jobs, while recent graduates do the lower value assignments.

Nearly all valuation firms have some way of categorising the work they handle. Many categorise their jobs by the purpose of the valuation or the property type; others classify their valuation assignments by the method of valuation, the amount involved, or the client. In some firms, two categories are adopted: the purpose of the valuation and the client.

Types of Valuation

The types of valuation carried out in Singapore may be broadly categorised by the purpose of the valuation and the property type. The purpose of the valuation can be further differentiated into statutory and nonstatutory valuations. Statutory valuations are those governed by statutes and legislation specific to Singapore. Statutory valuations are performed in other countries, but because the legal systems differ, statutory valuations also differ. In

Singapore, the most common statutory valuation is for property tax purposes, i.e., clients seek the services of the valuer to contest the chief valuer's assessment of their property. Among nonstatutory valuations, mortgage valuations are the most common followed by valuations for sale or purchase.

Breaking down valuations by property type, the largest category is valuations of residential properties, followed by valuations of commercial properties (office and retail centres), industrial properties (factories and warehouses), vacant land, and special properties (hotels).

Valuation Methods

In Singapore, all five methods of valuation—direct comparison, income, cost, profits, and residual methods—are used to some extent. These methods are widely recognised by the appraisal fraternity and their application has been well documented. Many techniques derived from these methods are also used, and in recent years innovative financial and econometric models have been introduced.

Direct comparison is the primary method used in Singapore, regardless of the purpose of the valuation. Notable exceptions are valuations performed for insurance purposes in which values are derived based on the cost of replacement. The widespread use of direct comparison is to be expected because, wherever comparable data are available, direct comparison provides an easy, logical, and defensible means of deriving property value. The real estate transaction data service that SISV provides its members captures up-to-date transaction information on the property market and is helping ensure the availability of data. Valuers also favour direct comparison since market experience is the prerequisite for its application. The other methods of valuation are used as secondary methods or to provide a check on the estimate derived by the principal method. The income method of valuation, for example, is usually applied as a check on the estimated value of income-generating commercial properties.

Thus, the direct comparison method is commonly used in Singapore for all property types (residential, commercial, and industrial) due to the availability of comparable evidence. For special properties such as hotels, recreational clubs, and institutional properties, methods such as the profits and cost methods are considered appropriate. If the property has a commercial use, either of these two methods may be applied. For hotels and commercially operated recreational clubs, the profits method is applicable; for institutional properties, the cost method is mainly used.

Further observations on the five methods of valuation used in Singapore follow.

Direct Comparison Method

One problem associated with applying the direct comparison method may be a lack of comparable data. Most valuers in Singapore feel that this is not a major problem, however, since the local market is small and the market structure is fairly well-defined. The transaction data service also ensures the availability of data. Another issue in direct comparison is whether appraisers apply a fixed methodology in estimating adjustments. Like most valuers in other countries, the majority of valuers in Singapore do not use a fixed methodology for adjustments. Instead they rely on their experience. The use of statistical techniques and mass appraisal methods is limited largely to the public sector, where the Inland Revenue Authority of Singapore (IRAS) has implemented the use of computer-assisted assessment methods.

Income Method

The accuracy and reliability of the traditional methods of income valuation have come under much criticism in recent years. Bearing the brunt of the attack are the hardcore, or layer, method used to value reversionary freehold (fee simple) interests and the dual rate method used to value leasehold interests.[2] Although most valuers in Singapore have learnt these traditional methods, the majority do not use them. Instead, most valuers apply discounted cash flow (DCF) concepts in the income approach. For freehold (fee simple) properties, direct capitalisation based on the market yield (direct cap rate) and net rental income is acceptable. For reversionary freehold and leasehold interests, most valuers resort to DCF analysis to arrive at the value of the property interest.

Cost Method

Despite its limitations, the cost method does have some applicability in valuation, e.g., for insurance purposes and for certain special properties. In the case of the latter, the cost or *contractor's test method,* as it is generally known, is used for the purpose of assessing property taxes.

Profits Method

The profits method is used in a few circumstances. For example, the valuation of hotels for property tax purposes is based on the profits from the hotel's operations. This method is also used in the market valuation of special properties that are commercially run and owner-occupied.

---

2. The dual rate method, which is used for valuing leasehold interests, reserves a portion of net income for investment in a sinking fund at an accumulative rate to recapture the initial outlay and capitalizes the remainder of the net income at an appropriate remunerative rate of return.

Residual Method

The traditional method for determining the value of a site with development potential is to estimate the hypothetical gross development value of the improved property and subtract the costs of the development. Given its simplicity, this method is frequently used in the appraisal of developments. Its main limitation, however, is that the method does not take into account the time value of money. This shortcoming can be overcome by the use of discounted cash flow analysis, in which periodic cash flows are broken down into various components and discounted to reflect their timing.

Valuation Report and Process

Most valuation firms adopt standards for valuation work. Usually the client's request is formally confirmed in writing, although some firms do accept verbal confirmation from established clients. The amount of time and human resources allocated to information gathering and research may vary depending on the type and nature of the valuation. Inspection of the subject property is mandatory and, in most cases, properties used as comparables are also inspected. After all the necessary groundwork has been laid, the valuation is conducted and the report is prepared. When more than one method is used to arrive at the estimated value, a reconciliation is shown. Valuation reports in Singapore generally follow the format used in other developed countries such as the U.K. and the U.S. In fact, the concept of open market value used in Singapore follows the RICS definition of open market value. Usually the same types of limiting conditions are attached to valuation reports.

Conclusion

Some of the issues facing valuers in Singapore and their implications for the future of the profession are briefly discussed below.

One key issue is the revision of the Auctioneers' Licences Act of 1906, which currently governs the professional activities of valuers, auctioneers, and estate agents. A separate act covering estate agents and one relating to valuers and auctioneers will give the valuation profession more power in regulating the activities of its practitioners through the establishment of a board of valuers and auctioneers. A code of conduct and ethics can also be adopted under the act, with supplemental guidance notes, practice rules, and regulations issued from time to time. These changes will undoubtedly enhance the standards of practice and professionalism.

Another major concern is the threat posed by related professions capable of providing similar services. This can be overcome through greater research and improvements in valuation practice. While a large number of valuers are already performing and including research in their appraisals, some smaller valuation firms may find the cost of research prohibitive. To improve existing practice, it is important to improve the flow of information. To some extent, the government's efforts in setting up economic and land use databases will help. Valuation firms need to upgrade their own research and information support teams. For smaller firms, information sharing might be necessary.

Finally, valuers need to consider using more finance-based methods to maintain a competitive edge. Firms should also expand the range of services they are equipped to provide in the face of increasing deregulation and the globalisation of financial and property markets.

Republic of Zimbabwe

Louis Taderera, ARICS

Louis Taderera is the principal valuer of Land Appraisal and Research Services, Ltd., a private company based in Bulawayo, Zimbabwe. He is also Projects Director of Karoo Investments, a construction company specializing in low-cost housing. Mr. Taderera has studied in both the United States and the United Kingdom. He holds B.A. and M.A. degrees (the latter in urban studies from Long Island University, Brooklyn Center, New York), a diploma in land management (Reading University, U.K.), and a diploma in surveying (College of Estate Management, U.K.). Mr. Taderera is an associate of several professional organizations, including RICS (general practice) and the Chartered Institute of Arbitrators (CIArb.). He is currently enrolled in the CIArb. fellowship assessment course and plans to specialize in the resolution of valuation and construction disputes. Mr. Taderera is also a member of the Real Estate Institute of Zimbabwe and the South African Institute of Valuers.

Mr. Taderera's involvement in urban development and property management spans 16 years in both public and private sectors. He has served as a regional valuer and estate surveyor for the Zimbabwe Ministry of Public Construction and National Housing. As Building and Estates Manager with the Post and Telecommunications Corporation (PTC), he was responsible for the development of PTC operational buildings. For the last seven years, Mr. Taderera has been a surveyor of farm and urban properties. His specializations include rating (assessment), property management, property development, and compensation claims for compulsory acquisition.

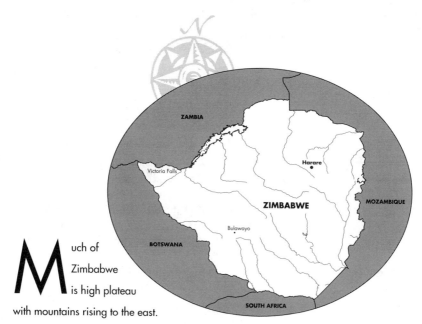

Much of
Zimbabwe
is high plateau
with mountains rising to the east.
Central and southwestern Zimbabwe is covered by veld, grassland with scattered shrubs
and trees, while the southeast has tropical hardwood forests. The north is also forested.
Much of the country has a subtropical climate and natural resources are ample. The
population is about 13 million. Principal cities are Harare (Salisbury) and Bulawayo.

Historical Background

Bantu peoples, the ancestors of the present-day inhabitants of Zimbabwe, arrived in the fifth century A.D. A kingdom centered on Great Zimbabwe (or stone fortress) was established by the Shona (Mashona) people in the eleventh century, reaching its apogee in the fourteenth and fifteenth centuries. Zimbabwe prospered from commerce in gold, which was mined in the interior and sold to Arab and Swahili merchants in the trading cities along the east African coast. Two successor Shona kingdoms were organized in the Zambezi valley to the north: Mutapa (or Mtapa) and Butua. Another Bantu people, the Ndebele (or Matabele), dispersed from South Africa in the 1830s and settled in the southern part of the country. The Ndebele and the Shona put up considerable resistance to the British. In 1889 the British South African Company formed by Cecil Rhodes secured mining concessions and land rights over the territories north of the Limpopo river that make up present-day Zimbabwe (known until 1980 as Southern Rhodesia).

The Dutch colonization of South Africa also had a strong influence on the development of present-day Zimbabwe. The colony established by the Dutch on the Cape of Good Hope in 1652 was taken over by Britain during the Napoleonic wars (1806-1814) while Holland was occupied by French armies. Between 1835 and 1843, many Boers, Afrikaner descendants of these Dutch colonists, chose to move into the interior to the northeast, where in the 1850s they establshed the independent Orange Free State and Republic of the Transvaal (with the Limpopo river as its northern boundary). British encroachments after diamonds (1867) and gold (1886) were discovered in the Boer territories led to the Anglo-Boer war (1899-1902). A British victory resulted in the creation of the Union of South Africa in 1910.

The strong link between British and Zimbabwean valuers is a legacy of the country's colonial history. Much infrastructure development and economic activity occurred as the frontier territories were first surveyed for mining and commercial agriculture. As European commerce and industry took root, professionally trained manpower was brought into the country and a new breed of land overseers emerged.

Between 1893 and 1965, land agency (brokerage) and valuation procedures and practices were based, to a great extent, on British standards. Most practitioners in the landed professions were, by birth or education, of English origin. As a result of both educational and professional affiliation, present-day Zimbabwean valuation surveyors very much resemble their British counterparts.

Legal Background

Historically the Dutch and, much later, the British played pivotal roles in the development of the legal framework under which both colonial and self-rule governments have operated in the administration of land. Much of current Zimbabwean property law has evolved from an amalgam of English common law and South African, i.e., Roman-Dutch, law as introduced into the Cape Colony by Dutch settlers in the seventeenth century. Property law also reflects adaptations from nineteenth-century European legal thinking, legislation, and case law.

The introduction of European law has to a great extent excluded traditional and indigenous systems of legality. These systems were characterised by pre-colonial social values, which tended to place more emphasis on collective social responsibilities than on individual freedoms, as reflected in European law.

Political Background

From 1923 on, "responsible self government" by British settlers replaced the British South African Company in the administration of the social and economic affairs of Southern Rhodesia.[1] Property matters were governed by a mixture of common law, Roman-Dutch law, and exclusionary land legislation.

Two factors have strongly influenced the practice of valuation in Zimbabwe: 1) the background and training of practitioners, and 2) pre-1980 land tenure legislation pertaining to land in urban, rural, and communal areas.

For more than 50 years, real rights to land were defined and granted on the basis of race. This resulted in a mixed economic system with two separate and unequal patterns of economic development, affecting both urban and rural areas. Land resources were divided and shared among the colonial government, the settler-farmers, and the indigenous communities. Settler-farmers with sound financial backing from the successive colonial governments were able to develop and improve the land they were granted. They had the right to trade this land on the market, but only to "persons of un-mixed European origin," a stipulation found in almost all pre-1970 deed-of-title transfers. The result is evident today throughout the country's urban centres, which have three characteristic property markets: a residential

---

1. In 1965 a white-minority government under Prime Minister Ian Smith unilaterally declared Rhodesia independent of Britain and for 11 years resisted demands of black Africans for majority rule. Sanctions imposed by the United Nations in 1967, heightened guerrilla warfare, and the withdrawal of South African troops forced Smith to meet with black nationalist leaders across the political spectrum (from moderates in the African National Congress to militants in the Patriotic Front). Smith's proposals for establishing a majority-rule government were not, however, acceptable. In talks sponsored by Britain in 1979, all groups agreed to a cease-fire and a plan of transition to black majority rule.

property market for the black population in former "African townships," a black/white residential property market in former "white only areas," and a limited commercial and industrial property market.

Property law is adapting to current sociopolitical developments in Zimbabwe. The past century has been a period of great socioeconomic and technical change, with cultural cross-pollination and the transfer of knowledge in the land management field. A sizeable minority of Zimbabwean civil servants involved in formulating and implementing economic development policies at the national and local government levels have been educated in South Africa, Britain, or other Commonwealth countries.

Economy

The economy of Zimbabwe is based on mining (copper, gold, chromium, nickel, tin), manufacturing (machinery, transport equipment), light industries (textiles, petroleum, chemical products), tourism, and agriculture. The country is self-sufficient and exports tobacco, corn, wheat, sugar, and cotton. Approximately three-fourths of the labour force is employed in agriculture (45% small-scale and 30% commercial farming) and another 15% work in service, transportation, and manufacturing industries. Many Zimbabweans are small entrepreneurs and craftsmen. Zimbabwe's principal trading partners are the European Community, South Africa, and the United States. Long droughts caused considerable hardship in 1982-1983 and again in 1992-1994.

Language

Many Zimbabweans understand English, which as the country's official language is used by civil servants and taught in the country's schools. Two Bantu languages are spoken by most of the population: Shona (67%) and Zulu-derived Ndebele (16%).

Currency

The monetary unit is the Zimbabwean dollar (Z$ or $).

Units of Measurement

Zimbabwe uses the metric system. Prices and rentals are quoted in dollars per square meter (m²).

Inflation

Zimbabwe's economic planners have recognised the need to redirect the developmental and socioeconomic priorities of the formerly colonial country and upgrade its rural infrastructure. Recent conditions have often been punitive. Thirty percent of the country's labour force is employed in agro-industry, which suffered the effects of severe droughts in the early 1980s and early 1990s. During both periods the country registered a negative growth rate. Since 1990 annual growth rates have ranged between –2% and +4%. A record high of +5% was achieved in 1996, the result of a good rainy season. The projected rate of growth for 1997 is +6%.

Under the Public Sector Investment Program of the last 15 years, the government has increased expenditures for the development of rural infrastructure and facilities and for social welfare projects such as free education and health care for minimum wage earners. There has also been an increase in unemployment as the labour force is swelled by 300,000 public school graduates each year.

Between 1980 and 1995, several economic programs were introduced, the principal one being the Economic Structural Adjustment Program I (1990-1995), which attempted to liberalize the economy, to make the production and service sectors more competitive, and to remove foreign exchange controls and thereby facilitate the development of import and export industries. The government is soon expected to introduce a new, five-year program to consolidate the economic gains made thus far and to improve the developing business and legal environment.

Annual inflation peaked at 45% in 1992 and reached its lowest recent level when it fell to 13.9% in November 1996. Interest rates have also dropped significantly, from a high of 39% in 1995 to an average rate of 26% in the last quarter of 1996. At that time the Bank of Zimbabwe reduced its discount rate from 27% to 23.5%. Since 1992 the bank has pursued a tight monetary policy to curb inflation. Annual inflation figures for retail prices follow.

1992	45.0%
1993	27.6%
1994	22.0%
1995	21.0%

Quarterly inflation rates for retail prices from 1996 to 1997 were

January 1996	28.0%
April 1996	24.1%
July 1996	22.0%
October 1996	20.0%
January 1997	15.0%

Estate Agents (Brokers) and Valuers (1945-1994)

At the end of World War II, the colonial government brought into the civil service personnel qualified in land surveying and valuation. Included in their ranks were professional associates of the Royal Institution of Chartered Surveyors, who headed the Revenue and the Land Surveying Departments of the colonial government. RICS associates also staffed the quantity surveying section of the Department of Public Works. Thus, new and highly qualified personnel were brought into the country and began to interact with local land agents. Also during the 1940s, a professional organization of land agents and valuers was founded, the Auctioneers', Estate Agents', and Valuers' Institute of Rhodesia. Later, legislation was passed to regulate and control the activities of the landed professions—the Estates Agents Act of 1970, as amended in 1985.

Since its founding in 1945, the Auctioneers', Estate Agents' and Valuers' Institute of Rhodesia had been the examining body responsible for the training of local valuers and estate agents. Valuation education had always been provided through a correspondence course. The syllabi and lecture notes on the various subjects covered by the examination were prepared by the Education Committee of the institute.

The members of the Zimbabwe Branch of the Royal Institution of Chartered Surveyors have been a major force in the training programme of the Auctioneers', Estate Agents', and Valuers' Institute. In the last five years, this branch has provided two successive institute chairmen, one serving as the Education Committee Chairman for the Estate Agents Council and the other as a valuation examiner for the institute. In 1979 the organization changed its name to the Real Estate Institute of Zimbabwe.

The institute's training programme is three years long. The principal subjects studied are building construction, mercantile law, town planning, valuation, and estate agents practice (brokerage). This course of study is divided into three parts. Those passing examinations for Part I are eligible to register under the Estate Agents Act. Students aspiring to be valuers are required to complete all three years and pass the final examinations before being issued a certificate recognising them as professional members of the institute.

The Estate Agents Act and Council

Any person representing himself as, or allowing himself to represented as an "incorporated estate agent," or using a name, title, or letter designation indicating that he is an incorporated estate agent must be a member or fellow of a recognised institute.

The preamble to the Estate Agents Act, promulgated in 1970 and amended in 1985, states as its purpose

> To establish the Estate Agents Council; to provide for the registration and regulation of the practice of estate agents in Zimbabwe; to provide for the establishment and operation of an Estate Agents' Compensation Fund; to regulate the keeping of moneys held by estate agents on behalf of other persons.

It then defines estate agents as:

> All persons doing for payment or reward [any of the following]:
>
> (a) ... in connection with the sale or proposed sale of immovable property belonging to another person,
>
>   (i) bringing together or taking steps to bring together the parties to the sale or proposed sale;
>
>   (ii) negotiating the terms of sale or proposed sale;
>
>   (iii) acting as an auctioneer for the sale or proposed sale,
>
> (b) valuing, for any purpose, immovable property or any part thereof; or
>
> (c) assessing the rental value of immovable property or any part thereof.

The real estate broker/agent, auctioneer, and valuer all fall under the same controlling body of rules and regulations for professional conduct.

For the purposes of reviewing qualifications and registering practitioners, the Estate Agents Council, as directed by the act, formed a Board of Examiners consisting of:

- Three members of the council,
- One member nominated by the Auctioneers', Estate Agents', and Valuers' Institute, and
- One member from the teaching staff of the University of Zimbabwe, who lectures on any of the subjects prescribed in the syllabus.

The Valuers' Act of 1995-1996

The years 1985 to 1994 saw a re-examination and revision of the Estate Agents Act to improve valuation standards in response to the country's developing economy. The previous acts lumped together the valuer and the estate broker, but the prevailing rules and regulations were only appropriate to the brokerage division. The Valuers' Act was promulgated and enacted in

1995-1996. The act was drafted after consultations and discussions among the Ministry of Public Construction and National Housing and other bodies such as the Estate Agents Council, the Real Estate Institute of Zimbabwe, and the Association of Building Societies.

The preamble to the Valuers' Act states its purpose: to establish a Valuers' Council, to provide for the registration of valuers and the regulation of valuation practice through the Valuers' Council, and to implement related matters. The act defines the "valuation of immovable property" as the preparation of a written estimate of value, which considers any right or interest with respect to the immovable property.

The function of the Valuers' Council is to do all things it considers necessary to ensure that the competence and conduct of valuers practising in the country meet a sufficiently high standard to protect the interests of the public.

The qualifications required for a person to register under the act include:

(a) professional membership in an institution which the Minister of Public Construction and National Housing (or any other minister to whom from time to time the President may assign the administration of the Act), after consultation with the Council, may prescribe; or

(b) a degree in valuation and estate management, land economics, or the equivalent, obtained from a university, polytechnic, or other institution of higher learning; or

(c) any other diploma or examination which the Minister may, after consultation with the Council, prescribe.

Valuation Practice

The following acts of the Zimbabwean Parliament are of primary concern to practising valuers:

- The Town and Country Planning Act of 1976
- The Land Acquisition Act of 1992
- The Urban Councils Act (Chapter 214) and
- The Rural Councils Act.

In addition, there are acts pertaining to statutory procedures involving riparian rights, mineral rights, and rights of way. (Statutory procedures refer to compulsory purchase, the exercise of eminent domain upon payment of just compensation.)

The 1947 Town and Country Planning Act retained the spirit of the U.K. acts pertaining to planning and local government administration in the post-1945 period. This act was superseded by the Town and Country Planning Act of 1976. It is important to note that, other than the Town and Country Planning Acts and some rules pertaining to land acquisition, there are no other such acts equivalent to those in the U.K.

U.K. acts that have a bearing on the valuation of landed property pertain to property ownership, transfer, and leasing. A Zimbabwean valuer must be aware of such acts where applicable. There are no equivalent acts in Zimbabwe that relate to the above-cited matters. The U.K. acts include the following:

- Law of Property Act
- Landlord and Tenant Act
- Leasehold Reform Act
- Agricultural Holdings Act

In the Zimbabwean acts, a "piece of land" is defined as land registered as a separate entity in a deeds registry and including anything permanently attached to, or growing on, such land and any interest or right in such land.

No land can be sold unless it has been surveyed and registered in the deeds registry in accordance with the Land Survey and Deeds Registry Acts.

The principles governing the U.K. Acquisition of Land Act (Assessment of Compensation Act) of 1919 have generally been followed in the Zimbabwean Land Acquisition Act of 1992 and are included in all legislation pertaining to compensation for land rights (eminent domain) in non-designated rural areas.[2]

According to these principles:

(a) No account shall be taken of the compulsory nature of the acquisition;

(b) No consideration shall be made of any change in the price or value of any land resulting from any action taken, or to be taken by the authority connected with the acquisition of the land, or resulting from the purpose for which, or in connection with which the land is being taken, or is to be used;

---

2. A non-designated rural area is any rural land that has not been identified for purposes of acquisition by the state under the Land Acquisition Act of 1992. In Zimbabwe, to designate land is to publicize that such land, as shown in maps on public display to which the public may voice its objections, has been set aside for specific purposes and acquisition by the relevant authority through approved measures for use as identified in the public notice.

(c) No regard shall be given to the special suitability or useful-ness of any land for the purpose that it is required by the acquiring authority if it is unlikely that, but for the acquiring authority's requirements, the land would have been pur-chased for that purpose on the open market.

(d) No regard shall be given to any increase in the price or value of any land where such increase is due to the use of the land in a manner which is illegal, detrimental to the land, or restrainable.

(e) If immediately before the date of publication of the prelimi-nary notice in the *Gazette* (the government periodical), land that is not designated as rural land had been used for a purpose and adapted to that purpose, in such a way that there is no general demand or market for the land so used and adapted, and if the justice of the court so requires, compensation shall be assessed on the basis of the reason-able cost of adapting other land in such a way that the claimant is restored as closely as possible to the position in which he was immediately prior to that date or any other basis which is considered fair.

Again, in compulsory land acquisitions, compensation is paid for:

(a) The loss of the land; and

(b) Any actual expense or loss which has been or may reason-ably be incurred or suffered directly as a result of the action taken by the acquiring authority, and which has not already been taken into account, directly or indirectly, in assessing compensation for the loss of the land, provided that, in relation to any damage to any area of the land or any build-ing or structure thereon, compensation for such damage shall not exceed the value of the area of land, building or struc-ture, as the case may be.

The Zimbabwean acts also stipulate that compensation shall be assessed in a manner so as to arrive at what is fair and reasonable, taking into account the value of the land, regard being given to its nature, location, and quality and any other factor bearing on its value.

Market Value

The development of property law in Zimbabwe has, to a certain degree, been linked to that of South Africa.

It would appear that, in South Africa, the meaning of *value* was first considered by De Villiers, J.P., in the 1911 case of *Pietermaritzburg Corporation v South African Breweries*. Here the judge discussed two meanings of the word *value*, namely:

(a) the expression of the utility of some particular object (called value in use) and

(b) the power of purchasing other goods which is the object's value in exchange.

He went on to say

> when the legislature prescribes that the value of the property has to be determined, it refers to the exchange value of the property, in other words, the amount of money for which the property can be exchanged or sold.

In another case, *S.A.R. v Theron* (1917), Justice Mason stated that

> when the phrase market value is used in connection with damages, what it means is the general selling price in that particular neighbourhood, and that general price is determined not only by the price at the public market, but also by the general prices throughout the district among people who deal in that particular commodity.

Except in valuation reports prepared by valuers who are members of the RICS, it has not been the general practice among Zimbabwean valuers to define market value or open market value in their reports.

The Rhodesian Land Acquisition Act of 1971, as amended in 1992, states in Section 26(2) (a) that

> in assessing compensation for land, the courts shall ... assess such compensation on the market value of the land immediately prior to the date of the publication of the preliminary notice which shall be taken to be the amount which the land would have realised if sold in the open market by a willing seller to a willing buyer, regard being given, where appropriate, to the nature of the land, its location and quality and any other factor which may in the circumstances be relevant.

Section 1999(1) of the current Urban Councils Act states that:

> the basis of valuation of any property shall be the estimated price which a buyer would be willing to give and the seller would be willing to accept if the property to be valued were brought to voluntary sale in the open market.

Valuation Standards

The admission of the Auctioneers', Estate Agents', and Valuers' Institute of Zimbabwe into membership in the International Valuation Standards Committee (IVSC) in April 1991 spurred an attempt to formulate valuation standards in the context of Zimbabwe's legal and economic development. However, there are no formal guidelines or valuation standards in Zimbabwe equivalent to the red book (the RICS manual) and white book *(RICS Valuation Guidance Notes)* in the U.K. or their American equivalent (USPAP).

In their "Accounting for Properties, Plant and Equipment," the International Committee (of the Auctioneers', Estates Agents', and Valuers' Institute of Zimbabwe) and the Institute of Chartered Accountants of Zimbabwe (ICAZ) provide the following definition of *property, plant, and equipment.*

> Property, plant, and equipment are tangible assets that:
>
> (a) are held by an enterprise for use in the production or supply of goods and services, for rental to others, or for administrative purposes and may include items held for the maintenance and repair of such assets;
>
> (b) have been acquired or constructed with the intention of being used on a continuing basis; and
>
> (c) are not intended for sale in the country of business.

Leasehold rights over assets which meet the criteria of (a), (b) and (c) may also be treated as property, plant and equipment in certain circumstances.

The two, above-cited organisations have also defined *fair value and recoverable amount.*

> Fair value is the amount for which an asset might be exchanged between a knowledgeable, willing buyer and a knowledgeable, willing seller in an arm's length transaction.
>
> Recoverable amount of an asset's value is what an enterprise can recover from future use of the asset, including its net realisable value on disposal.

In the scale of fees published by the Auctioneers', Estate Agents', and Valuers' Institute of Rhodesia (1 July, 1976) a *valuation* is defined as

> a report prepared by a valuer in accordance with his client's instructions ... [which] may be supported by full written details of the property concerned, together with his valuation.

Later amendments have improved the definition of valuation to state:

a formal report prepared by a valuer ..... stating the valuer's opinion on the open market value of any property in terms of its capital or rental value as of a certain date.

Regardless of the purpose of the valuation, Zimbabwean valuers generally provide property details in valuation reports—both physical and legal information on properties as contained in the title deeds and town planning schemes (land use maps) where relevant. Valuers also state assumptions and caveats pertaining to specialist (specialized) knowledge outside their area of competence or situations where financial records on the property have not been accessed or investigated.

The following assumptions [and limiting conditions] are normally included in a valuation report under the heading "Valuation Notes":

(a) neither a structural survey has been requested nor has such a survey been conducted on the plumbing, electrical or any other service installations;

(b) in assessing the property value, any repairs or rehabilitation that may be warranted are assumed to be commensurate with the normal upkeep and maintenance of the property, and the condition of the property is assumed, in all respects, to be fair and satisfactory;

(c) the existing land and improvements thereon comply with current by-laws and regulations (either statutory or non-statutory).

The Valuation Notes section usually includes a clause on the confidentiality of the contents of the report and restrictions on publication without the prior approval of the valuer and the manner in which the valuation conclusions may appear.

Most valuation reports contain the following information, which will depend on the type and location of the property to be valued:

1. Confirmation of the client's instructions and the purpose of the valuation.

2. Property description per title deed records, i.e., the stand number (lot or tract number) of a parcel of land, the situation and address, the area and relevant survey diagram, title deed numbers, year of purchase, and the declared purchase price.

3. Encumbrances or restrictions regarding use, servitude (whether subject to easements), information on the local authorities, and town and country planning (land use) conditions. Also included would be information on

any mortgage, lien, or caveats that may be registered against the title deed to the property, including the mortgage or loan amount, registration numbers, and the name of the bond holders.

4. Tenure, i.e., whether freehold or leasehold, including a list of tenants and lease details where possible.

5. Soil types, topography, drainage, and vegetation (for farms and development sites).

6. Facilities and services, e.g., sources of water and electricity, types of roads.

7. Suitability of the property for its existing or intended use.

8. Accessibility to other facilities and markets.

9. A considered opinion synthesizing the relevant, logical arguments that support the valuation conclusion, as derived or deduced from investigations and survey and market research.

10. Caveats and assumptions, i.e., a note on limiting conditions and any assumptions made

11. A valuation certificate.

The valuation certificate would be stated as follows:

> I have inspected the property known as Stand or Farm #...........
> situated in the District of .... and having made careful investigations
> and consideration thereof, am of the opinion that the current market
> value of the land and permanent improvements erected thereon, and
> as described in this report for .... purposes, is Z$ ....
> (amount written out in words).

As a result of the qualification requirements stipulated in the 1995 Valuers' Bill and the introduction of valuation as a subject offered by the Department of Rural and Urban Planning of the University of Zimbabwe, the next five years will likely be a period of reformation in the valuation profession, both in regard to valuation standards and the training of valuers.

Valuations Based on Open Market Value

Where information on property prices is readily available and subject to audits by revenue officers, it is possible to estimate the value of an interest in property in the near future with some degree of accuracy.

The open market value of residential freehold interests is based on evidence of recorded sales in the deeds office. Advertisements for such properties in the local and national papers may reflect sellers' expectations. They establish the call prices and are indicators of the range of property prices in the respective property market.

Requests for valuation certificates require the valuer to express in monetary terms the price that a particular property would likely fetch if it were to be placed on the open market for sale at a given time under conditions prevailing prior and up to the date of instruction. The time period which a valuer chooses to bracket the sales and the quality of evidence identified in the particular locality bear on the open market value conclusion.

In all valuations, the valuer expresses his or her opinion of value in terms of both the physical and economic characteristics of the subject property as compared to similar properties that have sold and the perceived behaviour and price expectations of sellers and bidders.

A valuer in a general practice office has three sources of information: 1) in-house information, which consists of the prices that sellers are asking as well as final negotiated purchase prices; 2) information from other practitioners and professional contacts (networking); and 3) the deeds registry.

An institutional lender is likely to be interested in the recoverable amount, including net realisable value on disposal (or reversion). Such a figure can be derived from, and supported by, the prevailing market prices.

Methods

Direct Comparison

Given a broad and active residential market where accurate information on sale prices is readily available, direct comparison is the most widespread method for estimating realistic open market values of residential properties in urban areas. The great number of residential districts that have been developed based on township development schemes (land use plans) over the last 40 years ensures sufficient data on comparable neighbourhoods, both for high- and low-density submarkets. The design, layout, and age of residential buildings show greater similarity than is found among buildings in industrial and commercial property markets.

Sample sales are obtained over a period, which may reflect a stagnant market, a market on the upturn, or a downward trend in house prices.

The price of the property most similar to the subject property is used as a base price, which the valuer adjusts upward or downward for any aspect of the property considered to produce a quantitative change in value.

It is best for the valuer to secure evidence from a locality as near to the subject as possible. Using the rating (assessment) information on relevant sales for which the property measurements have not changed since the valuation roll (assessment roll) was compiled, the valuer is able to establish periodic market trends. It is common to cross-check an estimate by calculating the ratio of the sale prices to the valuation roll figures. This assumes that the valuation roll was based on a sufficiently comprehensive analysis of property values to generate near-accurate figures that reflect market price levels at the time the roll was prepared.

Unit Value Method

Since the general revaluation (reassessment) in Harare, the capital of Zimbabwe, in 1975, the unit value method[3] of analysis and valuation has been used to arrive at value estimates for residential properties.

Historical construction costs of the main house, site features, and ancillary buildings are used to establish respective cost ratios. The areas of site features and ancillary buildings are converted into percentages based on their value relative to the main house, which is given a unit value of 1.0. Thus, each feature and ancillary building represents a percentage of 1.0. Although the values estimated for the ancillary features may sometimes be arbitrary, the percentages generally correspond to the relative costs and sometimes to the degree of utility. When there is reliable sales evidence, valuation "in terms of main space" (I/T/MS) seems as valid an approach as the zoning method, developed by Trustram Eve in the U.K., which is used to estimate the rental value of shops.

Sales Analysis Example

Sale property data (comparable sale data)

Property:	Stand 1455
Situated:	# 21 Harare Drive
Suburb:	Woodhall
Price and date of sale:	$165,000; 10 September 1995
Date of construction:	1975
Area in terms of main space:	246.2
Construction:	Rendered brick under concrete tiled roof, woodblock flooring.

---

3. The unit value method relies on ratings (assessments) and sale prices of comparable properties. Based on a cost analysis, each of the components of the comparable property is assigned a relative unit number. The relative unit number for the component is then multiplied by the area that the component occupies. The resulting unit numbers are totaled, and the price of the comparable is divided by the total to arrive at a unit value. This unit value is then applied to the total unit number estimated for the subject property.

Item	Area in m²	Relative Unit	No. of Units	Price Z$	Unit Value
Main building	150	1	150.0	165,000	
Veranda	12	0.35	4.2		
Garage	20	0.40	8.0		
Workers' quarters	40	0.40	16.0		
Boundary wall	80	0.10	8.0		
Land	4,000	0.015	60.0		
Total units (I/T/MS)			246.2		$670.18

Subject property

Item	Area in m²	Relative Unit	No. of Units	Price Z$	Unit Value
Main building	165	1	165		
Veranda	10	0.35	3.5		
Garage	18	0.40	7.2		
Workers' quarters	35	0.40	14		
Land	3,500	0.015	52.5		
Total units (I/T/MS)			242.2	$670.18	$162,317

Value of the house, say Z$162,500 (rounded)

Capitalisation of Income/Investment Method

When the capitalisation of income method is applied to income-generating properties, market rental levels provide base indicators of future realisable incomes. The method may be applied to commercial properties, such as shops and office buildings, or to any other property whose rental income is known or can be derived from a market of comparable properties, i.e., current/recent lettings (leasings) and sales of investment properties. For properties that are let (leased), the capital value of the freehold is the total value of rental income over the lease term plus the value of the reversion.

In practice, the three indicators used in the method are market-derived, i.e., established through analysis of comparable market evidence. These indicators are

1. The capitalisation rate for the rental income over the term,
2. The capitalisation rate for the reversion, and
3. The rental levels used to estimate the value of the reversion.

It should be noted that the method may also be applied to apartment block flats and supermarket complexes, but only when very little sales evidence exists and more data on lettings (leasings) is available.

Capitalisation Example

The property to be valued is under a fixed-rental lease with a term of five years.

Current gross rental income	$10,000 per annum
Less outgoings (operating expenses)	$ 1,000 per annum
Net rental income	$ 9,000 per annum

The value of the lease is calculated as follows:

Net rental income	$ 9,000 per annum
Capitalised @ 15% for five years (market rate)	
(*PV* of $1 per period)	× 3.3522
	$30,170

The value of the reversion is then calculated.

Estimated rental income in five years	$15,000
Less estimated outgoings (operating expenses)	$ 2,000
Net rental income	$13,000
Year's purchase in perpetuity after five	
years at 10%	6.20921
	$80,720

Thus, the value of the property is $30,170 + $80,720 = $110,890, or $111,000 (rounded)

Although discounted cash flow analysis is now applied to value income-producing properties, the capitalisation method more generally used applies an all risks yield (overall cap rate) derived from market sales of known income-producing properties.

Some practitioners who value leaseholds with fixed rents make use of the going mortgage interest rate to determine the opportunity cost of money and apply it as the discount rate. They capitalise the reversion using a market-derived all risks yield (reversion yield or terminal cap rate), which tends to be lower than the discount rate.

Profits Method

The profits method is mainly used to value specialist (specialized) properties that are sold as business concerns operating within the properties. In Zimbabwe, the profits method is used to value hotels, motels, safari lodges, and cinemas for which profit and loss accounts (operating statements) are available. In most cases, these properties tend to enjoy a degree of monopoly and hence lack competitors from which to obtain sales evidence for reasonable comparisons.

The valuation format is as follows:

1.	Gross earnings	$...............................
2.	Less purchases	....
3.	Gross profit	$...............................
4.	Less working capital	....
5.	Net profit	$...............................
6.	Less operator's profit	....
7.	Net annual rent	$...............................
	Capitalisation factor @ a market rate	....
	Capital value	$...............................

This format follows general practice in the U.K. Figures from the subject property's profit and loss account (operating statement) should be analysed and compared with those of other, similar properties to be sure they are realistic and sustainable.

Other Methods

Two other methods, i.e., the residual and contractor's methods, are used, primarily to establish book values for accounting purposes. They may also be applied when there is a lack of comparables and the properties are specialist (specialized) buildings designed for specific operations.

Bibliography

Abrahams, B. G. *A Handbook of Real Estate in Zimbabwe.* Harare, Zimbabwe: Auctioneers', Estate Agents', and Valuers' Institute of Zimbabwe, 1982.

Christie, R .H. *Rhodesian Commercial Law.* Cape Town, South Africa: Juta & Company Ltd, 1961.

Millin, Philip and George Willie. *Mercantile Law of South Africa.* 10th ed. Johannesburg: Hortors Limited, 1941.

Moyana, Henry V. *The Political Economy of Land in Zimbabwe.* Gweru, Zimbabwe: Mambo Press, 1984.

Penny, Peter. *Economic and Legal Aspects of Real Estate in South Africa.* Cape Town, South Africa: Juta & Company Ltd., 1970.

Public Relations Department (Salisbury). *Rhodesia Facts and Figures for the Settler.* Glasgow, Scotland: Robert MacLehose and Company Ltd, 1951.

Thompson, F.M.L. *Chartered Surveyors: the Growth of the Profession.* London: Routledge and Kegan Paul, Ltd., 1968.

Wright, H.C. *City of Harare Revaluation Circular Nos. 5 & 6.* Harare, Zimbabwe, 1990. (Note: General valuations are undertaken and new valuation rolls become effective at intervals of not less than three years and not more than seven years. The minister in charge of general valuations may, however, extend the interval up to 10 years by notice in the government *Gazette.* The last general valuation of Harare was carried out in 1974, and the interval until the next general valuation was undertaken was extended several times. In 1990 the current general valuation roll became effective.)

18

Mexico

Julio E. Torres Coto M., B.E. (Civ. E.), M.Sc. (Val.)

Julio E. Torres Coto M. holds a bachelor's degree in civil engineering from the National Autonomous University of Mexico and a master's degree in valuation from the Autonomous University of Baja California at Tijuana, where he teaches valuation in the graduate program of the faculty of economics. Mr. Torres Coto is President and CEO of AEIOU, S.C., a professional corporation specializing in structural engineering, consulting, and the valuation of urban, rural, and industrial property. He has served as the President of the National Association of Mexican Valuation Institutes (1988-1989), as Chair of the Permanent Commission for Valuation Education of the Pan-American Union of Valuation Associations (UPAV) since 1960, and as a member of the Management Board of the International Valuation Standards Committee (IVSC) (1996-1999). He is a founding member of the Colegio de Ingenieros Civiles de Tijuana, the Instituto Mexicano de Valuación de Baja California, and the Colegio de Valuadores del Estado de Baja California. Mr. Torres Coto is the author of several published papers and a book on professional ethics to be published by the Autonomous University of Baja California. He is also a member of several social and service organizations and has served as Chairman of the Board of Trustees of the Autonomous University of Baja California.

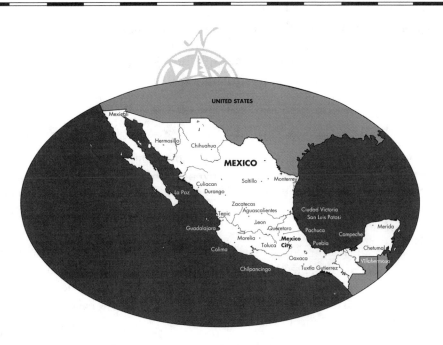

A central plateau bounded by two mountain ranges, the Sierra Madre Occidental and Sierra Madre Oriental, makes up much of Mexico. The northern section of the plateau is arid; the densely populated center is a region of broad, shallow lakes; and the plateau's southern edge is formed by mountains, some with active volcanos. South of the central plateau are two other regions of rugged mountains, the Sierra Madre del Sur (Guerrero and Oaxaca) and the Cordillera of Chiapas. A coastal plain extending along the Gulf of Mexico tapers out into the Yucatán peninsula. A coastal plain also extends southward along the Gulf of California, across from which lies the sierran peninsula of Baja California. Mexico's economy consists of manufacturing, agriculture, stockraising, and extractive industries (lead, copper, petroleum). Climate varies with elevation, i.e., the Yucatán and coastal lowlands are tierras calientes (hot regions), while much of the central plateau is tierra templada (temperate). Mexico's principal cities are Mexico City, Guadalajara, Monterrey, Puebla, and León.

Political Structure

From the early sixteenth to early nineteenth centuries, Mexico was a Spanish colony known as the Viceroyalty of New Spain. An insurrection that began in 1810 eventually succeeded and Spain recognized Mexico's independence in 1821. An empire was briefly established and then overthrown by a revolt in 1823. The Federal Republic was created under the Constitution of 1824.

With the exception of the short-lived Second Empire of Maximilian (1864-1867), the country has formally been a democratic republic since 1824. At times, Mexico has been a decentralized federation of states and at other times it has had a unitary or centralized government. Since the enactment of the present constitution in February 1917, Mexico has been a federal republic, the Mexican United States (Estados Unidos Mexicanos), and formally under democratic rule.

The federal government of Mexico is divided into three branches: an executive branch, represented by the office of the president and a large body of Cabinet members; a legislative branch composed of the two houses of Congress, the Senate and the Chamber of Deputies; and a judicial branch headed by the Supreme Court of Justice of the Nation.

The president is elected for a single, six-year term and is ineligible for reelection. He alone appoints secretaries to the various Cabinet positions. Different Cabinet secretaries oversee foreign relations, education, the economy, commerce and industry, transportation, mining, energy and natural and nonrenewable resources, health and welfare, and housing and urban development.

The federal Congress is divided in two houses or chambers. The Chamber of Senators, or Senate, consists of 128 senators, four from each of the 31 states and four from the federal district, the seat of the national capital (Mexico City). All senators are elected in one election for six-year terms. Two of the four senators from each state are elected directly by the majority vote of its citizens and two are named from the party that obtains the largest plurality among the remaining parties in the election. The Chamber of Deputies contains 500 deputies, each elected for a three-year term. Three hundred of the deputies directly represent the citizenry of the states and the federal district; the number of deputies representing each state is based on population. The other 200 deputies are selected according to the proportional distribution among all the parties that obtain more than $1\frac{1}{2}\%$ of the total vote.

Senators and deputies are not immediately eligible for reelection. A full term must transpire before they can run again, but they may enter the election for the other chamber.

Ministers of the Supreme Court are appointed for life terms by the Chamber of Senators upon the recommendation of the president.

The constitution lays down the principle that all governmental authority not specifically delegated to the federal government is reserved for the states. Most regulations governing real estate are drafted at the local level, but must conform with, and are subject to the dictates of, Article 27 of the general constitution which establishes that:

> The ownership of all land and water within the boundaries of the national territory originally belongs to the Nation, which has held and continues to hold the right to transfer ownership of land and water to private parties as to constitute private property.

The intent of the article is very wide-ranging. It establishes and limits the power of eminent domain. It defines the power of the state to regulate human settlement; to subdivide great landed estates (latifundios); to plan and regulate the founding, maintenance, improvement, and expansion of population centers; to enact the establishment and operation of "ejidos" (public or communal lands);[1] and to promote the development of small rural property.

Article 27 also dictates the

> nation´s inalienable and imprescriptible[2] (absolute) right to direct ownership of the continental shelf and all natural resources contained therein, and also within the shelves of all islands thereupon; of all minerals and substances beneath the surface of the ground, including solid fuels, petroleum, hydrogen carbides, be they solid, liquid or gaseous; and of the air space; of all water in the territorial seas, in lakes and lagoons, in estuaries and rivers, in springs associated with any of the above and, though [the article] allows the owner of the land on which a well is drilled to use the underground water, it also establishes the right of the Federal Executive to regulate such use, to ban it, and also to ban the right to drill in specific areas.

The right to use or exploit resources is subject to a concession granted only by the federal government through the executive branch.

> Only Mexican nationals or foreigners who formally consider themselves as Mexican nationals in regard to such property, may acquire ownership of real estate, upon agreeing not to invoke the protection of their governments in relation to such properties; however, within a

---

1. See footnote 3.
2. Prescription refers to a claim on, or title to, property established by virtue of immemorial possession.

strip of land one hundred kilometers wide along the borders and fifty kilometers wide along the shorelines, no foreigner may hold direct ownership over lands or waters.

Land use planning by means of national, state, municipal, and city or town master plans or *urban development plans,* as they are officially designated, is prevalent in all states and in most of the larger cities and metropolitan areas of Mexico. Zoning, as such, is enforced only in Mexico City. The concept of urban or city planning, although not new in Mexico, has only been codified since the General Law on Human Settlements was approved in late 1976. Thus, some city plans are relatively recent and enforcement varies in different states and municipalities.

By constitutional fiat, the rights to levy taxes on immovable property, its subdivision, division, consolidation, transfer and improvement, as well as those taxes based on the change in the value of real estate, are exclusively reserved for the municipalities. However, depending on the mandates of state law, assesments may be carried out either by the state or the municipality.

Property Rights

In Mexico, private ownership of real property is clearly defined by both the constitution and historic tradition. Limitations are well established. Although the law provides for the subdivision of very large landed estates *(latifundios)* for the creation of *ejidos,*[3] landed communities, and small rural properties, due process must be followed in all instances. Illegal confiscation of property does not occur and the power of the state to exercise eminent domain is clearly defined and regulated by federal and state law. Within the limitations established by the constitution, the ownership of real property is subject to the four powers of government: taxation, eminent domain, police power, and escheat.

- *Taxation* is the right of government to raise revenue through assesments on goods, products, rights, and interests.

- *Eminent domain* is the right of the government to take property for public use upon payment of just compensation.

- *Police power* is the right of the government to protect public safety, health, morals, and general welfare.

---

3. An *ejido* in the traditional sense refers to a town's common land. In Mexican agrarian legislation, however, it is specifically a tract of rural land placed under the common ownership of an existing or new community whose members are obligated to work it. This type of ownership was defined in the Constitution of 1917 and, until the 1993 amendment, it was considered inalienable and neither transferable nor distrainable (appropriable to pay off debt). The 1993 amendment and more recent Agrarian Reform Law now allow individual ownership of *ejido* lands and, subject to certain limitations, the possible selling and mortgaging of individual parcels.

- *Escheat* refers to the reversion of property to state ownership when the owner of the property dies without a will or ascertainable heir.

Mexico's legal system, which was inherited from Spain, preserves the tradition of Roman law as codified under Emperor Justinian[4] and by King Alfonso[5] in the *Las Siete Partidas* (The Seven Divisions). As Mexico modernized during the nineteenth century, the Napoleonic Code was adopted as a legal model. Thus, property rights are usually defined in terms of the Roman rights *jus fruendi, jus utendi et jus abutendi,* (the right to enjoy, the right to use, and the right to consume), tempered by the profound social concern of the 1917 constitution.

The concept of the bundle of rights inherent in the ownership of all real estate, which is recognized in common law countries, is not foreign to Mexico. However, the rights involved in the "bundle" may be perceived differently in the Mexican legal tradition. The right to use and the right to enjoy are clear and undisputed; the third right, however, is considered differently in the bundle of rights and modified into the right to *dispose* of the real estate.

Mexican law recognizes four different forms of land tenure: 1) individual private ownership, private co-ownership, and condominium private ownership; 2) communal tenure without private ownership rights, e.g., *ejido* lands held either communally or individually; 3) government lands which may belong to the public domain[6] of the nation, one of the states, or a municipality and as such are inalienable and imprescriptible (absolute) and cannot be sold or acquired by any means; and 4) government lands that belong to the private domain[7] of the nation, a state, or a municipality, in which case they receive the same treatment as private property. Strict limitations affect land legally defined as *small rural property*, in effect reducing the inherent property rights.

Language

Spanish is the universal language of the country. Several Indian languages and dialects are spoken in parts of Mexico, particularly in the south and southeast, but the use of Spanish prevails even in those areas. All business is

---

4. Justinian, the sixth-century Byzantine emperor, codified Roman law in the great *Corpus Juris Civilis.*

5. Alfonso X was the thirteenth-century king of Castile and León .

6. Government lands in the public domain include those assigned to serve a public use, e.g., roads, streets, schools, hospitals, national and state parks. These lands also include federal reserves, all land that has not been legally transferred from the nation to private parties, and land reclaimed from seas, rivers, lakes, or estuaries belonging to the public domain.

7. Government lands in the private domain include lands "that are susceptible to alienation by private parties"—i.e., lands that may be sold or in some other way transferred to private ownership, and all land and buildings acquired by the government through legal means.

conducted in Spanish. Students in secondary schools study English as a second language and most educated Mexicans understand and speak some English, many fluently. French is the third language used in the country and it is not difficult to find professionals with a working knowledge of four or five European languages.

Currency

The Mexican peso has historically been the unit of monetary measure. A monetary reform in 1992 established the *nuevo peso* (new peso) as a transitional unit to reduce the number of digits required when computing old pesos, which were devalued as a result of rampant inflation. All domestic transactions were priced in new pesos, expressed as N$1.00, with one new peso being equivalent to one thousand old pesos ($1,000.00). In 1996, the word *new* in new peso and the N before the $ sign were dropped. In other words, one peso now equals one new peso or 1,000 old pesos. It is not uncommon, however, for real estate prices to be quoted in U.S. dollars.

Units of Measure

Mexico uses the metric system. Real estate sizes are quoted in square meters, the symbol for which is m^2. Income and expenses are always quoted in pesos per square meter per month. Building and construction costs are usually quoted in pesos per square meter.

Inflation

Inflation is a very real fact of life in present-day Mexico, even though this has not always been the case. Between January of 1951 and December of 1960, the average rate of annual inflation was 9.54%; from 1961 to 1970, the rate averaged 4.10%; by 1974 the rate of inflation hit double digits and it continued to escalate rapidly during the 1980s. By 1986 it had risen to 105.75%, peaking the following year at 159.16%, the highest rate in Mexico's history. Strict financial and monetary policies brought the rate below 60% in 1988 and back to a single digit in 1993 and 1994, when it closed at 7.05%.

At the time of this writing, Mexico is weathering a severe economic crisis that affects both the Mexican stock market and the exchange rate of the new peso vis-a-vis the U.S. dollar. As a by-product, inflation was over 40% by the end of 1995 and may continue at high levels into the future. National policy aims to keep the rate of inflation as low as realistically possible to preserve the competitiveness of Mexico's exports.

Inflation in Mexcio is measured by the Indice Nacional de Precios al Consumidor (National Index of Consumer Prices), known as the INPC. This index is updated monthly by the Banco de Mexico, the central bank, and by the Instituto Nacional de Estadistica, Geografia y Informatica (INEGI), the national agency in charge of compiling statistical information. The INPC is a measure of the average increase or decrease in the price paid for a fixed basket of market goods and services. Inflation rates and other pertinent statistical information are published monthly by both the Banco de Mexico and INEGI; financial newspapers and the financial pages of most journals quote this information as do the quarterly bulletins of the Asociacion Nacional de Institutos Mexicanos de Valuación, ANIMV (National Association of Mexican Valuation Institutes).

As a result of persistent inflationary pressure in the late 1970s and the 1980s, the appraisal profession was forced to address how inflation is considered in discounted cash flow analysis. Abundant literature has been produced on this subject. Information is contained in the proceedings of the Convenciones Nacionales de Valuación (National Valuation Conventions), held annually under the auspices of ANIMV, and in the educational publications of the association.

Typical Lease Structure

Office

Lease terms are dictated by the civil codes of each of the 31 states and the federal district. Generally, leases for commercial property (office and retail space) are limited to a term of 15 years. Depending on local custom and anticipated inflation rates, contracts are often written for shorter periods, sometimes as short as one year with voluntary yearly renewal options.

Office space is typically leased by the unit. Rent is established on a gross monthly basis, with increases stipulated yearly or more often depending on the rate of inflation.

Building operating costs include expenses for property management, mainte-nance and repairs, utilities for common areas (e.g., entry, hallways, stairs and elevators), and real property taxes. These are generally borne by the owner, as are capital expenditures for structural repairs, leasing commissions, debt service (mortgage) payments, and any depreciation or replacement allowance.

Whenever possible, utility costs for individual units are separately metered and paid for by the lessee.

Retail

As noted, there is a 15-year limitation on lease terms for retail properties and other commercial real estate. In larger cities and metropolitan areas, 10- to 15-year rental contracts are not uncommon. In smaller cities, one- to five-year contracts with voluntary renewal upon revision of the rent appear to be the rule.

The gross monthly rent for the unit is customarily stipulated in leases for retail properties. In general, lease provisions are similar to those that apply to office buildings. The exception is a unit in a planned shopping center, where a tenant is expected to pay base rent plus a pro rata share of shopping center expenses, including the maintenance costs for common areas (e.g., parking, gardens, and mall) and publicity and promotional expenses. The landlord covers management or general administration costs, property taxes, capital expenditures, and the depreciation or replacement allowance.

One common arrangement in planned shopping centers, however, is the sale of the entire center or a major part of it as condominiums so that most of the shops and stores are owned by the individual operators.

Industrial

For properties under industrial use, the law allows rental terms of up to 20 years. Many foreign firms locate a "twin plant" in Mexico, particularly along the northern border (e.g., *maquiladora* assembly plants) and try to obtain 20-year contracts with rents usually set in U.S. dollars. Lessors favor shorter-term contracts which allow for periodic revision of the rent. The same holds true for land leases where the lessee builds the facility to house the operation.

Long-term leasing has never been, and still is not, the general rule in Mexico. The concept of leasehold is foreign to most Mexican property owners and developers, and it is not widely understood even by real estate profesionals in the country.

Typical lease terms for industrial properties provide for the lessee to assume the cost of all utilities, either by contracting directly with the purveyor or by paying pro rata through the lessor. Commercial and industrial tenants and a large proportion of apartment house tenants directly contract with the utility company and pay for their own water, electricity, and gas. In older apartment buildings with a single water connection, it is sometimes necessary to prorate the water bill.

Property tax is assumed to be the sole responsibility of the owner of the land or, in the case of an improved site, the owner of the property.

Most contracts state that any and all improvements or additions are subject to the prior consent of the owner and shall become part and parcel of the property. In certain exceptional situations, improvements may be built in lieu of rental payment. This requires a special arrangement, however, particularly for commercial and industrial properties since the cost of the improvements must be reported as income and the added improvement will affect the tax situation of the lessor.

The costs of tenant improvements, adaptations, and finishing out are always assumed by the lessee, who is also responsible for returning the premises to the original state at the termination of the lease, although this commitment is not always honored. The maintenance and upkeep of industrial and most commercial buildings is left to the tenant for the duration of the lease. Major repairs, however, are almost always covered by the owner upon termination of the contract, along with whatever general maintenance may be required at that time.

Valuation Standards

At the federal level, the valuation field is overseen by three different agencies of the federal government: the Comisión Nacional Bancaria, or CNB (National Banking Commission), the Comisión Nacional de Valores, or CNV (National Securities Commission),[8] and agencies of the Ministry of Finance and Public Credit and the Comisión de Avaluos de Bienes Nacionales, CABIN (Commission for the Valuation of National Properties). This last agency works under the Ministry of Social Development which, among other things, is the care-taker of all national properties, particularly real estate in the public domain. At the state level, the departments of finance and, in some instances, the municipal treasuries oversee valuation activities.

To date, there has been no factual or formal coordination of the three federal agencies nor any attempt to attain it. Each commission works independently within the terms of the respective enabling legislation. For the first two commissions (CNB and CNV), valuation is only one of the many aspects of economic activity that they oversee, whereas the third (CABIN) is specifically and solely involved in the field of valuation.

Both the banking and securities commissions have the power to establish general directives and regulations that industries under their supervision must observe. They do this through circulars and memoranda.

The Comisión Nacional Bancaria has a history, dating back to the 1950s, of issuing circulars that deal with diverse aspects of real property appraisals. These circulars have focused on matters ranging from the content and form of the appraisal report to the designation and recognition of valuers. The latest

---

8. The Comisión Nacional Bancaria and the Comisión Nacional de Valores have merged into a single entity, the Comisión Nacional Bancaria y de Valores (CNBV), which assumes the responsibilities of the former CNB and CNV as regulator of banks and securities. As regards valuation, all circulars in effect at the time of the merger remain in effect. These are discussed later in the chapter.

such documents are Circulars 1201 and 1202, published in March of 1992. Circular 1201 updates the regulations that apply to all bank appraisals and restates the requirements that valuers register with the commission before being allowed to appraise for the banking and insurance industries. Circular 1202 dictates the format and content of the real estate valuation report for all bank appraisals.

For Mexican banks, one very important aspect of valuation is the fact that the respective bank is liable. Circular 1202 states that

> ...in all cases and for all applicable legal purposes, the bank ....is responsible for the moral character and technical qualifications of the person which it recommends for registration (as valuer), and also for the reasonable accuracy of the appraisals which they (the appraisers) shall prepare, and also that such valuations be done according to the present disposition (statement) and such others of legal or adminis-trative character as may apply.[9]

Circular 1201 is quite explicit as to the contents of appraisals of urban prop-erty (both land and improvements), but deals mostly in generalities regarding industrial property, machinery and equipment, and agricultural property. The circular goes into great detail about the requirements for provisional and permanent registration as a bank valuer, the procedures for going about either type of registration, and the inspection and supervision of valuers by the commission.

The Comisión Nacional de Valores entered the valuation field during the late 1970s in response to a need for information on the effect of rampant inflation on the value of fixed assets of corporations whose securities were quoted in the Bolsa Mexicana de Valores, B.M.V (the Mexican stock exchange). The first circular on this matter, published May 22, 1980, emphasized the need to disclose the effects of inflation on the financial information released by all corporations whose issues were bought or sold in the B.M.V. The "disposi-tions" (statements) of Circular 11-6, published June 10, 1982, dealt with all the details of the valuation of fixed assets. It has become the practical, though not official, standard on this matter.

The Comisión de Avaluos de Bienes Nacionales (CABIN) is a three-member body with support staff in Mexico City and regional delegations, also headed by three-member bodies or boards. All CABIN members are engineers or architects. Field work is done by a corps of independent fee appraisers

---

9. Comisión Nacional Bancaria, *Circular 1201, Disposition (Statement) Eighteen,* March 11, 1992, Mexico, D.F.

authorized by and registered with the commission or the delegation. Each appraiser prepares a detailed report and submits it to either the regional delegation or the central body. Through their boards, these CABIN bodies have the power not only to review, but also to interpret, correct, and modify the report before issuing a resolution on the range of value of the property or the range of rent the government may pay or charge, depending on whether the government is the lessee or the lessor.

The concept of *range of value* is paramount in all instances where the federal government is involved and in all CABIN valuations. The philosophy behind the concept is that the commission and, of course, the valuer must provide a negotiating space within which officials of the executive branch may move to reach an agreement on the purchase or sale of real estate within the private domain of the nation, or on the rent to be paid to or charged by agencies of the federal government.

CABIN published the *Guia de Valuación de Bienes de Propiedad Particular o del Dominio Privado Gubernamental* (*Guide to the Valuation of Private Property or [Property in] the Private Governmental Domain*) on August 24, 1987. This manual provides guidelines and completed samples of the form approved by CABIN at that time for valuations of land and buildings in urban areas, the establishment of rental amounts, and valuations of industrial complexes. However, neither the circulars of CNB and CNV nor the CABIN guide constitutes formally recognized standards for the valuation profession in Mexico.

ANIMV authorized *Standard for the Valuation of Real Estate* in its convention, although this worthwhile effort was not officially recognized. The profession has recognized the "Panamerican Standard for the Valuation of Real Estate," approved at the Extraordinary Panamerican Valuation Congress (UPAV) held in Lima in December of 1989 to commemorate the one hundredth anniversary of the establishment of the *Cuerpo Técnico de Tasaciones del Perú*, the oldest, legally recognised body of valuers in the Americas. The fifteenth Panamerican Valuation Congress, held in Puebla, Mexico, in 1992, adopted the TIAVSC (IVSC) *Guidelines and Background Notes on the Valuation of Fixed Assets*, as translated into Spanish and Portuguese.

The Federal Law on Metrology and Standards[10] is the latest act of the Federal Congress of Mexico to address standards. For the first time in Mexican history, this law distinguishes between two types of standards: official standards (*Norma Oficial Mexicana, or NOM*) and voluntary standards (*Norma*

---

10. "Ley Federal de Metrología y Normalización," *Diario Oficial de la Federación,* July 1, 1992, Mexico, D.F.

Mexicana, or NMX). Official standards (NOM) can only be formulated by government agencies. Voluntary standards (NMX), however, may be prepared by the appraisal industry and submitted to the government for review and approval.

The law provides for the establishment of industry boards or committees empowered to formulate and propose standards. One such body is the Organización de Nacional de Normalización de la Construcción y la Edificación, or ONNCE (National Organization for Construction and Building Standards), within which ANIMV, as an active member, is working on standards for the valuation industry.

In October 1995, ANIMV enacted the *Normas Profesionales de Valuación* (Professional Valuation Standards), a comprehensive set of 13 standards that address most aspects of valuation. The standards include chapters on the qualifications of a professional valuer, the definition of market value and values other than market value, and the contents of the valuation report and certification of value. Specific individual standards cover the valuation of urban properties; rural properties; industrial plants, machinery, and equipment; and properties in foreign countries. These are the first formal valuation standards to be enacted in Mexico. The association expects that, in time, a voluntary standard (NMX) may be adopted on the basis of the *Normas Profesionales de Valuación*, and that this voluntary standard may evolve into an official standard (NOM) once the government recognizes the importance of standards to the valuation industry.

Licensing/Certification

According to Article V of the Mexican federal constitution, all persons in the country may practice the art or profession of their choice without hindrance. However, the article goes on to indicate that it is up to the law of the states to establish which professions shall require "titles" and the requisites for obtaining them. By tradition and custom, those professions for which titles are required have been the learned professions; the title is granted by a university or technical institute after the individual has completed at least four years of academic work, submitted a written thesis, and passed an oral examination before a board of at least three professors.

To date, the valuation profession is not one for which most states require a title, nor are there as yet stringent requirements for entry into the profession at the national level.

Historically, it has been common for titled professionals, usually architects and engineers, to enter the profession some three to five years after receiving their degree and to obtain proficiency in valuation through either an apprenticeship or traineeship. In recent years, things have begun to change. Some of the member institutes in ANIMV, emphasizing the need to protect the public as well as official agencies, have obtained legislation in their states requiring registration of valuers. Spearheaded by these initiatives, ANIMV has undertaken a two-fold effort to professionalize the industry.

First, ANIMV has established a wide-ranging postgraduate program that involves not only the association and its 50 member institutes, but also some of the most important public universities in the country (among them the National University and the Universities of Baja California, Nuevo León, Puebla, Veracruz, Occidente, and Yucatán). Typically the program leads to a master's degree in real estate valuation, but in some instances it goes further and embraces more specialized areas of valuation, including the appraisal of agricultural and industrial properties and machinery and equipment.

Second, efforts have been made to regulate the profession by passing adequate legislation in the states. This legislation would place valuation on the same level as other titled professions and would limit practice to persons with the academic credentials and experience required by the law. To date, some ten states have enacted such legislation and at least five others are currently considering it.

As stated earlier, both CNB and CNV register valuers employed by industries that these commissions regulate and CABIN registers valuers employed in its own service. Requirements for registration are not identical, but they have the following elements in common: the applicant must be a Mexican national, hold a university degree in engineering or architecture, and pass an examination. CNB uses a written examination, while the examination for CNV has written, oral, and practice components. CNB also requires that the candidate be recommended by a banking institution, that he or she belong to a professional association *(colegio)* in the field in which his or her university degree was earned, and also that he or she belong to a professional body of valuers. Neither CNV nor CABIN has these requirements.

In states and municipalities where laws and regulations have been enacted for the registration or licensing of appraisers/valuers, the professional must show evidence of the following: receipt of a degree in a profession related to valuation, registration with or authorization by CNB, membership in the relevant *colegio* and valuers' society, and bona fide residency in the state or municipality. Some laws currently under consideration also require proof of completion of postgraduate work in valuation.

Appraisal Reporting Requirements

Banking institutions, the Comisión Nacional Bancaria (now CNBV), and, to some extent, the treasury departments of the states and the federal district have been the principal forces in the development of appraisal reporting requirements. The Asociación Hipotecaria Mexicana, S.A., a government bank established in the early 1930s, was the first mortgage underwriting institution created after the banking system was modernized. Following the tradition of cadastral valuations, the bank adopted the form appraisal, which is still the universally accepted method for reporting appraisals.

Banco Nacional de Mexico, S.A. (Banamex) contributed to improvement of the form when it entered the mortgage market during the 1950s. Other banks designed their own forms and thus influenced the modification of the form used by the Asociación Hipotecaria. By 1960, the treasury of the federal district was also specifying requirements that the form include certain minimum information, particularly technical data, for appraisals undertaken for tax purposes.

Since 1974 CNB has specified minimum requirements for the contents of forms, issuing regulations in different circulars and memoranda and occasionally publishing model forms.

At present, the authorized form is sanctioned by and contained in Circular 1202 of March 12, 1992. The information that form reports must contain is clearly spelled out in the text of the circular, which also specifies the format of such reports. Most valuers follow CNB guidelines and the CNB format is generally accepted for appraisals conducted for all uses, be they judicial, administrative, or private. A copy of the form is shown Figure 1.

A minimum of seven pages of detailed information is required by CNB. The valuation report form for improved urban lots contains the following sections and must include all the stipulated information.

I. Background. Information on the person requesting the valuation, the valuer's name and registration/license data, the date of the appraisal, the type of property being valued, the legal description and location of the property, the type of ownership, the purpose of the valuation, and the cadastral identification number. In appraisals for banks, the name of the bank is also included in this section.

II. Urban Characteristics. Classification of the area, the type of buildings prevalent in the area, the percentage of built-up lots, the type and density of population, environmental contamination, land use and zoning, road access and type of roads, and type and quality of utilities and urban services. If a high degree of contamination is present, the report of a competent professional must be included.

Figure 1. CNB Valuation Report Form

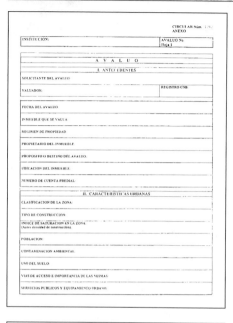

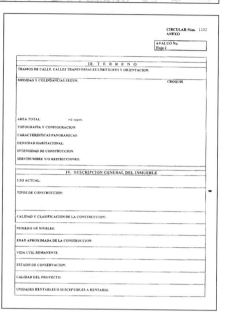

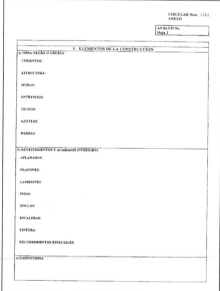

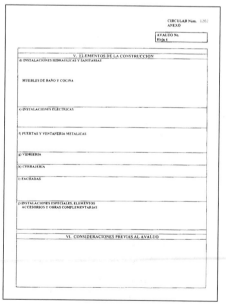

Figure 1. CNB Valuation Report Form (continued)

Form 1 (left):

CIRCULAR Núm. 1202
ANEXO

AVALUO No.
Hoja 5

VII. VALOR FISICO O DIRECTO

a) DEL TERRENO:

LOTE TIPO O PREDOMINANTE:

INVESTIGACION DE MERCADO:

VALORES DE CALLE O DE ZONA:

FRACCION	SUPERFICIE m2	VALOR UNITARIO $/m2	COEF.	MOTIVO DEL COEF.	VALOR PARCIAL
					$

TOTAL _____ m2   SUBTOTAL (a) $ _____

VALOR UNITARIO MEDIO DE: $

b) DE LAS CONSTRUCCIONES:

TIPO	AREA m2	VALOR UNITARIO DE REPOSICION NUEVO	DEME-RITO %	VALOR UNITARIO NETO DE REPOSICION	VALOR PARCIAL
					$

SUBTOTAL (b) $ _____

c) INSTALACIONES ESPECIALES, ELEMENTOS ACCESORIOS Y OBRAS COMPLEMENTARIAS: SUBTOTAL (c) $ _____

VALOR FISICO O DIRECTO (a) + (b) + (c) $ _____

Form 2 (right):

CIRCULAR Núm. 1202
ANEXO

AVALUO No.
Hoja 6

VIII. VALOR POR CAPITALIZACION DE RENTAS

a) RENTA REAL O EFECTIVA: $ _____

b) RENTA ESTIMADA O DE MERCADO: $ _____

RENTA BRUTA TOTAL MENSUAL: (EFECTIVA O ESTIMADA) $ _____

IMPORTE DE DEDUCCIONES   (%)
(Descripción)

RENTA NETA MENSUAL: $ _____

RENTA NETA ANUAL:

CAPITALIZANDO LA RENTA ANUAL AL ____ % TASA
DE CAPITALIZACION APLICABLE AL CASO, RESULTA UN
VALOR DE CAPITALIZACION DE: $ _____

IX. RESUMEN

VALOR FISICO O DIRECTO: $ _____

VALOR ... CAPITALIZACION DE RENTAS: $ _____

VALOR DE MERCADO: $ _____

Form 3 (bottom):

CIRCULAR Núm. 1202
ANEXO

AVALUO No.
Hoja 7

X. CONSIDERACIONES PREVIAS A LA CONCLUSION

XI. CONCLUSION

VALOR COMERCIAL
(CON LETRA) $ _____

ESTA CANTIDAD REPRESENTA EL VALOR COMERCIAL AL DIA _____ DE 19___

XII. VALOR REFERIDO (En su caso)

PARA LOS EFECTOS A QUE HAYA LUGAR, EL VALOR REFERIDO DEL INMUEBLE AL DIA

PERITO VALUADOR   INSTITUCION

_____   _____
FIRMA   FIRMA

_____   _____
NOMBRE   NOMBRE
No. DE REGISTRO C.N.B. _____   (DELEGADO FIDUCIARIO
                                      O FUNCIONARIO AUTORIZADO)

_____   CARGO _____
ESPECIALIDAD
                            CLAVE: _____
_____
PERIODO DE VIGENCIA

III. Land. Clear indication of the particular section of the street or road on which the property is located, the cross streets at each end of the block, and the orientation of the lot; the metes and bounds, total area, topography, and shape of the plot; panoramic features, allowable or actual housing density, allowable or actual percentage of lots built up, and restrictions and liens.

IV. General Description of the Property. The current use of the land and building(s), types of buildings on the lot, number of storeys, approximate age of each of the buildings, remaining economic life, state of maintenance, quality of the architectural design, and number of leasable units.

V. Description of Building Elements. A detailed description of building components for each type of building identified, including, as a minimum, the foundations, structural elements, walls, floors, roofs, fences, and property walls; wall finishes, ceilings, ceramic tiles in baths and kitchens, flooring, stairs; paint, special wall or floor treatments; type of carpentry (doors, closets, cabinets); water and sewage lines and other installations, bath and kitchen fixtures; electrical installations; metal doors and windows, glazing, brass fixtures; description of facades including type of finishes; and a complete description of all accessory installations, special equipment and additional works (patios, HVAC, elevators, water tanks, etc.).

VI. Considerations Before the Valuation. A discussion of the reasons specific unit values were selected, the sources used for information, the market research consulted, and any other relevant aspects of the property that affect its value in any manner. A description of the approaches employed is also required here.

VII. Physical or Direct Value. Indicated by the cost approach. The predominant lot type is described and its unit value is indicated; buildings are valued on the basis of depreciated replacement cost new.

VIII. Value from the Capitalization of Rent. Indicated by the income approach. This analysis may be performed by either the traditional method, based on market rent and a capitalization rate, or by determining the rentability of the fixed asset, taking into consideration the effect of inflation, the type of contract, the annual depreciaton of the improvements, and the level of taxes. The capitalization rate is derived from investment and capital markets and must reflect the risk associated with the investment as well as going rates in national and international capital markets.

IX. Summary. A recapitulation of the value indications obtained from the cost and income approaches and from market investigation.

X. Considerations Before the Conclusion (Reconciliation). An analysis and discussion of the value indications from the different approaches, which should logically lead to the concluded value indication presented in the following section.

XI. Conclusion.

XII. The Value Referenced (Valor Referido). If the value required is for a date other than the current date, pertinent discussion and calculations are presented and summarized in this section.

Finally, the appraiser (and bank officials, if the appraisal is being prepared for a bank) shall certify and sign the report. The addenda must include a location map, plot and building plans, and a photographic attachment. Valuations of vacant urban lots omit sections V and VIII, and parts of section IV.

The valuation of condominiums must comply with specific requirements established by the civil codes and condominium laws. These requirements stipulate that the report discuss the classification or type of condominium (usually vertical for industrial or single-family residential, horizontal for high-rise residential, or a combination of these) and the use (residential, commercial, office, industrial, parking, or mixed use). The valuation must also clearly indicate the percentage of undivided interest as set forth in the *escritura de condominio* (condominium deed) or as authorized by the proper authority.

These laws also specify that a complete description of the whole property be made, even though the valuation may be of a single unit. This general description starts with a discussion of the characteristics of the building and improvements and continues to present a detailed description of the unit being valued. Also, mention must be made of parking facilities and whether a space is specifically assigned to the unit and considered part of the condominium property, or whether the unit owner only has the right to use a parking space.

Condominium valuations must include the three approaches. Particular attention is given to the mandatory procedure to be followed in the cost approach to estimate physical or direct value. First, the percentage of total land value attributable to the condominium unit is estimated to include a percentage of the total value of all open and improved areas. Then the value of the individual unit and its accessories is determined using replacement costs and a separate calculation is made to derive the replacement cost of built-up improvements and common facilities and installations. The sum of these three partial values is taken to be the physical or direct value of the condominium unit.

Although not common, narrative reports are not unknown in Mexico and some valuers favor them in certain instances. One such situation is a judicial valuation in which the valuer acts as an expert witness. Mexican expert witnesses are expected to submit written testimony, which may be cross-examined by attorneys for either or both parties during the court proceedings. One witness presents a report for each party and, in cases where the testimony differs, the judge designates a third witness. Trial by jury being the exception rather than the rule, judicial outcomes depend on the rulings of judges. Thus, it is necesary for a witness to document and support all pertinent and relevant information clearly for the judge who must be convinced. It is the judge's sole prerogative when passing sentence to follow or accept any or none of the conclusions in any or none of the witnesses' reports. The testimony or reports of the expert witnesses in no way bind the judge, they only inform him. Thus, reports need be extensive, explicit, and clear. Narrative reports are useful in judicial proceedings while terse form appraisals are not. Narrative reports follow the same general table of contents for form reports established by CNB.

Definition of Market Value

There is to date no official definition of market value. CNB requires that all real estate valuations contain

> ...the physical and capitalized values, which must be based on a market study of the area, in which consideration is necessarily given to those factors or particular conditions that influence or may influence significant variations in the values...[11]

CNV establishes that the

> ...basis of the valuation of fixed assets of a corporation shall determine a value that shall be understood as an estimate of the physical value [of the fixed assets] in use, under normal conditions of operation.

CABIN is concerned with the determination of a maximum price or a minimum price, depending on whether the public agency that requires the valuation is buying or selling the property. Its directives emphasize that commercial value is derived from an exhaustive market investigation, which leads to the identification of the prices at which real estate is being rented or sold, and that this investigation must take into account the background and present condition of the property as well as its physical, political, and legal potential.

---

11. Comisión Nacional Bancaria, *Circular 1201, Disposition (Statement) Four*, March 11, 1992, Mexico, D.F.

None of the commissions has considered or found it necessary to draft a definition of the elusive concept of market value, nor has the judicial system shed any light on this void. The Mexican accounting profession has not defined the concept and the appraisal industry itself has not proposed any definition.

In practice, most Mexican valuers adopt some form of the Appraisal Institute's definition of market value or one taken from the literature of the American Society of Appraisers. But these are individual positions. To date, there is no officially accepted definition of market value and no evidence to suggest that an official definition is truly required.

The absence of an official definition may stem from the fact that it has generally not been possible to obtain factual market information regarding real estate sales. Appraisers have tended, therefore, to rely on value indicators derived from the cost and income approaches and have only very recently considered market information, which is still largely unreliable or nonexistent.

While the definition of market value quoted below may be the most widely used, it is not an officially recognized definition.

> Market value is the most probable amount, in terms of money, that a property may be expected to produce in a competitive and open market, under all conditions for a just sale, in which both the buyer and the seller are acting prudently, knowledgeably, and assuming that the price is not affected by any undue stimulus.[12]

Income Approach

The income approach (*enfoque de ingresos/rentas*) is based on the principle of anticipation, which states that value is the present worth of future benefits. This principle governs the sale and purchase of most income-producing properties. That is to say, such properties are usually bought and sold on the basis of their income-producing potential.

According to the *Norma para la Valuación de Bienes Raices* (*Standard for the Valuation of Real Estate*) approved by the Seventeenth National Valuation Convention held in Guadalajara in September 1980, the income approach, or capitalization method, is founded on the fact that the rent generated by real property represents the interest paid on capital under normal conditions. The standard equates the value of the property with equity value.

---

12. Instituto Mexicano de Valuación, A.C., *Norma para la Valuación de Bienes Raices (Standard for the Valuation of Real Estate)*, proceedings of the XVII National Valuation Convention, Guadalajara, 1980, p. 59.

The standard goes on to state that the capitalization procedure analyzes the amount an investment is worth in terms of the net profits, or their equivalent, that the property may generate by the capitalization of its net income. To estimate value using this method, the valuer must consider the types and levels of rents in the area, investment risks, capitalization rates, operating and maintenance expenses, repairs and reserves for replacements, and fixed costs (taxes, fees, and amortization) of the property type.

The standard states that the income approach should not be used as the sole procedure to obtain an indication of the market value of a property because variable elements such as depreciation allowances and capitalization rates may skew the results. (According to the standard, estimates of these elements are not considered dependable.) It recommends that the income approach, or capitalization method, be used to provide a comparison to the results obtained through the other approaches.

Two methods of capitalization are recognized in the standard. In the direct capitalization method, which is most frequently used, "the value of real property is obtained by means of applying an overall capitalization rate *(tasa global)* to the net rent or its equivalent." The indirect residual capitalization method, which is not often used, is described as follows:

> while giving due consideration to the net rent or its equivalent, this method determines the values corresponding to the land and improvements; these values are obtained by capitalizing the net rent *(renta liquida)* corresponding to the land and improvements.[13]

Cash Flow Analysis

Valuers of income-producing property typically prepare a cash flow analysis *(analisis del flujo de caja)*. Standard appraisal practice requires an analysis of gross income, which gives due consideration to the amount, quality, and durability of the income stream. These three elements are basic to the valuer's understanding of the capacity of a property to generate income.

Information about the amount, quality, and durability of income on a monthly basis is usually provided by the owner and verified by the valuer during inspection of the property. The valuer typically analyzes records for the three preceding years. Market rent is assigned to each leasable vacant unit and to new properties that remain vacant, and a presumed date of lease commencement is established.

---

13. Ibid., pp. 68-69.

Next, other sources of income are identified and included in the analysis. Deductions for collection losses, tenant turnover, and vacancies are then made to obtain effective gross monthly income. From this figure, deductions are made for fixed expenses, maintenance and repairs, reserves for replacements, and other reasonable operating expenses to obtain net monthly income, which is then converted into an annual net income and discounted directly

Traditional Capitalization

The capitalization procedure traditionally used is based on the assumption that the property is held in perpetuity. Thus, the simplified capitalization formula expresses the value of the property as the net annual income that the property is capable of producing divided by a representative capitalization rate.

$$CV = NAI/R$$

where:

$CV =$ commercial value indication by capitalization
$NAI =$ net annual income
$R =$ applicable capitalization rate

Net annual income is the net monthly income multiplied by 12. This formula is expressed as

$$NAI = NMI \times 12$$

where:

$NMI =$ net monthly income

Net monthly income, in turn, equals the gross monthly income less estimated allowable deductions. The formula is:

$$NMI = GMI - \%D$$

where:

$GMI =$ gross monthly income
$\%D =$ total deductions as percentage of income

Substituting the second and third formulas into the simplified formula results in the general equation shown below:

$$CV = NAI/R$$
$$CV = (NMI \times 12)/R$$

General equation:

$$CV = (GMI - \%D) \times 12/ R$$

This procedure is relatively straightforward and easy to use, but it has several flaws that must be addressed when it is applied in the real world, particularly in a highly inflationary economy. First, it disregards the effects of inflation on the income flow. Second, it gives no weight to the type of contract binding the parties concerned (e.g., quarterly, semiannual, annual, or "frozen"). Further, it gives no consideration to the rate of return on the investment after inflation and does not quantify the depreciation of assets over time. And finally, the inherent difficulty of establishing the capitalization rate should not be forgotten.

Capitalization Factors

While the traditional capitalization procedure may prove useful for an income analysis covering a relatively long period over which inflation remains manageable, the rampant inflation of the late 1970s and 1980s rendered the approach inapplicable. To address this problem, the profession had to develop a clear and reliable procedure that would give due consideration to the rate of inflation in the analysis of future income streams generated by rents. This was accomplished by the introduction of a new procedure employing a capitalization factor developed to quantify the effect of the inflation rate as a variable.

The capitalization factor can be determined once the valuer knows how long it will take to recover the capital invested in the fixed asset(s). This period is estimated by equating the future value of the net income generated with the future value of the capital investment in the fixed asset(s).

In terms of accrued increments, the future value of income *(FVI)* is a function of the net income *(NI)* produced by the investment and the corresponding summation over the whole recovery period at the reinvestment rate *(tasa pasiva)* as well as the periodicity at which income or rents are increased. Through complex mathematical derivation and the substitution of terms in the general equation, a very simple formula is obtained:

$$CP = NI \times FC$$

where:

$CP =$ equity or value of the capital investment in the fixed asset(s)
$NI =$ net income produced by the investment
$FC =$ capitalization factor

The formula shows that the capitalization factor is a function of the length of time required to recover the capital investment, the rate of inflation, the reinvestment rate *(tasa pasiva)*, and the periodicity at which the flow of income is modified (rents are usually increased).

To facilitate application of the formula, tables have been prepared for both accrued incremental cash flows and capitalized incremental cash flows.

Cash Flow Analysis Example

Consider an office and retail shop building on a 500 m² lot with 1000 m² of built-up area, of which 750 m² are rentable. The building must undergo remodeling at a cost of $ 459,000.00. The remodeling will take six months. Average monthly rent in the area is $ 20.00 per m². The capitalization or risk rate is 9%, the cost of capital is 1.5% per month, and the lease is subject to annual revision with rental increments projected at 27%.

Analysis of Component Values

First, the value of the land is obtained from market analysis or owner information:

$$500 \text{ m}^2 \times \$340.00 \times 1 = \$170,000.00$$

In the above equation, an adjustment coefficient[14] of 1 is used to indicate that the land is a typical lot that requires no adjustments. Should adjustments for size, shape, or topography be necessary, an appropriate coefficient or factor, usually less than 1, would be applied.

Next, the value of the remodeled building is estimated, assuming accrued depreciation at 11%:

$$1,000 \text{ m}^2 \times \$1,193.40 \times 0.89 = \$1,062,126.00$$

Unit value of building after remodeling = $1,193.40

Time held:	15 years
Owner:	Private individual (not a corporation)
Total gross monthly income:	750 m² × $ 34.00 = $ 25,500.00
Average period of occupation:	Five years
Average time vacant:	Five months
Maintenance requirements:	4% of building elements per annum
Management costs:	6% of gross income

---

14. Government cadastral bureaus determine the unit value of land in areas defined as *uniform zones. Valor unitario de calle or valor de calle* is the typical unit value of lots located on the street. To adjust this typical or average value to indicate the value of the specific site, a factor of less than 1 is usually applied. Lots with a superior view or corner location carry a premium. The adjustment factors are determined by formulas developed by different cadastral offices in the country, the most widely used being those of the federal district (Mexico City), the state of Mexico (the state north and west of the federal district), and the state of Jalisco (Guadalajara).

Amount of Deductions

Vacancies	$0.05 \times \$25,500.00$	$ 1,275.00
Property tax:	$ 4,080.00/12	$ 340.00
Maintenance:	$0.04166^* \times \$25,500.00$	$ 1,062.33
Management:	$0.06 \times \$25,500.00$	$ 1,530.00
Fiscal depreciation:	$0.0042 \times \$ 1,062,126.00$	$ 4,460.92
Allowable fiscal deductions:		$ 8,668.25
Taxable base:	$\$25,500.00 - \$8,668.25 = \$16,831.75$	
Income tax:		$ 4,169.80

Total deductions

   = vacancies

   + property tax

   + maintenance

   + management

   + depreciation

   + income tax $12,838.05

Net monthly income $25,500.00 - $12,838.05 = $12,661.95

* The maintenance factor is obtained from the following table, published by ANIMV in *Valuación de Construcciones*, p. 109. The criteria suggested are as follows. Once the percentage of building components or elements that receive annual maintenance is established, it must be divided by 12 to obtain the monthly percentage (0.4/12 = 0.03333). In Mexico, the gross monthly income for rental properties is roughly 0.8% of the total value of the building, therefore 0.03333/0.8 = 4.1666% of the gross monthly income, assuming maintenance is performed on a yearly basis. The table provides factors for maintenance periods of one to eight years and for maintenance percentages of 1% to 8% of the total building components. (Asociación Nacional de Institutos Mexicanos de Valuación, A.C., *Valuación de Construcciones*, course notes, p. 109, 1992.)

Maintenance Factors

Maintenance Period	Percentage of Elements Due for Maintenance							
	1%	2%	3%	4%	5%	6%	7%	8%
Each year	10.4	20.8	31.2	41.7	52.1	62.5	72.9	83.3
Every two years	5.2	10.4	15.6	20.8	16.1	31.2	36.4	41.7
Every three years	3.4	6.9	10.4	13.9	17.4	20.8	24.3	27.8
Every four years	2.6	5.2	7.8	10.4	13.0	15.6	17.2	20.8
Every five years	2.1	4.2	6.2	8.3	10.4	12.5	14.6	10.7
Every six years	1.7	3.5	5.2	6.9	8.7	10.4	12.1	13.9
Every seven years	1.5	2.9	4.5	5.9	7.4	8.9	10.4	11.9
Every eight years	1.3	2.6	3.9	5.2	6.5	7.8	9.1	10.4

To obtain the capitalization factor *(CF)*, the tables are consulted for the following data.[15]

Risk rate: $TR = 9\%$; lease renewal: $K = 12$ month period; prevailing rate: $i = 2\%$; reinvestment rate: $r = 1.5\%$.

Capitalization Factor* for K = 12, r = 1.5%											
TR	5	6	7	8	9	10	11	12	13	14	15
i											
0.25	69.3	65.5	61.7	58.2	55.2	52.1	49.7	47.0	45.0	42.8	41.4
0.50	79.3	73.7	68.5	63.9	60.1	56.2	53.3	50.1	47.7	45.1	43.6
0.75	91.8	83.8	76.6	70.6	65.7	60.8	57.4	53.5	50.8	47.7	46.0
1.00	107.6	96.0	86.2	78.4	72.1	66.1	62.0	57.4	54.2	50.5	48.6
1.25	128.0	111.2	97.7	87.5	79.5	72.0	67.1	61.6	57.9	53.6	51.4
1.50	154.3	130.1	111.5	98.2	88.1	78.8	72.9	66.3	62.0	57.0	54.5
1.75	188.7	153.6	128.2	110.8	98.0	86.5	79.5	71.5	66.6	60.6	57.9
2.00	233.9	183.2	148.4	125.7	**109.5**	95.2	86.9	77.3	71.6	64.7	61.6
2.50	373.8	268.1	203.0	164.5	138.4	116.6	104.8	91.1	83.4	73.9	70.0
3.00	625.8	406.1	284.7	219.7	177.9	144.7	127.8	108.3	98.0	84.9	80.0
3.50	1089.6	634.2	408.5	298.8	232.0	181.5	157.6	129.8	116.1	98.2	92.0
4.00	1958.1	1016.4	597.9	306.8	306.8	230.2	196.5	156.8	138.6	114.2	106.3

* Leoncio Angulo V. and Juan Carlos Peiro G. *Rentabilidad de Activos Fijos Considerando El Efecto Inflacionario,* Instituto Mexicano de Valuación de Sinaloa, A.C., Culiacan, 1990.
K = Periodicity at which income is augmented
r = Reinvestment rate *(tasa pasiva)*

Thus, $CF = 109.5$ and

$$CV = FC \times NI = 109.5 \times \$12,661.95 = \$1,386,483.50$$

The cost of remodeling, however, has not been deducted. The analysis may be taken one step further to obtain the value of the building in its present state before remodeling:

$$VBR = \$1,386,483.50 - \$459,000.00 = \$927,483.50$$

where:

VBR = Value before remodeling

15. Asociación Nacional de Institutos Mexicanos de Valuación, A.C., *Valuación de Construcciones,* course notes, 1992.

Sales Comparison Approach

The sales comparison approach *(enfoque de la comparación de ventas)* is not widely used because it is difficult to obtain factual market information due to several factors. Sales records of private corporations are considered confidential information and few, if any, Mexican corporations are willing to let outsiders investigate their records. In the case of real property operations, it is always possible to obtain information from outside sources because of the requirements of both federal and state law. For example, a notary public must attest to these transactions; an appraisal must be made by a qualified valuer and certified by an established credit and trust institution; and the operation must be recorded at the *Registro Público de la Propiedad y de Comercio* (Public Registry of Property and Commerce) as well as the cadastral bureau. Thus, it should be possible to obtain information on normal real estate transactions without much difficulty.

However, normal real estate transactions also must satisfy certain protocols and formalities. In the coastal and border areas, there is the requirement that both parties be Mexican nationals or Mexican corporations without any foreign stockholders, even those authorized by the corporate charters or the Ministry of Foreign Relations to own land. Or the parties to the transactions may be foreigners and corporations with foreign stockholders who have special authorization to hold or use land under trust. If the property is contained within a subdivision, the subdivision must also be authorized under state law and must be duly registered with the proper local offices so that a notary public can formalize the transaction and the corresponding agencies can record it. Where it is impossible to comply with these conditions, private contracts may be entered into, but they are usually not registered.

Further, in dealings between individuals, it is accepted practice to quote an amount lower than the actual transaction price in order to reduce the tax base. The overall effect of these factors is to produce totally unreliable information in many of the official records. Thus, factual published or quotable data is lacking.

Most information for developing market-oriented valuations must come from other sources. The most reliable source for the appraiser has been direct interviews with the parties concerned, sometimes with access to records and always with the obligation to maintain confidentiality. The second major source of information, again confidential, is real estate agents and brokers. The third is listings of property offered for sale or rent. Listings are abundant, but they are usually skewed and do not indicate the real price of the completed transaction.

In recent years, some organizations and commercial interests in the larger metropolitan areas have attempted to gather factual market information on real estate transactions. If this trend continues and if the tax authorities begin closer monitoring of real estate operations, as they appear to be doing, reliable published and quotable information will become available for sales comparison analyses.

Without reliable information, any and all valuations that rely heavily on market analysis must be based on the study of data obtained either indirectly, without proper documentation, or directly from the source. Unfortunately, the valuer will not be allowed to quote or expressly identify these direct sources.

Cost Approach

Traditionally, the cost approach *(enfoque de costo)* has been the most widely used indicator of value, and the indicator most respected by banking institutions. This is due to the fact that appraisals for banks originated in mortgage institutions established by the central government to finance housing in planning or under development. All appraisers at the time were civil engineers or architects, fully conversant and familiar with building and construction costs. Their interest represented that of the lender and, to a lesser extent, that of the borrower. They sought to ascertain that the "value" of the building to be developed would equal the physical cost of developing it.[16] Thus, their understanding of value reflected the amount of investment necessary to achieve a finished, saleable product. This was value to the engineer, the builder, and the bank. No economic considerations were involved since the housing was financed by the federal government, mostly for an avid market of its own employees, at very low rates.

Engineers and architects still constitute the core of the appraisal profession and their influence on valuation thought is paramount. Since they customarily deal with physical concepts, it is no accident that they rely heavily on the cost approach in valuations of improved property. The *Comisión Nacional Bancaria* (National Banking Commission), the regulatory agency for the banking industry, requires that all appraisals for bank purposes include this approach. An example of a cost approach appraisal follows.

Summary of a Cost Approach Appraisal

First, the replacement cost new of the buildings and accessories is calculated.

---

16. The Spanish term for a value indication derived from the cost approach is *valor físico o directo,* i.e., physical or direct value. See item VII in the earlier section on the appraisal report form and requirements.

Type of Construction	Quantity m²	Direct Cost ($)	Indirect Cost as % of Direct Cost	Replacement Cost New ($)
Quality modern	200.00	1,193.00	140	334,152.00
Economical modern	20.00	733.50	140	21,658.00
Boundary wall	22.00	316.20	140	9,738.96
Patio	60.00	35.70	140	2,998.80

Then the net replacement value and remaining usable life of the buildings and accessories are calculated.

Type of Construction	Replacement Cost New ($)	Depreciation %	Net Replacement Value ($)	Total Usable Life (Years)	Remaining Usable Life (Years)
Quality modern	334,152.00	5	317,444.40	80	72
Economical modern	21,658.00	10	19,492.20	60	54
Boundary wall	9,738.96	10	8,765.06	60	54
Patio	2,998.80	5	2,848.86	80	72
			348,550.52		

Value of land: $300.00 \text{ m}^2 \times \$255.00/\text{m}^2 \times 1 = \$76,500.00^*$

* The adjustment coefficient of 1 used in this equation is explained in footnote 14.

Value by cost approach:

$$\$76,500 + \$348,550.52 = \$425,050.52$$

Value estimation may sometimes call for the use of a commercialization factor, which considers special aspects of the location or the desirability of the property. In this case, the factor is 10%. Thus, the commercial value of the property is estimated at:

$$CV = \$425,050.52 \times 1.10 = \$467,555.57$$

After the figure has been rounded to the nearest thousand, the value estimate is quoted as:

$$CV = \$468,000.00$$

Reconciliation

The Comisión Nacional Bancaria (CNB) has established guidelines for general practice. The final discussion in the report should provide the results of the cost approach and income approach analyses, plus any additional market or sales comparison information that may have been obtained, before the final conclusion of value is presented. In this discussion, referred to as *consideraciones previas a la conclusión* (considerations before the conclusion), the valuer ponders the merit of each approach in light of the particular problem involved and the relative weight of the value indications obtained and then offers an explanation for the final estimate of value. Established practice and CNB regulations prohibit the averaging of value indications to arrive at a final value conclusion.

Availability of Data

In the Mexican real estate market, factual market data is not readily available. Some attempts to remedy this situation have been made in Mexico City, by far the largest market in the country, and in Guadalajara, the second largest market. Listings are published in these two centers. While listings can provide some useful information, published listings are not commonly available throughout the country.

The exchange of information among valuers is a very common practice and has given rise to the creation of data banks at some of the institutes that belong to ANIMV. Most notable are the data banks in Monterrey, Guadalajara, and Puebla. The weekly and, in some instances, biweekly meetings of institute members provide a forum for the exchange of much useful information.

The sources of information listed below are available to all.

Demographic and Economic Data

- Instituto Nacional de Estadística, Geografía y Informática (INEGI)
- Banco de Mexico
- Municipal offices (state and city)
- Local chambers of commerce, chambers of industry, and specialized business areas
- Specialized publications and periodicals of national banks
- Articles in local and business papers
- ANIMV and association bulletins

Real Estate Market Data (Market Size, Occupancy, Rent Levels)

- Local offices of real estate brokerage, management, and appraisal firms

- *Asociación Mexicana de Profesionales Inmobiliarios, AMPI* (Real Estate Society) publications

- *Asociación Nacional de Institutos Mexicanos de Valuación, A.C.,*[17] (National Association of Mexican Valuation Institutes), Mexico City

- Local Mexican valuation institutes

- Appraisal offices

- Cadastral offices (in some cities)

Rent and Sales Comparables

- Valuers (membership directory available from ANIMV, A.C.)

- Real estate brokers and managers

- State offices (in states with rent control regulations)

Appraisal Organizations

Asociación Nacional de Institutos Mexicanos de Valuación, A.C.
Asturias # 52-8vo. piso
Insurgentes-Mixcoac
03920 México, D.F., México
Tel. 915-598-7423 Fax. 915-598-7428

President (1996-97)
Ing. Eduardo A. Camelo Verduzco
José María Pino Suarez 225-201
86000 Villahermosa, Tab.
Tel. (919) 3 14 01 34, Fax. (919) 3 12 40 08

---

17. The acronym A.C. stands for *Asociación Civil,* indicating a nonprofit corporation.

19

El Salvador

Carlos A. Portillo

Carlos A. Portillo is General Manager of Vappor, S.A. de C.V., an appraisal firm in San Salvador that specializes in the valuation of real estate, machinery, and agricultural equipment. Mr. Portillo's educational background is in civil engineering. He has also worked as a supervisor in the appraisal and soil classification sections of the Catastro Fiscal (Department of Property Assessment) in the Ministry of Public Finance of El Salvador.

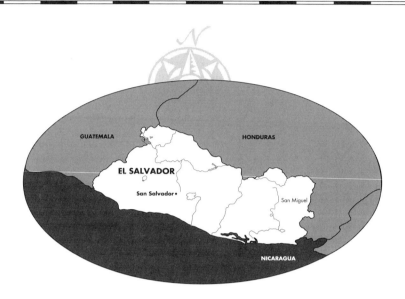

El Salvador is located on the Pacific coast of Central America. The country consists of a tropical coastal plain in the south, which rises to the cooler plateau and valley region of the north. San Salvador is the principal city.

Political Structure

El Salvador declared its independence from Spain on September 15, 1821, becoming a part of a Central American federation that lasted until 1838. The first constitution of the republic of El Salvador was promulgated in 1856. The powers of the Salvadoran government are divided among three branches: the executive, the legislative, and the judicial.

The executive branch consists of a Cabinet of Ministers, which includes the president and vice president of the republic and the ministers of state. The president and vice president are elected by popular vote for a period of five years. Neither is eligible for reelection. The president appoints the ministers and vice ministers of state.

The Cabinet of Ministers is responsible for drafting the general plan of the government, which includes policy directives in the following areas: labor and social security, education, science and culture, public health and social assistance, public works, finance and economy, and agriculture.

The legislative branch comprises the unicameral legislative assembly made up of 84 deputies who are elected by popular vote for a period of three years and are eligible for reelection. The election of deputies to the assembly is based on a system of proportional representation.

The judicial branch includes the Supreme Court of Justice, the chambers of second instance (appellate courts), and other courts. The president of the Supreme Court of Justice is elected by the legislative assembly. This official is also the head of the judicial branch.

Governmental regulations dealing with real estate emanate from the executive branch. The zoning of land use is governed by laws and regulations, which are enforced through the combined efforts of the Ministries of Public Works and Agriculture and the municipal governments.

In El Salvador the only law that actually affects real estate is a tax law involving transfers of real estate *(impuesto sobre la transferencia/enajención)*. This tax is paid on the purchase of real estate by the buyer. The tax must be paid when the purchase price exceeds ¢250,000 (Salvadoran *colones*).

The real estate transfer tax is levied at a rate of 3% of the amount in excess of ¢250,000 and paid to the central government. The annual amount of revenue collected from this tax is very small in relation to the revenue collected from other types of taxes, such as the income tax *(impuesto sobre la renta)* and the value-added tax *(impuesto sobre el valor añadido)*, or IVA.

Property Rights

The constitution of El Salvador guarantees citizens the right to ownership and possession of property. The civil code, established in 1859, mandated the establishment of a national registry of deeds. Following the promulgation of this code, the National Registry of Deeds and Mortgages *(Registro Nacional de las Escrituras y Hipotecas)* was set up. Regulations issued by the registry, dating back to 1897, identify its purposes: to make public information about property within the territory of the country, to maintain historic property records, and to enable interested parties to find information on the mortgages encumbering a property so as to prevent other parties from being defrauded.

The possession of real estate is subject to the following powers of government: taxation, the maintenance of economic order (toward which end, eminent domain and police powers may be exercised), and escheat.

Taxation

The state has the power to determine necessary taxes *(impuestos, contribuciones)* and assessments *(tasaciónes, gravamanes)* by promulgating relevant legislation.

Real estate assessment law is drawn up by the executive branch, but must be approved and decreed by the legislative assembly. In El Salvador, fiscal laws that at one time directly affected real estate, such as the Territorial Tax Law and Inheritance Tax Law *(Patrimonio)*, have been abolished. Only the tax law, which is applied when a property is purchased, remains.

Economic Order

The economic order of the country is based on principles of social justice to ensure its inhabitants a suitable life. The government can legally expropriate real estate for public use if it can be demonstrated that such use is in the societal interest and fair compensation is paid. The government also has the power to limit or restrict the use of a property, to require the owner to police the property, and to take measures to promote the general welfare, public health, and morals.

Intestacy

The civil code establishes procedures to be followed in cases of intestacy. If a person dies and leaves no heirs or successors, the property is passed on to the national university or to the hospitals.

Language

The official language of El Salvador is Spanish. There are centers for bilingual education in the country where the English language is taught. Most of the population, however, is not bilingual.

Currency

The *colon* (¢) is the Salvadoran currency. There is a market in foreign currency, which the U.S. dollar dominates. Many real estate purchases and rentals are transacted in U.S. dollars.

Units of Measure

Because El Salvador uses the metric system, the basic unit of measurement is the meter. For real estate transactions, however, Salvadorans also use the square *vara* as a unit of land measurement. The square meter is used as the unit of measurement for all improvements. The symbol for square *vara* is v^2 and the symbol for square meter is m^2. One square *vara* equals 0.6989 square meters; 0.1328 square *varas* equal one square foot; and 7.5313 square feet equal one square *vara*.

Inflation

Among the countries of Latin America, El Salvador has one of the lowest inflation rates. In El Salvador, it may be very difficult to undertake retrospective appraisals because a civil war was waged in the country for 12 years, from 1980 to 1992, when peace agreements were signed.

Since 1992 annual inflation rates have ranged between 8.9% and 19.9%. The rate of inflation is measured by changes in the prices of goods and services. The General Directorate of Statistics and the Census maintains a register of consumers prices and variations in these prices are measured to establish the rate of inflation in a retail price index *(indice de precios al consumo/IPC)*.

The inflation values or figures registered annually are published by the Banco Central de Reserva (Central Reserve Bank) and are available to anyone.

Typical Lease Structure

Office

Many commercial, financial, and other service sector businesses operate on leased premises. Contracts for residential real estate are considered permanent (i.e., the length of the leases is indefinite), and the rights and obligations of the contracting parties are stipulated in the law of tenancy. Contracts for commercial and industrial real estate are for fixed terms with durations of five to 10 years. The rights and obligations of the lessor and lessee are addressed in the civil code.

In leases for commercial and industrial real estate, percentage increases in monthly rent are set at the beginning of the annual lease period. Percentage increases oscillate between 10% and 15% per year.

The forces of supply and demand determine rent levels. In intensive commercial development zones, rents are high, reflecting the desirable location; in zones of lesser demand, monthly rents are set according to the commercial (market) value of the real estate. Most monthly gross rents range between 1.0% and 1.5% of the commercial (market) value of the property.

The tenant pays rent monthly and in advance; rent is only paid for use of the physical space. Maintenance, utility, and building security expenses are paid by the owner.

Retail

There are few shopping centers in El Salvador. Businessmen interested in developing this type of property do so to sell the units under a system of joint-ownership of property *(copropiedad)*. The new joint owners are generally professionals or businessmen who require their own offices. Leases for units in retail centers exist, but these contracts only provide for use of the unit for a fixed term, usually between five and 10 years. At the end of the term the tenants are expected to vacate.

Monthly gross rent is generally fixed at between 1.0% and 1.5% of the commercial (market) value of the property. Because of regulations and covenants, annual rent increases generally range between 10% and 15%.

Appraisal Standards

No collegial organization exists for real estate appraisers in El Salvador. Consequently, there are no professional standards or requirements and no manuals or texts to provide assistance or guidance to appraisers. Appraisal services are offered by professionals such as engineers, architects, and economists, or by people with experience in real estate.

Licensing/Certification

No institutions exist to monitor the professional activities of appraisers. Appraisers are generally trained in the business enterprises, financial institutions, and government offices where they work. This informal training is provided according to the employer's needs.

Within the government, the Ministry of Public Finances is probably the only entity that has developed a formal training program for appraisers. Nevertheless, the people who undergo such training are not officially recognized or accredited as real estate appraisers.

Appraisal Reporting Requirements

Because there is no association to oversee the preparation of appraisal reports, Salvadoran appraisers may submit their reports in any format they chose. Generally, however, most reports follow the format outlined below.

Contents of an Appraisal Report

I. Title page. Identifies the type of property to be appraised, the owner's name, the purpose of the appraisal, the name of the person who requested the appraisal, and the date of the appraisal.

II. Generalities. Contains a brief description of the property to be appraised, indicating the type of property; its existing use and potential use (commercial, residential, industrial, etc.); its location; factors that influence its value (property-specific and external); ease or difficulty of street access; type of construction, design, age, and state; and description of the layout of components.

III. Registration data. Includes the owner's name and information in the registry of deeds and mortgages that might affect the property.

IV. Location. Cites the postal address and legal description of the site or property to be appraised.

V. Land. Includes a brief description of the site characteristics, e.g., the area, shape or configuration, level in relation to the street, elevation, boundaries, grade, the width and length in relation to frontage; and the names of the current owners of adjacent properties.

VI. Utilities. Refers to basic government-provided utilities and amenities which are available to the property; these may include drinkable water, sewage, electricity, streetlights, sidewalks, causeways, and streets.

VII. Building. Includes a detailed description of the building materials (adobe, wood, reinforced concrete, or *bahareque,* i.e., walls of cane plastered with mud and chopped straw); specifies the type and quality of the materials and finishings of the following components: the roof, ceilings, walls, floors, doors, windows, other accessories and installations; also describes the labor and any technical assistance used in the construction.

VIII. Conclusions and purpose of the appraisal.

IX. Certification of the appraisal.

Definition of Market Value

There is no legally prescribed definition of the term *market value* in El Salvador. However, in 1964 the government of El Salvador, in consultation with the firm of Collet and Clapp, Inc., prepared a manual on real estate appraisal procedures. This manual adopted the following definition of *commercial value*, from a publication of the International Association of Assessing Officers *(Asociación Internacional de Funcionarios Valuadores)*:

> Commercial value is the exact amount of money that is paid in market (purchase-sale) transactions of real estate, merchandise or services, occurring within a reasonable period of time, under conditions where both contracting parts are capable of acting prudently, and both are reasonably well informed.

Income Approach

The income approach *(enfoque de ingresos/rentas)* rests on the principle that the future benefits a real estate investment can generate provide a prudent investor with a basis for determining the price he or she should pay for the real estate. While the conversion of income into present value by means of an appropriate discount rate is an entirely acceptable method for determining property value and is especially applicable to properties that produce income, discounted cash flow analysis is rarely applied by appraisers in El Salvador. Without an appraiser association to impose regulations and practice standards, Salvadoran appraisers generally rely on the comparative and replacement cost methods to develop value estimates.

Because of the limited scope of the local real estate market, Salvadoran appraisers treat profits and rental incomes from real estate in terms of investment value *(valor subjectivo)*. Profits from the sale of real estate are fixed according to the owner's asking price at the time of property resale; strong demand has resulted in a high volume of market (purchase-sale) transactions. These circumstances allow people who want to invest in real estate to operate in the market very simply. They purchase a real estate investment with the certainty that, in a very short time and with little capital expended on upgrading the real estate, they will be able to sell the property at three to four times the price they paid.

Despite these conditions, capitalization methods are available for appraisers to use, and under certain circumstances, these methods may be required. There are two, well-known methods by which income capitalization is applied: direct capitalization of overall property income (present value of ¢1 in perpetuity),[1] and separate capitalization of income to the land and the improvements.

---

1. The present value of ¢1 in perpetuity is the reciprocal of the capitalization rate, e.g., if the capitalization rate is 10%, the present value of ¢1 in perpetuity would be 1/10%, or 10.

The first method is based on the following simple equation:

$$V = \frac{I}{R}$$

where
V = commercial value of the property being appraised
I = annual net income to the property
R = overall capitalization rate *(tasa global)*

The second method is based on the following equations:

$$I = (T \times I_n) + (C \times I_n) + (C \times a)$$

where
I = annual net income to the property

T = value of the land

I_n = annual net return rate *(tasa anual de interés neto)* earned by the real estate

C = value of the buildings

a = annual amortization of debt on the buildings

and

$$C = \frac{I - (T \times I_n)}{(I_n + a)}$$

$$T + C = \frac{I - (C \times a)}{I_n}$$

The following sample appraisal is based on these equations.

Separate capitalization of income to the land and building:

Annual net income	¢2,293,500.00
Value of the land	¢2,445,120.00
Annual net return rate	0.096000
Amortization (94 remaining years; 1/94)	0.010638

By substituting these values into the following equation, the value of the building may be derived:

$$\text{Building value} = \frac{2,293,500 - (2,445,120 \times 0.096)}{0.096 + 0.010638} = ¢19,306,143$$

Using this derived value of the building in the equation below, the value of the land and building is estimated.

$$\text{Land + building} = \frac{2,293,500 - (19,306,143 \times 0.010638)}{0.096} = \textcent 21,751,263$$

Market value = ¢21,751,263

Sales Comparison Approach

The applicability of the sales comparison approach *(enfoque de la comparación de ventas)* in estimating real estate value depends on the amount of data available concerning sales of properties that are similar to the subject property. When the market values of comparable properties are known, it is easy to estimate the value of the subject property. In El Salvador the comparative method is used for appraising both single-family and multi-family residential real estate.

Generally, commercial or industrial real estate is appraised by means of other procedures, e.g., the capitalization of income or through a combination of replacement cost and income methods.

Cost Approach

Used to estimate the value of buildings, the cost approach *(enfoque de costo)* is based on the theory that the value of a building at any particular time tends to approximate the cost that would be incurred to replace the building in its existing state or condition. One of the limitations of this approach is that it cannot be used to establish land value. For this reason, some Salvadoran appraisers do not consider it to be an effective approach to value. Neverthe-less, the cost approach is often used to check the estimated value of the building component after the overall property value is derived by the com-parative or income approach.

Appraisers who estimate the replacement cost of buildings consult cost estimating manuals for different types of construction costs. This information is applied using special quantitative techniques (e.g., comparative unit method, unit-in-place method).

A sample appraisal based on replacement cost follows.

Replacement cost estimate

Land value		¢2,000,000.00
Replacement cost new	¢2,000,000.00	
Less normal depreciation	¢ 600,000.00	
(2,000,000 x 0.30)		
Value of the building		¢1,400,000.00
Indicated value		¢3,400,000.00

Reconciliation

In El Salvador the simple format that appraisers use for their reports does not generally include a section dedicated to the conclusions of the appraisal. Since appraisals are generally based on only one method, reconciliation is not required.

In some cases, however, an appraiser will support the value conclusion by including in the report a detailed explanation of the most significant characteristics of the real estate appraised.

Availability of Data

Governmental offices maintain records of all property purchases that take place in the country, but this information is not generally available. Some private firms collect information on the costs of new housing, which is available for purchase. Appraisers generally maintain their own databases of comparable sale and rental data that they obtain either in the field or from listings advertised in the newspapers. The newspapers are one of the best sources of information available to appraisers.

Listed below are sources of information that appraisers may use or consult.

Demographic and Economic Data

- Construction industry councils
- Libraries
- Articles in local newspapers or business publications
- Chambers of commerce and industry
- Banco Central de Reserva (Central Reserve Bank)
- National Geodetic Institute

Comparable Rent and Sale Data

- Local appraisers
- Registry of Deeds and Mortgages
- Local newspapers

Bibliography

Chandías, Mario E. *Tasación de Inmuebles Urbanos (Appraisal of Urban Real Estate)*. Buenos Aires, 1954.

Código Civil de El Salvador (Civil Code of El Salvador).

Constitución de la República de El Salvador (Constitution of the Republic of El Salvador).

Gobierno de El Salvador (Government of El Salvador) y Collett and Clapp, Inc. *La Valuación de La Propiedad Raíz (The Valuation of Real Property)*. San Salvador, El Salvador, 1964.

Ley de Catastro de El Salvador (Law of Land Registry of El Salvador).

Pulidos, Raúl J. *Analisis de Valor de Capitalisatión para Inmuebles e Inversiones (Capitalization Analysis of Value for Real Estate and Investments)*. Mexico City, 1973.

State of California, Property Tax Department, State Board of Equalization. *General Appraisal Manual.* Sacramento. California, 1975.

State of California, Assessment Standards Division, State Board of Equalization, *Catalog of Drill Problems.* Sacramento, California, 1979.

Colombia

L. Jorge Hurtado

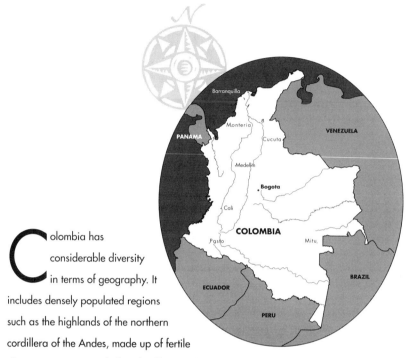

Colombia has considerable diversity in terms of geography. It includes densely populated regions such as the highlands of the northern cordillera of the Andes, made up of fertile plateaus *(mesetas)* and alluvial valleys, and the tropical Caribbean coast as well as sparsely populated plains *(llanos)* and rainforests *(selvas)* in the southeast, which is drained by the Orinoco and Amazon river systems. Coffee is grown in the Andean highlands. The climate varies with elevation. The Caribbean and southeast are hot *(tierras calientes),* while the Andean highlands are temperate or cool *(tierra templada or terra fria).* Principal cities are Bogotá, Medellin, Cali, Barranquilla, and Cartagena.

Political Structure

The Republic of Colombia has been under democratic rule since the Days of Independence, dating back to 1821.[1] Three branches make up the central government of Colombia: an executive branch consisting of the president and Cabinet members; the legislative branch, or Congress, consisting of the Senate and the Chamber of Deputies; and the judicial branch, within which the highest court is the Supreme Court.

The president of Colombia is elected for a single, four-year term. Re-election is not permitted. The president appoints Cabinet ministers for defense, education, transportation, urban and economic development, foreign affairs, health, and housing.

The Congress is divided into two chambers. The Senate consists of 102 senators elected for four-year terms. The Chamber of Deputies consists of 162 deputies, who are also elected for four-year terms. Both senators and deputies are elected by direct vote and may be re-elected. The apportionment of deputies among the administrative divisions of the country is based on the population count in the national census, which is taken every 10 years.

Members of the Supreme Court are appointed for life. Customarily, justices of the court decide the age at which they will retire.

In recent years, the administration of Colombia has become more decentralized. The country is divided into three types of administrative units: departments, which are headed by a governor; municipalities, which are run by municipal councils; and cities, which are run by mayors. All these officials are freely elected, although previously they were appointed by the president and the Cabinet.

General guidelines on rural and urban land use are laid down by the national authorities. Land use regulations and their enforcement are the responsibility of local authorities, development corporations, and city governments. Environmental regulations are subordinate to economic development projects.

Property taxes are levied locally. There is a national value-added tax, the proceeds of which go into the coffers of both national and local governments. Property taxes are manageable, but property owners have expressed concern over special assessments for public works.

---

1. A federation of Colombia, Ecuador, and Venezuela, known as Gran Colombia, emerged from the wars of independence (1811-1824). In 1830 the federation broke up, and Ecuador and Venezuela became independent. With the backing of the United States, Panama seceded from Colombia in 1903.

Property Rights

The assignation of property rights dates to colonial times. Land not granted to individuals by the time of independence was held as state property by the national and local governments. In the past, all government takings have been compensated as a matter of law. Property ownership is subject to the four powers of government: taxation, eminent domain, police power, and escheat.

Taxation is the right of government to raise revenue through assessments on goods, products, rights, and interests. Local governments levy property taxes, and the national government levies taxes on the ownership of assets, including real estate.

Eminent domain is the right of government to take property for public use upon payment of just compensation. When local and national governments take property for public use, compensation may be based on a value other than market value, such as assessment value.

Police power is the right of government to protect public safety, health, morals, and the general welfare. Land use and zoning regulations are based on the police powers of the local and national governments.

Escheat gives the state ownership of property when an owner of property dies without a will or ascertainable heirs.

A common concept, known as the *bundle of rights,* is inherent in the ownership of real estate. The bundle of rights is frequently compared to a bundle of sticks, with each stick representing the right to do something with property. For example, an owner of property may sell, lease, or give the property away.

Ownership of all the rights in the bundle is known as fee simple *(dominio absoluto, pleno dominio).* This is considered the highest form of ownership. A fee simple estate implies absolute ownership, unencumbered by any other interest. In urban areas, fee simple ownership of condominium units in commercial, office, industrial, and residential properties has become very popular. Condominium ownership has even been used for land in subdivisions and investment units in hotel properties. Lately, resort properties have begun to come under timeshare ownership *(utilización compartida).*

A leased fee *(derecho sobre dominio alquilado)* is a legal estate in which some of the rights, such as the rights to the use and occupancy of the property, have been conveyed by a lease *(contrato de arrendamiento)* to others. Most multitenanted buildings are owned in leased fee.

A leasehold *(derecho de arrendamiento, bienes forales)* estate is one in which a tenant leases the land from another party and owns the building(s) or improvements attached to the land until expiration of the lease. Most leases, including land leases *(contrato de alquiler de terreno)*, are short term. Under most land leases, ownership rights to the buildings and improvements revert to the landowner upon termination of the lease. All buildings and leasehold improvements *(mejoras a la propiedad alquilada)* permanently attached to the land revert to the owner of the land and buildings.

Language

Spanish is the language of Colombia. The second language of choice is English, followed by French.

Currency

The peso Colombiano (PC or C$) is the monetary unit. Colombia has been an advocate of the "crawling peg"[2] to protect its foreign exchange and develop its exports. All real estate transactions are priced in pesos, although from time to time transactions are contracted in U.S. dollars. The exchange rate as of 1995 was about C$900 to one U.S. dollar.

Units of Measure

Colombia uses the metric system. In real estate, however, two nonmetric measures are used: a linear measure, the *vara* (80 cm. or 31.2 inches), and an area measure, the *fanegada* (6,400 m² or 1.58 acres). Real estate prices are generally quoted in pesos per square meter; the prices of rural property are quoted in pesos per hectare (1 ha. = 10,000 m²). Rents are quoted in pesos per square meter per month.

Inflation

Inflation generally runs 20% to 40%. Income analysis is frequently conducted in real or constant pesos. The government reports various price indices; the one in most common use is the consumer price index. The minimun wage is adjusted anually at the beginning of the year.

Although most price controls have been abolished, gasoline prices are regulated and there are provisions for the rent control of some properties. The regulation of rent applies to urban real estate, especially multitenanted properties. There is some flexibility, however, since rents are based on assessed values and property owners have the option of estimating their own assessments on an annual basis. Monthly rentals are set at 2% of the as-

---

2. A policy aimed at maintaining a favorable balance of payments and preventing the flight of domestic capital.

sessed value of the property. Since assessment values are reported at 80% of market values, monthly rent is 1.6% of market value.

Lease Structure

Because of inflation and rent controls, most leases run for a one-year term and are subject to renewal. In practice, tenants with annually renewable leases tend to stay for medium to long terms. Leases with terms of more than one year generally contain escalation clauses and/or may refer to hard currency.

Most leases contain important expense pass-throughs, especially when the property leased is in a residential or commercial condominium. As a rule, the leasing of real estate excludes all services, even minor maintenance and cleaning.

Rental insurance is available in Bogotá and other major cities through select insurance companies. The tenant pays for this insurance, which covers delinquency in rental payments and protects the landlord. The insurance company checks the qualifications of the tenant with the owner and rental agent.

Leasing commissions *(honorarios de gerencia de los negocios)* start at about 8% of rental income, and real estate agents may charge up to a month's rent for new clients.

Valuation Standards

Appraisers are organized in the Consejo Nacional de Avaluadores (National Council of Appraisers). The council administers a national registry *(registro nacional)* that is open to all appraisers and is maintained by the two major appraisal organizations: the Sociedad Colombiana de Avaluadores (Colombian Society of Appraisers) and the Federación Colombiana de Lonjas de Propiedad Raíz, (Colombian Federation of Real Estate Boards), which is known by the acronym Fedelonjas.

The Sociedad Colombiana de Avaluadores is the Colombian member of the Pan-American Union of Valuation Associations (UPAV) and has four seats in the National Council of Appraisers.

Fedelonjas has six seats in the National Council of Appraisers and administers 15 regional appraiser councils. Fedelonjas represents the real estate industry, from which most of Colombia's appraisers come. The membership of Fedelonjas easily outnumbers that of the society.

The National Council of Appraisers promotes the professionalism of appraisers by supporting education initiatives and the participation of universities.

The Universidad del Externado, which offers extension courses to off-campus students, has been an important supporter of this initiative.

The National Council of Appraisers prints the *National Registry of Appraisers* every two years and has the technical support of the Instituto Geográfico Agustín Codazzi (IGAC), the national government agency responsible for all geodesic surveys and studies.

Although appraisal work is not regulated, appraiser organizations have proposed that designated valuers be recommended and/or required for assignments for financial and governmental institutions.

The real estate boards provide valuation services for appraisals that require outstanding expertise or involve the sale of properties to government entities. With the support of their membership and the direct participation of their technical staff and appraisal committee, the real estate boards perform valuation studies. Such board or corporate appraisals are more expensive and do not, therefore, compete openly with the work of individual appraisers.

Appraisers quote minimum fees that are set in proportion to estimated property values. The minimun fees range from C$1.75 per thousand pesos to C$10.75 per thousand pesos on a progressive scale. Minimum fees may be lower for financial institutions, multiple assignments, and updates of previous assignments. Real estate boards charge three times the minimum fees for their appraisals.

Licensing/Certification

Licensing is limited to those included in the national registry. To be included, an appraiser must join either a real estate board or the Columbian Society of Appraisers. Good character, respectability, and experience as a bona fide appraiser are required and the recommendations and sponsorship of colleagues is very important. Board membership is oriented toward business entities, while membership in the society is essentially on an individual basis, although business entities can be members. Inclusion in the national registry is identified by the initials RNA, followed by a numerical sequence, in the appraiser's letterhead or after the appraiser's signature.

Many public and private institutions prefer, and sometimes even mandate inclusion in the national registry. Membership in a real estate board *(lonja)* is very prestigious and because of the large national presence of *lonjas*, such membership is readily identifiable to the general public.

Those listed in the national registry have made great inroads, obtaining assignments in the financial sector and with government agencies. More and more valuers are required to hold national registry credentials.

Appraisals for certain government transactions must be supported and/or performed by the Instituto Geográfico Agustín Codazzi (IGAC); in these cases no other appraisals may be used, regardless of the appraiser's certification or membership.

Appraisal Reporting Requirements

Lending institutions, investors, government agencies, and the general public rely on appraisers to perform their work diligently. Appraisals that meet professional requirements are needed to support sales and acquisitions, insurance policies and claims filed, the estimation of ad valorem taxes, analyses for credit and collateral, the issuance of stock, and current cost accounting among other uses.

To help the general users of real estate appraisals, guidelines in Colombia typically require that the following items be included in appraisal reports:

1. Name of the client and/or final user
2. Definition of the property, specifying
   - Address
   - Ownership
   - Type
   - Location
   - Neighborhood
   - Area accessibility
   - Site accessibility
   - Public transportation
   - Utilities
     - Water
     - Sewage
     - Electricity
     - Telephones
     - Sidewalks
3. The current use of the property
4. A legal description and topographical data
   - Ownership
     - Property record
     - Parcel identification

- Property defects
- Topography
  - Shape
  - Slope
  - Frontage and depth
5. The property boundaries
6. A building description
   - Type of construction
   - Age
   - Conservation and maintenance
   - Floors and levels
   - Materials and specifications
   - Layout of components
7. Economic conditions
   - Building activity
   - Market supply and demand
8. Planning board controls
   - Zoning definitions
   - Rights of way
   - Building height
9. General considerations
   - Neighborhood
   - Location
   - Site
   - Topography
   - Lot size
   - Improvements
   - Specifications
   - Maintenance
   - Design and finishes
   - Age
   - Current use and income

- Sales activity
- Current supply and demand

10. Final considerations
- Record of sales
  - Address
  - Lot size
  - Improvements
  - Recorded price
  - Date
- Listings
  - Address
  - Lot size
  - Improvements
  - Recorded price
  - Date

11. The appraisal estimates
- Site valuation
- Valuation of the improvements
- Value conclusion

Addenda
- Drawings
- Photographs

According to appraisal requirements, valuers need to rely on market observation. No formal consideration is given to either the income or the cost approach, although income and cost analyses may be performed. Separate valuations of the site and improvements are required, based on the appraiser's best judgment of these values. The estimated value of the improvements is not based on the cost approach.

It should be noted, however, that appraisers generally do not acknowledge that the improvements may add little to property value or even penalize it. The physical existence of the improvements is considered sufficient evidence that they add positive value to the land. When there is no market evidence of land values, e.g., in stable, built-up neighborhoods, appraisers must provide their best judgment as to the value of the land and improvements without recourse to data that might provide some indication of land value.

Definition of Market Value

There is no universally accepted definition of market value *(valor de mercado)*. The closest appraisers come to defining the concept is their general acceptance of a distinction between commercial and technical appraisals. This differentiation originates in the use of the appraisal and the selection of the approach to value.

Commercial appraisals rely on market evidence and trends and are used to support sales and offerings, mortgage financing, and the estimation of ad valorem taxes. *Commercial value* is synonymous with *market value* and is the basis for the purchase and sale of property, mortgage underwriting, and other business transactions.

Technical appraisals rely on cost evidence and are used to support insurance underwriting and claims filing, the issuing of stock, and current cost accounting.

Income Approach

The income approach *(enfoque de ingresos/de rentas)* is rarely used in Colombia. The best applications of this approach are found in appraisal studies that compare market evidence based on income streams and in appraisals that support rent estimates and arbitrage.

When the income approach is applied, gross rent *(renta bruta)* is estimated and a direct capitalization rate *(tasa de capitalizacíon)* is favored over a rent multiplier *(multiplicador de renta)*. Any income projection *(projeccíon de renta)* is made in terms of constant pesos, employing inflation-neutral interest and discount rates.

Rents for urban real estate generally fall under governmental regulation. Rental increases are subject to officially published inflation rates. Acceptable monthly rentals are set at 1% of twice the amount of the current ad valorem tax base *(base impositiva)* or assessment of the property. Since the ad valorem tax base represents 80% of the property's market value, it is generally accepted that monthly rental rates are 1.6% of market value.

Rental rates for residential and commercial property are quoted monthly. Commercial rents are quoted in pesos per square meter. Most leases run for one year with renewal subject to an increase in rent. Typically, the landlord requires a three-month deposit and rental insurance in case of delinquency in rental payments. Insurance is available through select underwriters.

Sales Comparison Approach

The sales comparison *(enfoque de la comparacíon de ventas)* or market approach *(enfoque de mercado)* is favored by appraisal practitioners and professionals. It is understood that sales comparison provides the most reliable estimates of commercial value. An appraisal based on the market approach is referred to as *avalúo comercial,* or commercial appraisal, since this type of appraisal provides an estimate of market value.

Sales data is hard to come by. Listing information can be directly investigated or may be found in select realty publications and media. There is no multiple listing service and property record information, although officially public, is not readily accessible.

Given these conditions, appraisers attach great significance to documented and undocumented listing information and hearsay. In many localities, appraisal value estimates become value indicators for future appraisal analyses. Therefore, there is always a risk of starting a "chain" of value estimates based on previous value estimates that were not sufficiently supported. The *lonjas* (boards) maintain a file of value estimates from appraisals performed by the board and its members.

Most *lonjas* have an appraisal committee and conduct appraisal roundtables on a regular basis. Appraisers and real estate brokers network extensively to secure information and other opinions on value. Roundtables provide a forum for exchanging information, analyses, and data regarding particular appraisal assignments. Such material is often presented and openly discussed.

Appraisal reports generally include estimates and opinions of value, but no specific references to market data, be it sales or listing information.Thus, formal discussions of market data or its relationship to the subject property are not found in appraisal reports. The evidence on which the value estimate depends is never presented to clients.

The land residual technique is not favored by practitioners. Some appraisers, who falsely present themselves as being highly competent technically, develop land values by means of the land residual technique. Applications of this technique are found in appraisals of urban land for commercial or residential condominium development. Such reports may include a discussion of zoning and development standards, but provide little or no support for the estimated sales prices of the condo units or space.

Cost Approach

Use of the cost approach *(enfoque de costo)* is generally limited to special-purpose properties. However, this restriction may be followed less rigorously in Colombia than in other localities. For example, a shopping center or an office building may be considered a special-purpose property in Columbia and valued as such by means of the cost approach.

The cost approach is used extensively for the appraisal of machinery, equipment, and other fixed assets. Most buildings that are fixed assets of corporations are appraised by means of the cost approach. Ad valorem taxation also promotes the use of this approach.

In mortgage underwriting, some financial institutions may require a cost estimate to compare against the market value estimate, although market or commercial value is always the basis of valuations of collateral for loans.

Insurance underwriting for real estate relies heavily on the cost approach. Many buildings are insured based on their replacement cost new, without any consideration of the age of the property, forecast market conditions, or property use that may accelerate obsolescence.

Reconciliation

Since the use of more than one approach is neither customary nor mandatory, most appraisals present only the estimate of value derived from the approach applied. When more than one estimate of value is developed, appraisers generally prefer to reconcile value indications by means of a simple or weighted average, rather than conclude a value by identifying which indication of value is more representative and reliable.

Highest and best use analysis, which in many instances may provide a basis for reconciliation, is not undertaken in preparing an appraisal or reporting the value conclusion.

Availability of Data

Reliable data is difficult to secure. Real estate brokers and agents in the valuation profession have an advantage over expert practitioners because brokers deal with market data daily. The local and national real estate boards are very supportive of appraisers in need of zoning infomation and generally act as liaisons with the planning board on behalf of appraisers.

Because first-hand information on sales transactions is limited, appraisers may have to rely solely on listings. Furthermore, since no multiple listing service exists and listings are sometimes kept confidential, only listing information published in the local media may be available. This situation requires clients to rely on knowledgeable local appraisers to perform valuations and, as expected, these individuals are generally brokers or agents.

As noted previously, real estate boards hold regular appraisal committee meetings for their members. Appraisals are discussed openly at these meetings and colleagues do their best to inform one another of value estimates, the characteristics of subject properties, and market trends. Some boards keep a record of value estimates, which are consulted by the members and used as bases for other assignments.

Appraisers also make use of information on building activity and market supply and demand, which is published by the builders' association. Rapid changes are occurring, however. Some local boards have already started limited multiple listing services and others regularly print current listings of sales and rentals.

The following data sources may prove useful:

Demographic and Economic Data
- Statistics of the Banco de la Republica (the state bank)
- Local chambers of commerce
- Print media
- Instituto Geográfico Agustín Codazzi (the government agency that carries out geodetic surveys)

Real Estate Market Data
- Local *lonja* (real estate board) chapters
- Statistics compiled by the builders' association
- *Construdata,* a publication written for developers which provides excellent insights on new condominium activity, including sales and cost information
- *La Guía,* a guide to new listings of residential and commercial construction in Bogotá
- *Inmuebles,* a guide to new listings of residential and commercial construction in Cali
- Local real estate newspapers, which may from time to time contain inserts of listings provided by important realtors
- Instituto Geográfico Agustín Codazzi (the government agency that carries out geodetic surveys)

Appraisal Organizations

- Sociedad Colombiana de Avaluadores (Colombian Society of Appraisers), Santa Fe de Bogotá.
- Federación de Lonjas de Propiedad Raíz (National Federation of Real Estate Boards), known as Fedelonjas, Santa Fe de Bogotá.
- Local real estate boards in the cities of Santa Fe de Bogotá, Medellin, Cali, Barranquilla, Cartagena, Bucaramanga, Manizales, and Pereira.

Argentina

Jorge M. Saravia, M.E. (Ind.E.)

Jorge M. Saravia is an industrial engineer who holds a bachelor of engineering degree from the Universidad Nacional de Buenos Aires and a master of industrial engineering degree from Cornell University. He is a member of the Tribunal de Tasaciones de la Nación. Mr. Saravia is a partner of Estudio de Ingeniería Saravia, a valuation and management consulting firm. He is the author of two books *Tasación de Activos Fijos Empresarios (The Appraisal of Fixed Assets of Business Enterprises)* published by Ediciones Macchi in 1986; and *Valuación de Activos Fijos y Revalúos Técnicos (The Valuation of Fixed Assets and Expert Reappraisals)* published by Estudio de Ingeniería Saravia in 1994.

Most of Argentina is a subtropical plain that comprises several distinct regions, e.g., the grass-covered pampas, part of the thicket forest Gran Chaco. and the semiarid tableland of Patagonia. Principal cities are Buenos Aires, Córdoba, Rosario, La Plata, Mendoza, and San Miguel de Tucuman.

Political Structure

Three, independent branches make up the federal government of Argentina: the executive branch, which includes the president and vice president as well as the various members of the Cabinet; the legislative branch, which comprises the Senate and the Chamber of Deputies; and the judicial branch, which includes the Supreme Court of Justice and the lower federal courts.

The president and vice president are elected for four-year terms and can be reelected for one additional term. The Senate is composed of three senators from each of the 23 provinces and three senators from the federal district, the city of Buenos Aires. The members of the Chamber of Deputies are elected for four-year terms. The number of deputies is based on the population of each province. Judges of the Supreme Court of Justice and of the lower federal courts are appointed for life by the president, with the approval of the Senate.

Political powers not specifically delegated to the federal government are vested in the 23 provinces.

Property Rights

Property rights are protected by the constitution. Confiscation of property is prohibited. Expropriation of property for public needs (the exercise of eminent domain) must be approved by congressional legislation. A property owner is entitled to the payment of just compensation, including the value of the property taken, direct damages to the remainder caused by the taking, and compensation for other costs incurred, e.g., the cost of moving.

The ownership of real property is subject to the powers of government. These include the power to tax property, to expropriate property, to exercise escheat, and to safeguard the general welfare, public safety and morals, and the rights of third parties.

The basic legislation governing real estate is found in the civil code, which was modeled after the traditions of Roman and French (Napoleonic) law. The civil code states that the owner of a parcel of land also owns any building attached to it. Thus, in Argentina there is no leasehold estate *(bienes forales)*, the ownership right to an improvement built on a parcel of land that is leased from another party, and no separate ownership of the leasehold improvements *(dominio de las mejoras a la propiedad alquilada)*.

The most common type of ownership for urban real estate is the *propiedad horizontal,*[1] a legal arrangement *(esquema legal)* in which each apartment in a building may have a different owner. Each owner is the exclusive owner of

---

1. This form of ownership corresponds to condominium ownership in other parts of the Western Hemisphere.

one or more apartments and, at the same time, a co-owner together with the owners of the other apartments of the land and all parts of the building in common use (e.g., the external walls, structural components, elevators, boilers, and common areas such as hallways and corridors). Each owner's share of the common use areas and components is stated in the title to the apartment. His or her apportionment of the common expenses for the building corresponds to this share. The owner's share of the common use areas and components of the building is inherent in the ownership of the apartment and cannot be sold independently. The ownership share for each apartment is determined when the building is registered as a *propiedad horizontal.* The share apportioned for each apartment is based on the estimated market value of the apartment on the date of registration in proportion to the total market value of all the apartments in the building. This original ownership share can be changed only with the unanimous approval of all the other apartment owners.

Language

Spanish is the official language of Argentina.

Currency

The Argentine peso ($) is the monetary unit. The value of the Argentine peso approximates that of the U.S. dollar and is officially tied to the U.S. dollar.

Units of Measure

Argentina uses the metric system.

Inflation

For many years, the rate of inflation in Argentina was very high, but since 1992 inflation has averaged less than 1% per year. Statistical indices of inflation such as the Consumer Price Index, the Wholesale Price Index, and the Cost of Building Index are compiled every month by the National Bureau of Statistics and the Census and by the corresponding agencies in some provincial governments. Index data are readily available through the press.

Typical Lease Structure

From 1946 to1984 legal regulations on the leasing of real estate were quite unfair to landlords. Leasing contracts were automatically renewed by law, and the updating of rental rates was also fixed by law. Percentage increases in the rents to be paid were significantly lower than the prevailing rates of inflation. In many instances, rents were lower than the operating expenses of the building, which had to be borne by the landlord. If a tenant was not willing to move out, the only legal way to terminate a lease was to grant the tenant a substantial indemnity payment.

As a result of these regulations, the market of real estate available for leasing progressively dwindled and almost disappeared. In 1984 a new legal framework was established to reverse the situation and, since then, the market for leased real estate has gradually begun to increase. The present state of affairs is reflected in the real estate advertisements in leading newspapers, where only about 20% of the advertisements pertain to rental offerings and 80% relate to sales offerings.

Rents are typically quoted in pesos per month. In the typical lease *(contrato de alquiler/de arrendamiento),* the tenant pays monthly rent plus all operating expenses such as maintenance, repairs, property management fees, real estate taxes, and utilities. Capital expenditures for improvements that could increase the value of the property are almost never included.

In general, the law prescribes a minimum lease term of three years for residential properties, excluding summer resorts and temporary lodgings. The minimum lease term for office, retail, and industrial premises is generally two years. The typical term for a lease is the legal minimum, but quite frequently leases contain an option for renewal at the end of the term at a rent already stated in the contract.

Valuation Standards

There are no uniform valuation standards for appraisers in Argentina. The only exceptions are in the area of eminent domain and appraisal assignments for federal government agencies. In these cases, appraisers usually follow the valuation criteria or methodologies used by the Tribunal de Tasaciones de la Nación, the federal agency that deals with valuations for eminent domain and federal acquisitions. Tribunal members hold tenure and therefore act independently of the government.

To securitize in international markets the mortgage loans they grant, some banks have recently started to request that appraisers use similar methodologies and follow standards similar to those applied by U.S. appraisers in comparable assignments.

Licensing/Certification

Licensing is legally required only of appraisers who perform valuations for cases brought before the courts. A license is automatically granted by the appropriate professional council of each province to college graduates who hold a degree from a university in an area of specialization that the university deems acceptable to perform appraisals, provided the university is academically recognized by the government. A license can be revoked for unethical behavior. The decision to revoke a license rests on the judgment of the appraiser's peers, and due process is guaranteed.

Appraisal Reporting Requirements

There are no uniform reporting requirements for real estate appraisers. Reports vary according to the needs of the client and the assignment at hand. A complete real estate appraisal report for a reasonably complex assignment will typically include the following components:

I.   **Introduction**

- Letter of transmittal

- Table of contents

- Certification of value

- Summary of conclusions

II. **The Appraisal**

- Statement of the purpose of the appraisal and its scope

- Summary of limiting conditions and specification of the date of the value estimate

- Definitions of the terminology used

- Identification of the property to be valued

- City, neighborhood, and locational data

- Site data and zoning category

- Description of the improvements

- Current offers and sales comparison analysis

- Highest and best use of the property as improved

- Additional analyses (If appropriate, the report may provide an estimate of land value, an analysis of the highest and best use of the land as though vacant, a cost analysis, an income analysis, a marketability study, and details of the tax and legal status of the property.)

- Other pertinent information

Definition of Market Value

There is no universally accepted definition of market value, but most local authorities and practitioners would agree that market value is generally understood to be the most probable price at which a property may be sold, in cash, after exposure on the market for an adequate period of time, where the buyer and the seller are each acting prudently, with adequate knowledge, and neither being subject to undue pressure.

Sales Comparison Approach

In Argentina, the sales comparison approach *(enfoque de la comparación de ventas)* is the most widely used method for valuing real estate. The market value of a property is estimated by comparing it to other, similar properties that have been sold or are being offered for sale. The more similar the properties being compared are, the more reliable the resulting estimate of value will be.

In comparing data from units that are being sold or offered within a *propiedad horizontal,* care should be taken to differentiate net area (of which the owner is the sole owner and user) from total area (calculated by adding to net area the owner's share of the total common use area of the building).[2]

Cost Approach

Depreciated replacement cost *(costo de reemplazo/reposition menos depreciacion),* not reproduction cost, is the approach to value normally used when the purpose of the assignment is to appraise value in use *(valor de uso),* e.g., the value of the fixed assets of a business as a part of a going concern. This approach is also used, with an appropriate allowance for market conditions, to estimate the market value of properties for which adequate market data is not available.

Income Approach

Until very recently, real estate was rarely owned for rental purposes. Properties were bought either to be used or to be held and eventually sold for capital gain. Properties very seldom were bought to be rented. Now the situation is changing. Nevertheless, for the time being, the income approach to appraising real estate, referred to as the *rents approach (enfoque de rentas),* is rarely used and hardly ever requested by clients.

Availability of Data

Market data is not easily obtained in Argentina and, with the exception of public auctions, final sale prices and conditions of sale are usually considered confidential. The same holds true of income and expense data.

---

2. The share of the total common area apportioned to the owner of an individual apartment is calculated by multiplying the total common area of the building by the share represented by the apartment being analyzed.

Data can be obtained from the sources listed below.

Demographic and Economic Data

- Instituto Nacional de Estadistica y Censos (National Institute of Statistics and [the] Census)
- Provincial bureaus of the census
- Articles in magazines and newspapers

Real Estate Market Data

- Local offices of real estate brokerage, management, and appraisal firms.

Rent and Sale Comparables

- Real estate brokers and managers
- Appraisers

Appraisal Organization

The primary appraisal group is

Instituto Argentino de Tasaciones
Cerrito 1250
1010 - Buenos Aires
Tel. 541-812-0440; Fax 541-812-0475

Bibliography

Guerro, Dante. *Manual de Tasaciones (Appraisal Manual)*. Buenos Aires: Editorial Alsina, 1984.

Saravia, Jorge M. *Valuación de Activos Fijos y Revalúos Técnicos (The Valuation of Fixed Assets and Expert Reappraisals)*. Buenos Aires: Estudio de Ingenieria Saravia, 1994.

Appendix A

International Associations of Valuers and Real Estate Professionals

Appendix A lists only those organizations that include national valuation and real estate associations in their membership. For information on prominent organizations in a specific country, such as the Appraisal Institute in the United States or the Royal Institution of Chartered Surveyors in the United Kingdom, the reader should refer to the section on professional associations provided in each chapter.

ASEAN Valuers Association. An association of southeast Asian valuers founded in 1981 to promote cooperation among practitioners in the six ASEAN nations, provide an organizational framework for collaborative projects, and encourage research and the exchange of information. The association offers seminars and training programs and holds biennial congresses. Its headquarters are located at the Institute of Surveyors of Malaysia in Selangor, Malaysia.

Appraisal Foundation. A U.S. educational foundation organized in 1987 to foster professionalism through the establishment of the Uniform Standards of Professional Appraisal Practice (USPAP) and qualifications for the state certification and licensing of U.S. appraisers. In recent years, organizations outside the U.S. have expressed interest in becoming affiliated with the Appraisal Foundation as the acceptance of USPAP in other countries increases. USPAP has been translated into Bulgarian, French, Spanish, Polish, and Russian. In 1997 the Appraisal Institute of Canada (AIC) became the first international sponsor of the foundation. Another organization from Canada, the Canadian National Association of Real Estate Appraisers, was admitted to the foundation's advisory council in 1996. The Appraisal Foundation has entered into a cooperative agreement with Central and Eastern European Valuer Association Network (CEEVAN) and has hosted two delegations from China for briefings on appraisal standards and appraiser qualifications.

CASLE (Commonwealth Association of Surveying and Land Economy). An academic society with membership drawn from Commonwealth countries.

CEEVAN (Central and Eastern European Valuer Association Network). An umbrella organization of appraisal organizations headquartered in Europe. Through this organization, the U.S.-based Eastern European Real Property Foundation and the Appraisal Foundation have provided technical assistance to newly formed appraisal organizations in Bulgaria, Hungary, Poland, Romania, Russia, Slovakia, and Ukraine.

EUROVAL (The European Property Valuers Association). An international association of property valuers with the following objectives: to promote study and research into all areas of property valuation (i.e., land, buildings, plant and machinery); to liaise with the European Commission on related issues; to establish a code of conduct for its member associations with power to exclude them for non-compliance; and to guide and help member associations in the development of the profession in Europe. EUROVAL and The European Group of Valuers Associations (TEGOVA) merged in 1997.

Contact:

EUROVAL, Secretariat
12 Great George Street
London SW1P 3AD
United Kingdom
Tel: +44 171 334 3728
Fax: +44 171 334 3844
e-mail: rel@rics.co.uk

EUROVAL
715, Chaussée de Waterloo
Bte. 30
B-1180 Brussels
Belgium
Tel: +32 2 344 48 60
Fax: +32 2 346 64 24

FIABCI (The International Real Estate Federation). Formerly the Fédération Internationale des Administrateurs de Biens et Conseils Immobiliers, but now the Fédération Internationale des Professions Immobilières. Founded in 1951, FIABCI is a worldwide organisation of real estate brokers which provides real estate professionals throughout the world with an efficient means of communication. Through FIABCI they can share their knowledge and experience with each other and with the international community and provide society with optimal solutions to its property needs. FIABCI operates chapters in 50 member countries, embracing more than 100 national professional associations and their individual members.

Contact:

FIABCI
23, avenue Bosquet
75007 Paris
France
Tel: +33 1 45 50 45 49
Fax: +33 1 45 50 42 00

FIABCI-USA
Susan Newman, Secretary General
1611 N. Kent St., Ste. 910
Arlington, VA 22209
Tel: (703) 524-4279
Fax: (703) 528-2392

FIG (The International Federation of Surveyors/Fédération Internationale des Géomètres). A federation of national professional associations of surveyors who provide advice on the management and use of land and property, developed or undeveloped, on or below the surface of land or water. Nearly 100 countries are represented in FIG, whose primary aims are to promote professional practice and to encourage the development of professional and academic standards. As a nongovernmental organisation recognised by the United Nations, FIG works closely with U.N. development agencies and acts as the international spokesperson for the surveying profession.

Contact:

FIG Bureau
12 Great George Street
London SW1P 3AD
United Kingdom
Tel: 0171 334 3796
Fax: 0171 334 3719
e-mail: figjw:rics.co.uk

International Confederation of Associations of Experts and Consultants (ICAEC)/Confederation internationale des associations d'experts et de conseils (CIDADEC). Organization of associations of experts, appraisers, and consultants in 25 countries which works to establish a level of uniformity among professional experts and technical consultants as regards law, principles and practice. The federation makes a special effort to accept professionals from Third World countries as members.

Contact:

Georges Sellon, Gen. Sec.
10, rue du Debarcadere
F-75852 Paris Cedex 17, France
Tel: 33 1 45745060
Rue ten Bosch
85-B-1050 Brussels

IVSC (The International Valuation Standards Committee). Formerly The International Assets Valuation Standards Committee (TIAVSC). A technical committee formed by members of the Royal Institution of Chartered Surveyors in 1981 to establish and publish international valuation standards and procedural guidelines for the valuation of fixed assets and to promote their worldwide acceptance and observance. Other objectives are to harmonize standards among the world's states and to make known differences in standards statements and/or applications of standards as they occur. It is a particular goal of IVSC that international valuation standards be recognised in statements of international accounting and other reporting standards and that valuers recognise what is required of them under the standards of other disciplines. IVSC membership consists of national valuation societies and institutions representing their respective states. The IVSC standards represent the consensus of 40 participating countries.

Contact:

> Philippe Malaquin
> 114, avenue de Wagram
> 75017 Paris
> France
> Tel: 33 1 42 27 80 36
> Fax: 33 1 46 22 16 80

See Appendix C for more information on the International Valuation Standards and the activities of IVSC and for a listing of member states and valuation associations.

North American Conference of Appraisal Organizations (NACAO). A body founded in the late 1960s which currently comprises 12 member organizations (including the Appraisal Institute, the Appraisal Institute of Canada, and the Asociación Nacional de Institutos Mexicanos de Valuación, A.C.), four observing organizations (including the Appraisal Foundation and Pan-American Union of Valuation Associations), and four allied organizations. NACAO's objectives are to encourage the flow of information among professional appraisal organizations, to foster an understanding of the problems and duties facing such organizations, to provide a forum where public and private agencies that use appraisal services can express their needs, to promote education and goodwill within the profession, and to develop and promote ethical standards and practice guidelines.

Pan Pacific Congress of Real Estate Appraisers, Valuers, and Counselors. An educational organization which comprises appraisal and counseling organizations from nations bordering the Pacific Ocean. The Pan Pacific Congress was founded in 1957 and its first conference took place in 1959. The Appraisal Institute (formerly the American Institute of Real Estate Appraisers, or AIREA) was a founding member. Sponsoring organizations (1993) include the Appraisal Institute of Canada (AIC); the Australian Institute of Valuers and Land Economists (AIVLE); the Chinese Institute of Land Appraisal; the Counselors of Real Estate (formerly the American Society of Real Estate Counselors, or ASREC); the Indonesian Society of Appraisers; the Institution of Surveyors, Malaysia (ISM); the Japanese Association of Real Estate Appraisal (JAREA); the Korea Appraisal Board (KAB); the New Zealand Institute of Valuers (NZIV); and the Singapore Institute of Surveyors and Valuers. The Institute of Philippine Real Estate Appraisers was a co-sponsoring member in the 1960s and 1970s; Hong Kong and Fiji have also been represented by unofficial groups.

The main objectives of the Pan Pacific Congress are to foster good relations particularly among the members of the Pan Pacific Congress and to promote the exchange of ideas, concepts, and appraisal techniques as well as standards for the profession of real estate appraising, valuing and counseling. Papers on property valuation are featured at Pan Pacific Congress programs held annually in cities of member organizations around the Pacific Rim. The Pan Pacific Congress does not have a permanent headquarters, but information can be obtained by contacting:

Russell Hunter, MAI
P.O. Box 22
Farmington CT 06034
Tel: 203 677-9646

TEGOVA (The European Group of Valuers Associations). Formerly TEGOVOFA (The European Group of Valuers of Fixed Assets) and renamed after its merger with EUROVAL (The European Property Valuers Association) in 1997. TEGOVOFA was established in 1977 for the following purposes: 1) to represent before the European Commission, European Parliament, and other European organisations within the European Union, the united views of asset valuers on matters concerning the valuation of fixed assets for financial statements and related subjects; 2) to recommend asset valuation standards and procedures for adoption throughout the European Union; 3) to promote the need for such valuation standards in the interests of the public and of asset valuers within the European Union; 4) to give guidance to asset valuers on European Union law; and 5) to represent the united view of European asset valuers to international organisations.

Since 1977, TEGOVOFA, whose members include representatives from the land professions of all member states of the European Union and associate members from nine other European countries, has established the only authoritative work of guidance for valuers of fixed assets for financial statements. Known as the *Guide Bleu,* this unique achievement anticipated the ideals of the Single European Act and has been particularly useful as fundamental source material in the creation of new market economies throughout Central and Eastern Europe. TEGOVA and IVSC are collaborating in the preparation and maintenance of updated valuation standards. New, revised European Valuation Standards are expected to be available soon.

Contact:

The Secretary General, TEGOVA
12 Great George Street
London SW1P 3AD
United Kingdom
Tel: +44 171 334 3728
Fax: +44 171 334 3844
e-mail: rel@rics.co.uk

UPAV or Pan-American Union of Valuation Associations/Unión Panamericana de Asociaciones de Valuación. UPAV was founded in Lima, Peru in 1949 and adopted its current name in 1957. The objectives of UPAV are to bring together and encourage exchanges among appraisal practitioners in the Americas; to publicize and promote standards and procedures approved by the Pan-American Congresses of Valuation or otherwise in force in various countries; to work for the improvement of standards and procedures employed in valuation; and to promote professionalism through the observance of an ethical code, technical education, and the passage of laws supportive of appraisers. Each country within UPAV is represented by an active member, but additional observer members from the same country may also be enrolled. For example, the United States is represented by the Appraisal Institute and the American Society of Appraisers is an observer member of UPAV. Included among the member organizations are the Appraisal Institute of Canada (AIC), the Argentine Appraisal Institute (Instituto Argentino de Tasaciones, or IAT), the Brasilian Institute of Valuation and Engineering Expertise (Instituto Brasileiro de Avaliações e Pericias de Engenharia, or IBAPE) the Colombian Society of Appraisers (Sociedad Colombiana de Avaluadores), the National Association of Mexican Valuation Institutes (Asociación Nacional de Institutos Mexicanos de Valuación, A.C.), the Expert Corps of Appraisers of Peru (Cuerpo Técnico de Tasaciones del Perú), the Institute of Appraisers of Puerto Rico (Instituto de Evaluadores de Puerto Rico) and the Society of Valuers of Venezuela (Sociedad de Ingenieros Tasadores de Venezuela [SOITAVE]). UPAV does not have a permanent office, but information can be obtained by contacting:

Larisa Phillips
Appraisal Institute Membership Services Department
875 North Michigan Avenue, Ste. 2400
Chicago, IL 60611-1980

Appendix B

International Economic Organizations and Treaties

Andean Pact. *See* **Latin American Integration Association (LAIA).**

The Asia-Pacific Economic Cooperation Forum (APEC). An organization of 18 members including Australia, Brunei Darussalam, Canada, Chile, China, Indonesia, Hong Kong, Japan, Malaysia, Mexico, New Zealand, Papua New Guinea, the Philippines, Singapore, South Korea, Taiwan, Thailand, and the United States. (Peru and Vietnam have petitioned to join and India and Russia have expressed interest in becoming members.) The goal of APEC is the promotion of economic and trade relations among Asian/Pacific Rim countries, especially through the dismantling of tariffs. Much-publicized APEC summits took place in Seattle in 1993 and Manila in 1996.

Note: The international economic organizations cited here are those that include among their members countries covered in this book. Other important organizations are not referenced, e.g., the Arab League, the Economic Cooperation Organization (ECO), the Nordic Council, and the Organization of Petroleum Exporting Countries (OPEC). Military treaty organizations, active or defunct (e.g., ANZUS, NATO, Warsaw Pact) have also been omitted. It is noteworthy that several international economic organizations are consciously modeled on the Common Market or NAFTA, e.g., APEC with its "Asian Tiger" and Pacific Rim members and LAIA comprising the "Latin American Pumas." For detailed information on these and other international organizations, see *Political Handbook of the World: 1995-1996* (Binghamton, NY: CSA Publications, State University of New York, 1996).

Association of Southeast Asian Nations (ASEAN). An organization formed in 1967 to promote economic, commercial, technical, and scientific cooperation among its six members, all noncommunist states of the region: Brunei Darussalam, Indonesia, Malaysia, Philippines, Singapore, and Thailand. The association's central secretariat is in Jakarta, Indonesia.

Bretton Woods Conference. A conference held in 1944 to address postwar reconstruction and the establishment of an international monetary system. *See also* **General Agreement on Tariffs and Trade (GATT)**, **International Bank for Reconstruction and Development (World Bank)**, and **International Monetary Fund.**

The British Commonwealth of Nations. A free association of independent nations and dependencies that share common ideals, institutions, and traditions based on their inclusion within the former British Empire. Initially comprising the United Kingdom and independent dominions of the former British Empire, i.e., British populated settlements such as Canada and Australia, the Commonwealth began to transform itself with the admission of the Republic of India in 1948. In the past, reciprocal tariff preferences existed between Britain and Commonwealth countries, but GATT has largely reduced the importance of these policies. Commonwealth countries covered in this book include Australia, Canada, India, New Zealand, Singapore, the United Kingdom, and Zimbabwe.

Caribbean Community and Common Market (Caricom). *See* **North American Free Trade Agreement (NAFTA).**

Central American Common Market (CACM). *See* **Latin American Integration Association (LAIA).**

The Common Market. *See* **European Community (EC).**

The Commonwealth of Independent States (CIS). A group formed upon the disbanding of the Soviet Union in December 1991, when 11 of the 12 former Soviet Republics (all but Georgia) joined the Commonwealth of Independent States. (Azerbaijan temporarily withdrew between 1992 and 1993.) This alliance of fully independent states was created for economic cooperation and joint defense. CIS is a free market for ruble-denominated trade (Uzbekistan briefly withdrew from the ruble zone in 1993.) CIS also attempts to monitor the security of former Soviet nuclear installations. In 1993, the effort to establish a joint defense force was abandoned. Within CIS, two "economic communities" are promoting regional economic integration: one between Kazakhstan and Uzbekistan (1994) and the other between Russia and Belarus (1997).

The European Community (EC). Since the ratification of the Maastricht Treaty in November 1993, the European Union (EU) is the collective designation for three organizations: the European Coal and Steel Community, the European Economic

Community (EEC or Common Market), and the European Atomic Energy Community (Euratom). The first of these organizations, the European Coal and Steel Community, was founded in 1951 and originated with an idea from the French statesman, Robert Schuman, to pool the iron resources of French Lorraine with the coal resources of the German Saar. The European Economic Community and European Atomic Energy Community, were subsequently established by the Treaty of Rome in 1957-1958. The European Community resulted from the merger in 1967 of the executive bodies of these three organizations. The EEC's six original members (Belgium, France, Italy, Luxembourg, the Netherlands, and West Germany) were joined in 1973 by Denmark, Ireland, and the United Kingdom; by Greece in 1981; and by Spain and Portugal in 1986. Some 60 nations in Africa, the Caribbean, and the Pacific (known as the the ACP countries) are affiliated under the Lomé Convention (Togo, 1975-1979). *See also* **European Monetary System (EMS), Maastricht Treaty.**

European Free Trade Association (EFTA). Formed in 1960 by six non-Common Market countries (Austria, Iceland, Finland, Norway, Sweden, and Switzerland) to work toward the elimination of custom duties and trade quotas, EFTA entered into a free trade agreement with the European Community in 1973. *See also* **European Community (EC).**

European Monetary System (EMS). A system founded in 1978 to stabilize exchange rates among the currencies of European Community nations (since 1972 the exhange rate of European currencies had been based on the U.S. dollar) and to lay the foundation for a common European currency (the euro). EMS created the European Currency Unit (ECU) as the unit of account or referent for all payments and reserves of EC central banks. The Exchange Rate Mechanism (ERM) keeps fluctuations in exchange rates within the range of 2.25%. In the early 1990s, the United Kingdom and Italy withdrew from the ERM. *See also* **European Community (EC), Maastricht Treaty.**

The French Community (Communauté). Formed in 1958 (and approved as part of the plebisite leading to the establishment of the Fifth Republic), the French Community was formed to link France, overseas French departments and territories (DOM-TOM, Départements d'outre-mer and Territoires d'outre-mer), and former French dependencies and colonies. Upon achieving independence from France, many African countries chose not to join the community, which has been inactive since 1960. France does maintain strong ties with her former colonies in military, economic, technical, and cultural areas.

General Agreement on Tariffs and Trade (GATT). A United Nations- sponsored treaty signed in 1947 to reduce trade barriers. In 1958 a U.N. agency was established in Geneva to promote the settlement of trade disputes (enfringements of copyright and intellectual property rights) and to negotiate trade liberalization. An eighth round of negotiations, held in Urugauy between 1986 and 1993, led to the establishment of the World Trade Organization (WTO) in 1995; the WTO has 122 contracting members, but not all major nations have been admitted to membership as yet, e.g., China.

Group of Three. *See* **Latin American Integration Association (LAIA).**

Group of Seven (G-7). Heads of state of the world's seven major industrial democracies who hold meetings periodically to discuss global economic issues. The group includes Canada, France, Germany, Italy, Japan, the United Kingdom, and the United States. Russia joined the group in 1997.

International Bank for Reconstruction and Development (IBRD). Also known as the World Bank, IBRD was organized as an agency of the United Nations in 1945; originally launched to help finance the reconstruction of Europe and Asia after World War II, the introduction of the Marshall Plan forced the bank to redirect its focus to lending programs for underdeveloped countries. IBRD extends development loans, promotes technical assistance, and encourages cofinancing projects by public and private sources.

International Monetary Fund (IMF). A United Nations agency established in December 1945 on the basis of the Bretton Woods Conference to promote international monetary cooperation, currency exchange stabilization, and the expansion of international trade.

Latin American Free Trade Association (LAFTA). *See* **Latin American Integration Association (LAIA).**

Latin American Integration Association (LAIA). Founded in 1980 as the successor to the Latin American Free Trade Association (LAFTA), an organization formed in 1960 to work toward the establishment of a Latin American common market. In view of the difficulties LAFTA had in dismantling trade barriers, LAIA has set more modest goals and has no timetable. The 11 LAIA members include Argentina, Bolivia, Brazil, Chile, Colombia, Ecuador, Mexico, Paraguay, Peru, Uruguay, and Venezuela. Its headquarters are in Montevideo, Uruguay. A group of five Andean countries (Bolivia, Chile, Colombia, Ecuador, and Peru) agreed in 1969 to begin the process of economic integration. Pledges by the Andean Pact or Ancom countries were made in 1994 to renew activities. In addition to LAIA and the Andean Pact, three other free trade blocs exist in Latin America: 1) Group of Three (Colombia, Mexico, and Venezuela), formed in 1994; 2) Mercosur (Southern Cone Common Market), 1991, whose members include Argentina, Brazil, Paraguay, and Uruguay (Mercosur and Ancom have reciprocity); and 3) Central American Common Market (CACM), 1961, whose members include Costa Rica, El Salvador, Guatemala, Honduras, and Nicaragua.

Maastricht Treaty on European Union. A treaty signed in December 1991 and ratified on November 1, 1993, which resulted in the creation of the European Union (EU). The Maastricht Treaty called for the strengthening of the European Parliament, the establishment of a central bank, the adoption of a common currency (the euro), and the pursuit of common defense policy. *See also* **European Community.**

Marshall Plan (European Recovery Program). *See* **Organization for European Economic Cooperation (OEEC).**

Mercosur. *See* **Latin American Integration Association (LAIA).**

The North American Free Trade Agreement (NAFTA). A treaty concluded by Canada, Mexico, and the United States in December 1992 to eliminate restrictions on the flow of goods, sevices, and investment in North America. NAFTA promotes North American economic integration, providing for full protection of intellectual property rights and including provisions for the settlement of trade disputes. While a free-trade agreement between Canada and the United States had been in effect since 1989, NAFTA has eliminated about half of the tariffs on trade between Mexico and the United States and will phase out all remaining tariffs and restrictions over a 15-year period. The Caribbean Community and Common Market (Caricom) is seeking parity with NAFTA, and Chile has requested admission.

Organization for Economic Cooperation and Development (OECD). An independent organization established in September 1961 to promote the economic and social welfare of member countries, international financial stability, and growth in developing countries. The OECD is the successor to the Organization for European Economic Cooperation (OEEC), which was established in 1947 to allocate Marshall Plan aid and to coordinate reconstruction programs. (The total cost of the Marshall Plan was $13 billion; plan aid was distributed between 1948 and 1951.) OECD members include 28 industrialized, "free-market" countries: Australia, Austria, Belgium, Canada, Czech Republic, Denmark, Finland, France, Germany, Greece, Hungary, Iceland, Ireland, Italy, Japan, Liechtenstein, Luxembourg, Netherlands, New Zealand, Norway, Poland, Portugal, Spain, Sweden, Switzerland, Turkey, the United Kingdom, and the United States. OECD headquarters are in Paris.

Organization of African Unity (OAU). Formed in 1963 by 32 African countries (membership had grown to 50 by 1997) to coordinate economic, political, scientific and cultural policies and to promote a common defense of the independence of its members. OAU has its headquarters in Addis Ababa, Ethiopia.

Organization of American States (OAS). Succesor organization to the Pan-American Union, which was founded in 1890. The 35-member OAS was formed in Bogotá, Columbia in 1948 and its headquarters are in Washington, D.C. The

OAS consists of a Permanent Council; a General Assembly; an Inter-American Economic and Social Council; a Council for Education, Science and Culture; a Juridical Committee; and a Commission on Human Rights. While not excluded from membership, Cuba is suspended from participation in OAS activities.

Pan-American Union. *See* **Organization of American States (OAS).**

The United Nations (UN). For UN agencies, *see* **General Agreement on Tariffs and Trade (GATT), the International Monetary Fund (IMF),** and **International Bank for Reconstruction and Development (IBRD).**

Visegrad Countries. A group consisting of Czechoslovakia (the Czech Republic as successor state since 1993), Hungary, and Poland. Representatives of these three states met in Visegrad, Hungary in February 1991 to coordinate efforts to join the European Community.

World Trade Organization. *See* **General Agreement on Tariffs and Trade (GATT).**

World Bank. *See* **International Bank for Reconstruction and Development (IBRD).**

Appendix C

The International Valuation Standards

The Need for International Valuation Standards

The growth of investment on a global scale brings with it increased demand for internationally accepted standards to ensure the security and enhance the quality of such investment. To address the need for common standards for reporting the value of assets owned or held by multinational corporations and institutional funds, valuation professionals on a technical committee of RICS established The International Assets Valuation Standards Committee (TIAVSC) in 1981. The key objectives of TIAVSC and its members are:

- To develop truly international standards of valuation and reporting that meet the needs of international property markets and the international business community;

- To develop valuation standards that meet the needs of developing and newly industrialized countries and to assist in the introduction and implementation of those standards; and

Note. The material in Appendix C was prepared by Julio E. Torres Coto M., the permanent representative of the *Asociación Nacional de Institutos Mexicanos de Valuación, A.C. (ANIMVAC)* to IVSC and a member of the current board.

- To identify where local or regional standards differ, and to work toward bringing greater compatibility between local or regional requirements and international valuation standards.[1]

  To achieve these objectives, the committee "... will seek to obtain a consensus of opinion from its members to ensure that the standards and guidance notes equate to the best professional practice consistent with practicality and acceptability to business undertakings and the public."[2]

Responsibilities of TIAVSC Members

The members will support the standards and guidance notes published by the committee and endeavor to secure the adoption of these in their states and to ensure that asset valuations related to financial statements conform to the standards and guidance notes. The constitution of TIAVSC further states that members will take appropriate steps to persuade all controlling and regulatory authorities, both statutory and voluntary, as well as societies of other related professions to ensure that published valuation standards comply with the committee's standards and guidance notes. It also sets forth members' obligation to play an educative role within their states in demonstrating the necessity of such standards and guidance notes to professional valuation practice.

Recognizing that there may be national requirements and regulations within the member states that do not conform to TIAVSC standards and procedural guidelines, the committee has suggested that such departures from the International Standards be brought to its attention and to that of interested national bodies.

TIAVSC as a UN Consultative Organization

TIAVSC has gained international recognition through its consultative role vis-a-vis the United Nations Economic and Social Council (since 1985) and the International Accounting Standards Committee (IASC). Between 1981 and 1996, TIAVSC published a series of 13 Guidance Notes and 20 Background Papers on the Valuation of Fixed Assets. These addressed some of the most diverse facets of the subject, including "Classification of Fixed Assets," "Valuation for Security Loans," "The Valuer's Relationship with the Client," and "The Valuer's Relationship with Other Professional Advisers."

---

1. TIAVSC "World Guidelines for Professional Valuers," a pamphlet on the International Valuatuion Standards Committee, TIAVSC, London, 1991
2. TIAVSC Constitution, Preface.

The Guidance Notes and Background Papers have been translated into Spanish and Portuguese and are widely distributed in Mexico and Brazil.

The International Valuation Standards

The current International Valuation Standards were developed in the early 1990s and published in June 1994. They represent a thorough revision of the committee's earlier publications. As stated by Lincoln W. North, the committee's chair at the time, the standards "... reflect the collective thoughts, experiences, and professional judgment of valuers from more than 30 nations."[3] The revised standards were reorganized and updated, but the underlying principles did not change. The earlier standards were revised "... to provide more explicit explanations of the various bases for valuations, to emphasize differences between valuations performed for financial or reporting purposes and those that may be performed under other circumstances, to clarify terms where international misunderstandings could occur, and to provide additional introductory materials designed to foster understanding and to improve application of the standards."[4]

The 1994 edition of the standards contains a preface, an introduction addressing the format of the standards, a chapter on general valuation concepts and principles, and the four International Valuation Standards themselves:

IVS-1 Market Value Basis of Valuation

IVS-2 Valuation Bases Other Than Market Value

IVS-3 Valuation for Financial Statements and Related Accounts

IVS-4 Valuation for Loan Security, Mortgages, and Debentures

The standards cannot attempt to provide a complete discussion of the valuation methodology and practice in all the member states. However, in an effort "... to further understanding among professional disciplines and to lessen the difficulties of language barriers..." each of the standards includes an opening section that describes the general valuation concepts and principles upon which the standard is based. IVS-1 deals with valuations based on market value and includes a definition of market value, the relationship of market valuations to accounting standards, and other matters such as reporting requirements and the characteristics of markets and data. Recognizing the need to use other bases of value according to the different purposes of, and requirements for, valuations, IVS-2 addresses valuation bases other than

---

3. *TIAVSC International Valuation Standards*, IVS 1 Through IVS 4 and Preface to the Standards. Toronto: The International Assets Valuation Standards Committee, 1994
4. Ibid.

market value, e.g., value in use, investment value, going-concern value, insurable value, assessed/rateable value, salvage value, liquidation/forced sale value, and special value. IVS-3 builds on the foundation laid by the first two standards and discusses asset valuations for financial statements, their relationship to accounting standards, and matters such as investment properties, individual versus aggregate utility, present versus future utility, and specialized/limited marketability assets. IVS-4 and future standards will deal with valuation issues common to business activities, but distinct from asset valuations as covered in IVS-3. It was considered necessary to discuss these issues because "... valuation reports such as those for lending, purchase and sale, business valuation and other [purpose]s are sometimes confused with those rendered under IVS-3."[5] The committee decided that by articulating specific Standards for diverse situations, the asset valuation standards would be more readily understood and applied.

Name Change and Activities of IVSC Since 1994

To better reflect the expanded scope of its activities, the committee changed its name in 1994 and is now known as the International Valuation Standards Committee (IVSC).

IVSC has developed Application and Performance Guidelines (APG), including APG 1 "Going Concern Concept of Valuation" and APG 2 "Valuation of Plant, Machinery and Equipment." It is curently studying issues such as the valuation of public sector assets, the valuation of inherited assets, business valuations, and the valuation of intangible assets, which may lead to the development of further standards or APGs.

IVSC has also been active in the field of education, sponsoring seminars and courses on various aspects of valuation in developing countries. Recently the committee participated in the World Valuation Convention held in Warsaw in October 1996. A mock arbitration was staged as part of the convention. In the near future, seminars on valuation practice are to be offered in Central and Eastern Europe, Southeast Asia (Hanoi and Ho Chi Minh City in Vietnam), and Latin America. The establishment of valuers societies in Central and Eastern Europe has been a special priority for the committee.

Although English is the committee's official language and the only authorized version of the standards is the English language version published by IVSC, the standards have to date been translated into Lithuanian, Russian, and Spanish.

---

5. Ibid., 1.

Work with International Professional Organizations

IVSC has a close working relationship with the International Accounting Standards Committee (IASC); the European Group of Valuer Associations (TEGOVA), formerly the European Group of Valuers of Fixed Assets/ TEGOVOFA; the International Federation of Accountants; the International Auditing Practices Committee; and the International Organization of Security Commissions.

IVSC's stated objectives in establishing such liaisons are "... to provide advice and counsel relating to asset valuation to the accounting profession, to coordinate Standards and work programs of related professional disciplines in the public interest, and to cooperate with these and other international bodies in the determination and promulgation of new Standards. These objectives are accomplished through direct liaison and through participation in international organizations such as the United Nations."[6] Since May 1985, IVSC has been listed in the roster of consultative organizations of the United Nations Economic and Social Council.

Membership in IVSC is limited to the most prominent valuation societies or associations in each state represented. On the model of the United Nations, which only recognizes states, each ISVC member state has but one vote. A management board with administrative duties has a secretariat with offices in Toronto and London. The respective addresses of these offices are:

15 Delisle Avenue	12 Great George Street
Toronto, Ontario (M4V 1S8)	London SW1P 3AD
Canada	United Kingdom

The present (1997) chairman is Philippe Malaquin of Paris, France, and the vice-chairman is Greg MacNamara of Hobart, Tasmania, Australia.

The management board meets twice annually, in the spring and fall. IVSC holds its general meeting in the fall, the venues for which are selected by the management board and are as widely varied as is the membership.

Member States and Valuation Societies

The following is a list of members states and valuation societies that belong to ISVC as of April 1997.

---

6. Ibid., 3.

Albania	The Albanian Society of Real Property Valuers
Argentina (proposed)	Instituto Argentino de Tasaciones (IAT)
Australia*	Australian Institute of Valuers and Land Economists (AIVLE)
Belgium	Union Belge des Géomètres
Brazil	Instituto Brasileiro de Avaliçõs e Pericias de Engenheria (IBAPE)
Bulgaria	The Bulgarian Institute of Business Appraisers
Cameroon (observer)	Association Camerounaise des Experts Immobiliers
Canada*	Appraisal Institute of Canada (AIC)
China	China Appraisal Institute
Czech Republic	Czech Chamber of Appraisers
Denmark	Dansk Ejendoms-moeglerforening
Egypt (correspondent)	Mr. Adel Hanafi Hussein
Estonia (observer)	Estonian Association of Appraisers
France*	Chambre des Experts (Fédération Nationale des Agents Immobiliers/FNAIM)
	Institut Française de l'Expertise Immobilière (IFEI)
	Compagnie Nationale des Experts Immobiliers (CNEI)
	Association des Evaluateurs d'Enterprise (AEE)
Germany	Bundesverband der öffentlich bestellten und vereidigten Sachverständiger (BVS)
	Bund der öffentlich bestellten Vermessungs-Ingenieure (BVDI)
	Deutscher Verein für Vermessungswesen (DVW)
Ghana	Ghana Institution of Surveyors
Greece	Body of Sworn-In Valuers of Greece
Hong Kong	Hong Kong Institute of Valuers
Hungary (observer)	Association of Hungarian Appraisers and Financial Analysts

* Indicates this country's delegate is a current member of the management board

Iceland	Icelandic Society of Appraisers
India	The Institution of Surveyors
Indonesia	Indonesian Society of Appraisers (MAPPI)
	Association of Indonesian Appraisal Companies (GAPPI)
Ireland	Society of Chartered Surveyors in the Republic of Ireland
	The Irish Auctioneers and Valuers Institute
Italy	Consiglio Nazionale Geometri
Japan	Japanese Association of Real Estate Appraisal
Kenya (observer)	
Korea	Korea Appraisal Board
Latvia	Latvia Association of Appraisers
Lithuania	Lithuanian Association of Property Valuers
Luxembourg	Institut National de l'Expertise Immobilière
Malawi*	Surveyors Institute of Malawi
Malaysia*	Institute of Surveyors Malaysia
Mexico*	Asociación Nacional de Institutos Mexicanos de Valuación, A.C. (ANIMVAC)
Netherlands	Nederlandse Vereniging van Makelaars in Onroerende Goederen (NVM)
New Zealand*	New Zealand Institute of Valuers
Norway*	Norges Takseringsforund (NTF)
Pakistan (observer)	Sarngati Pakistan Chowk
Poland	The Polish Federation of Valuers' Associations
Romania	The National Association of Romanian Valuers
Russia	Russian Society of Appraisers
Singapore	Singapore Institute of Surveyors and Valuers
South Africa*	South African Institute of Valuers
Spain	Asociación Española de Sociedades de Tasación (Asociación Española de Tasadores y Empresas de Valoración/ATASA)

* Indicates this country's delegate is a current member of the management board

Sweden	The Swedish Association of Real Estate Economists (SFF)
Switzerland	Schätzungsexperten-Kammer (SVIT)
	Chambre d'Experts en Valuations Immobilierès (USPI)
Trinidad and Tobago	Association of Professional Valuation and Land Economy Surveyors of Trinidad and Tobago
Ukraine	Ukrainian Society of Appraisers
United Kingdom*	Royal Institution of Chartered Surveyors (RICS)
	Incorporated Society of Valuers and Auctioners (ISVA)
United States*	The Appraisal Institute
	American Society of Appraisers
Venezuela (proposed)	Sociedad de Ingenieros Tasadores de Venezuela (SOITAVE)
Zambia	The Surveyors Institute of Zambia
Zimbabwe (observer)	

* Indicates this country's delegate is a current member of the management board

Glossary

accommodation. In British and Commonwealth usage, the composition of a property in terms of lettable (leasable) area, floors, and the number of finished/unfinished rooms or rooms for specific functions (bedrooms, bathrooms).

accounts method. *See* **profits method.**

(French) **acte.** French term for deed.

Note. *The Glossary of Property Terms* (1989/1990), compiled by Jones Lang Wootton in association with The Estates Gazette Limited and South Bank Polytechnic, is an especially useful source on valuation terminology in the United Kingdom. *The Multilingual Dictionary of Real Estate: A Guide for the Property Professional in the Single European Market* (1993), edited by L. van Breugel, B. Wood, and R. Williams and published by E & FN Spon, an imprint of Chapman and Hall, provides the equivalents of more than 1,150 real estate terms in British English, German, Spanish, French, Italian, and Dutch. Many of the French and German terms appearing in this glossary were taken from 1981 translations of the seventh edition of *The Appraisal of Real Estate,* undertaken by the Association for Professional Real Estate Publishing in Geneva, Switzerland. A useful source for Spanish (Latin American) to English terminology is Santiago Briceño's *Terminologia de Valuacion de Bienes Inmuebles,* sponsored by the Pan-American Union of Valuation Associations (UPAV) and the Society of Valuers of Venezuela (SOTAVE) in Caracas (1979). The Japanese terms in this glossary are those used in the 1995 Japanese translation of *The Appraisal of Real Estate,* done by the Japanese Real Estate Institute. Excellent Romanji guides to Japanese are published by Charles E. Tuttle Co. (Rutland, Vt. and Tokyo)—*Tuttle Dictionary of Legal Terms* (Richard S. Keirstead, 1993) and *Japanese Business Dictionary* (Boye Lafayette de Menthe, 1991)—and by Kodansha International (Tokyo, New York, and London)—*Kodansha's Romanized Japanese-English Dictionary* (Timothy J. Vance, 1993).

(French)   **actifs immobiliers.** French term for building assets. (Note: The terms actif and passif come from accounting, i.e., actifs are assets and passifs are liabilities and equities.)

(Spanish)   **activos fijos.** Spanish term for fixed assets.

alienation. In British and Commonwealth usage, the right to transfer title to property.

all risks yield (ARY). The remuneration rate of interest used in appraisal to reflect prospects and risks (*RICS Appraisal and Valuation Manual*, Guidance Note 4.7.2, London, 1996). In British and Commonwealth usage, all risks yield is the overall capitalization rate applied in direct capitalization; the reversion yield is a terminal capitalization rate.

alternative use value. In British and Commonwealth usage, the value of a property under a potential alternative use; required when the estimate of market value under the existing use differs substantially from what could be obtained for the vacant possession sale of the property. *See also* **existing use value, open market value.**

appraiser. A valuer. Foreign language equivalents are: évaluateur, expert, kanteishi, otsenshchik, valuador. *See also* **assessor, surveyor.**

(Russian)   **arenda.** Russian word for lease. *See also* **pravo arendi.**

(Spanish)   **arrendamiento.** Spanish term for rent.

articling. In British and Commonwealth usage, an apprenticeship.

artificial or "fictitious" person. A legal entity such as a partnership or corporation, in contrast to a natural person. *See also* **legal entity.**

assessor. A fiscal official who values real property for purposes of ad valorem taxation. *See also* **rateable value, rates/rating, tasador, taxateur.**

auctioneer. A person who sells property at public auctions, typically in cases of repossession for default or insolvency.

(Spanish)   **avaluador.** *See* valuador.

(Spanish)   **avalúo comercial.** A term used in many Latin American countries for a market value appraisal; literally, commercial appraisal. *See also* **commercial value.**

averaging of value indications. The practice of using the average of the different indications derived from multiple approaches to value; discouraged or enjoined by many organizations, but employed in some countries.

(French)   **bail** (plural **baux**). French term for lease.

barrister. In British and Commonwealth usage, a lawyer who has the right to speak and argue as an advocate in higher courts of law. *See also* **solicitor.**

(German) **Barwertkalkulationen.** German term equivalent to discounted cash flow analysis.

(Spanish) **base impositiva.** Spanish term for assessment base or property tax base.

basis of valuation. In British and Commonwealth usage, the defined value, which may or may not be based on the highest and best use of the property, e.g., open market value, existing use value, alternative use value.

(German) **Bebauungsplan.** German term for development plan. (*Bau* is the word for building.) *See also* **Flächennutzungsplan.**

(German) **Beleihungswert.** German term for loan value.

BEMs. An acronym for big emerging markets, e.g., Argentina, Brazil, China, India, Indonesia, Mexico, Poland, South Africa, South Korea, and Turkey; usage from the U.S. Commerce Department. *See also* **NICs.**

(German) **Beteiligungsklauseln.** German term for participation or percentage rent (lease) clause.

(German) **Bewertung.** German term for valuation or assessment. *See also* **Schätzung.**

(Spanish) **bienes forales.** Spanish term for leasehold estate; generally the leasehold interest in the land upon which the tenant builds improvements, which the tenant owns until the expiration of the lease. (The adjective foral is from the noun fuero, which means a charter/statute/code of laws or an exemption/privilege). *See also* **derecho de arrendamiento, propiedad alquilada.**

(Spanish) **bienes raices.** Spanish term for real estate. *See also* **immovable property, propiedad raíz.**

(French) **bien(s) fonds.** French term equivalent to real estate or landed property. *See also* **immovable property, propriéte foncière.**

block. In North American usage, an area bounded by four streets; in British and continental usage, a building complex in which residential, retail, and office units are located.

(German) **Bodenrichtwertkarte.** Standard land value map compiled by German appraiser committees from all the property sales in a locality.

bourse. Stock exchange. The term has been adapted by many European langauges: bourse (des valeurs) in French, (Wertpapier) börse in German, borsa in Italian, (fondovaya) birzha in Russian, bolsa in Spanish.

broker. An agent who negotiates a sale and/or purchase transaction. *See also* **courtier, estate agent, Makler.**

(German) **Bruttoeinkommen.** German term for gross income.

bundle of rights. A concept originating in common law that describes the rights inherent in the ownership of real estate, which may either be kept intact or separated and transferred. The bundle of rights is analogous to a bundle of sticks with each stick representing a right to do something with the property, e.g., to use it, to sell it, to lease it, to bequeath or give it away, to control its use (e.g., restrictive covenents), or to grant easements for entry and egress (e.g., rights-of-way). For a discussion of the bundle of rights concept in Latin American countries with a tradition of Roman law, see Chapter 18—Mexico.

(Japanese) **bunjō manshon.** Japanese term equivalent to condominium property (not the legal estate).

business cycle. *See* **conjuncture.**

cadastre. A land registry or official register for survey and ownership data and property value. Compare cadestre in French; catasto in Italian; catastro in Spanish; Kataster in Czech, German, and Polish; and Kadastr in Russian.

capital gains tax. A tax on the gain accruing to a taxpayer through the sale of a capital asset. In the United States, capital gains were taxed as ordinary income between 1986 and 1997, but are now subject to reduced tax rates. In the United Kingdom, capital gains are payable on all realized property gains except those from a principal residence.

capitalization factor. A factor used to adjust a value indication derived by the income approach for the effect of inflation on value. The capitalization factor applied is a function of the length of time required to recover the capital investment, the rate of inflation, the reinvestment rate, and the periodicity at which the flow of income is modified (i.e., increased). The Spanish term is factor de capitalización.

capitalization in perpetuity. *See* **present value of £1 in perpetuity, year's purchase in perpetuity.**

capitalization rate. Any rate used to convert an income stream into value, e.g., overall capitalization rate (all risks yield), building or land capitalization rate, equity capitalization rate, or discount rate. Foreign language equivalents are: Diskontsatz, Gesamtrate, global rate, kangen rimawari, tasa de descuento, taux d'escompte. *See also* **income multiplier.**

(Spanish) **capital propio.** Spanish term equivalent to equity capital. *See also* **fondos propios.**

(French) **capital social.** A French term equivalent to equity capital. (Note: Social refers to the société or firm, not society at large.) *See also* **fonds propres.**

capital value. In British and Commonwealth usage, the value of an asset as distinct from its annual or periodic value, i.e., its rental value. The concept is integral to the profits method. See Chapters 4 and 5—Australia and New Zealand.

capital value band. *See* **council rate/tax.**

caravan park. In British and Commonwealth usage, a trailer park.

(Japanese)   **chin-ryō.** Japanese term for rent or rental amount; kariru is the verb "to rent."

(Japanese)   **chinshaku ken tsuki shoyū ken.** Japanese term for leased fee estate.

(Japanese)   **chintai keiyaku.** Japanese term for lease; chintai pertains to rental, keiyaku means contract; alternative terms are shakuyu shōsho and riisu (apāto riisu). *See also* **shōsho.**

(Japanese)   **choh.** Japanese unit of measurement. One choh equals approximately 9,900 square meters or 106,500 square feet.

(Spanish)   **colegio.** Spanish term for professional association.

command economy. A centrally planned economy that is primarily responsive to the directives of the planning body rather than the forces of supply and demand, as in a market economy. A command economy is generally associated with state ownership of industrial enterprises, agricultural land, and banking.

commercialization factor. A factor used in Mexico to adjust a value indication derived by the cost approach for the effect of the special location or desirability of a property; in Spanish, factor de comercialización.

commercial value. A term used in many Latin American countries as the equivalent of market value; in Spanish, valor comercial. *See also* **avalúo comercial.**

common law. System of law that evolved in England based on legal precedents; differs from Roman law or law codes derived from Roman law, e.g., the Napoleonic Code. For insight into the adoption of common law in the United States, see Herbert Pope, "The English Common Law in the United States," *Harvard Law Review,* vol. XXIV (1910-1911). *See also* **bundle of rights.**

common law or old systems title. The term used in Australia for a system of land registry based on the principle that title is established in deeds. *See also* **registry system, Torrens system.**

comparison approach. *See* **sales comparison approach.**

compulsory acquisition. In British and Commonwealth usage, the exercise of eminent domain upon payment of just compensation. *See also* **injurious affection, severance.**

compulsory purchase. In British and Commonwealth usage, the exercise of eminent domain upon payment of just compensation; a taking.

(Italian/ Spanish)   **condominio.** The term for condominium in Italian and Spanish.

condominium. Shared ownership of a freehold, such as a unit in an apartment block (building); includes both the individual unit and a proportionate share of common areas. Foreign language equivalents are: bunjō manshon, condominio, copropriété, flying freehold, propiedad horizontal, propiedad por pisos, strata title, Wohnungseigentum.

conjuncture. The term in many European languages for market conditions, the current phase in the business/trade cycle, or the economic outlook. Compare conjoncture in French, Konjunktur in German, congiuntura in Italian, konjunktura in Czech and Polish, kon'yunktura in Russian, and coyuntura in Spanish. Keiki is the Japanese equivalent.

consumer price index (CPI). A measure of the cost of living and inflation based on the price of a fixed market basket of goods and services as a percentage of the price of the same goods and services in some base period; used in North America and Australia. (There are other important measures of inflation, e.g., the Wholesale or Producer Price Index and Employment Cost Index.) In the United Kingdom, the retail price index (RPI) is used and in Latin America, the indice de precios al consumidor/consumo (IPO). *See also* **Lebenshaltungskostenindex.**

contractor's test method. *See* **cost approach.**

contract rent. In North American usage, the rent specified in the lease contract; passing rent in Britian and the Commonwealth. Foreign language equivalents are: derzeitige Miete, loyer contractuel, renta de contrato.

(Spanish) **contrato de alquiler.** A Spanish term for lease. *See also* **contrato de arrendamiento.**

(Spanish) **contrato de alquiler de terreno.** Spanish term for land lease.

(Spanish) **contrato de arrendamiento.** A Spanish term for lease. *See also* **contrato de alquiler.**

(Spanish) **copropiedad.** Spanish term referring to the ownership of a condominium unit; joint ownership.

(French) **copropriété.** French term equivalent to fee simple ownership of a condominium.

cost approach. A valuation procedure in which a property value estimate is derived by estimating the current cost to construct a property, deducting an estimate of depreciation, and adding the cost of land and entrepreneurial profit; called the contractor's or contractor's test method (in Britian and Commonwealth countries) or the summation approach. Foreign language equivalents are: enfoque de costo, genka hō, méthode de détermination de la valeur intrinsèque, Sachwertverfahren, valor fisico o directo.

(Spanish) **costo de reemplazo.** Spanish term for replacement cost.

council rate/tax. Municipal or county assessor's tax in British and Commonwealth usage; applied in the United Kingdom and based on the capital value band in which the property is placed.

county planning scheme. *See* town planning scheme.

(French) **courtage/courtier.** French term for brokerage/broker; equivalent terms are kurtaż in Polish and kurta<u>zh</u> in Russian.

court of first instance/second instance. *See* **first instance, court of; second instance, court of.**

covenant. A binding agreement setting forth the obligations of the subscribing parties, e.g., a lease specifying the obligations of the landlord and tenant. In British and Commonwealth usage, the term may refer to the character or ability of a tenant to comply with the terms and conditions of the lease, and the word is often used in descriptive phrases such as "tenant in good covenant" (tenant in good standing), "covenant strength" (creditworthiness), and "covenant value" (a component of value attributable to a creditworthy tenant).

(Indian) **crore.** Indian unit of monetary measurement equivalent to 10 million rupees; written as Rs <u>1</u>,00,00,000.00. *See also* **lakh.**

the Crown. The sovereign ruler. In Britain, Australia, and New Zealand, all lands are theoretically vested in the Crown and held under tenure from the Crown. Equivalent to state as used in North America.

current cost accounting basis. Accounting concept that states the value of fixed assets held by a business in terms of their current, rather than historic, costs.

(German) **Dauernutzungsrecht.** German term equivalent to long-term lease.

deed. A written legal instrument that conveys an estate or interest in real property when it is executed and delivered. Foreign language equivalents are: acte, escritura, shōsho, Übertragungsurkunde. *See also* **common law or old systems title, registry system, Torrens system.**

demised premises. In British and Commonwealth usage, leased space.

depreciated replacement cost (DRC). In the United Kingdom and Commonwealth countries, a method of valuing properties with unusual physical or locational characteristics for which comparable data do not exist. An estimate of the market value of the land under the existing use is developed, to which an estimate of replacement cost new is added, and from which an estimate of depreciation is deducted. For a complete definition, see *RICS Appraisal and Valuation Manual,* Practice Statement 4.8 and 4.82, 1995. *See also* **cost approach.**

(Indian) **depreciation value.** In India, the amount by which the value (cost new) of a property has been reduced by depreciation. *See also* **depreciated replacement cost.**

(Spanish)   **derecho de arrendamiento.** A Spanish term for leasehold estate. *See also* **bienes forales.**

(Spanish)   **derecho sobre dominio alquilado.** A Spanish term for leased fee estate. *See also* **dominio alquilado.**

(German)   **derzeitige Miete.** German term for contract rent. *See also* **vertraglicher Mietbeziehungsweise Pachtzins.**

developer's test or development approach. A type of income capitalization recognized as a separate method in the United Kingdom and Commonwealth. *See also* **income capitalization approach.**

direct capitalization. *See* **income capitalization**.

direct comparison approach. *See* **sales comparison approach.**

(German)   **Diskontsatz.** German term for discount rate.

distrainable. *See* **distraint.**

distraint. The seizure or appropriation of property to pay off a debt or obligation.

(Spanish)   **dominio.** Spanish term for ownership.

(Spanish)   **dominio absoluto** or **pleno dominio.** Spanish terms for fee simple.

(Spanish)   **dominio alquilado.** Spanish term for leased fee. *See also* **derecho sobre dominio alquilado.**

(French)   **droits au bail.** French term equivalent to leasehold estate (position du locataire). *See also* **locataire, tenure à bail.**

(French)   **droits de propriété de la chose soumise à bail.** French term equivalent to leased fee estate (position du propriétaire). *See also* **propriétaire.**

dual rate method. A method for valuing terminable income streams, e.g., rents, in Britain and the Commonwealth. Part of the net income is set aside to be reinvested in a sinking fund at a rate that ensures recapture of the initial capital outlay; the remainder is capitalised at an appropriate rate of return. *See also* **income capitalization approach.**

(Polish)   **dzierżawa.** Polish term for a lease or leasehold interest.

(Indian)   **earning value.** In India, the present value of a property that will yield future income; also called investment value.

economic rent. A traditional term for market rent. Foreign language equivalents are: loyer economique, renta economica, wirtschaftlicher Mietbeziehungsweise Pachtzins.

(German)   **Eigenkapital.** German term for equity capital.

(German)   **Eigentum.** German term for property, equivalent to fee simple.

(German)   **Einheitswert.** German term for assessed value.

(Spanish)   **ejido.** In Mexico, public or communal land cultivated collectively by the inhabitants of a village. Under the Constitution of 1917, ejido lands could not be transferred or appropriated to pay off debt. A 1993 amendment and more recent Agrarian Reform Law allow individual ownership of ejido lands, and even make it possible to mortgage or sell individual parcels.

emerging markets. *See* **BEMs.**

eminent domain. The right of government to appropriate private property for public use; equivalent to compulsory acquisition in British and Commonwealth usage.

(French)   **emplacement.** French term for siting or location.

(Spanish)   **encomienda.** A land grant in Spanish New World colonies and the Philippines; literally, a trusteeship or commission. The encomendero (grantee) was charged with judicial functions and the collection of taxes and rents from the native or mestizo laborers attached to the grant.

encumbrance. A debt or charge legally secured to property; also, an easement, restrictive covenant, or right-of-way.

(Spanish)   **enfoque de costo.** Spanish term for the cost approach.

(Spanish)   **enfoque de ingresos/rentas.** Spanish term for the income approach.

(Spanish)   **enfoque de la comparación de ventas.** Spanish term for sales comparison approach.

English system. In North America, the pound-foot system of measurement; called the imperial system in the United Kingdom and Commonwealth.

(French)   **épargne immobilière et foncière.** French term for savings and loan institution.

epitome of leases. Lease summaries in British and Commonwealth usage.

equated or **equivalent yield.** British and Commonwealth term for the internal rate of return. In New Zealand, the calculation of an annuity.

equitable interest. In British and Commonwealth usage, a third party right in or charge against a property, e.g., restrictive covenants, easements, or mortgages.

equity. The ownership claim on property; total property value less all debt claims and liens against the property. *See also* **Eigenkapital, fondos propios, fonds propres** or **fonds du tiers, mochibun.**

(German)   **Erbbaurecht.** German term for an estate similar to a leasehold; literally, hereditary building right.

(German)   **Ertragswertverfahren.** German term for the income approach.

escheat. The reversion to the state of property left by a person who dies intestate, i.e., with no designated heirs.

(Spanish) **escritura.** The Spanish term for deed.

estate agent. Real estate broker in British and Commonwealth usage.

estimated realisation price (ERP). The anticipated resale price of a property before the deduction of selling costs. For a complete definition, see *RICS Appraisal and Valuation Manual,* Practice Statement 4.5, 1995. *See also* **prospective value.**

(French) **évaluateur.** French Canadian term for appraiser.

existing use value. In British and Commonwealth usage, the value of a property under its current use (as currently improved). Properties considered essential to the operations or activities of the corporation or company that owns them are valued under the existing use. *See also* **alternative use value, open market value**

expense pass-alongs, expense pass-throughs, expense recoveries. Lease provisions that allow increases in operating expenses to be assumed by the tenants.

expert. Connotes a valuer or appraiser in many European languages, e.g., expert in French, esperto in Italian, experto in Spanish, Gutachter or Sachverständige in German, znalec in Czech, and rzeczoznawca in Polish.

(French) **expertisse.** French term for appraisal.

(Spanish) **factor de capitalización.** *See* **capitalization factor.**

(Spanish) **factor de comercialización.** *See* **commercialization factor.**

fair market value. *See* **market value.**

(Indian) **fancy value.** In India, the price a purchaser is prepared to pay for a property that he or she absolutely must have; also called desired value.

fee simple absolute/estate. The highest form of property ownership, unencumbered by any other interest or estate, subject only to the four powers of government; also called freehold title. Foreign language equivalents are: dominio absoluto, Eigentum, pravo chastoi sobstvennosti, tanjun fudōsan ken, toute propriété, vlastnictví, własność.

finish. *See* tenant finish.

first instance, court of. A trial court with original jurisdiction over a case. *See also* **second instance, court of.**

first refusal. *See* **right of first refusal**.

fitout. Tenant finish in British and Commonwealth usage.

five-method paradigm. The five methods of valuation, recognized as distinct appraisal approaches in the United Kingdom and Commonwealth countries; includes the direct comparison, cost, income, profits, and residual or development methods. These methods are discussed at length in Chapters 2 and 4—United Kingdom and Australia. *See also* **three-approach paradigm.**

(German) **Flächennutzungsplan.** German term for development or zoning plan. *See also* **Bebauungsplan.**

flat. An apartment unit in British and Commonwealth usage.

(Spanish) **flujo de caja.** Spanish term for cash flow.

flying freehold. British term similar to the American term, condominium; can also describe ownership of the air space over another freehold.

(Spanish) **fondo fiduciario de inversion en bienes raices.** Spanish term for real estate investment trust.

(Spanish) **fondos propios.** Spanish term for equity. *See also* **capital propio.**

(French) **fonds propres** or **fonds du tiers.** French terms for equity (Note: Du tiers refers to the "third part" on an accounting sheet—after assets and debentures). *See also* **capital social.**

foot-pound system. *See* **imperial system.**

freehold. Fee simple absolute.

freeholder. Owner of the fee simple estate.

(Japanese) **fudōsan.** Japanese term for real estate.

(Spanish) **ganancia(s).** Spanish term for profit or gain; sometimes used interchangeably with renta.

(Spanish) **ganancias reales.** Spanish term for net profit or income; used in Mexico.

(Spanish) **gastos de operación.** Spanish term for operating expenses.

(Japanese) **genka hō.** Japanese term for cost approach. (Genka means cost price and kenchiku genka is building cost.)

(Japanese) **gentei kakaku.** Japanese term for limited market value; applicable when a building owner purchases the site upon which the building stands or when two or more sites are combined (plottage).

geometer/geometry. A term used in many European languages for land surveyor/surveying, e.g., expert géometrè in French, geometra in Italian. *See also* **surveyor.**

(German) **Gesamtrate.** German term equivalent to overall capitalization rate

Glasgow lease. In British and Commonwealth usage, a perpetually renewable ground lease, usually with fixed rental, which gives the lessee priority to renew the lease; used in New Zealand.

global rate. An overall capitalization rate; in French and Spanish, taux global and tasa global.

Gordon (constant) growth model. A model developed and popularized by Myron J. Gordon in the 1960s for the analysis and valuation of financial securities; sometimes used for valuing commercial property. By incorporating an expected constant growth component, the Gordon growth model allows alternative investments to be compared directly. For further discussion, see *The Appraisal Journal* (January 1994) and Chapters 2 and 14—United Kingdom and Japan.

gross external area (GEA). In British and Commonwealth usage, the aggregate surface area of a building, including each floor. According to the RICS/ISVA Code of Measuring Practice, GEA includes external walls and projections; internal walls and partitions; columns, piers, stairwells, and lift wells (elevator shafts); tank and plant rooms; fuel storage areas; and enclosed parking areas. Excluded are open balconies, open fire escapes, open parking areas, terraces, and coalhouses.

gross floor area. *See* **gross external area**.

gross internal area (GIA). Similar to gross external area, except that the measurements are made to the internal face of the perimeter walls at each floor level. In the United Kingdom, GIA is used for industrial buildings, warehouses, supermarkets, and department or variety stores. *See also* **net internal area**.

(Indian) **ground.** A unit of measure used in India; equivalent to 223 m^2 or 2,400 sq. ft.

ground lease. The lease to the land on which tenant-owned buildings stand; typically long-term.

(German) **Grundstück.** A German term for a site or land parcel; may be used for real estate or landed property. *See also* **immovable property, Liegenschaften**.

(Indian) **guideline value.** In India, the value of a parcel of land as recorded in the local registrar's office and used to determine stamp duty when property transfer documents are registered.

(German) **Gutachter.** German term for appraiser; literally, one who opines a value for goods or property.

hard core method. A method used in the United Kingdom in which open market rent is directly capitalized and the resultant value is then adjusted for passing or contract rents above or below market levels; also known as the layer or hard core and top slice method. The hard core method is considered one of the three variations of direct capitalization. For examples, see Chapter 2 (United Kingdom) and the appendix to Chapter 4 (Australia). *See also* **income capitalization approach**.

hoarding rental. In British and Commonwealth usage, the rent paid for a billboard.

(Spanish)   **honorio(s) de gerencia de los negocios.** Spanish term for leasing commission(s).

(Thai)   **hope value.** In Thailand, the enhancement in the value of a property anticipated under a specific use, which may or may not come to fruition.

(Japanese)   **hoshō kin.** In Japan, earnest money equal to several months' to several years' rent; the amount is refundable.

(Greek)   **hypotheke.** Greek word meaning "pledge," which is the root of the word for mortgage in most European languages, i.e., hypotéka in Czech, hypothèque in French, Hypothek in German, ipoteca in Italian, hipoteka in Polish, ipoteka in Russian, and hipoteca in Spanish.

immovable property. The term used for real estate in many European languages—e.g., nemovitost in Czech, immoblier in French, Immobilien in German, bene immobiliare in Italian, nieruchomosci in Polish, nedvizhemoe imushchestvo in Russian, and bienes inmuebles in Spanish. *See also* **movable property.**

imperial system of measurement. The system of weights and measures (e.g., pounds, feet, yards, miles, acres) formerly used in the United Kingdom; replaced with the metric system to facilitate Britian's entry into the European Community. Although many Commonwealth countries no longer use the imperial system, elements of the system are still used in the United States, where it is called the English system or foot-pound system.

(Italian)   **imposta communale sugli immobilia (ICI).** Italian term for the annual tax on the value of real estate paid by the owner; not a tax on real estate income.

imprescriptible. *See* **prescription.**

income capitalization/capitalisation approach or investment approach. Approach to value which includes direct capitalization and discounted cash flow techniques. British and Commonwealth valuers distinguish three variations of direct capitalization, depending on the treatment of income: term and reversion, hard core or layer, and shortfall methods. (See the appendix to Chapter 4 for examples.) Income capitalization may also be performed by means of a single rate or a dual rate method (see separate entry). The profits method and development or residual method are related techniques that are generally recognized as separate methods in the United Kingdom and Commonwealth. Foreign language equivalents are: enfoque de ingresos/rentas, Ertragswertverfahren, méthode du revenu prévisionnel, shū-eki kangen hō.

income multiplier. The ratio between the sale price or value of a property and the average annual income or income expectancy; may be based on potential gross, effective gross, or net operating income. The multiplier is called year's purchase in British and Commonwealth usage, multiplicateur in French, Multiplikator in German, and multiplicador in Spanish.

indefeasible title. Absolute title which cannot be annulled, voided, or undone by any condition. *See* **Torrens system**.

(Spanish) **indice de precios al consumidor/consumo (IPO).** Spanish term for consumer/retail price index.

injurious affection. In British and Commonwealth usage, the diminution in value of an interest in land resulting from the exercise of statutory powers, i.e., eminent domain. *See also* **compulsory acquisition, severance**.

(Spanish) **inquilino.** Spanish term for tenant.

in terms of main space (I/T/MS). *See* **unit value method**.

international company. A company that produces goods in one country to be distributed in another country. *See also* **multinational company**.

intestacy. Dying without leaving a valid will. *See also* **escheat**.

(Spanish) **inversion(es).** Spanish term for investment(s).

(German) **Investitionswert.** German term for investment value.

investment method. A method of estimating land value by capitalizing the ground rent, often by applying a multiplier (year's purchase); an income capitalization technique used in Britian and Commonwealth countries.

investment property. A property purchased with the intention of enjoying the income and/or capital appreciation over the holding period; in the United Kingdom, an investment property that is extraneous to the operational requirements of the corporate owner and is valued at current open market value; also called a surplus property. *See also* **existing use value, open market value**.

investment value. The specific value of an investment to a particular investor or class of investors based on individual investment objectives; distinguished from market value, which is impersonal and objective. Foreign language equivalents are: Investitionswert, valuer d'investissement, valor subjectivo.

(Japanese) **joh.** Japanese unit of measurement equal to approximately 1.65 square meters or 17.75 square feet.

just compensation. In condemnation, the amount of loss for which a property owner is compensated when his or her property is taken; generally (but not necessarily) held to equal market value. *See also* **compulsory purchase**.

(Japanese) **kakaku.** Japanese term for value or price paid. *See also* **gentei kakaku, seijō kakaku, tokutei kakaku**.

(Japanese) **kangen rimawari.** Japanese term for capitalization rate. Sōgō kangen rimawari is overall capitalization rate; warikubi ritsu is discount rate.

(Japanese)   **kantei.** Japanese term for appraisal; alternative terms are hyōka and kantei hyōka.

(Japanese)   **kanteishi.** Japanese term for appraiser. Fudōsan kanteishi is a licensed real estate appraiser, and fudōsan kanteishi ho is a licensed assistant real estate appraiser.

(German)   **Kapitalisierungsrate** or **Kapitalisierungssatz.** German terms for capitalization rate.

(Japanese)   **kenri kin.** In Japan, key money equal to two months' to six months' rent; the amount is nonrefundable.

key money. Payment made by an incoming tenant to the landlord; a type of security deposit. *See also* **kenri kin.**

(Japanese)   **kin.** The Japanese word for gold; used for a monetary payment or deposit. *See also* **hoshō kin, kenri kin, shiki kin.**

(Indian)   **lakh.** Indian monetary unit equivalent to one hundred thousand rupees, written as Rs 1,00,000.00; used together with the crore.

landed property. Unimproved land, either vacant or under agricultural use. *See also* **Gründstuck, propriété foncière, tochi, zemlevladeniye.**

land residual technique. In Russian usage, the development approach in which land value is calculated as anticipated sales proceeds, less the direct and indirect costs of development, less entrepreneurial incentive. *See also* **residual method.**

land title system. A Canadian system for registering title documents modeled after the Torrens system.

latifundi(um ia). Large landed estate(s); latifundio(s) in Spanish.

layer method. *See* **hard core method.**

lease. As a verb, to transfer the rights of use and occupancy to another party by means of a lease contract; to let in British and Commonwealth usage. As a noun, the term refers to the contract specifying the terms and conditions of this arrangement. Foreign language equivalents are: arenda, bail, chintai keiyaku, contrato de aquiler, Mietvertrag, najem, Pacht(vertrag). *See also* **sublease/sublet.**

leased fee estate. An estate in property in which some rights, such as the rights to use and occupancy, have been transferred to another by means of a lease. The landlord, or lessor, is the possessor of the leased fee estate. Foreign language equivalents are: chinshaku ken tsuki shoyū ken, Dauernutzungsrecht, derecho sobre dominio aquilado, droits de propriété de la chose soumise à bail, vladeniye nedvizhimim imushchestvom, vzyatim v arendu.

leasehold estate. The interest in property held by the tenant (lessee or renter) through a lease transferring the rights of use and occupancy for a stated term under certain conditions. Foreign language equivalents are: derecho arrendamiento, droits au bail, dzierżawa, Erbbaurecht, pravo arendi, shakuchi ken.

lease structure. The terms, conditions, and provisions that characterize lease contracts.

leasing commissions. Fees paid to an agent for leasing tenant space; may be paid at the inception of the lease or spread over the term of the lease or lease renewal.

(German) **Lebenshaltungskostenindex.** German term for cost of living index; used for indexing leases in other central European countries, e.g., the Czech Republic.

legal entity. An artificial or fictitious being that is considered under law to possess a separate existence, generally for tax purposes. *See also* **artificial person, natural person.**

let. *See* **lease.**

licensed premises. In British and Commonwealth usage, a property such as a pub or restaurant where alcoholic drinks are sold.

(German) **Liegenschaften.** A German term for real estate or landed property. *See also* **Grundstück, immovable property.**

(French) **locataire.** French term for tenant or lessee.

(Spanish) **lonja.** Spanish term for public exchange building. In Colombia, lonja refers to a real estate board.

(French) **loyer contractuel** or **loyer en cours.** French terms equivalent to contract rent (or passing rent in British and Commonwealth usage).

(French) **loyer économique.** French term for market rent.

(Czech/Polish) **majetek/majątek.** Czech/Polish term for property; from the Slavic verb, mít/ miec: to have, possess, or own. *See also* **immovable property.**

(German) **Makler.** The German word for broker; the same or similar terms are used in several other European languages: makelaar in Dutch, moegler in Danish, makler in Czech and Polish, and maklyer in Russian.

market economy. An economy that operates through free competition among producers and retailers, with consumer behavior reflecting individual preferences and purchasing power; as opposed to a command economy.

market rent. The rental income a property would most likely command in the open market (open market rent). *See also* **economic rent.**

market value. "The estimated amount for which an asset [property] should exchange on the date of valuation between a willing buyer and a willing seller in an arm's-length transaction after proper marketing wherein the parties had each acted knowledgeably, prudently, and without compulsion." (IVSC). Foreign language equivalents are: Marktswert, rino<u>ch</u>naya stoimost', seijō kakaku, valeur vénale, valor de mercado, valor venal, Verkehrswert. *See also* **alternative use value, existing use value, investment value, open market value.**

(German)   **Marktmiete.** German term for market rent. *See also* **wirtschaftlicher Mietbeziehungsweise Pachtzins.**

(German)   **Marktwert.** German term for market value. *See also* **Verkehrswert.**

(Thai)   **marriage value.** The enhancement in property value that results from assemblage or merger with other assets (land or buildings) or the combination of individual interests in the same asset (the right of occupancy); used in Britain, the Commonwealth, and Thailand. In North American usage, plottage may be considered a specific example of marriage value.

(Spanish)   **mejora(s).** Spanish term for improvement(s).

memorial. In British or Commonwealth usage, a written statement of facts sent to authorities in support of a petition, remonstrance, or protest.

(French)   **méthode de détermination de la valeur intrinsèque.** French term for the cost approach.

(French)   **méthode des données du marché.** French term for the sales comparison approach.

(French)   **méthode du revenu prévisionnel.** French term for the income capitalization approach.

metrication. Conversion to the metric system.

metric system. A decimal system of weights and measures which was adopted in France in 1799 and is the basis for the International System of Units/Système internationale d'unités (SI).

metrology. A system of weights and measures.

(German)   **Miete.** German term for rent. *See also* **derzeitige Miete, Pachtzins.**

(German)   **Mieter.** German term for lessee or tenant.

(German)   **Mietvertrag.** German term for lease contract or tenancy agreement. *See also* **Pacht (vertrag).**

(Japanese)   **mochibun.** A Japanese term for equity or asset buildup; an alternative term for equity is jiko shihon, literally (the company's) own capital.

(Indian)   **monopoly value.** In India, the premium price paid for the last vacant plot in an area undergoing development.

mortgage. A pledge of a described property interest as collateral or security for the repayment of a loan under certain terms and conditions. For foreign language equivalents, *see also* **hypotheke, teitō.**

movable property. A term used in many European languages for personal property and/or furniture—e.g., biens meubles in French, Möbel in German, movitost in Czech, ruchomosci in Polish, dvizhemoye imushchestvo in Russian, bienes muebles in Spanish. *See also* **immovable property.**

multinational company. A company with both production facilities and distribution networks in more than one country. *See also* **international company.**

(Spanish)   **multiplicador de renta.** Spanish term for rent multiplier.

multiplier. *See* **income multiplier, year's purchase.**

natural person. A real human being, as opposed to an artificial or fictitious person. *See also* **legal entity.**

(Czech/Polish/ Russian)   **nájem, najem, nayom.** The term for lease in Czech, Polish, and Russian. In Czech and Polish, it is the typical commercial or residential lease; in Russian, nayom refers to a Soviet-style lease for public housing units. *See also* **arenda.**

net floor area. Equivalent to net internal area.

net internal area (NIA). In the United Kingdom, the usable space within a building, measured to the internal surface of the structural, external, or party walls, but excluding areas occupied by pillars, internal structural walls, washrooms, lifts (elevators) and plant rooms, stairways and lift wells (elevator shafts), space used for public circulation (entrance halls, lobbies, and corridors), and parking areas; used to measure office space, retail space, and high street shops (main street or strip commercial). *See also* **gross internal area.**

(German)   **Nettoeinkommen.** German term for net income.

NICs. Acronym for newly industrialized countries, e.g., Singapore, South Korea, and Taiwan in Asia and Argentina, Brazil, and Mexico in Latin America; usage from *The Economist. See also* **BEMs.**

(Spanish)   **normalización.** Spanish term for adoption of, or compliance with, professional standards.

(Spanish)   **norma(s).** Spanish term for (professional) standard(s).

occupational lease. An arrangement in which the tenant occupies the space being leased (the demised premises) rather than subleasing the space to a subtenant; used in Britian and the Commonwealth.

open market rent. *See* **market rent.**

open market value (OMV). In British and Commonwealth usage, market value: "the best price at which the sale of an interest in property would have been completed unconditionally for cash consideration on the date of valuation," under specified conditions. For a complete definition, see *RICS Appraisal and Valuation Manual,* Practice Statement 4.2.1, 1995. *See also* **alternative use value, estimated realisation price, existing use value**.

open market value method. In British and Commonwealth usage, the sales comparison approach.

operating expenses. The periodic expenditures required to maintain a property and continue the production of gross income; the terms outgoings and service charges are used in the United Kingdom and Commonwealth.

operational entirety. A unit of a business conducted from one property (RICS); in British and Commonwealth usage, the business enterprise operated from a property that generates income, e.g., a hotel, restaurant, pub, theatre, cinema, petrol filling station, golf club, race course, caravan park (trailer park). *See also* **profits method.**

operational expenses. *See* **operating expenses.**

opportunity cost of capital rate. The general rate of interest chargeable on borrowed capital.

(Russian) **otsenka, otsenshchik.** The Russian terms for appraisal and appraiser. *See also* **tsennost'.**

outgoings. Operating expenses in British and Commonwealth usage

overrented In British and Commonwealth usage, a situation that results when passing or contract rent exceeds open market rent.

(German) **Pacht(vertrag).** German term for lease. Note: Pacht derives from the Latin pact(um/a) meaning agreement. *See also* **Mietvertrag.**

(German) **Pachtzins.** German term for rent; literally, the amount of rent specified by a lease. *See also* **Miete.**

pass-alongs, pass-throughs. *See* **expense pass-alongs, expense pass-throughs.**

passing rent. In British and Commonwealth usage, contract rent.

(Spanish) **patrimonio.** Spanish term for inheritance, the monetary worth of all hereditary rights and obligations that devolve upon an heir, or the tax on this estate; patrimonio familiar means family inheritance. Patrimonio may also be used in the sense of equity or net worth, e.g., patrimonio social refers to the capital of a sociedad (firm or company).

percentage rent. Payment by a retail tenant of a portion of annual gross sales above a stipulated level (breakpoint) to the landlord. *See also* **turnover rent.**

perch. Unit of measure in the imperial system; one perch equals 30.25 square yards.

personal property or **personalty.** *See* **movable property**.

physical or **direct value.** Spanish term (valor fisico/directo) for a value indication derived from the cost approach; used in Mexico.

(French) **plan d'occupation des sols.** French term equivalent to land use plan. *See also* **schema directeur d'aménagement.**

(Spanish) **planificación del uso de la tierra.** Spanish term for land use planning.

(Spanish) **plano regulador.** Spanish term for zoning map.

plinth. The base on which a structure stands; in India, a unit of measurement that refers to the built-up covered area at the floor level of the basement.

(Russian) **pomest'ye.** The Russian word for estate, which carries pre-1917 connotations. The Russian term pomest'ye nakhodyashcheyesya v chastoi sobstvennosti is equivalent to fee simple, literally, the estate found in private property. *See also* **pravo chastoi sobstvennosti.**

powers of government. In relation to real property, the four powers exercised by government: taxation, eminent domain, police power, and escheat.

(Russian) **pravo arendi.** Russian term for leasehold (estate). *See also* **arenda.**

(Russian) **pravo chastnoi sobstvennosti.** A Russian term equivalent to fee simple (estate). *See also* **sobstvennost'.**

premises. A tract of land and the building(s) on it; in British and Commonwealth usage, generally demised property.

prescription. A claim on, or title to, property established by virtue of immemorial possession.

(Indian) **present value.** A value derived by discounting forecast income and reversion; in Indian usage, cost less depeciation.

present value of £1. British term corresponding to the present value of $1; the reciprocal of the amount of $1 or compound interest factor.

present value of £1 in perpetuity. In British and Commonwealth usage, the reciprocal of a direct capitalization rate; a form of capitalization in perpetuity. *See also* **year's purchase in perpetuity.**

present value of £1 per annum. British term corresponding to present value of $1 per period.

(Indian) **prevailing market rate.** In India, the unit rate (value) at which the subject parcel of land would be sold in the market.

privatization. The process of transferring ownership of state-run enterprises (industries, farms) and apartment buildings to individual shareholders or tenants. Privatization is a requisite step for command economies making the transition to market economies.

probationer. In British and Commonwealth usage, a candidate for an appraisal designation.

profit rent. The difference between the rent from subtenants and/or rent for the space occupied by the lessee and the total rent payable to the landlord; used in Britian and the Commonwealth. *See also* **shortfall method.**

profits and loss account. In British and Commonwealth usage, an operating statement.

profits method. A type of income capitalization recognized as a separate valuation method in the United Kingdom and Commonwealth; also called the accounts method. The profits method is used when a specific business activity or enterprise contributes to the income-generating capacity of the property, e.g., in the valuation of hotels, restaurants, pubs, theatres, cinemas, petrol filling stations, golf clubs, race courses, and caravan parks (trailer parks). *See also* **income capitalization approach.**

(Spanish) **projección de renta.** Spanish term for rental/income projection or forecast.

property. Foreign language equivalents are: Eigentum, propiedad, propriété, majetek, shoyū-butsu, sobstvennost'. *See also* **immovable property, movable property, real estate, real property.**

property unit trust. The term used in the United Kingdom for a real estate investment vehicle similar to a real estate investment trust in North America.

(Spanish) **propiedad alquilada.** Spanish term for leasehold. *See also* **bienes forales.**

(Spanish) **propiedad horizontal.** Spanish term for a condominium property; used in Argentina. Note that terminology varies within the Spanish-speaking world. In Spain, the term used is propiedad por pisos, literally, ownership by floors or apartments. In Mexico, the term is condominio.

(Spanish) **propiedad particular.** Spanish term for private property.

(Spanish) **propiedad por pisos.** *See* **propiedad horizontal.**

(Spanish) **propiedad raíz.** Spanish term for real estate or real property. *See also* **bienes raices, immovable property.**

(Spanish) **propietario.** Spanish term for landlord.

(French) **propriétaire.** French term for landlord.

(French) **propriété foncière.** French term equivalent to real estate or landed property.

prospective value. Forecast of the value expected at a specified future date. *See also* **estimated realisation price.**

provident fund. In British and Commonwealth usage, a fund that provides for future needs, e.g., an old-age pension. *See also* **superannuation fund.**

quantity survey method. A cost-estimating method in which the quantity and quality of all materials used in a building and all categories of labor required are estimated and unit cost figures are applied to arrive at a total cost estimate for labor and materials.

quit rent. The payment a freeholder makes to the lord of the manor to be released from obligatory labor or military services; abolished in the United Kingdom in 1936.

rateable value (RV). In British and Commonwealth usage, the assessed value on which poundage is charged. (Poundage refers to the tax rate on the assessed value.) *See also* **council rate/tax, uniform business rate.**

rates/rating. Assessment(s) in British and Commonwealth usage.

real estate. Physical land and the appurtenances (structures or improvements) attached to it. Foreign language equivalents are: fudōsan, Gründstuck, propiedad raíz, propriété foncière.

real estate investment trust (REIT). A form of securitized real estate investment in which many investors pool their capital to acquire or finance a variety of properties; similar to a mutual fund for real estate. Such an investment is a property unit trust in British and Commonwealth usage, fondo fiduciario de inversion en bienes raices in Spanish, and société civil de placement immobilier in French.

real property. All interests, benefits, and rights inherent in the ownership of physical real estate. *See also* **bundle of rights, fee simple absolute/estate, leased fee estate, leasehold estate.**

recoverable amount of an asset. In British and Commonwealth usage, the amount an enterprise can recover from future use of the asset, including its net realisable value on disposal (or reversion).

registry system. A system for recording title to land and transfers of title originating in North America. *See also* **common law or old systems title, Torrens system.**

(Indian) **reinstatement value.** In British and Commonwealth usage, refers to insurable value; in India, the term is used interchangeably with replacement value.

reinvestment rate. The rate at which the return on, or profit from, an income stream is reinvested.

(French) **rendement.** French term for yield.

(Spanish) **rendimiento.** Spanish term for yield.

(German) **Rendite.** German term for yield.

(German) **Rendite-Satz.** German term for yield rate.

rent. An amount paid for the use of land, improvements, or a capital good. Foreign language equivalents are: arrendamiento, chin-ryō, loyer, Miete, renta.

(Spanish) **renta.** Spanish term for rent or income; sometimes used interchangeably with ganancia(s).

(Spanish) **renta bruta.** Spanish term for gross rent or gross income.

(Spanish) **renta de contrato.** A Spanish term for contract rent.

(Spanish) **renta de mercado.** A Spanish term for market rent. *See also* **renta economica.**

(Spanish) **renta economica.** A Spanish term for market rent. *See also* **renta de mercado.**

(Spanish) **renta liquida.** Spanish term for net rent or net income.

(Spanish) **renta neta.** Spanish term for net rent or net income; may be used interchangeably with renta liquida or renta real.

(Spanish) **renta real.** Spanish term for net rent or net income (Mexico); literally, real rent; may be used interchangeably with renta liquida.

rental. In British and Commonwealth usage, the rent payable.

rental value. In British Commonwealth usage, the rent the property might reasonably be expected to command in the market; equivalent to market rent in North American usage. *See also* **capital value, profits method.**

(French) **rente.** French term equivalent to (annual) income, annuity, or stock. (Action is the French term for share.)

(French) **rentier.** French term equivalent to an annuitant or stockholder.

residual method. A type of income capitalization recognized as a separate method in the United Kingdom and Commonwealth; also called the development method or developer's test; used to value property with development or redevelopment potential. *See also* **income capitalization approach, land residual technique.**

resumption. In Australia, the taking of land by the state through compulsory acquisition (eminent domain).

(French) **revenu brut.** French term for gross income.

(French) **revenu locatif.** French term for rental income.

(French) **revenu net.** French term for net income.

reversion yield. In British and Commonwealth usage, a terminal capitalization rate. *See also* **all risks yield.**

right of first refusal. A tenant's option to exercise a prior claim to purchase a property or renew a lease at the same price/rent and on the same terms/ conditions offered by a third party, which the owner/landlord has shown a willingness to accept.

(Russian)   **rino<u>ch</u>naya ekonomika.** Russian term for market economy. *See also* **command economy.**

(Russian)   **rino<u>ch</u>naya stoimost'.** Russian term for market value.

Roman law. System of law based on the Roman legal tradition, which is the basis for most legal systems in continental Europe. Under Roman law, property rights are defined in terms of jus fruendi, jus utendi, and jus abutendi (the right to enjoy, the right to use, and the right to consume). *See also* **bundle of rights, common law.**

Ross formula. A method of determining a deduction for depreciation which originated with F.W. Ross, a master builder in late 19th century Germany. The formula applied is $D\% = (1/2 \times [A^2/L^2 + A/L]) \times 100$ where $D\%$ is the estimated percentage deduction for depreciation, A is the age of the structure, and L the life expectancy for the structure.

(German)   **Sachverständige.** German term equivalent to appraiser. *See also* **expert.**

(German)   **Sachwertverfahren.** German term for the cost approach.

sales comparison approach. A set of procedures in which a value indication is derived by comparing the subject property to similar properties that have been sold recently and applying adjustments to the sale prices of the comparables based on the elements of comparison. Foreign language equivalents are: enfoque de la comparación de ventas, méthode des donèes du marche, torihiki jirei hikaku hō, Vergleichwertsverfahren.

(German)   **Schätzung.** German term for appraisal or estimate; Abschätzung and Einschätzung are alternative forms. *See also* **Bewertung.**

(French)   **schema directeur d'aménagement.** French term equivalent to large-scale development plan. *See also* **plan d'occupation des sols.**

scheme. In British and Commonwealth usage, a development plan. *See also* **town planning scheme.**

second instance, court of. An appellate court in which the rulings of lower courts are reviewed. *See also* **first instance, court of.**

(Japanese)   **seijō kakaku.** Japanese term equivalent to market value; literally, normal value.

sensitivity analysis. Any method used to isolate how a change in one or more variables (set of parameters) may affect an outcome, e.g., an economic forecast, an investment risk scenario, an estimate of prospective value; a tool to assist in decision-making.

service charges. In British and Commonwealth usage, the payment a tenant makes to the landlord for services, repairs, maintenance, insurance, and management; in North America, the tenant's share of operating expenses.

servitude. British and Commonwealth term which indicates whether a property is subject to easements.

severance. In British and Commonwealth usage, the right to compensation that may result from the physical separation of land through condemnation by a public authority. *See also* **compulsory acquisition, injurious affection, solarium.**

(Japanese)   **shakuchi ken.** Japanese term for leasehold.

(Japanese)   **shihon (kin).** Japanese term for capital. *See also* **mochibun, shū-eki.**

(Japanese)   **shikichi.** Japanese term for site or parcel of land. *See also* **tochi.**

(Japanese)   **shiki kin.** In Japan, a refundable security deposit paid by the lessee in an amount ranging from six months' to one year's rent.

shortfall method. One of three variants of direct capitalization used in the United Kingdom and Commonwealth; based on profit rent. For examples, see Chapter 2 (United Kingdom) and the appendix to Chapter 4 (Australia). *See also* **income capitalization approach, profit rent.**

(Japanese)   **shōsho.** A Japanese term for deed; literally, a written instrument.

(Japanese)   **shoyū butsu.** Japanese term for property, possessions, belongings; alternative term is zaisan, meaning assets or accumulated wealth.

(Japanese)   **shū-eki.** A Japanese term for yield; alternative term is rieki.

(Japanese)   **shū-eki kangen hō.** Japanese term for income capitalization approach.

(Russian)   **sobstvennost'.** Russian term for property; chastnaya sobstvennost' is private property. *See also* **immovable property, movable property.**

(French)   **société civile de placement immobilier.** French term equivalent to property unit trust. (Note: One of the meanings of the French word placement is investment.)

solarium/solaria. Additional compensation paid in a compulsory acquisition or governmental taking; used in Australia. *See also* **severance.**

solicitor. In British and Commonwealth usage, a lawyer who drafts legal documents (wills and deeds), prepares cases for barristers, advises clients on legal matters, and represents them in lower courts. *See also* **barrister.**

stand. In Commonwealth countries, the lot or tract to which a parcel of land belongs.

strata title. In Australia and Singapore, freehold title to a horizontal plane (or stratum) of a building; similar to condominiums in North America or flying freeholds in the United Kingdom; may also refer to a building erected on the basis of air rights.

subdivision. A tract of land that has been divided into blocks or plots with streets, roadways, open areas, and other facilities appropriate to its development as residential, commercial, or industrial sites; also, a residential development. In British or Commonwealth usage, the term estate or village is used.

subjective value. A concept similar to investment value; in Spanish, valor subjectivo.

sublease/sublet. An arrangement in which a lessee's rights to use and occupy a property are conveyed to another, the sublessee.

succession. In British and Commonwealth usage, the right to inherit property or title.

summation approach. *See* **cost approach.**

superannuation fund. In British and Commonwealth usage, a pension fund. *See also* **provident fund.**

surplus property. In the United Kingdom, an investment property considered extraneous to the operational requirements of the corporation or company that owns it. Such properties are valued at their current open market value. In contrast, properties considered essential to the operations or activities of the corporation or company that own them are valued at existing use value or market value under the existing use.

surveyor. In North America, a person who surveys or measures land; in British and Commonwealth usage, a person who both surveys and values land and buildings. *See also* **geometer/geometry.**

(Japanese)   **tan.** Japanese unit of measurement equal to approximately 990 square meters or 10,650 square feet.

(Japanese)   **tanjun fudōsan ken.** Japanese term for fee simple (estate).

(Spanish)   **tasa de capitalización.** Spanish term for capitalization rate.

(Spanish)   **tasa de descuento.** Spanish term for discount rate.

(Spanish)   **tasa de rendimiento.** Spanish term for yield rate.

(Spanish)   **tasador or tasador fiscal.** The Spanish term for appraiser or assessor used in many Latin American countries. *See also* **valuador** or **avaluador.**

(Spanish)   **tasa global.** Spanish term for an overall capitalization rate.

(Spanish)   **tasa pasiva.** Spanish term for a reinvestment rate.

(French)   **taux de capitalisation.** French term for capitalization rate.

(French)   **taux d'escompte.** French term for discount rate

(French)   **taux de rendement.** French term for yield rate.

(French)   **taux global.** French term for overall capitalization rate.

(French)   **taxateur.** French term for assessment or taxation agent; variants of this term are used in several European languages—e.g., Taxator in German, taksador (takserings-) in Norwegian, taksator in Polish. *See also* **tasador.**

(Japanese)   **teitō.** A Japanese term for mortgage; alternative terms are mōgēji and tanin shihon, literally, the other (party's) capital.

tenant finish. Costs incurred by a landlord to fix up space for a new tenant; called tenant fitout in the United Kingdom and Commonwealth.

tenant improvement (TI). *See* **tenant finish.**

(French)   **tenure à bail.** French term equivalent to leasehold. *See also* **droits au bail.**

term and reversion method. One of the three variants of direct capitalization used in the United Kingdom and Commonwealth. For examples, see Chapter 2 (United Kingdom) and the appendix to Chapter 4 (Australia). *See also* **income capitalization approach**.

three-approach paradigm. The three valuation approaches recognized by North American appraisers as distinct, but interdependent, methodologies: the sales comparison, cost, and income capitalization approaches. *See also* **five-method paradigm.**

(Japanese)   **tochi.** Japanese term for land or ground. *See also* **shikichi.**

(Japanese)   **tokutei kakaku.** Japanese term for unique value, e.g., the value of an old religious building with no planned change in its use and no prospects for market exposure.

(Japanese)   **torihiki jirei hikaku hō.** Japanese term for sales comparison approach.

Torrens system. A legal system under which title to freehold land depends on registration and certification. The purpose of the Torrens system of title registration is to establish indefeasible title so that interested parties can be assured that only the rights and claims so registered have legal standing. Developed in 1857 by Sir Robert Torrens, an Australian, the system is used in Australia, New Zealand, Canada, parts of the United Kingdom, and 10 states of the United States. It is also being adopted in Singapore. Chapters 3 and 4 (Canada and Australia) discuss systems of land registration. *See also* **common law or old systems title, registry system.**

(French)   **toute propriété (bien en toute propriété).** French term equivalent to absolute ownership (fee simple absolute or freehold).

town planning scheme. In British and Commonwealth usage, a municipal land use map.

trade cycle. *See* **conjuncture.**

trading potential. In British and Commonwealth usage, the goodwill "attached to an operational entity...which is personal to the present owner or management, and which would not pass with the property on a sale with vacant possession." (*RICS Appraisal and Valuation Manual*, Practice Statement 2.7.3.); applies to properties such as hotels, private hospitals/nursing homes, and entertainment/recreational facilities.

(Russian)   **tsennost'.** Russian term for value; the plural, tsennosti, refers to securities. *See also* **otsenka.**

(Japanese) **tsubo.** Japanese unit of measurement equal to 3.3 square meters or 35.5 square feet.

turnover. In North American usage, the ratio of new tenants to remaining tenants.

turnover and turnover rent. In British and Commonwealth usage, the volume of business measured in sales receipts; in North American usage, turnover equates to gross sales and turnover rent is called percentage rent.

(German) **Übertragungsurkunde.** German term for deed; literally, transfer document.

underrented. In British and Commonwealth usage, a situation that results when passing (contract) rent is less than open market rent.

uniform business rate (UBR). The tax payable on all commercial property in the United Kingdom.

unit title. In New Zealand, freehold title held by a registered proprietor to a unit in a scheme (development plan) defined in three dimensions, hence also called strata title.

unit value method. A method of appraising residential properties in Commonwealth countries which relies on ratings (assessments) and the sale prices of comparable properties. Based on a cost analysis, each of the ancillary components of a comparable property is assigned a relative unit number in terms of (the) main space or dwelling (I/T/MS), which is given a unit value of 1.0. The relative unit number for the component is then multiplied by the area the component occupies, the resulting unit numbers are totaled, and the price of the comparable is divided by the total to arrive at a unit value. This unit value is then applied to the total unit number estimated for the subject property to calculate the property value. *See also* **zoning method**.

(Spanish) **utilización compartida.** Spanish term for time-share property.

vacant possession. In British and Commonwealth usage, units of commercial space that are available for immediate leasing at market rental levels; describes a commercial property available for sale with full rights of occupancy.

(French) **valeur.** The French term for value; the plural, valuers, is used for assets or securities.

(French) **valeur d'investissement.** French term for investment value.

(French) **valeur vénale.** French term for market value.

(Spanish) **valor comercial.** Commercial value; used in many Latin American countries as the equivalent of market value. *See also* **avalúo comercial**.

(Spanish) **valor de mercado.** A Spanish term for market value. *See also* **valor venal**.

(Spanish)	**valores.** Spanish term for securities, as in bolsa de valores, stock exchange; literally, values.
(Spanish)	**valor fisico o directo.** Spanish term for a value indication derived by the cost approach; used in Mexico; literally, physical or direct value.
(Spanish)	**valor referido.** Spanish term qualifying a value indication for a specific date referenced in the report.
(Spanish)	**valor subjectivo.** Spanish term for a concept similar to investment value.
(Spanish)	**valor unitario de calle** or **valor de calle.** Spanish terms for the typical unit value of lots located on the streets of an area defined as a uniform zone; determined by cadastral bureaus, which also develop formulas to derive applicable adjustment coefficients or factors; used in Mexico.
(Spanish)	**valor venal.** Spanish term for market value. *See also* **valor de mercado.**
(Spanish)	**valuador** or **avaluador.** Terms used for appraiser in many Latin American countries; sometimes used synonymously with tasador, but generally tasador suggests an assessor.
	value. Foreign language equivalents are: kakaku, t̲sennost', valeur, valor, Wert.
	value-added tax (VAT). In many European countries, a tax levied at the time of sale or transfer of real property and based on the increment in value the property has incurred as a result of improvement (development/redevelopment) or appreciation. Value-added taxes may also be levied at each stage in the manufacture and distribution of a product as it passes to each successive processor and, ultimately, to the consumer. In the United Kingdom, the VAT is normally payable on rents and service costs. In France, it is known as taxe à la valeur ajoutée; in Italy, imposta sur valore aggiunto (IVA); in Columbia and El Salvador, impuesta sobre el valor añadido (IVA).
	valuer. A person who estimates the value of real property. Foreign language equivalents are: évaluateur, expert, kanteishi, ot̲senshc̲hik, valuador. *See also* **assessor, surveyor.**
(French)	**valuer locative.** French term for rental value.
(Spanish)	**vara.** Unit of measure used in certain Latin American countries. For exact equivalents, see Chapters 19 and 20—El Salvador and Columbia.
(German)	**Vergleichswertverfahren.** German term for sales comparison approach.
(German)	**Verkehrswert.** German term equivalent to (fair) market value. *See also* **Marktwert.**
(German)	**Vermieter.** German term for lessor or landlord.
(German)	**vertraglicher Miet-beziehungsweise Pachtzins.** German term for contract rent; literally, contractual rent in respect to rental. *See also* **derzeitige Miete.**

(Russian) **vladeniye nedvizhimim imushchestvom, vzyatim v arendu.** Russian term for leased fee (estate); literally, the possession of real estate held under a lease.

(Czech) **vlastnictví.** Czech term for fee simple interest.

(German) **Wert.** German term for value. *See also* **Bewertung.**

(German) **Wertminderung.** German term for depreciation.

(German) **wirtschaftlicher Miet-beziehungsweise Pachtzins.** German term equivalent to market rent (passing rent); literally, economic rent in respect to rental. *See also* **Marktmiete.**

(Polish) **własność.** Polish term for fee simple interest.

(German) **Wohnungseigentum.** German term for fee simple ownership of a condominium.

year's purchase (YP) A multiplier used in Britain and the Commonwealth which is the reciprocal of the yield rate (equivalent to the present value of $1); applied to annual net income (NI) to derive capital value (CV).

year's purchase in perpetuity. British and Commonwealth usage for the present value of $1 in perpetuity; can be calculated as 100 divided by the yield rate or 1 divided by the interest rate expressed as a decimal. For example, *YP* in perp. at 8.5% = 100/8.5 or 1/0.085 = 11.7647. *See also* **present value of £1 in perpetuity**.

yield. *See* **Rendite, rendement, rendimiento.**

(Indian) **zamindar.** Term used in Moghul and British India for collectors of revenue levied on the tenant cultivators, who worked the large estates owned by the zamindars.

(Russian) **zemlevladeniye.** Russian term for ownership of landed property.

(Spanish) **zonificación.** Spanish term for zoning.

zoning. Public regulation of the character and density of real estate use; division of an area by a planning authority into zones for particular uses. Foreign language equivalents are: Bebauungsplan, Flächennutzungsplan, plan d'occupation des sols, planificación del uso de la tierra, plano regulador, schema directeur d' amenagement, scheme, zonificación.

zoning method. A method of estimating the rental value of shop or retail space based on its division into strips parallel with the frontage; developed by Trustram Eve in the United Kingdom and used in New Zealand and Zimbabwe. *See also* **unit value method.**